Management in Education
Reader 2

The Open University
Faculty of Educational Studies

Management in Education (E321)
Course Team

Carolyn Baxter
Oliver Boyd-Barrett
Lydia Campbell
Sheila Dale
Digby Davies
Lance Dobson
Tony Gear (chairman)
Philip Healy
Donald Holms
Vincent Houghton (deputy chairman)
Christine King
Royston McHugh
Reg Melton
John Miller
Edward Milner
Colin Morgan
Robert Nicodemus
Gerald Normie
Gwynn Pritchard
Adam Westoby

Management in Education
Reader 2

Some Techniques and Systems

Edited by
Lance Dobson, Tony Gear and Adam Westoby
for the Management in Education Course Team
at The Open University

Ward Lock Educational
in association with
The Open University Press

ISBN 0 7062 3471 5 paperback
      0 7062 3470 7 hardback

First published 1975
Reprinted 1976

Set in 10 on 11 point Plantin and printed by
Willmer Brothers Limited, Birkenhead
for Ward Lock Educational
116 Baker Street, London W1M 2BB
Made in England

Contents

Acknowledgments

The Open University and publishers would like to thank the following for permission to reproduce copyright material. All possible care has been taken to trace ownership of the selections included and to make full acknowledgment for their use.

Russell L. Ackoff for "A management scientist looks at education and education looks back"; George Allen and Unwin Ltd for "The contemporary system in outline" by Graeme C. Moodie and Rowland Eustace from *Power and Authority in British Universities* by Graeme C. Moodie and Rowland Eustace 1974; Tyrrell Burgess Associates Ltd in *Higher Education Review*, "Accounting information in universities" by by M. A. Sims and "Towards an economic theory of higher education" by Maurice Peston; Council for Educational Technology (CET) for "Making claims for computers" by Richard Hooper; Tony Gear for "Applications of decision trees to educational planning"; reprinted from *Higher Education* (1974) no. 3 pp. 353–64, with permission of Elsevier Scientific Publishing Company, Amsterdam, "U 68—a reform proposal for Swedish higher education" by Gunnar Bergendal; reprinted from *Instructional Science* (1973) no. 2 pp. 1–52, with permission of Elsevier Scientific Publishing Company, Amsterdam, "Behavioural objectives—a critical review" by Michael Macdonald-Ross; this article first appeared in *New Scientist*, London, the weekly review of science and technology: "Models for thinking with" by Maurice G. Kendall; North East London Polytechnic and The Anglican Regional Management Centre in *Occasional Papers in Education Management* (1974), "The secondary school timetable: a matrix approach" by Harry L. Gray; Organisation for Economic Cooperation and Development (OECD), Paris, in *Methods and Statistical Needs for Education Planning* (1967), "Educational planning and manpower" edited by Gareth L. Williams; copyright The Open University for "Basics of timetabling" by John E. Brookes, "Decisions, decisions. . ." by Alan Harris, "The development and use of mathematical models in educational planning" by Peter H. Armitage, "A discussion of the use of PPBS and MBO in educational planning and administration" by John L. Davies, "From learning to earning: an economic analysis" by Gareth L. Williams, preliminary report of on-going research at The Open University (Tony Gear) in collaboration with Corporate Management Consultants Ltd (John S. Gillespie) and Cumbria County Council (William H. Stubbs)—"Allocating budgets to colleges of further education: a case study in Cumbria" by Tony Gear, John S. Gillespie, and William H. Stubbs, "The recent history of planning teacher numbers" by Peter H.

Armitage, and The Open University Press edited extracts from the OU (1974) E221 *Decision Making in British Education Systems,* Unit 15 *Introduction to Planning and Decision Models*—"Management problems and school leadership" by Peter Snape (with an appendix on network planning by Tony Gear); *Socio-economic Planning Sciences* for "How did we ever make decisions before the systems approach?" by Roger L. Sisson, "On some basic steps in the application of systems analysis to instruction" by Alexander M. Mood, and "Potential economies of scale at the University of Bradford" by John Dunworth and Anthony Bottomley; Pitman Publishing for "Government of polytechnics" by Michael Locke from *Polytechnics: A Report* by John Pratt and Tyrrell Burgess (1974); Walter H. Worth for "Colleges and governments".

1 Education as a System

INTRODUCTION
An education system presents itself as an immense accumulation of institutions. All institutions have two things in common: they are in part autonomous, setting their own goals and pursuing them by means which they decide internally, and at the same time they are dependent, sometimes closely and sometimes much more remotely, upon the other parts of the system to which they belong. This Reader deals (especially in the second section) with some of the quantitative techniques which may be used for decision-making within institutions. But it seems correct to open the Reader with the section entitled "Education as a System". Its purpose is to illustrate some of the ways in which society as a whole makes demands upon the education system, sets limits to the ways in which it decides and achieves its objectives, and affects the framework of management and planning by which an education system as a whole attempts to guide itself.

In "Decisions, Decisions . . ." Alan Harris examines, from the standpoint of analytic philosophy, some of the central characteristics of educational decisions. He argues that no decision, at any level, can properly be considered "value-free". Peter Armitage's first article, "The Development and Use of Mathematical Models in Educational Planning", then looks at some ways of planning decisions within simplified models of education systems.

One of the most important areas of decision-making in education has to do with its capacity to supply the trained manpower required in the economy. The articles by Gareth Williams, "Educational Planning and Manpower", and by Peter Armitage, "The Recent History of Planning Teacher Numbers", review part of the experience and techniques developed since the Second World War in the general area of "manpower planning". Peter Armitage's article deals more specifically with some of the problems which arise from the fact that an education system uses a large part of its resources to supply its *own* future requirements for trained employees.

The next article, "From Learning to Earning; An Economic Analysis", by Gareth Williams, presents a somewhat different approach to tailoring the "output" of an education system to the demands of the labour market, and raises the question of the relevance of orthodox economic theory to education. It centres upon the concern now arising over significant levels of unemployment or inappropriate employment among highly educated sections of the labour force, and discusses this concern in the context of the theory that education raises the productivity (and therefore the earn-

1

ings) of employees by providing them with "human capital". Although it is true that "manpower planning" techniques and theories of "human capital" are distinct approaches (the latter basing themselves on the earnings of educated labour, while the former concentrate upon attempts to estimate the numbers required, regardless of their expected earnings), the methods bear upon many of the same problems.

Whatever goals (and methods for achieving these) may emerge or be set for an education system, and whatever the values and priorities, implicit or explicit, attached to these goals and methods, the development of the system is always affected by the fact that the institutions within it must possess (and in any case come into being already possessing) a significant degree of internal autonomy. Autonomy exists also in each region and level of education, though in many different ways in different national systems.

The final three readings in this section approach some of the problems involved in the organization of the system as a whole. Gunnar Bergendal's article, "U68—A Reform Proposal for Swedish Higher Education", provides an account of the Swedish plan to reorganize higher education on a regional basis, subordinating much of the traditional autonomy of the universities to regional bodies responsible for higher and further education as a whole. Walter Worth's paper, "Colleges and Governments", deals (more contentiously) with some proposals to integrate traditionally independent higher education institutions within a coherent system in the Canadian province of Alberta.

The last paper is the most speculative in the section. Russell Ackoff's "A Management Scientist Looks at Education and Education Looks Back" insists that there is a crisis of method and outlook running throughout the management of education and argues that only a "renaissance" in the thinking both of educators and of management scientists concerned with education can begin to provide solutions to this crisis. Perhaps his most controversial suggestion is that the reform of an education system may most usefully go forward if it is conducted within the framework of an "idealized design" for the system—as if it were possible, somehow, to wipe the slate clean of existing institutions and organizations.

Adam Westoby

1.1 Decisions, Decisions . . .

Alan Harris

One of the simplest of all educational situations, I suppose, is the Robinson Crusoe sort—one person learning first to survive and then to do more than merely survive. But even this situation, before the arrival of Friday, is complicated enough to demonstrate the different sorts of *decisions* that Crusoe had to take about his own education. They can be described as follows:

1 DECISIONS CONCERNING IMMEDIATE NEEDS

What were the first things, in this particular situation and given his own existing knowledge, that Crusoe needed to learn? The situation dictated that he should learn to build a shelter and to obtain food (but note that when he attempted to educate Friday his priorities were altogether different—to teach him first English and then Christian beliefs).

2 DECISIONS CONCERNING FUTURE NEEDS

Having survived the first few weeks, Crusoe began to look ahead. He had to learn how to survive indefinitely on the island and also, if possible, to escape from it. Thus he had to decide on the relative importance of learning to domesticate wild goats and to grow crops, and of learning to build a suitable boat.

3 DECISIONS CONCERNING VALUES

This is not a separate category, for *all* his decisions so far have involved evaluations. Thus his selection of immediate priorities reflected the fact that he valued his life and therefore survival. His decisions about future needs meant evaluating not merely survival but survival in comparative comfort, and the return to his former way of life (via escape).

But so generally are such elemental values taken for granted that they hardly needed to be entertained at a conscious level. It is not until the more basic human needs are satisfied that important conflicts begin to arise within an individual's value system, or between the value systems of different individuals.

Source: Commissioned for this volume by The Open University.

4   DECISIONS CONCERNING EDUCATIONAL METHODS

In the case of Crusoe it would hardly make much sense to say that he decided not only *to learn to build a boat* but also about the *best way* to learn to build a boat. But when he tried to teach Friday how to speak English he may well have made such a decision. And if he had known as much as we do now about teaching languages then he would have had a greater array of possibilities from which to choose.

All four types of decision can be seen in any situation where a country's educational provision is systematically organized.

1   In a developing country the emphasis on *immediate needs* is patently very great. The sheer physical survival of the people is a priority, and not one which is likely to cause theoretical arguments.

2   Note though that in Tanzania, where a very sophisticated programme of educational reform is currently in progress, *self-reliance* has become the prime educational aim. Not only will we survive, says the Prime Minister, Julius Nyerere, but we will survive *independently*. No one will question survival as a basic aim; but what is to count as survival *as human beings* does in fact involve all sorts of value judgements about future needs, and here may begin debates about priorities. Which is more important, for example: to educate people to farm more efficiently, which will bring benefits very quickly, or to educate many of them to become technologists, which may have long-term advantages?

3   So far we have mentioned decisions of a utilitarian sort. Though these necessarily involve evaluative choices they are all to do with long- or short-term *needs*. But not all curriculum decisions can be seen as need-based or utilitarian. Does one *need* Mozart or Shakespeare? Does one *need* witty conversation, grace of bodily movement, elegance of mathematical proof? Educational decisions not so directly connected to basic needs are more complex. Should we "transmit" the existing values of our culture to children? If so, which ones, since only a selection can find a place in the school curriculum? What criteria do we have for this choice? Should we decide to help pupils to *challenge* contemporary values and, if so, can we do this without simply indoctrinating them with a *new* set of values?

4   The last question takes us into educational methodology. Given some measure of agreement about aims, what methods should we decide to adopt? Should there be institutions called schools? Or are there alternatives? If we have schools, should they be comprehensive? Should children be streamed, or put in "family groups", or setted? Should the curriculum be "subject-based" or "integrated"? Again it is impossible to escape from the fact that all educational questions necessarily involve

questions about values. Here we are talking about methods of communicating valued sorts of education, but the methods themselves involve value judgements. If our aim is to produce autonomous human beings, can we justify indoctrination, or punishment, or the *imposition* of our own interests and values via the curriculum—or are such processes (whatever ends they facilitate) intrinsically immoral?

In an article as short as this, over-simplification is inevitable. I hope, however, that I have made my main point: that there is no decision about education which is "value-free" or "neutral"; *Management in Education* is about what education *ought* to achieve as well as about *how* to achieve it.

1.2 The Development and Use of Mathematical Models in Educational Planning

Peter H. Armitage

During the past generation there has been a considerable interest and some progress in the development of models of educational systems. At the national level the main concern has been with calculations having some relevance to questions such as "How much higher education should there be?" and "How many teachers do we need or can we afford?"

The ways in which these calculations were shaped requires brief description. The National Advisory Council on the Training and Supply of Teachers was set up in 1949 and produced a series of reports up to 1965. (It then quietly died, only to be reincarnated in new form in 1973.) In its Ninth Report (1965) demand and supply were examined separately, and the numbers needed and the numbers likely to be produced were compared at the end to reveal the prospect of shortfall or surplus.

The demand calculations were particularly simple. The current official projection of the future school population was taken and the expected numbers in primary classes, in the first five years of secondary courses and in sixth-form groups were each subjected to a pupil–teacher ratio. The results were added together to give the grand total of teachers required, as shown in Figure 1. There was difficulty in arriving at the ratios and controversy about them but, for present purposes, that argument can be ignored.

The supply calculations can be generalized as in Figure 2. It was necessary to distinguish between those who were already teaching, those who intended to become teachers and those who had been teachers but were now otherwise engaged and might return to service. To project the future teacher force, patterns of wastage had to be assumed for present teachers and entry and re-entry patterns had to be assumed for prospective teachers. The calculations were executed in much greater detail at various times, with the process repeated for different groups—men, single women, married women, graduates, non-graduates, trained mathematicians and scientists, etc. The whole exercise constituted a primitive manpower model.

Source: Commissioned for this volume by The Open University.

Figure 1 The National Advisory Council's view of demand

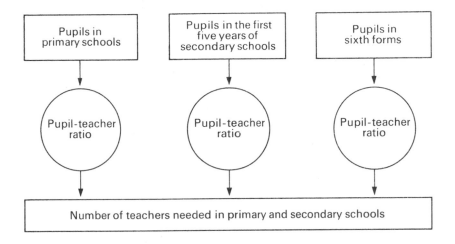

Figure 2 The National Advisory Council's view of supply

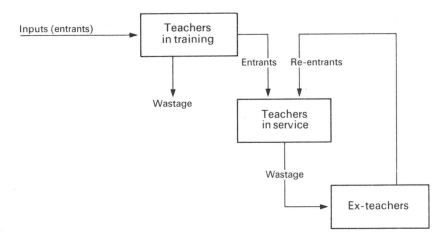

The study of higher education carried out in the early sixties by the Robbins Committee (1963) was more grandiose. Robbins was invited to review the pattern of full-time higher education in the light of national needs and resources, and to advise on principles of long-term development, on what institutional changes might be necessary and on how to plan and co-ordinate development. The starting point was to define "higher education" and it was identified, not without some criticism, as being all students in universities and colleges of education and all those in

Figure 3 The Robbins Higher Education model

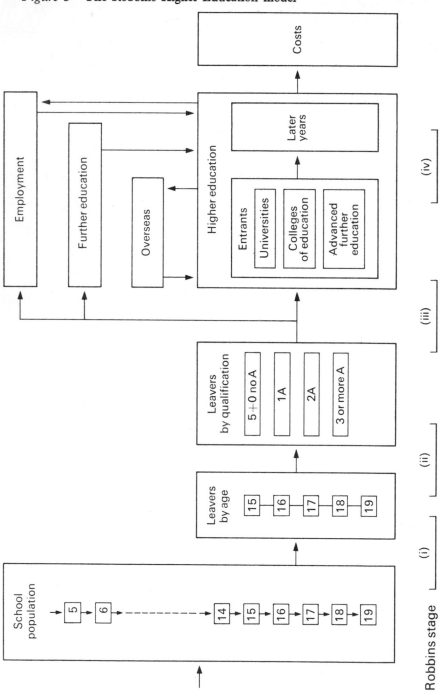

further education who were following advanced courses. As entrants to higher education came from the schools, non-advanced further education, employment and overseas, attention had to be widened.

Robbins described the calculation procedure:

(i) We first look at the size of the age groups relevant to higher education.

(ii) Then we estimate what proportions of these age groups are likely to reach the level of attainment appropriate for entry.

(iii) We next consider how many of those so qualified should be assumed to enter. This in effect involves two assumptions:

  (a) how many will try to enter higher education (the application rate);

  (b) what proportion of applicants with given attainments should be given places (the degree of competition).

(iv) Finally, we decide on assumptions about the future length of study.

The procedure can be visualized as in Figure 3.

The whole model can be seen as a sequence of separate stages, each of which can be completed one at a time to give an output projection which becomes the input into the next stage. Hence, given a population projection, there is a succession of projections on the school population, school leavers, qualified school leavers, entrants to higher education, places in higher education and, if required, costs in higher education. The calculation is highly repetitive and can be exemplified by considering just one stage. Given a projection of qualified school leavers, it is necessary to decide how many will want and should be allowed to go forward to

Table 1 Robbins's assumptions on the percentages of school leavers entering different sectors of higher education[1]

Number of A level passes	University	College of education	Advanced further education
Boys			
3 or more	84	4	4
2	34	13	11
1	7	17	18
None[2]	1	8	3
Girls			
3 or more	69	16	2
2	18	41	5
1	—	39	6
None[2]	—	16	1

higher education. Robbins laid down the axiom that "courses of higher education should be available for all those who are qualified by ability and attainment to pursue them and who wish to do so". However, entry standards were vague and there was no measure of desire.

The snag was overcome by assuming that specified percentages with each level of qualification should go forward, as shown in Table 1. The relation of these assumptions to the axiom is tenuous but flows of students can be determined and the total entrants summed.

Similar calculations to those made by Robbins were published in an Educational Planning Paper (Department of Education and Science, 1970), and enrolment models of this kind have been developed in many other countries. They are founded on the identification of a number of structural elements corresponding to educational processes so that the state of the system at any given time is described by the stocks of students or teachers in that process at that time. The flows of students from any process in one year to another process in the next have to be defined, together with any newcomers to the system. A typical equation in the model is:

$$n(s,t+1) = \sum_r f(r,s,t) + u(s,t) \tag{1}$$

where $n(s, t+1)$ is the stock of people in process s at time $(t+1)$; $f(r,s,t)$ is the flow of people who are in process r at time t and move to s in time $(t+1)$; and $u(s,t)$ are the new entrants to process s at time $(t+1)$ who were not in the system at time t.

Given base year stocks, a projection is possible if assumptions are made about all future flows and inputs. It is difficult to make direct assumptions about flows as they will reflect such phenomena as demographic variations. It is much easier to standardize the flows in the form of transition proportions, $p(r,s,t)$, so that:

$$p(r,s,t) = f(r,s,t)/n(r,t) \tag{2}$$

and then make assumptions about these proportions. The complete model now takes the familiar form:

$$\mathbf{N}(t+1) = \mathbf{P}(t) \cdot \mathbf{N}(t) + \mathbf{U}(t) \tag{3}$$

where $\mathbf{N}$ and $\mathbf{U}$ are column vectors and $\mathbf{P}$ is a square matrix summarizing the assumed information on the interconnections between the processes. A projection requires knowledge of the base year stocks, $\mathbf{N}(t)$, and comprehensive assumptions about all future inputs, $\mathbf{U}(t+T)$, and transitions, $\mathbf{P}(t+T)$.

These models have seen much service and their use so far might be broken down into three stages. In the first stage a single projection was offered as either the total evidence relevant to decision-making or as the outcome corresponding to a chosen set of decisions. It must be remembered that in the days of hand calculations a highly detailed projection was an impressive feat. Robbins produced the projection that went as far as the Committee thought would be acceptable to the Government. The 1970 Planning Paper displayed "one possible pattern of development" in "a working document intended to assist discussion" but carrying "no implications whatever for future Government policy or finance".

In the second stage of usage, these models were used to prepare a number of projections. The explanatory introduction to the Planning Paper had noted that "different assumptions at any point in the calculations would have led to results differing to a greater or lesser extent" and "a considerable range of projections with differing scales and patterns of development could be devised". Disagreement about the "reasonableness" of assumptions is bound to occur and curiosity will raise a number of "what . . . if" questions. The exploration of alternatives is readily achieved, given the facility of a computable model. When a limited number of projections are generated, they can be compared and one can be selected as preferred. It has become fashionable to admit the existence of at least three variants, usually labelled "low", "central" and "high". It was implied in some of the comment on the White Paper (Department of Education and Science, 1972) that the numbers quoted related to a projection chosen by the Secretary of State from several variants. (On this occasion, no full projection was published.) The process of selection characterizing this stage of usage is sometimes thought of as choosing between options.

So far the model has been regarded as a machine for making projections without the declaration of any motive. Robbins discussed meeting the demand for higher education and meeting the needs of the nation as alternatives and found the latter, manpower approach, was not practicable in 1963. For this reason, it is often wrongly stated that Robbins adopted a "social demand" approach; in fact, the Committee wandered far enough away from its guiding principle for the approach to be neither one thing nor the other. Similarly the National Advisory Council on the Training and Supply of Teachers did not adopt a full-blown manpower approach by searching for a policy that would balance supply and demand. In retrospect, the Council's reports appear to be commentaries on the progress made in turning shortfall into eventual surplus. Abroad (France, Eastern Europe) and at institutional levels (universities in the USA) there has not been the same reticence about stating objectives, and this opens the way to a programming approach. Provided some objective can be agreed upon, it can be "optimized" subject to any stated constraints. The third stage of educational model building would aim to get as near as possible to some target or purport to look for the best policy according to some criterion, without necessarily enumerating or comparing a great many alternatives.

Clearly there is much scope for the improvement of educational models. Their development so far has been heavily influenced by the desire to make the most of available data and by the fact that much data collection has been for accountancy rather than operational reasons. The simple enrolment models are conceived in terms of counting bodies and their role is seen as passive and pseudo-objective. The driving force lies in the transition matrix and everything hinges on the validity of the transition proportions. An empirical approach encourages assumptions about future values of the transition proportions which merely extrapolate their behaviour in the recent past. This is not good enough, for the assumption must also reflect some judgement on the impact of new policies. Unfortunately past data offer no guidance here and it is only possible to guess the impact of innovations which, like raising the school-leaving age, have already been implemented but have not yet produced known consequences.

It seems to me that we must be much more fastidious in the information we seek. It is often claimed that one of the prime virtues of educational model building has been to direct attention to collecting data on flows which had suffered neglect in the previous concentration upon stocks. There is some truth in this but we must go further. Flows do not just happen; they depend upon both the demand for places and the previously arranged supply. Consequently they should be defined:

$$f(r,s,t) = \text{Min}[d(r,s,t), s(r,s,t)] \tag{4}$$

where $d(r,s,t,)$ is the demand for places in s at time $(t+1)$ by those who are in r at time t, and $s(r,s,t)$ is the supply of places in s at time $(t+1)$ allocated to those in process r at time t. Sometimes flows will be determined by demand, sometimes by supply. Robbins's belief that there was too much pressure in the competition for places in the universities and colleges of education implies that flows were being determined by supply (and the notion that Robbins intended to meet social demand is contradicted by his acceptance of the persistence of this pressure). A projection based on the extrapolation of flows observed during a period when they were determined by supply will go badly astray when supply overtakes demand, resulting in empty places. This possibility cannot be anticipated unless we can go behind the flows and measure the demand, the diversions from one sector to another and empty places.

This suggestion is tantamount to proposing an entirely new model. Instead of the linear, free-forward model of equation (3), the new model would be nonlinear and the resolution of the dual forces of demand and supply. Characteristically the equations of the new model would be:

$$n(s,t+1) = \text{Min}[\mathbf{D}(s,t+1), \mathbf{S}(s,t+1)] \tag{5}$$

where $\mathbf{S}(s,t+1)$ is the supply of places to be provided in process s at time t and the matching demand can be written:

$$\mathbf{D}(s,t+1) = \sum_r d'(r,s,t) + u(s,t) \tag{6}$$

where $d'(r,s,t)$ comprises all those students in r at time t for whom a place in s at time $(t+1)$ is the first choice, and also those students for whom it is not the first choice but would be an acceptable alternative when they are unable to obtain a place in some other sector. The demand corresponding to a particular flow could therefore be defined:

$$d'(r,s,t) = p'(r,s,t)n(r,t) + \sum_s o(r,\bar{s},s,t) \tag{7}$$

where the prime in $p'(r,s,t)$ again indicates first preference and $o(r,\bar{s},s,t)$ is the number overspilling from non-s into s. This kind of model requires statements about preferences and selection procedures, i.e. the priorities of the students and "suppliers".

While recognizing the desirability of keeping models as simple as possible, I feel that it would be necessary to assert that overspills have never occurred and never could, for this degree of complexity to be avoided. There is the further attraction that the new model has parameters, the $S(s,t+1)$, which relate closely to the decisions that may be taken by central decision-makers in the allocation of resources. The claim that the model can be used to choose between options stands up when the outcome of a particular set of parameter values corresponds with an identifiable policy. It does not hold when, as in the earlier models, the transition proportions are only implicitly connected with decisions.

The whole conception of choosing between options is still troublesome. It is meaningful to the administrator because he thinks of a number of policy instruments under his control that can be varied. For the model builder the combinations of possible actions constitute an extensive policy space inviting a formidable search problem. The administrator may have knowledge, experience or intuition allowing him to discount a large part of the theoretical horizon of possibilities but there must be a suspicion that he may not fully appreciate the range of options open to him. By taking a savage view of "reasonable assumptions", the model builder can present the administrator with as few alternatives as he feels he can manage. Little further reduction may be needed for the politician to be given the single answer we are told he must have. There is a strong chance that we are deceiving ourselves if we think the result sensible.

The lay idea that options are being chosen presupposes that we are discriminating between definite and precise alternatives and this may seem to be the case when deterministic models provide unique outcomes for particular sets of parameter assumptions. Of course we cannot be so certain, and when uncertainty is taken into account it may become impossible to distinguish between the outcomes of different options. We were told earlier that "everybody knows about margins of error" but it

13

would be more true to say that "everybody knows about uncertainty and has remarkable success in forgetting about it".

As ignoring uncertainty can lead to completely wrong conclusions, we must be wary. Feasible outcomes can easily be dismissed in the process of a group reaching a consensus and there is also strong temptation to eliminate uncertainty prematurely. The initial input to the Robbins model is the official population projection of the Government Actuary's Department and it is used as the best available information. However, when this singular projection is fed into the next stage, the range of outcomes in school population projections must be diminished because the possible variability of input is not represented. If calculations proceed in the same way, so that the range of outcomes at each stage is condensed into a single input for the subsequent stage, then the perception of possible futures at the end of the line will be nonexistent or, at best, vestigial. Uncertainty should surely be carried right up to the point where a decision has to be taken, and only then should a single answer be produced by taking an expected value.

The outstanding question is, what is it that we are trying to find the expected value of? This brings us back to what it is that we are all trying to do. I can sustain no faith in the model that is uncontaminated by purpose and do not believe in the supposedly detached, all-purpose model placed at the disposal of anyone who wishes to use it. Now objectives are notoriously difficult to get at but there must be at least a momentary revelation whenever a decision-maker acts. As there will never be agreement on clear-cut, unchanging objectives, models must be set up in the actual decision process so that they are open to continual discovery of purpose. Indeed I would go further and suggest that we need batteries of models related to the aims of different decision-makers at different points in the system, including both students and teachers. Some test of the validity of conclusions from one model would come from checking in other models, and we might learn about the interplay of conflicting objectives. Unlike models so far, which have been cut off from non-educational forces, this complex of models would be more exposed to economic, social and political stimuli.

This is a tall order, but at least it does not fall into the folly that we are wiser than we really are. The technical improvement of models is necessary but far less important than better communication between all the decision-makers and their model builders. If achievement to date is not impressive, then it must be remembered that educational planning is in its infancy. I have no doubt about the vital role that mathematical models will play in future.

NOTES

1 These percentages were observed for 1961 and assumed to hold to 1967, when they would increase by 2 per cent per year until 1972,

after which time they would be fixed at this new (10 per cent higher) level.

2 No A-level passes, but 5 or more O-level.

REFERENCES

DEPARTMENT OF EDUCATION AND SCIENCE (1970) *Student Numbers in Higher Education in England and Wales*, Education Planning Paper No. 2, HMSO.

DEPARTMENT OF EDUCATION AND SCIENCE (1972) *Education: A Framework for Expansion*, Cmnd 5174, HMSO.

NATIONAL ADVISORY COUNCIL ON THE TRAINING AND SUPPLY OF TEACHERS, NINTH REPORT (1965) *The Demand for and Supply of Teachers*, HMSO.

ROBBINS COMMITTEE (1963) *Higher Education*, report of the Committee (Chairman: Lord Robbins) appointed by the Prime Minister, Cmnd 2154, HMSO.

1.3 Educational Planning and Manpower

Edited by Gareth L. Williams

ELEMENTS OF AN EDUCATIONAL FLOW MODEL

Demand for places by pupils

The point of departure for this approach to educational planning is that access to all branches of education should be available to all those wishing to enter them who are qualified to do so, by ability and attainment. This is certainly the most frequent basis on which educational decisions are made, and even educational plans that purport to be based on other methods often base a large part of their estimates on what students and their families are thought to be demanding.

Traditional methods of forecasting the demand for places have depended upon forecasts of enrolment ratios in each branch of education based on projections of trends and correlations with national income and the demographic, geographic and socio-economic structure of the population, etc. The principal weakness of such methods is that they cannot easily take into account the interrelationships between the various branches of education. In recent years, the techniques of making such projections have developed rapidly. The present chapter outlines the type of forecasting and planning models that are coming into use for forecasting student enrolments on the basis of individual demand for places, and for formulating educational policies on the basis of these forecasts.

In order to understand the mechanics of this approach to educational planning and indeed much of educational planning in general, it is convenient to start by examining the educational system as if it were a rather complex mechanised production system. The basic raw materials are human beings, usually children. As these raw materials proceed through the educational system, from one branch to another, they are transformed by the actions of teachers and educational equipment into educated, or at least partially educated, people. These educational processes usually take place in schools or universities.

Source: Edited extracts from Organisation for Economic Co-operation and Development (1967) *Methods and Statistical Needs for Educational Planning*, pp. 17–31, 43–67.

The "inputs" into the educational process are thus children, teachers, equipment and buildings. The "outputs" are various types of educated people. In the first instance, attention may be concentrated on the "raw material" inputs only—pupils and students.

The initial input into the educational system in any country with effective compulsory education laws is very closely related to the number of births the relevant number of years previously. During the whole of the period of compulsory education, total enrolments of pupils at each age differ very little from total population at that age and by far the most important basis for global enrolment projections is a reliable set of demographic forecasts. It is not a function of this manual to describe methods of making demographic forecasts. It is assumed that the educational planner will have before him detailed forecasts by individual year of age of the population of school age throughout the planning period. If these do not exist, the educational planner must make his own forecasts, using the best demographic techniques available.

Above the age of compulsory education, less than 100 per cent of each age group will be in school and for even the simplest global forecasts of total enrolment it is therefore necessary to apply "enrolment ratios" expressing the percentage of people of each age who are expected to be seeking education. Methods of estimating future enrolment ratios include the use of trend projections and international comparisons, and the straightforward setting of targets based on social, political or other criteria. The formulation of trend projections may, of course, be quite sophisticated, taking into account the socio-economic structure of the school population, its regional distribution, etc.

It is not, however, sufficient merely to make global projections of total enrolments, for at least two quite separate reasons. In the first place, no educational system is fully "comprehensive" in the sense that all pupils have exactly the same educational experience while they are at school or university. Total enrolments are distributed amongst different types of school, different educational specialisations, different geographic regions, etc. To be useful, forecasts of enrolments must take account of these differences, and also of the movements of pupils between the different elements of the educational system at each age. Secondly, children themselves are not homogeneous. They enter the educational system from different environmental conditions and with different inherent abilities. As they pass through the different levels of the system, such differences are often magnified rather than diminished, both because the basic aim stated (at the beginning of this chapter) means that children with different abilities can benefit best from different educational experiences and because the structure of modern society and of modern knowledge is such that what is required is not simply "educated people", but a wide range of people with different skills, talents, aptitudes and attitudes. Thus, while total enrolments are heavily influenced by demographic factors, the actual inflow of pupils into any particular branch of education is determined by a large

17

number of other factors which exert an influence from both the input and the output sides.[1]

A basic forecasting model of enrolments
Most children begin their full-time education with a period of legally compulsory attendance[2] which in modern societies is usually fairly well enforced. As has been suggested above, therefore, prediction of total numbers in compulsory education is largely a matter of demographic forecasting. Four special reasons must, however, be mentioned which suggest that even for compulsory education, global forecasts of enrolments are not adequate.

a   Most countries permit pupils the opportunity of attending non-public schools if their parents wish it. While the educational planner is usually primarily interested in making estimates for the public sector, he cannot do so accurately without knowledge of the likely proportion of enrolments in the private sector. In addition, there is in some countries a transfer from the private to the public sector at certain points and also flows from the public to the private sector that might look like drop-outs, if they are not carefully observed.
b   Knowledge of the detailed geographic distribution of enrolments is vitally important at the compulsory school level. Children of these ages cannot be expected to travel great distances to school. The rate of growth of population and the proportions in different age groups are likely to differ in different geographical areas.[3]
c   Decisions are made during the period of compulsory education, often quite early, which materially influence the career of the pupil when the period of legally compulsory education ends. Information about these decisions, which in practice means attendance at different types of institution, or entering different educational "streams" within an institution, is vital for forecasting developments in subsequent branches of the system.
d   In many educational systems pupils frequently "repeat grades" which means that there is a greater concentration of pupils in the lower than higher grades. Apart from the importance of this phenomenon in itself from the point of view of the analysis of the efficiency of the system it has important implications for the type of teachers needed.

Another important factor affecting the number of pupils in compulsory education is the length of the period of compulsory education. It is difficult to state how assumptions about the future length of compulsory education should be made. It can, of course, be assumed that it will remain the same in the future as at present, unless specific political decisions to change the period of compulsory education have been or are likely to be made. Reasons why the educational planner may himself take the initiative in proposing a change in the period of compulsory education include:

a In order to set a period of compulsory education similar to that of other countries at equivalent stages of economic growth;
b In order to extend the educational opportunity of children from social groups who, for one reason or another, are not taking advantage of the educational facilities available;
c If it is believed that pupils leaving school at the end of compulsory education are inadequately prepared for labour-force participation; or if, for other reasons, there is a lack of employment opportunities for school leavers.

After the end of compulsory education, it becomes much more difficult to predict the numbers of pupils in each branch of education. Apart from the obvious fact, previously mentioned, that it is no longer possible to use 100 per cent enrolment ratios and, therefore, to rely mainly on demographic forecasts, there is the further complication that the educational system usually becomes much more complex. Private education is often relatively more important in the higher stages of secondary education. Furthermore, whereas the number of different streams and types of institution is usually quite limited in earlier education, at the more advanced stages there are often a large number of different streams catering for different needs on the part of pupils. An important problem for the planner is to decide how many of these separate streams it is necessary to identify in detail. Another complication is the existence of part-time education.[4] All of these different options have different implications for the needs for teachers, building and finance in the public educational system, and effective planning requires reliable forecasts of the number of pupils likely to follow each stream.

The decision to follow a particular educational stream is not necessarily a final decision. As educational systems become more flexible, pupils move from one stream to another at different points in their career. Moreover, a stream at one level of the educational system may feed several streams at a higher level, and conversely one stream at a higher level may be fed by several streams from a lower level.

Many pupils leave school after the end of compulsory education and thereafter some leave each year, some having successfully completed courses, others not, until by the age of 30 very few people are still full-time students. Apart from the need to make estimates of school leavers at each age for his own purposes, the educational planner has some responsibility to make such estimates by age and by qualification for the benefit of economic planners who require information on potential new entrants to the labour force.[5]

It is particularly important to have good estimates of the number of students who wish (and who have the required ability) to transfer from one branch of education to another at the important thresholds[6] of the system. Apart from the end of compulsory education, the most important of these is the move from secondary to higher education.

Estimates of future student numbers in any particular branch of education have usually been made on an *ad hoc* basis. If, for example, estimates of the likely number of entrants to universities are required, attempts are made to predict the number of secondary-school leavers who will be qualified and seeking admission to universities.[7] Recent work, however, has concentrated on a more systematic approach, trying first to describe in quantitative terms the interrelationships between the various branches of education and then to use these as a basis for forward estimates. At its most ambitious, this may lead to the construction of a computable model of the whole educational system which can be used to:

(i)   Demonstrate how the educational system would be likely to develop, given no change in its present structure;

(ii)   Show the likely effect of various policy decisions (e.g. to raise the compulsory school-leaving age) on the number of pupils in each branch of education;

(iii)   Determine how the educational system should be made to develop if specific targets are to be achieved in some future year.[8]

The basic form of the model is the simple input-output matrix shown in Table 1. In this table a number of branches of education have been distinguished from 1 to r. For the sake of exposition the first few branches of education (primary education, etc.) have been written in. The row totals of the matrix show the number of pupils in each branch of education in a particular year, say t_0. The column total shows the number of pupils in each branch of education in the following year, t_1. Since, during the year, some children will enter the system and some will leave, it is necessary to have a further row and column headed "outside education", which may be further subdivided, if it is necessary to know where the entrants and leavers are coming from and going to. The rest of the cells of the table show how the stock of pupils of year t_0 is distributed in year t_1. Alternatively, it can be considered as showing whence the pupils of year t_1 came. The figures in the matrix are purely illustrative, and are intended to help in interpreting it. To take the example of secondary general education, the interpretation is as follows: in year t_0, there were 300 pupils in this branch of education. By t_1, these were distributed as follows: 200 were still in secondary general education, 10 were in secondary vocational education, 40 were in other branches of education (here unspecified), and 50 had left the educational system. Similarly, to look at the table the other way, there were 312 secondary general pupils in t_1. Of these, 100 had come directly from primary school, 200 were already in secondary general education the previous year, 10 came from vocational education, and 2 came from outside the educational system (presumably re-entrants or immigrants). The matrix can be viewed in more general terms: if attention is directed towards the row heading "r" and the column heading "s", it can be seen that the typical element in the matrix is the flow $f(r,s)t_0$. The row totals must equal the numbers of individuals in each branch of education at time t_0, i.e. $n(r)t_0$. The column totals must be the quantities $n(s)t_1$.

Interesting methodologically are the 10 pupils who moved from vocational to general secondary education, and the 10 who moved the other way. Ordinary stock statistics (i.e. the row and column *totals*) would not record these movements at all, yet such transfers can be very interesting. Apart from the importance of distinguishing the various components of net changes in student numbers during a year, these cross flows reveal the importance of an integrated flow framework. Without such a framework, pupils who leave general schools to enter vocational schools are often recorded as drop-outs, and thence "wastage" despite the fact that they have merely transferred to another branch of the system.

It is, of course, possible and for most practical purposes essential to enlarge Table 1 considerably. In the first place, it is very useful to have the length of cycle of education represented by each row and column heading correspond to the period t_0-t_1. In practice, since t_0-t_1 usually represents a single school year, this means that the row (r) and column (s) headings should correspond to a single grade or year of study. If (r) and (s) represent an educational cycle of longer duration than the period t_0-t_1, an unduly high proportion of pupils will be in the diagonal term, in which it will be impossible to distinguish course repeaters from normal promotions within the branch of education. More important, however, a model based on such data will be of little more use than normal "stock"

Table 1 Summary example of flow tabulation (Stocks of students in years t_0 and t_1 and flows occurring between the two points in time)

Origin t_0 Destination $t_1 \rightarrow$ ↓	1	2	3	4	S	R	Total in t_0
1 Primary education	800	100	50			50	1 000
2 General secondary education	0	200	10	40		50	300
3 Vocational secondary education	0	10	60	4		26	100
r					$f(r,s)t_0$		$n(r)t_0$
R	300	2	0				
Total in t_1	1 100	312	120		$n(s)t_1$		

projections, since unless it can reasonably be assumed that each member of a particular cell has the same probability of going to any other particular cell, the different probabilities for individuals within the cell have a profound effect on the numerical results. Where a cell is an aggregation of pupils from several grades, it is quite clear that the probability of pupils successfully completing the course from the last grade is likely to have a positive value, whereas for all other grades it will be zero. Except in the case of a stable school population (or one in which the number of pupils in all grades is growing at the same constant rate), in order to predict successful completions accurately it is necessary to know numbers in the last grade, the last grade but one, etc. [. . .]

The same need to make each cell contain as homogenous a group of pupils as possible as far as their future possibilities are concerned suggests that the classification scheme for the flow tabulation should also take account of a number of individual characteristics of pupils, sex, socio-economic background, innate ability, etc., since the transition coefficients are likely to be different for pupils with different characteristics under these headings. One difficulty is that these tabulations soon become very large. The basic model described by Redfern (Moser and Redfern, 1965), if constructed, would have had nearly 500,000 cells. Where the individual characteristics are invariant with regard to time, (e.g. sex) or vary in a simple predictable way, (e.g. age), it is often most convenient to think of separate tabulations for pupils with each characteristic.

The need to assume the same probability for all pupils within one cell creates another problem in that it cannot be assumed, as the simple flow formulation described above does, that previous educational experience does not affect present probabilities for future performance. For example, a pupil who in arriving in a certain grade has previously repeated one or more grades may well have a set of future probabilities attached to him different from a pupil who has reached the same level without repeating. This problem can be dealt with conceptually in terms of second, third and higher order Markov claims. In practice, this means that as well as tabulations showing the distribution of t_1 pupils in t_0, it is also necessary to obtain data on their distribution according to their activity at time t_{-1}, t_{-2}, etc. Clearly, this presents certain problems of data collection, though it can easily be handled with an individualised data system in which the links between the various years can be made automatically.

It is also likely that marks gained in earlier examinations are significantly related to a pupil's later transition probabilities; for example, success in examinations for university entry is often correlated with marks obtained in examinations at the beginning of secondary school. [. . .]

In order that the matrices may be used for forecasting, the absolute figures of Table 1 can be converted into a set of coefficients showing the proportions of pupils in one branch of education who are in any other branch in the subsequent time period. The basic "transition co-efficients" are obtained by dividing each element of the matrix by the corresponding row total. Thus in terms of Table 1, by dividing the elements of the matrix $f(r,s)t_0$ in each row r, we obtain the transition proportions $p(r,s)t_0$, i.e.

$$p(r,s)_{t_0} = \frac{f(r,s)_{t_0}}{n(r)_{t_0}}$$

These transition proportions show the proportions in which the individuals in process r at time t are redistributed between various processes during the unit period between time t_0 and t_1. The totals of the transition proportions for each row, of course, add up to 1 since the whereabouts of all the pupils or teachers of year t_0 has to be accounted for in year t_1.

Past data on flows between the different parts of the educational system can now be used in preparing projections of a part of, or the whole of the educational system. A soundly based projection can be made, using demographic forecasts of the initial inflow into the system, to which are applied the current values of, trends in, or likely developments of, the transition proportions. An integrated projection model of the whole educational system can be built up from the recurrence relationship:

$$n(s)_{t_1} = \Sigma n(r)_{t_0} \cdot p(r,s)_{t_0}$$
where $n(s)_{t_1}$ = each column total
where $n(r)_{t_0}$ = each row total
$p(r,s)_{t_0}$ = relevant transition proportion.

Thus if numbers of pupils in each branch of education at time t_0 are given along with data on demographic trends and assumptions about transition proportions in subsequent time periods, numbers in each activity in later periods can be forecast.

Teacher flows
Similar techniques can be used for projecting numbers of teachers, though with some reservations. In the case of pupils the educational system can be considered as a fairly well-defined system which pupils enter in a steady flow, and within which they move, following a number of quite well-defined patterns determined by the structure of the system. Flows within the system are of relatively minor importance in the case of teachers and such movements as do take place do not follow a well-defined structural pattern. In the case of teacher flows, therefore, attention is devoted mainly to the teachers entering and leaving the profession and their reasons for doing so, whereas many of the most interesting pupil transfers are those within the system itself.

A further difference is that the values of the transition coefficients for teachers entering and leaving the profession are less likely to remain stable or to follow well-defined trends. In the case of pupils, the transition proportions are unlikely to change sharply from one year to the next, because most of the fixed facilities remain intact, and new buildings are in most cases only a small proportion of existing capacity; furthermore, pupil flows depend very much on the traditions and inherent propensities of the society. For example, if in year "t_0" families wish to send 5 per cent of their 18-year-old children to university, they are unlikely to want, or be able to send 10 per cent in year "t_1". However, the proportion of, for example, university graduates who take up secondary-school teaching may be subject to many economic and educational policy influences that can change markedly from one year to the next.

Teacher flow "tabulations" remain, however, the most coherent way of showing the sources of supply of new teachers and the destination of those leaving the profession, thus permitting an analysis of teacher demand and supply problems, which are among the most important facing educational planners. In such a tabulation the row and column headings would correspond to the main sources of supply of teachers (e.g. teacher training colleges, universities, married women, other professional occupations) and the main destinations of those leaving the profession (retirement, marriage, other occupations, etc.). A summary of such a tabulation is shown in Table 2. In this table, the area marked A would show those people who were pupils in period t_0 and also pupils in t_1. That marked B shows those who are teachers in t_0 and who have become pupils in t_1. C shows those outside the educational system in t_0, but who have become pupils by t_1. D are those people who are students in t_0 and teachers in t_1. E are those who are teachers in t_0 and t_1 (the figures within the sub-matrix will show movements of teachers between the different branches of education during the year). F shows those outside the educational system in t_0 who have become teachers in t_1. This part of the matrix is a very important feature of teacher supply estimates, showing as it does the number of married women who are returning to the profession, and the number of people who are being attracted into teaching from other professions. G shows those pupils who have left the educational system and who have not become teachers between t_0 and t_1. H is another important area of the matrix: it shows the number of teachers who left the profession over the year. I shows the number of people who were neither pupils nor teachers in both t_0 and t_1. [...]

Comments on the use of flow matrices
If the data are available, the mechanical use of these matrices of transition proportions for forecasting purposes is straightforward. It has been outlined above (p. 23). In the examples that have been shown, the values of the transition coefficients have been assumed constant, but it is not much more difficult to incorporate trend changes in the transition co-

Table 2 Summary example of teacher flow tabulation

Origin in t_0 ↓	Destination in $t_1 →$	1	2	3	4	5	6	7	8	9	Total t_0
Pupils in primary and secondary education	1										
Pupils in teacher colleges	2	A			D			G			
Pupils in universities	3										
Teachers in primary and secondary education	4										
Teachers in teacher colleges	5	B			E			H			
Teachers in universities	6										
Other active labour force	7										
Other adult population	8	C			F			I			
Other population	9										
Total t_1											

efficients, if data are available to estimate the trends. "However, this amounts to saying that we can forecast the future state of the system if we know accurately its present state and are prepared to assume what movements are going to take place over the period of interest. . . . These calculations are possible because we are either given or have presumed everything we need to know and because the system is still highly simplified. This is no longer possible when the system is made more complex" (Armitage and Smith, 1966).

The important part of the exercise is that of making estimates of likely developments in the transition coefficients. This, at its simplest, is a four-stage exercise.

a The determination of which transitions are important, and the establishment of a system of classification and set of tabulations to enable these transition coefficients to be identified.
b The estimation of their values in the base year.
c Identifying the individual characteristics of pupils that affect the transition coefficients, and ascribing a numerical value to the influence of these characteristics, perhaps by using separate matrices for each individual characteristic. In principle, it is possible to identify an almost unlimited number of individual characteristics that may be important. The only limitations are practical ones.
d Using the estimates of detailed transition coefficients for each homogeneous group of pupils derived from (c) above, to estimate probable developments in the global transition rates from forecasts of likely rates of growth of different socio-economic groups, urban and rural population, etc.

B

Some of the practical limitations on the degree of detail possible or desirable in identifying individual characteristics of pupils are outlined below:

a   The capacity of the computing facilities available. Even the largest modern electronic computers do not have unlimited capacity and a forecasting model which attempted to take account of the inter-relationships between all possible factors affecting transition co-efficients would be very large indeed. There is also an administrative and economic constraint. Computer time is expensive and the addition of extra variables needs to be justified in terms of their likely effect in improving the forecasts.

b   The basic data which it is worthwhile to collect. Some of the information on individual pupil characteristics may be very difficult and costly to obtain; for example, the relationships between distance from residence and educational institution, and educational attainment. In some cases, it is simply not justified. In others, one detailed survey may provide data which can be considered valid for a number of years. In fact, very few data on transition proportions are as yet available in most countries.

c   The degree to which the effect of a particular characteristic is likely to affect the results. For example, although the occupation of his parents is widely recognised as a factor influencing a child's educational decisions, there is unlikely to be much information gained by listing each individual occupation separately, since it is when occupational differences are wide enough to reflect broader social differences that they materially affect attitudes to education. It is, however, necessary from time to time to conduct special surveys to obtain information on all possibly significant characteristics of at least a sample of pupils in order to decide which are, in fact, the important ones.

d   The limits beyond which disaggregation is in any case not worthwhile. Unless the structure and dynamics of the components of the system are fully understood, there is no evidence that forecasts of trends in highly disaggregated components of a system will be more accurate than more aggregated projections. In addition, excessive disaggregation leads to such a small number of observations in each group that the estimates of probabilities within each group are heavily influenced by random disturbances. If, for example, there are only five persons in a particular group an atypical move by one of them will cause a 20 per cent error in the estimate of the transition coefficient for that group.

e   The possibility of making forecasts of the number of people with particular attributes. For example, if it is found that there are marked differences between rural and urban participation, for this information to be of any use for forecasting it is necessary to predict developments in urban and rural population. [...]

Critique of demand for places model
Like all "methodologies of educational planning", the approach has many conceptual weaknesses and is justified mainly by the consideration that some forward estimates must be made as a basis for decisions that will in any case be taken about schools and universities to be built, teachers to be trained, etc. Many of these decisions will have very long-term implications, and it is desirable to consider as accurately as possible their likely results.

The main criticism of the approach is that although it is purportedly based on estimate of the "demand for places" by individuals, what the data actually show is a mixture of demand for places, and supply of places or capacity available. This is seen most clearly in relation to the so-called "bottleneck" problem. In many cases the number of students who enter for example universities, or at least certain "restricted" faculties, is determined by the number of places available.[9] In this case, it is somewhat unrealistic to interpret the statistics of the numbers of students who enter universities as an indication of the demand for university places. There is little evidence that if more university places were available, there would not be enough students to fill them.

The situation is, however, even more complicated. Even if an attempt is made to measure the demand for university places by collecting information on the number of students who apply for these places, it is not at all clear that applications for entry to university are not influenced by students' own estimates of the number of places available. An additional complication caused, in part, by the bottleneck problem, is that transition coefficients cannot be considered independent of one another, since removal of a bottleneck at one point will have implications for a wide range of pupil choices. This increases the complexity of the basic research to be undertaken before such models can make their maximum contribution to forecasting and planning.

Criticisms are also possible from a broader social viewpoint. In most modern educational systems, education is supplied to individuals free, or at least much below its real costs to the community. Demand in this case does not have the same connotations that it normally has in economics. This is particularly relevant in cases where students receive financial grants which can be used explicitly or implicitly to influence individual demand, by encouraging students either to remain in the educational system when they might otherwise leave, or to enter institutions or specialised courses when, given no financial incentives, they might prefer others. One answer to these criticisms is that they apply equally to most traditional methods of forecasting demand for places by students, only in the absence of a comprehensive descriptive model they are not recognised.

It is not necessary to regard Table 1 as indicating anything very profound about the demand for places in educational institutions, but rather as a convenient descriptive formulation of the basic dynamics of the educational system, just as statistics of the number of pupils and teachers at a point in time can give a reasonable picture of the static situation of the system. The analytical framework can be used in a variety of ways, of which the simple prediction model outlined in this chapter is only a first step. The ultimate objective will be to develop planning models which are part of the decision-making structure itself in such a way that there is continuous feedback between the projections of the model and the actual decisions and actual developments in the real world.[10] [. . .]

MANPOWER REQUIREMENTS

Reasons for estimating manpower needs as a basis for educational planning
The "demand for places" approach to educational planning uses as its starting point the input into the various branches of the educational system. The manpower approach starts with the required outputs. Just as [we have] considered, therefore, the factors affecting the *inputs* into the various branches of education—demographic factors, socio-economic factors, job opportunities, policy decisions, etc.—so [we] must investigate the factors affecting the required outputs of the system. [. . .]

A problem that has worried economists ever since they have become interested in education is that "output" cannot be very well defined, much less measured, in education. This makes it difficult to analyse cost/benefit relationships. Various attempts have indeed been made to measure the economic output of education, ranging from the measurement of the earnings differential between educated and uneducated people to assuming that the part of economic growth that cannot be statistically "explained" in terms of growth in the capital stock and increase in the labour force is due in some measure to education.[11] Whatever the intellectual merits and demerits of these different attempts to measure educational output, most of them have not proved very useful in providing policy makers with the information that will help them decide how much of the available resources to devote to education; and how to distribute these between the various levels and types of education.

The manpower approach to educational planning does not attempt to deal directly with the problem of defining or measuring educational output. It is concerned simply with one aspect of educational output, the skills, talents, aptitudes and attitudes with which education can provide the future working population. The "rationale for according manpower forecasts a prominent role in assessing educational needs is perfectly straightforward. It runs something like this: a nation with plans or aspirations for economic development cannot afford to slight the preparation of its human agents of production. The creation of a new steel works, for example, is meaningless unless provision is also made for the scientists, engineers, managers, skilled workers, clerical staff, etc. necessary to operate it. Since one of the functions of an educational system in society is to provide its work force with the abilities required for productive activity, it follows that the system must be reasonably well geared to the production requirements of the economy. Moreover it is the *future patterns of* requirements that must guide today's educational decisions. The reason is that the "lead time" in producing qualified manpower is exceptionally long" (Parries, 1963).[12]

One of the basic difficulties of this approach to educational planning is to interpret the meaning of "requirements". In the simplest sense manpower "requirements" are interpreted as meaning that there are fixed relationships between various types of manpower inputs and economic output. Carrying it a stage further this means that there is a somewhat rigid complementarity between physical capital inputs and qualified manpower inputs, and also between the inputs of different types of qualified manpower. Clearly this narrow interpretation is open to criticism. In the first place, many types of qualified manpower are only remotely connected with physical outputs. It would be difficult, for example, to show how gross national product would be affected if there were a thousand more or fewer lawyers.[13] In the second place, even in production sectors some substitution between different qualifications is clearly possible. This may mean that a particular function (e.g. administration) can equally well be performed by people with various different qualifications, or that different functions can themselves be combined in different ways to give the same output.[14]

A further difficulty in forecasting manpower requirements, particularly in economically advanced countries, is to predict the effects of technological progress. Although some progress is being made, (see, for example, Jantsch, 1966) it remains extremely difficult to foresee the effects of such developments on manpower needs a decade or more hence. In many cases the new technology creates new occupations. It is safe to say that no manpower forecasts that might have been made in the early 1950s in North America or Europe could possibly have foreseen the phenomenal demand for a whole range of skills associated with computer technology a decade later. Of the various groups with whom the educational planner must associate closely, among the most important are those whose concern is forecasting technological developments. Because of the uncertainties of technological progress, if for no other reason, manpower forecasting is likely to remain an art rather than a precise science; which does not, however, mean that quantitative techniques have an unimportant role.

In the present state of the art of manpower and educational planning, therefore, it is probably more useful to think in terms of educational output "targets" than of manpower "requirements" rigidly based on a desired rate of national income growth. For some occupations, certainly, and for some educational qualifications, these targets may be interpreted as showing the amount of certain types of manpower that should be forthcoming if certain specific production targets are to be met. In other cases, educational output targets will be much more loosely linked to general economic and social aspirations—so many doctors per head of the population, etc. The art of manpower forecasting for educational planning is to find reasonable and generally acceptable bases for the establishment of targets. Clearly such an approach is in many ways not so intellectually satisfying as the attempt to establish manpower "requirements" linked directly to certain GNP growth targets: it is, however, more realistic. Public debate about the reasonableness or otherwise of the targets is as important a part of the educational planning exercise as the calculation of sophisticated forecasting coefficients. [. . .]

Methods of estimating future values of qualified manpower coefficients

(a)   Occupational forecasts
The present section considers methods by which target estimates of future occupational and educational needs can be made. It should be admitted that much of the existing work gives inconclusive results and any attempt to estimate qualified manpower needs should be considered as fundamental research and as a contribution to knowledge of the subject as much as practical preparation for any particular educational planning exercise.

It is assumed here that total employment figures and output figures by branch of economic activity are provided to the educational planner by the economic planning authorities.[15]

One very straightforward method of estimating occupational needs is to project the trends over a number of years in the occupational structure in each branch of activity. Sometimes the proportion of the total labour force in each occupation is projected, and in other cases the total number in each occupation has been related directly to output. Unfortunately, very few countries have sufficient data at the present time to make such calculations, and no countries have sufficient data for reliable regression analysis of time series. Eventually, this situation will be rectified as a result of the amount of manpower forecasting that is currently being undertaken in a large number of countries, but it is likely to be many years before sufficient data will have been generated to test the validity of such trend estimates. One particular danger with this method is the likelihood in many cases of projecting "non-optimum" situations since there are often strong reasons for supposing that the base period situation is itself not an optimum.

Another technique that has been quite widely used is that of simply taking as a pattern for some future date the current occupational structure of one or a number of other countries considered to have suitable economic and social structures. Alternatively, more sophisticated comparisons relating for example sectoral productivity to occupational structure in each country may be made.[16] Use of international comparisons in this way means making some rather restrictive assumptions about technological progress. It also requires good international data which hardly exist at the present time and it is necessary to adopt a moderately cautious attitude to existing data. However, since there are now several dozen countries with information on their occupational structures (see OECD, 1967) it is possible to undertake regression analyses of occupational structures with labour productivity, etc. with some degree of statistical confidence, provided all the usual reservations are made about classification problems and the difficulties of interpreting the results of international comparisons.

A further way to estimate the future occupation composition of employment is to examine current differences in manpower structures among firms in the industry. A comparison of advanced high labour/productivity firms with average productivity firms can indicate the likely directions of change of occupational structures. A variation of this approach is to investigate the occupational structures associated with new net investment. It is also, of course, possible to base estimates on firms' own ideas of likely occupational changes[17] though it is probably better to use this as a test of the reasonableness of estimates based on other approaches rather than as a basic method of estimation.

For some occupations, requirements are closely related to variables other than output or productivity and can be independently estimated. The most obvious example is perhaps the requirements for teachers themselves, which can be related to the projected school population.[18] The requirements for doctors and various other professional groups can be similarly estimated.

(b) Educational output targets

The calculation of educational requirements once occupational needs have been assessed can similarly be done in a variety of ways. One approach is to attempt to ascertain the "optimum level" of education for specific occupations, by analysing the functions of people in these occupations (see, for example, Eckhaus, 1962). It can then be stated that all persons in these occupations will "require" the appropriate levels of education. For certain occupations this method is appropriate. Doctors and some other professional groups again come to mind.

Other occupations cannot be equated with specific educational needs either because the occupation is not sufficiently precisely defined or because a wide range of educational preparation is appropriate for satisfactory performance of the tasks involved. For this reason it makes very little sense to attempt to group occupations according to the estimated educational needs. The appropriate method of analysis is to have data on the complete education/occupation matrix, showing not only the average but also the distribution of educational backgrounds of people in each occupation. The projection of this matrix can be done in a wide variety of ways, but in general some attempt should be made to ascertain whether the people at the lower end of the educational scale in each occupation are performing their tasks adequately, and whether they are old people who will, when they retire, be replaced by younger people with a qualification structure corresponding more to that of the younger age groups.

A further problem under this heading concerns the extent of the educational information required. In general, to be able to base educational plans on manpower forecasts it is necessary to have information on the *amount* of education required (measured probably in years of study) and *type* of education (shown probably as subject of specialisation) at least of the higher levels.

A conceptual framework for quantitative analysis of manpower structures
[...] A useful conceptual framework for analysing qualified manpower structures in an integrated dynamic manner is a demographic flow matrix similar to that developed for the educational system. The matrix should be constructed in such a way that it can be linked with the educational flow matrix on the one side, and with the input/output matrices of the economic planner on the other. It would show what happened to students leaving the educational system when they entered the labour force or the economically inactive population and would subsequently plot their economically significant movements until they retired or died.

A fundamental problem in constructing the matrix is to decide which of the movements of qualified manpower are economically significant from the point of view of educational planning. The discussion of the previous paragraphs indicates that from the point of view of manpower forecasting techniques currently in use, the most important features are the following:

1   Changes in branch of economic activity.
2   Changes in occupation or function (including movements from outside the labour force into the labour force and vice versa).
3   Changes in educational qualification.

It is necessary, therefore, to construct a set of flow tabulations that would permit the identification and analysis of movements of manpower from one economic occupational and qualification category to another, to be identified and analysed. [...] To permit such a table to be constructed, it would be necessary to record any change during the course of the period covered by the table in an individual's occupation, branch of activity or educational qualification. In addition to the characteristics mentioned above, others which might usefully be taken into account include place of residence, place of work, income, employment status, age and sex.

Transition proportions could be calculated in a way similar to that suggested for pupils, and likely and desired developments in these transition proportions could provide a basis for forecasting or planning manpower structures in any future time period. This tabulation can, in fact, be considered as an extension into other occupational fields of that suggested [earlier] for teachers. The arithmetical methods of making projections would be almost identical with those used in making projections of likely student numbers and, as in the case of students, the difficult part of the exercise is the calculation of the relevant transition coefficients—in this case the proportion of school and university leavers of various types who enter different occupations each year, the proportion with each qualification who change their occupation, and/or branch of activity, or who acquire another qualification.

To an even greater extent than in the case of students, the forces acting on the various transition proportions are extremely complex. In this case, salary and wage differentials, job opportunities, proportion prospects, social status of different occupations all play their part. In order to be able to use the model effectively, it would be necessary to have information on the extent of the influence of, and likely development in all these factors.

Before such a comprehensive demographic accounting model can be developed, many conceptual and practical problems must be overcome. The practical problems are concerned mainly with data needs. The first is the establishment of a classification and tabulation scheme which will enable the economically significant movements of manpower to be traced. [...]. The second problem is to decide on the length of the accounting period. If the accounting period is too long (between two decennial population censuses, for example), very many significant movements of qualified manpower are likely to take place which will not be recorded. The best way of obtaining the data to construct such a manpower flow matrix would be to extend the individualised data system suggested for the educational population to include the whole population. If each member of the population were given an identification code at one census, and if each time he changed his occupation, or obtained a new qualification, or retired from the labour force, this fact were recorded, it would be possible to construct a manpower flow matrix for any length of accounting period that was considered necessary.

The conceptual problems spring largely from the fact that very little is known about the dynamic structure of the labour force and so it is difficult to prepare a schematic framework which takes into account all the relevant flows. In the case of the educational system, as has been suggested, pupils normally proceed from one grade or one year of study to the next in accordance with the formal structure of the educational system. It is the absence of such a formal structure that makes it so relatively difficult to deal with many branches of vocational education and sometimes higher education within such a framework.

At the present time, what can be validly claimed for a manpower flow matrix of the type described in this section is that it appears to be a useful way of analysing the dynamic structure of the labour force and is a promising link between economic and educational planning. As in the case of the educational flow tabulation, it directs the attention of the planner towards the vitally important transition coefficients and the factors influencing them. It can also be used as a basis for various types of simulation models in order to test the outcome of different assumptions about educational and manpower policy. [. . .]

A question that needs to be asked is how much of the educational system might be influended by manpower forecasts. In most [advanced] countries manpower forecasts are unlikely to give much guidance for the development of primary and lower secondary education. One view is that manpower forecasts are of most help in indicating the necessary orientation of the system between different types of education in the secondary and higher levels. In this case, of course, the information on *type* of qualification would be more important than that on *amount* of education.

A final point that should be made about estimating educational needs on the basis of manpower forecasts is that nothing has been said in this summary about estimating the extent to which courses leading to different educational qualifications actually do qualify people to perform the functions that they purport to. Is a man with a university degree in civil engineering actually competent to build bridges? Could his training be improved in such a way as to make him a better civil engineer or a better citizen? This is a vitally important area that has been inadequately taken into account by quantitative educational planning. Ultimately, it is to be hoped that plans for curricula and school and university organisation will be closely linked to plans concerning the number of pupils who should be pushed through the system and there are many indications that current thinking on the subject of manpower aspects of educational planning is moving in this direction.

AN INTEGRATED CONCEPTUAL FRAMEWORK FOR EDUCATIONAL PLANNING
For purposes of description the manpower requirements approach to education planning and the approach known as "demand for places" or social demand have been presented as if they were mutually exclusive. Indeed much of the controversy of recent years has implied that the educational planner has to make an initial decision as soon as he starts that he will adopt one or the other. It may be shown, however, that conceptually one approach does not preclude the other. In fact any realistic educational planner uses both. This section seeks to present a framework within which they can be brought together.

The most important anomaly of using the manpower approach in isolation is that unless account is taken of the available inflows into the educational system it is very easy for the "required outputs" to imply inflows that are not available, either because there are not sufficient children of educable age,[19] or because they do not want to enter the branches of education that "manpower requirements" say they should.[20] Similar anomalies occur if plans for educational development are based on "demand for places" alone. The most important is that very many young people do regard their education as an investment in themselves that will increase their earning capacity during their adult lives. Many individuals, therefore, certainly make at least implicit manpower forecasts, and the important problem is how to make the estimates as informed as possible. There is also the broader socio-economic issue that many kinds of education, particularly at the higher levels, are extremely expensive, and unless society is likely to be rewarded for this expenditure by the increased productivity[21] of the beneficiary this represents a misallocation of resources. Although manpower requirements alone are an inadequate basis for planning the future structure of the educational system, the absence of estimates of manpower needs makes it extremely difficult to plan the structure of the system, particularly as regards the balance between specialised faculties in higher education[22] and technical and vocational education.

At the technical level the interdependence of the two approaches is clear. It is possible to think of a three-sector scheme consisting of the overall demographic and social situation, the educational system and the economy. In a highly simplified case it may be assumed that the demographic situation determines what education people will be seeking, that the economic situation determines the need for educational outputs of different types and that the two are linked by the educational system. Looked at in this way, the model becomes not merely a device for projecting educational outputs given certain inputs, but a valuable planning tool providing an analytical basis for harmonising economic needs for qualified manpower of different types and individuals' desires for the type of education that best suits them. One of the most important jobs of the educational policy maker is to influence social demand so as to ensure a harmony between the outputs demanded by manpower considerations, and the outputs which arise from the individual's demand for education. The job of the educational planner is to provide him with the appropriate information to bring about this harmony.

A schematic view

A way of viewing the educational system and its relationship to other features of society is shown schematically in Figure 1. This diagram should be interpreted as follows. The three main factors involved in educational planning are demography (shown here as births), the educational system, and the economy and society at large. These are linked by flows of new entrants, pupils and graduates (shown here as unbroken arrows, the most likely direction of flow being indicated by the arrow) and flows of ideas, decisions and influences (shown by the broken arrows, the arrows pointing to the dependent variable). The interpretation of the diagram and areas in which statistical data are required are discussed in more detail in the following paragraphs. A useful way of looking at the data-gathering problem is to consider the exercise in three parts:

(i) Data on the pupils within the educational system;
(ii) Data on other educational inputs: teachers, capital equipment, etc.;
(iii) Supplementary demographic, economic, sociological and political information and also whatever assumptions are made about qualified manpower needs.

Flows within the educational system
The most important of the flows of pupils, students and graduates are

Figure 1 Schematic representation of educational system and its relationship with the economy

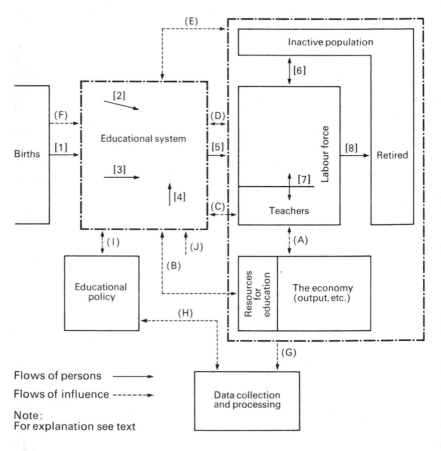

numbered 2–9 in Figure 1. Flows numbered 2, 3 and 4 symbolise the various flows within the educational system. There are, of course, an extremely large number of possible flows which could be identified. It could be maintained that every time a decision or an action is taken by the pupil himself or by others, which affects probabilities about the future course of action of a pupil, this decision should be quantified and recorded.[23] Such a model is too complex to be recommended for general usage at present. There are, however, a number of points in the system where it is usual for decisions to be made which have a major effect on the child's future career. For prediction and decision-making purposes it is important as a minimum to be able to put quantitative values to the coefficients which show the directions and magnitude of the flows of pupils at these critical points. These critical points may be thought of as junctions of a railway system in which an apparently insignificant change in the position of the track at a particular point can have a considerable effect on the ultimate destination of the train. The junctions are the decision-making points of the educational system. The analogy with the railway system can be extended in that, by suitable manipulation of the points, the policy makers can decide how many trains to send in each direction. Also if no route is provided from A to B when the best available information shows that there ought to be one, a new track can be laid. This would correspond to a major reform of the educational system. The main decision-making points in the educational system of many [advanced] countries are enumerated below.[24]

a The decision whether to attend a publicly or privately[25] controlled institution upon first entering education, and at subsequent stages.
b The point in his educational career where the pupil ceases to follow courses that are common to all and enters one of a number of different institutions or streams in which pupils have different expectations of subsequent educational experience. In many educational systems this is often considered to be the point at which primary education ends and secondary education begins and occurs while full-time education is still compulsory.
c The end of full-time compulsory education, at which point the pupil must for the first time make a decision about whether to stay in the full-time educational system, to leave it completely, or to undertake part-time education. This decision must be frequently retaken until the pupil finally does leave the educational system. His choice here is often very strongly influenced by the previous decisions made under (b).
d The decision at the end of secondary education whether to enter a university or equivalent institution full time, to enter another type of full-time institution of higher education, to enter one of these types of institution part time, or to leave the educational system altogether.
e The decision upon leaving full-time education from whatever level,

at whatever stage, whether to enter the active labour force and, if so, into what branch of economic activity and what occupation.

Flows into and out of the educational system and the labour force
Other movements of people which are directly relevant for educational planning are shown as 1, 5, 6, 7, 8, in Figure 1. Flow number 1 represents the intial inflow of young people into the educational system. Flow number 5 represents school and university leavers of all types. It includes successful completers and dropouts from all branches of education, all of whom should be distinguished in any statistical tabulation scheme. It includes also persons who become teachers, persons who enter other parts of the labour force, and persons who do not enter gainful employment upon leaving the educational system. These also should all be distinguished. Flows numbered 6 and 8 represent movements between the active and inactive population. Number 6, which corresponds to population of working age, shows movements of people (especially women) between labour force and inactive population. This is a two-way flow whose direction and magnitude depend on a variety of economic and social conditions. Flow number 8 shows retirements. In general this is a simple one-way flow whose magnitude can be determined with some degree of accuracy from population forecasts by age. These data are clearly important for the calculation of replacement needs of various types of qualified manpower.

Flow number 1 presents little difficulty. As far as educational planning is concerned it can be treated as an exogenous variable and the number of children to enter compulsory education will correspond closely with the number of births the appropriate number of years previously. It is also of course necessary to have data on migration, which is particularly important for regional planning. The educational planner should reasonably expect to have continually updated population forecasts at no more than five-year intervals for at least 25 years ahead. These should include forecasts by individual ages for the population aged 0–30.

Data on the labour force and the inactive population help to provide the information on outputs corresponding to the input data provided by demographic statistics. In an ideal planning framework the educational planner would be able to expect from the manpower planners reliable estimates of the required output of each type of educational qualification for a sufficient number of years into the future. He would also have information about whether the content of the educational qualifications is adequate from the point of view of manpower needs. Unfortunately, such a state of affairs does not now exist and is unlikely to exist in the near future although manpower forecasting is becoming a specialised activity complementary to educational planning. One reason why the educational planner must sometimes himself make the manpower projections he needs is that a very important part of educational planning is, and must be, a very long-term process. Such long-term peering into the future is not so vitally important to many other types of economic planning. The educational planner should, however, make use of already worked-out manpower implications of existing economic plans. Such plans are now far more often established in the context of ten- to fifteen-year perspectives which are necessary for some types of infrastructure investment. This begins to approach the needs of the educational planner.

Teacher flows
Flow number 7 shows movements between one particular occupation—teachers—and the rest of the labour force. It is a two-way flow whose direction and magnitude clearly depend on changes in the relative attractiveness of teaching and other professions. Knowledge about the direction and magnitude of this flow, and on the factors influencing it is among the most important information needed by educational planners.

The educational planner is interested in data on the stock, supply and wastage of teachers for two rather separate reasons. In the first place it can be considered that for teaching, as for other professions, the educational system should ensure that roughly the right amount of people are forthcoming to meet requirements. Secondly, since teachers are one of the important inputs into the educational system, the system itself establishes the requirements. If there are not enough teachers with any particular qualifications the system cannot operate efficiently. If a teacher, or a person who is qualified to teach, enters another profession or the inactive labour force, this, *from the viewpoint of the educational system,* is a loss, even if the missing teachers take up other socially useful occupations like social work or bringing up a family. It is also the case that teacher supply is an area where the educational policy maker can probably exercise more influence on the orientation of the educational system than in most others.

The educational planner thus has a general and a specific interest in the utilisation of teacher qualifications. The specific interest is clearly very important and for this reason alone detailed information on the factors affecting the inflow and outflow of teachers is required. As far as the more general interest is concerned, teaching is no different from any other profession, and the question arises whether all the inter-occupational and inter-industry flows of people with all types of educational qualification should be recorded. [. . .] Ideally the educational planner would have at his disposal details of all inter-occupation and inter-industry movements of people with each educational qualification but in practice this must be a long-term aim. [. . .]

The factors influencing flows of students, teachers and other qualified manpower
In addition to the flows of people in Figure 1, there are a considerable number of what might be called flows of "influence". These are the factors which influence the values of the various coefficients describing

39

the flows of people. They are shown in the diagram by the letters A to J. There are undoubtedly a large number of such influences on the size and orientation of the educational system. Those shown here have been selected as being considered the most important in the present stage of thinking about educational planning. They are considered briefly in the following paragraphs.

Flow A links the labour force with the rather abstract concept, economic activity, which can be thought of as the magnitude and structure of the national product at any period in time. It is a reciprocal relationship; the size and structure of GNP affect the requirements of different types of labour, and the availability, distribution and utilisation of different types of labour affect the size and structure of the GNP. In terms of statistical needs it means that the educational planner, if he is to consider manpower requirements, needs forecasts of national product by industry of origin for the last year of his planning period and preferably for some of the intervening years. They should be accompanied by labour productivity estimates by branch of economic activity. Ideally he should use the detailed inter-industry input-output matrices of the economic planner.[26]

At the same time as much information as possible should be gleaned to show how the level and structure of economic activity is related to educational inputs. In the present state of our knowledge on this subject it means as much information as possible from time-series, from international comparisons and from inter-firm comparisons of how productivity changes, technology changes, new investment, etc. affect or are affected by the utilisation of people with different types of educational qualifications. This is the information that is vital for constructing an occupation by education by branch of activity matrix, or set of alternative matrices for any future year.

The flow that is labelled B links the economic activity box to the education box. It shows the forces which determine how much of its real resources an economy chooses to devote to education at any particular point in time. It is a two-way flow: the desired size and quality of the educational system indicates needs and the state of the economy determines how many resources society can afford to devote to education. There are thus, in fact, a number of different forces pulling against each other and the resultant is the actual resources devoted to education in any particular period. [...]

The flow marked C between teachers and the educational system has as least two different meanings corresponding to at least one influence in each direction. Of these the more straightforward is that which makes teachers the dependent variable. In this case it shows that the size and structure of the educational system determines the numbers and the type of teachers that are required. Various types of statistical information are necessary to make this calculation; as a minimum the numbers of pupils in each branch of education must be estimated and targets set for pupil/

teacher ratios. More sophisticated data are required to estimate teacher needs in particular disciplines, to take account of the use of part-time teachers and so on.

The reverse flow, which makes the educational system the dependent variable, is a rather more subtle concept. It arises from the key strategic position in the educational system that is occupied by teachers. Education is for the most part what teachers teach pupils.[27] The attitudes, aptitudes and skills acquired by pupils in the educational system are for the most part acquired with the help of teachers. If there are insufficient teachers to teach a particular subject, either some pupils will not be able to learn that subject, or those that do learn it will learn it less well than they otherwise would. Similarly, if teachers are heavily biased in favour of particular types of education, this bias is likely to influence pupils when they make their critical educational decisions. This influence has often led to an excessive emphasis on "academic" branches of education. These two factors can mean also that a shortage of specialised teachers can set up a tendency to reinforce itself. A shortage of mathematics teachers discourages pupils from studying mathematics. This lowers the supply of people qualified in mathematics, raises the employment opportunities outside teaching of those that are so qualified, and thus diminishes the future supply. Many aspects of this factor, particularly those involving attitudes, are not susceptible to general statistical reporting. They should, however, be the subject of intensive research by psychologists, sociologists and educationalists. At a more general statistical level, however, teacher shortages by specialisation should be defined and measured at regular intervals.

The flow marked D shows the effect of the labour-market situation on the educational system and vice versa. It indicates the extent to which the labour-market situation affects the choice made by pupils within the educational system. This may make itself felt either simply through employment opportunities available or through movements in relative wages and salaries. If, for example engineers' salaries are rising relatively to those of other professions, other things being equal, this is likely to encourage young people to study engineering in the schools and universities. Conceptually it is possible to consider this problem in terms of elasticities—an X per cent rise in the salary of profession A relative to salaries in other professions is likely, other things being equal, to increase the number of pupils who study subject Q by Y per cent over the following S years. In practice such an analysis would be extremely difficult to conduct statistically since the "other things" would very rarely stay equal for long enough to test the hypothesis. It does, however, give an additional reason, beside manpower forecasting for collecting detailed data on the deployment and utilisation of educational qualifications. Even if it cannot be shown that the economy requires specific numbers of people with various types of qualification it should at least be possible to ensure that the talents and qualifications that young people acquire in schools and universities are not going to be completely useless in their adult life. It will be recalled that the direct manpower supply influence has been treated under the heading of flows of people.

The flow that is marked E groups together all of what can be called the socio-economic influences that affect pupils' educational careers. There are a very large number of such influences, of which those which research has shown to be the most important are listed below[28]:

(i)   the occupation of the child's father;
(ii) the education acquired by the child's parents;
(iii) the income of the child's family;
(iv) the distance of the family residence away from educational institutions at the various levels;
(v)   race and religion.

It is not unreasonable to expect ultimately to obtain statistical information on all these factors at least on an irregular sample basis. It might be desirable to start by obtaining data on the socio-economic background of children as they crossed each of the important thresholds outlined earlier.

The flow marked F indicates the inherent individual characteristics acquired by the child at birth and in the very early years of his childhood, with which he enters the educational system for the first time. It would include characteristics such as intelligence, health, creativity, dexterity, etc. all of which exercise an influence on a child's educational experience under any educational system. It is, however, extremely difficult, if not impossible, to integrate these factors into a formal statistical framework. In the first place many of them cannot be measured. Secondly, even those that might be measurable cannot be reliably measured at very early ages. Thirdly, one of the functions of education is to develop the inherent capabilities of children, at least those that are considered to be socially desirable. The inherent characteristics of children are modified by their educational experience. Many educational systems by concentrating on the abilities that children already have widen the dispersion of ability—others try to close the gap by devoting special attention to children who are less able in particular fields. It is clearly impossible to collect regular statistical information of this nature on children entering school. Nevertheless the importance of this factor should not be forgotten, and it may be desirable, particularly for short-term forecasting, to use some measure of current or past performance as an indicator of future performance.

The flows marked G, H, I and J can be considered together as those which represent the planning and policy-making complex of the educational system. Flow G is fairly straightforward. It simply shows that somewhere in the educational policy-making machinery a mechanism should exist for collecting and processing all types of data, that are relevant for the formulation of educational policy. Many of the statistical data that should be collected are considered in the present handbook. The flow marked H indicates that once the data have been collected and processed the results should be fed into the policy-making machinery as a basis for decision-making and also that the needs of policy makers and administrators should to some extent determine what data are collected and processed. The collection of information on educational research itself must be a part of any statistical programme for educational planning purposes.

Flows marked I and J are rather more difficult to interpret. The flow marked I leaving the educational policy box shows that nearly all aspects of the educational system are subject to some measure of control or influence by the educational policy makers. Clearly, the extent and methods of this control or influence depend upon the administrative structure of the national educational system or systems. It will range from limited intervention to ensure certain minimum standards in educational institutions, through partial or full financial control, to full central control of curricula, etc. It may or may not encompass control of teacher recruitment, regulations of school construction, the prescribing of certain textbooks and so on. One task that needs to be undertaken by any planning authority that wishes to be really effective[29] is a thorough analysis of the decision-making mechanisms and the forms of control available to the central policy-making authorities. Of the flows into the educational policy box, that from the data-processing mechanism marked H has been considered above. Finally, the flow marked J is open-ended indicating that, even if all the other factors influencing the system are enumerated, analysed, assigned numerical values and evaluated, the system is still open and subject to very many influences which cannot be neatly integrated into any formal analytical framework. For example, not only educational policy itself may affect the educational system, but also economic, military or foreign-policy decisions. For example, a decision to institute or to end conscription of young men for military service will have substantial effects on the educational system, at least in the short period. This open-ended flow is also a reminder that the educational planner and policy maker must take into account such unquantifiable but important factors as public opinion, ideological prejudices and changes in educational theory.

A useful way of looking at the educational planning problem is to consider the educational planner as testing the effects on the system of various "inputs" of "policy". He continues to do this until he achieves the "best" result, taking into account the values of society as expressed through its policy makers. This "best" result is extremely difficult to define but can probably be thought of as the result of applying some social cost/benefit calculus.[30] In principle, the planner may in this way test policies concerning the whole educational system or such specific issues as whether a particular school should recruit an additional mathematics teacher.[31] He will not, however, be able to make the tests effectively until he has quantitative data to complete an analytical framework similar to that outlined in this chapter. While it may be wrong to think of educational planning as a mechanical statistical exercise, it is impossible to rationalise many aspects of educational decision-making without assigning, at least implicitly, quantitative values to most of the magnitudes that have been discussed.

NOTES

1 The same conclusion holds even if the educational system is geared to diminishing the inherent and required differences between children rather than magnifying them.

2 It is, however, becoming increasingly common for children to enter school before they reach compulsory school age either for educational reasons or to permit their mothers to enter the labour force. Forecasts of their number depends on a variety of social factors, including, of course, the age of commencement of primary education.

3 The question of geographical breakdown of all estimates and plans is beginning to interest educational planners to a greater and greater extent as they move from general target setting to operational plans. This is not a field in which it is possible to make many general statements about appropriate detail in breakdowns, etc. This handbook is concerned with the global planning framework within which regional and local planning is likely to take place. It may, however, be remarked that the educational planner has a great need of detailed estimates of internal population movements, which hardly exist at present in most countries. In the context of compulsory education it may be noted that ideally demographic forecasts are needed for each existing and potential school catchment area. This probably necessitates considerable local participation in the planning process.

4 In some countries a period of compulsory part-time education follows compulsory full-time education for those pupils who discontinue their full-time education at this point.

5 Two important trends are worth noting in this connection. One, is the tendency for pupils to leave education for a year or more and then re-enter the system—often in connection with military service or similar activities. The second is the increasing importance of continuing education and training throughout adult life. Such "lifelong education" is becoming more and more formalised.

6 Or "filters", as they are sometimes called.

7 Cf. Robbins Committee (1963); see also Moser and Layard (1964).

8 Cf. Moser and Redfern (1965). The present section relies heavily on this paper [and on Thonstad (1969) and Alper, Armitage and Smith (1969)].

9 Even in cases where entry to universities is apparently open to all who qualify, there are reasons to suppose that apparently objective

qualification standards are not unrelated to the number of places available.

10 For initial thoughts on such developments, see Alper (1966) and Armitage and Smith (1966).

11 For a summary and evaluation of different attempts at estimating the economic output of education see Bowen (1964).

12 This chapter leans heavily on the work of Parnes and on Hollister (1966).

13 The fact that highly qualified manpower is often concentrated in service sectors aggravates this problem.

14 For a useful discussion and some empirical evidence see Blaug, Peston and Ziderman (1966).

15 For a description of the way such estimates may be made see Beckerman (1964) and Tinbergen (1966).

16 For a discussion of the use of international comparisons as a basis for forecasting qualified manpower needs see Layard, Saigal and Ziderman (1966).

17 In certain centrally planned economies there is a manpower planning unit in each enterprise which makes detailed forecasts of the firm's manpower needs in the same way that investment plans are made. These are integrated into a coherent educational plan by the central planning authority. See Skorov (1964).

18 Though it may be useful to check projected pupil/teacher ratios against the ratios in other countries at similar levels of National Product per capita.

19 See, for example, some of the results of the country studies in OECD (1965).

20 For example, many educational plans based on manpower needs suggest a very rapid expansion of "second level" manpower and a less rapid expansion of 'third level" manpower. To attempt to base educational policy on this finding without radically altering the structure of the educational system (after analysing social demand patterns) merely leads to social frustration, since the present structure of secondary education in most countries is such that students who successfully complete secondary education expect to have the opportunity to enter higher education.

21 It is, of course, possible to adopt an extremely broad concept of productivity in this context, to take account of those professions whose incomes are low in relation to the benefits society derives from their services.

22 The Robbins Report (Robbins Committee, 1963) on higher education in the United Kingdom, one of the most complete investigations of a country's higher education system ever produced, could say virtually nothing about the balance of faculties in higher education because it made no investigations of requirements of highly qualified manpower, apart from teachers.

23 A forecasting technique based on this approach is developed in Orcutt.

24 It should be mentioned that though for the sake of exposition the decisions are described as if they are made by the pupils themselves, it is clear that many of the decisions are in fact made by other people —families or various public and private bodies—and that all decisions are heavily influenced by a number of factors (often measurable) other than the unadulterated desires of the individual student. [. . .] Much of the art of educational planning consists in identifying these influences and measuring their effects.

25 "Public" and "private" in this context are taken to summarise a number of possible administrative arrangements.

26 It is important to distinguish between: national product by industry of origin and the pattern of final demand. GNP projections are usually demand projections and when disaggregated by means of income elasticity estimates the pattern of final demand by branch of activity can be determined. The manpower planner, however, needs estimates of net output by industry of origin. These can be obtained from the final demand estimated by means of input-output matrices. For a full discussion of this point, see Beckerman (1964).

27 This statement is not intended to provoke any profound discussion of educational or learning theory. It merely states that the point at which "education" takes place is usually when "teachers" come into direct or indirect contact with "pupils".

28 See, *inter alia*: Halsey (1961) and Orcutt, Greenberger, Korber and Rivlin (1961).

29 And which has been undertaken by very few educational planning authorities at the present time.

30 A preliminary mathematical treatment of this type is contained in Benard (1966).

31 This begins to become an operational research approach to educational planning. Cf. Beer (1962). The next methodological developments in educational planning will probably move in this direction.

REFERENCES

ALPER, P. (1966) "The Introduction of Control Concepts in Educational Planning", *Mathematical Models in Educational Planning*, OECD.

ALPER, P., ARMITAGE, P. and SMITH, C. (1969) *Decision Models for Educational Planning*, Allen Lane, The Penguin Press.

ARMITAGE, P. and SMITH, C. (1966) "The Development of Computable Models of the British Educational System and Their Possible Uses", *Mathematical Models in Educational Planning*, OECD.

BECKERMAN, W. (1964) "Long-term Projections of National Products", and "Projections and Productivity Concepts", *Planning Education for Economic and Social Development*, OECD.

BEER, S. (1962) "An Operational Research Project for Technical Education", *Operational Research Quarterly*, June 1962.

BENARD, J. (1966) "An Optimization Model for Education and the Economy", *Mathematical Models for Educational Planning*, OECD.

BLAUG, M., PESTON, M. H. and ZIDERMAN, A. (1966) *The Utilization of Education Manpower in Industry*, Chapman and Hall.

BOWEN, W. G. (1964) "Assessing the Economic Contribution of Education: An Appraisal of Alternative Approaches", in Harris, S. (ed.) *Economic Aspects of Higher Education*, OECD.

ECKHAUS, R. S. (1962) "Education and Economic Growth", in Mushkin, S. (ed.) *Economics of Higher Education*, US Department HEW.

HALSEY (ed.) (1961) *Ability and Educational Opportunity*, OECD.

HOLLISTER, R. G. (1966) *The Technical Evaluation of the Mediterranean Regional Project*, OECD.

JANTSCH, E. (1966) *Technological Forecasting in Perspective*, OECD Document DAS/SPR/66.12.

LAYARD, R., SAIGAL, J. and ZIDERMAN, A. (1966) "Educational and Occupational Characteristics of Manpower: and International Comparisons", *British Journal of Industrial Relations*, July 1966.

MOSER, C. A. and LAYARD, P. R. G. (1964) "Planning and Development of Higher Education in the United Kingdom: Some Statistical Problems", *Journal of the Royal Statistical Society*.

MOSER, C. A. and REDFERN, P. (1965) "Education and Manpower: Some Current Research", in Berners Lee, D. M. (ed.) *Models for Decision*, English Universities Press.

OECD (ORGANISATION FOR ECONOMIC CO-OPERATION AND DEVELOPMENT) (1965) *Econometric Models of Education*.

OECD DIRECTORATE FOR SCIENTIFIC AFFAIRS (1967) *Statistics on Occupation and Education from 48 Countries*.

ORCUTT, G. H., GREENBERGER, M., KORBER, J. and RIVLIN, A. (1961) *Micro-analysis of Socioeconomic Systems, A Simulation Study*, Harper and Row.

PARNES, H. S. (1963) "Manpower Analysis in Educational Planning", in Parnes, H. S. (ed.) *Planning Education for Economic and Social Development*, OECD.

ROBBINS COMMITTEE (1963) *Higher Education*, report of the Committee appointed by the Prime Minister (Chairman: Lord Robbins), Cmnd 2154, HMSO.

SKOROV, G. (1964) "Manpower Approach to Educational Planning: Methods Used in Centrally Planned Economies", in *Economic and Social Aspects of Educational Planning*, UNESCO.

THONSTAD, T. (1969) *Education and Manpower: Theoretical Models and Empirical Applications*, Oliver and Boyd.

TINBERGEN, J. (1966) "Projections of Output and Employment", in *Lectures and Methodological Essays on Educational Planning*, OECD, Directorate for Scientific Affairs.

1.4 The Recent History of Planning Teacher Numbers

Peter H. Armitage

Whether there is, or will be, a sufficient teaching force is a matter for permanent concern. Begging the question of criteria of sufficiency, it is interesting to trace in brief outline the efforts that have been made in the past generation to address this problem.

The duties of the Minister and of the local education authorities with respect to the training of teachers were set out in section 62 of the Education Act (1944):

> 62. (1) In execution of the duties imposed on him by this Act, the Minister shall, in particular, make such arrangements as he considers expedient for securing that there shall be available sufficient facilities for the training of teachers for service in schools colleges and other establishments maintained by local education authorities, and for that puprose the Minister may give to any local education authority such directions as he thinks necessary requiring them to establish maintain or assist any training college or other institution or to provide or assist the provision of any other facilities specified in the direction.
>
> (2) Where by any direction given under this section a local education authority are required to perform any such functions as aforesaid, the Minister may give such directions to other local education authorities requiring them to contribute towards the expenses incurred in performing those functions as he thinks just.

At the same time the McNair Committee on the recruitment and training of teachers recommended close association in each area between the university, the training colleges, local education authorities and serving teachers in an Area Training Organisation. By 1947 these ATOs began to share in the responsibility for shaping and developing future policy and the Minister appointed two Interim Committees for Teachers, one for England and the other for Wales, to secure the widest possible

Source: Commissioned for this volume by The Open University.

advice in developing national policy. In 1949 these committees were replaced by the National Advisory Council on the Training and Supply of Teachers and the new body was to play a significant role for the next sixteen years.

The original purpose was "to keep under review national policy on the training and conditions of qualification of teachers and on their recruitment and distribution in ways best calculated to meet the needs of the schools and other establishments" (National Advisory Council on the Training and Supply of Teachers, First Report, 1951, p. 3). In this report the Council considered many aspects of this purpose but soon became preoccupied with the problems of supply and recruitment. Three developments were then dominant in their minds: first that the post-war bulge of births would reach the schools in the early 1950s; secondly that the school-leaving age had been raised to 15 in 1947; and thirdly that, in contrast with the pre-war situation, an era of full employment had been entered. The short-term view was:

> Even if all the colleges and departments are filled in 1951, the supply of teachers by 1954 may very well fall slightly short of effective requirements, though these are calculated on a basis which provides little or no improvement in staffing standards compared with those of 1950. This emphasizes the over-riding importance of ensuring, in 1951 and later years, that the colleges and departments are filled to capacity with suitable candidates for training [p. 12].

Though they had "no firm basis for estimating the effective demand for teachers after 1954", their long-term view was that 1950 staffing standards could not be maintained without an increase in training places; they cautiously considered preparations for this to occur in 1952, though "the final steps for admitting more students, however, should in our view be deferred until better information is available both as to the prospects for employment from 1954 onwards, and as to the recruitment of students into the colleges in 1951" (p. 13).

By the time the Council reached its Fifth Report (1956), the outlook had changed profoundly:

> It had been expected that, as the special post-war teacher training schemes came to an end, the teaching force would cease to increase at the same rate as in the late 1940s. There was in fact some slowing down, but it was less than had been expected. Recruitment started to improve. More important, wastage among serving teachers fell ... more married women continued teaching than had been expected. ... Classes remain large and there is no room for complacency, but, in spite of an increase in school population between January 1950 and January 1955 of 865,000 or 15 per cent, the situation has not been, and is not now, as bad as had been

feared. Thus it becomes desirable in all prudence to begin to look beyond the time strain to the state of the schools as it will be when, in the not too far distant future, the large numbers of children born in the immediate post-war period pass out of the schools and the school population begins to fall fairly fast. The fall will not have quite the dramatic speed of the rise in the early 1950s; but it will be sufficient to make it no longer unrealistic to think in terms of the introduction of a longer training college course, a reform with which the Council has always been sympathetic [pp. 1–2].

When the three-year course was introduced, there would be a year of intermission with an estimated fall in the teaching force of 3,000, so the Council was highly concerned about timing. It was felt that a suitable time should occur in the period of the declining school population of the early 1960s but the recommendation still required some justification:

To the reader in the mid-1950s it may seem surprising that the possible difficulty of absorbing into employment all the trained teachers available is a factor of which account need be taken in considering the introduction of the three year course in the early 1960s. There is, however, a limit to the number of additional teachers which the schools can absorb and the country afford in a period of declining school population. Without introduction of the three year course or some other equivalent restriction of recruitment (and without some major new source of demand for teachers), it is not impossible that there may be some difficulty in the early 1960s, as there has never been in the 1950s, in maintaining full employment in the teaching profession. In such circumstances it seems wise not to bank up too many teachers for employment so soon, but rather to adjust the flow of training in good time by the introduction of the three year course [p. 11].

By the time this was implemented the situation looked different again. This time the unexpected occurrences were the upsurge in numbers of births from 1955 onwards and the high wastage of teachers, particularly young women, in the late 1950s. At this point the Minister was urging consideration of short-term measures to help the schools and the Council was emboldened to look ahead for a period of twenty years and make a variety of forecasts on a number of different assumptions. These showed that from 1970 onwards there was likely to be a sufficient supply of teachers to meet current policy objectives in the secondary schools but that "the position in the primary schools will get worse and stay worse over the whole period under review" (Seventh Report, 1962, p. 26). The Council considered that it had established "that the shortage of teachers was not a temporary difficulty, but a persistent and deep rooted problem" (Ninth Report, 1965, p. 1).

In its Ninth Report the Council updated its forecasts and considered "possible remedies for the continuing shortage of teachers which we foresee" (p. vii). Now there was the prospect that all qualified teachers must be professionally trained and that the school-leaving age would be raised to 16; both these factors were taken into account, together with the aims on class sizes. It was estimated that the number of teachers in maintained primary and secondary schools would have to grow from 280,000 in 1963 to 500,000 in 1983 on then current policy objectives and to 570,000 on proposed objectives. The Council reckoned that it would take thirteen years before supply matched demand in terms of eliminating classes of 30 in secondary schools and 40 in primary schools, with a further five-year delay if the target for the younger classes was also reduced to 30. The Council urged the greatest possible acceleration of the already accepted expansion proposals of the Robbins Report (1963), and recommended that the target date for an intake of 40,000 students a year should be advanced by three years from 1974 to 1971. These recommendations led to the very rapid expansion of the colleges of education in the rest of the 1960s and the successful campaign to encourage large numbers of married women to return to teaching.

The Council showed considerable awareness in its reports of its own shortcomings and was in some danger of falling apart when it concluded its Ninth Report. While supporting the main recommendations, ten members of the Council signed a supplementary minority report (Ninth Report, 1965, pp. 88–9) because "we do not believe that progress at this pace is acceptable", and further recommended "that the Secretary of State should take steps to secure the application of a four-term year in such number of colleges for such periods of time as he considers necessary and desirable". A lengthy note of dissent (pp. 90–98) was also added to state another position:

> In summary, whilst endorsing the report insofar as it recommends a rapid and large increase in the number of places for teacher education, I dissent from it insofar as:
> 1 The Council has under-estimated the demand for teachers, and has set its sights too low;
> 2 It has fundamentally accepted the structure and the scale of provision of higher education recommended by the Robbins Committee although this is inadequate and unsuitable to provide the supply of teachers we need;
> 3 It has based its long-term recommendation on insufficient data;
> 4 Its proposals may imply discrimination against women in the allocation of places in higher education;
> 5 It has shown insufficient sense of urgency with respect to the short-term problem of teacher supply;
> 6 It has mistakenly accepted the view that the universities should not be compelled to make a more positive response to the national

need for teachers;

7 It has attached insufficient importance to the need to raise the status of the colleges of education and to improve the educational opportunities they provide;

8 It has failed to emphasise sufficiently the need for a great increase in research work in education and social science relating to the problems of teacher supply.

E. E. ROBINSON

We find ourselves in broad agreement with the analysis and conclusions in the above note of dissent, though we consider that the proposal for a four-term year in colleges of education also deserves further examination.

C. F. CARTER

J. VAIZEY

Some time later, Anthony Crosland, who had been Secretary of State at the time of the Ninth Report, declared that he had never had any intention of reappointing the Council: "I thought that was a job that should be done inside the Department and not by an amorphous outside body. If the Department couldn't do that job, which was central to all its activities, it ought to pack up" (Kogan, 1971). Later still the James Committee of Inquiry declined to

go into detail into the reasons for the failure of the National Advisory Council. Some of the reasons seem to be that it was too big; that it found itself advising on matters which fell solely within the discretion and responsibilities of the Government and was thus taking decisions that were essentially political; and that it was hampered by working too much, in practice if not in theory, on the principle of mandation [James Committee of Inquiry, 1972, p. 57].

In contrast the view of Lord Boyle, who was Minister at the time of the Robbins Report, should be recorded:

I do believe that there were gains, certainly at that time, in having an outside advisory body which secured a large amount of publicity for their recommendations; and I am not at all sure the James Committee has been altogether wise in accepting it as axiomatic, with very little attempt at justification, that the Department should have the sole—and not just the ultimate—responsibility for deciding the target of student places [Boyle, 1972].

In the mid-sixties, when the Council ceased to exist, forecasting exercises were continued in the *Statistics of Education* published by the Department of Education and Science (1967 and 1968). However, it was found that the validity and practicability of equating pupil/teacher ratios with limits on class size, which had been assumed by the Council, was doubtful:

> Though the proportion of oversize primary classes has diminished more rapidly than might have been expected, the reverse has been true of secondary classes. Secondary schools, in deploying teachers, seem to have pursued a number of objectives of which reducing the number of classes over 30 was only one. For example, schools may have decided to use additional teachers not so much to reduce the numbers of oversize classes as to reduce still further the size of small classes in which they group the slow learners, or to use more than one teacher with a large class, or to broaden the option in the sixth form and elsewhere. It is right that school authorities should be left free to decide such questions themselves, but an incidental result is to make it difficult, if not impossible, to calculate how many teachers are needed to eliminate oversize classes [Department of Education and Science (1968) *The Supply of Teachers*].

At first the Department of Education and Science continued to use the old pupil/teacher ratios intended to eliminate oversize classes, but soon abandoned them. It was now no longer possible to forecast how many teachers would be required, though it was still easy to compare the forecast supply with the forecast school population to give an estimated "overall pupil/teacher ratio". Whereas the former method revealed future shortages which alarmed the Council, the overall pupil/teacher ratio had been improving and was expected to continue to improve. No attempt was made to say what the overall ratio should be or what supply would correspond to any specified overall ratio, and interest shifted from numbers to other aspects.

When the James Committee was appointed to inquire into the present arrangements for the education, training and probation of teachers, it paid particular attention to the content and organisation of courses, the extent to which intending teachers should be trained with other students and the role of different types of institutions. The Report recommended a major restructuring of teacher training, including the introduction of the two-year Diploma in Higher Education, but it did not consider the future demand and supply. It did, however, reflect the changing official mood:

> To put it bluntly, the supply of new teachers is now increasing so rapidly that it must soon catch up with any likely assessment of future demand, and choices will have to be made very soon between various ways of using or diverting some of the resources at present invested in the education and training of teachers [James Committee of Inquiry, 1972, p. 75].

This culminated in the decisions of the 1972 White Paper (Department of Education and Science, 1972). Although it was thought opportune to expand in-service training for teachers so as to reach the target of three per cent release by 1981 and to extend provision on nursery schools, it was necessary to contract the training system. The full position was summarised:

148. The Government's plans will require more teachers. Earlier sections have already indicated a potential demand by 1981 (subject to uncertainties about the future birth-rate) made up as follows:

  (i) about 465,000 (full-time equivalent) qualified teachers needed not merely to maintain existing staffing standards for pupils aged five and over, in the face of increased numbers and the changing age distribution, but also to secure the progressive further staffing improvement for which the Government are planning (paragraph 51);
 (ii) upwards of 25,000 for pupils below the age of five, to staff the planned expansion of nursery education (paragraph 32);
(iii) about 20,000 to permit, without loss of staffing standards, the release of teachers for in-service training and of probationers who will be undertaking additional training during their induction period following the Government's acceptance of these recommendations of the James Report (paragraph 72).

In order to be ready to meet these needs when the time comes, the Government propose—as in paragraph 52—that planning should be directed to securing the employment of about 510,000 (full-time equivalent) qualified teachers in maintained schools by 1981.

149. The attainment of a teaching force of this size will not require its present net growth by 18,000–20,000 a year to be continued indefinitely. There must soon, therefore, be some reduction in the rate of recruitment. The schools recruit their teachers mainly from three sources: direct from three- and four-year courses in the colleges and polytechnic departments of education; direct from the one-year postgraduate courses in universities and colleges; and from among the large numbers of qualified teachers, mainly married women, who are out of service and can be attracted back into the schools. The effect on the colleges of the reduction in recruitment will depend in part on the preference of employers among these three sources.

150. On present trends the best estimate which the Government can make is that the number of initial training places required in the colleges and polytechnic departments of education by 1981 will be 60,000–70,000 compared with the 1971–72 figure of about 114,000.

This will involve stronger competition for entry to training than in the past with the welcome result that standards will be raised substantially [Department of Education and Science, 1972].

These plans and figures were attacked by the National Union of Teachers (Drake, Morris and Ryba, 1973) and the Association of Teachers in Technical Colleges. Though the numbers seem to be very definite, they are not offered with quite the same air of finality as in the past. It was made clear in parliamentary debates that they would be subject to continuous revision and that they were not predictions. This was amplified in some press reports:

> Thus Mrs Thatcher chose the figure of 510,000 teachers as a matter of policy rather than being presented with an arbitrary figure by statisticians as a result of single-value forecasting techniques. She could equally have chosen 480,000 or, say, 570,000. Briefing by the Civil Service was available for other figures.

At this time profound changes were taking place which were bound to affect the way future supply problems would be regarded. First, there was the reorganisation of the colleges of education, for which there was no precedent. This was partly a rationalisation of the system of producing teachers but it was specifically intended to reduce the number of initial training places in 1981 to about 60 per cent of what they were in 1971.

Secondly, the reorganisation of local government portended far-reaching consequences for education as a whole and particularly for teacher supply, as the local authorities are responsible for the employment of teachers and their salaries. The costs of education had become such a burden upon local finance that some advocates of reforming the rating system were already suggesting that responsibility for teachers' salaries should be transferred to the central exchequer. The Government have not so far favoured this suggestion but it proved necessary in fixing the 1974–5 rate support grant to make a special supplementary allowance. It seems probable that the question of transferring teachers' salaries to central funds will recur. If this switch ever takes place, a reversal of present attitudes might follow. The Secretary of State could be expected to become more cautious in the production of teachers than under a system where, having decided what an adequate supply would be, the main concern is ensuring that the teachers are employed. On the other hand, unless restrained in some new way, the local authorities could wish to employ and could call for as many teachers as possible, in contrast with the present situation where not filling teacher vacancies may be the principal method of meeting short-term financial pressures.

Thirdly, all those involved have become more articulate and developed greater expectations not only of being consulted, but of participating in the decision-making process. In many respects the Advisory Committee for the Supply and Training of Teachers (ACSTT) set up in 1973 may resemble its predecessor, and its work may develop along similar lines, but it is operating in a decision environment that has been transformed. Of course, many elements of the supply situation persist. The prospective size of the school population is still, and must always remain, a dominant consideration. The steep decline in the annual number of births in the first half of the seventies had a considerable effect upon these projections. When the 1972 White Paper was formulated, the projected number expected to be in maintained nursery, primary and secondary schools in 1981 was 9.6 million, and in 1986, 9.7 million. Two years after the White Paper, revised projections put these estimates at 8.7 and 8.0 million respectively. Clearly estimates of teacher needs significantly change if, looking about seven years ahead, you expect about 900,000 or ten per cent fewer pupils or, looking twelve years ahead, you expect 1,700,000 or about 20 per cent fewer. It was pointed out that "the educational policy objectives set out in the 1972 Education White Paper could now be achieved with fewer than 510,000 teachers by 1981. Put another way, 510,000 teachers could represent much more generous policy than when it was first adopted" (Department of Education and Science, 1974, p. 1).

Given that the Secretary of State had now adopted the policy objective of securing as soon as possible a supply of teachers sufficient to avoid the need for maintained schools to have classes of over thirty, the Ninth Report pupil/teacher ratios were revived "as a convenient, though approximate definition of the standards required". Some alternative estimates of future requirements were set out as follows:

Estimated for	1981		1986	
Projection made in	1972	1974	1972	1974
Teachers needed	Numbers in thousands			
to achieve White Paper standards	513	467	517	429
to achieve Ninth Report standards	560	511	565	469

Source: Department of Education and Science (1974), p. 4.

It marked a significant step forward that these officially projected variants were presented publicly, with the desire that "widespread consultations" should take place before "final decisions are taken".

REFERENCES

BOYLE, E. (1972) "Ministers and Educational Reports", *Universities Quarterly*, Winter 1972, p. 5.

DEPARTMENT OF EDUCATION AND SCIENCE (1967) *Statistics of Education*, HMSO, Vol. 4, pp. 77–91.

DEPARTMENT OF EDUCATION AND SCIENCE (1968) *Statistics of Education*, HMSO, Vol. 4, pp. 85–98.

DEPARTMENT OF EDUCATION AND SCIENCE (1968) *The Supply of Teachers*, Reports on Education No. 51, HMSO, p. 2.

DEPARTMENT OF EDUCATION AND SCIENCE (1972) *Education: A Framework for Expansion*, Cmnd 5174, HMSO, p. 43.

DEPARTMENT OF EDUCATION AND SCIENCE (1974) *Pupil and Teacher Numbers*, Reports on Education No. 80, HMSO.

DRAKE, K., MORRIS, N. and RYBA, R. (1973) *How Many Teachers?* a report prepared for the National Union of Teachers.

EDUCATION ACT (1944) Ch. 31, HMSO.

HENCKE, D. (1973) "Forecasting Errors Can Be Very Expensive", *Times Higher Education Supplement*, 3 August 1973, p. 5.

JAMES COMMITTEE OF INQUIRY (1972) *Teacher Education and Training*, report by the Committee of Inquiry (Chairman: Lord James of Rusholme) appointed by the Secretary of State for Education and Science, HMSO.

KOGAN, M. (1971) *The Politics of Education:* Edward Boyle and Anthony Crosland in Conversation with Maurice Kogan, Penguin.

MCNAIR COMMITTEE (1944) *Teachers and Youth Leaders*, report of the Committee (Chairman: Sir Arnold McNair) appointed by the President of the Board of Education, HMSO.

NATIONAL ADVISORY COUNCIL ON THE TRAINING AND SUPPLY OF TEACHERS:

   (1951) *Training and Supply of Teachers*, First Report, covering the period July 1949 to February 1951, HMSO.

   (1956) *Three Year Training for Teachers*, Fifth Report, HMSO.

   (1962) *The Demand for and Supply of Teachers 1960–80*, Seventh Report, HMSO.

   (1965) *The Demand for and Supply of Teachers 1963–86*, Ninth Report, HMSO.

ROBBINS COMMITTEE (1963) *Higher Education*, report of the Committee (Chairman: Lord Robbins) appointed by the Prime Minister, Cmnd 2154, HMSO.

C

1.5 From Learning to Earning: An Economic Analysis

Gareth L. Williams

INTRODUCTION

It is by now well known that, following more than a decade of unprecedented demand by employers for their services, secondary-school leavers and higher-education graduates are finding it more difficult to find what has traditionally been considered suitable employment. The employment difficulties of graduates in many countries are causing concern and are probably at least partly responsible for the reduction in the growth of higher education which has been experienced in several Western European countries since 1970, as well as in North America.[1]

At the same time a sub-culture of educated young people has developed at the margins of the economy and of society. Such young people find casual employment in catering and other personal service industries but rarely enter the formally organized labour market. Little at present is known about the causes of this phenomenon or the likely prognosis—about whether these "drop-outs" are eventually absorbed into orthodox employment or whether a new class of educated proletariat is in the process of being created in Western societies.[2]

The problem is not, however, confined to young people with high educational qualifications. Others also often have difficulty in finding suitable employment. In the few cases where data are available on unemployment levels by age and educational qualifications it is normal to find that less well educated juveniles have higher unemployment rates than their more educated contemporaries. The issue is really one of initial entry into the labour force rather than one of unemployment among the educated.[3] Particular educational qualifications, and the attitudes engendered in obtaining these qualifications, may be a help or a hindrance in finding jobs, but the fundamental problem is created by the transition, usually very abrupt, from full-time education to full-time employment.

Nevertheless, there are three reasons why it is convenient from the point of view of exposition to pay special attention to those young people who have continued with their full-time education beyond the minimum

---

Source: Commissioned for this volume by The Open University.

permissible school-leaving age. First, in many cases they stay on at school at least partly in the hope of obtaining more lucrative employment as a result. Thus these are the people who suffer the worst disappointments; it is their thwarted expectations and dashed hopes, with the accompanying implications for society as well as the individual, that give the greatest cause for concern in the issue of education and employment. Secondly, society as a whole has paid the substantial direct costs of their education partly for similar reasons. In particular, it was generally believed in the 1960s that more secondary and higher education was a way of overcoming juvenile unemployment. It is the discovery that this is not so, except in the naive sense that if someone is in school full time he cannot be unemployed at the same time, which necessitates some new thinking about education/labour-market relationships. Finally, many of the issues are more clear cut in the case of specialized manpower and therefore it is helpful to think first in these terms.

EDUCATIONAL QUALIFICATIONS AND THE LABOUR MARKET

One apparently straightforward explanation of the employment difficulties of educated young people is that the expansion of the 1960s resulted in too many qualified people in relation to unskilled and semi-skilled workers. There are, however, two empirical observations that cast doubt on such a simple explanation. First, unemployment of educated young people is almost always lower than amongst less well educated. Secondly, it is difficult to reconcile this explanation with the existence of educated unemployment at various levels of educational development throughout the world. It has been claimed by some commentators (Conroy 1972) that in New Guinea unemployment of primary-school leavers results from there being too many of them, despite the fact that only a minority of the population receive any primary education at all. In another group of countries in the developing world—as is shown in many of the reports of the Employment Missions of the International Labour Office (1971–3)—the fear is that there are too many secondary-school graduates, again despite there being only a minority of the population receiving any secondary schooling at all. In Western Europe the problem is believed to be concentrated at the graduate level, whereas in the United States the main anxieties appear to be about the employment opportunities for Ph.D.s and those with other postgraduate degrees (e.g. Carter 1973). If there are limits to the numbers of jobs suitable for educated people, why are these limits so different in different countries of the world? Before rejecting entirely this explanation of educated unemployment, however, we should note that it is, to a large extent, simply a variation of the manpower-forecasting approach to educational planning which was so popular in much of the literature of the 1960s.

A more plausible view is that there are limits to the rate at which the economy can increase its absorption of educated manpower. In other words, there are limits to the rate of growth of secondary and higher education if their graduates are not to experience employment difficulties.

In the long run, as technologies, social structure and cultural attitudes change there are probably no limits to the number of qualified people who can usefully be employed. Either technological progress will enable all unskilled and semi-skilled jobs to be done mechanically or in the "learning society" of the future it will become increasingly acceptable for workers at all levels of occupational hierarchies to have high levels of education. In any case, the hierarchies themselves may largely disappear. In the short run, however, there may be very definite limits to the rate at which the economy can absorb larger numbers of educated people. Such limits can occur for technological, structural and cultural reasons. Technologically the number and types of manpower that can be productively employed at any point in time are fixed within narrow limits. Unemployed literature graduates can, in the short run, in no way help to overcome a shortage of engineers. In the longer run, however, technologies (and the term is to be interpreted in a broad sense) are likely to adapt to the labour available. One example, the case of political-science graduates in Germany, is described by Hartnung (1970). According to this study there was no obvious economic demand for 80 per cent of such graduates. However, after a particular post had once been filled by a graduate, employers tended to specify a degree as necessary for subsequent recruits to that post.

Cultural reasons for slow adaptation of the labour market to educational expansion occur because employers have fixed ideas about the right proportions of different kinds of manpower to recruit. Many have conventional notions about the type of job appropriate for a university graduate and that for secondary-school leavers. These ideas are often slow to change despite the fact that increasingly school leavers with intellectual ability have been able to acquire higher education. It is only slowly that even such employers as the civil service and large banks are recruiting graduates for jobs that were previously considered as more suitable for secondary-school leavers.

The structural problem occurs because many of the occupations which recruit highly qualified manpower are hierarchical with well-established rules governing promotion and recruitment. A sudden influx of young people with high formal qualifications and high expectations may well upset delicately balanced career structures. Furthermore, the considerable security of tenure enjoyed by many qualified employees when they have become established in their jobs means that if there is a reduction in the rate of growth of demand for manpower, employers dismiss existing employees only as a last resort. The brunt of any adjustment is borne at the point of initial recruitment.[4] This will exaggerate any impression of imbalance between the outputs of the educational system and the needs of the labour market. One view is that employers treat their qualified manpower similarly to their fixed capital: once they have purchased it they are committed to it and it is new investment which is reduced in periods of slackening demand. Fluctuations in the recruitment of new graduates are similar to fluctuations in new capital formation as economic growth rates change. Like the capital-goods industries, the upper part of the education system suffers a magnified effect of such fluctuations.

EMPLOYERS' ATTITUDES

The ease of the transition from full-time education to full-time employment is obviously influenced by employers' attitudes to educational qualifications. These are not easy to ascertain and the evidence is conflicting.

Throughout the 1960s it was widely believed by educational planners that educational qualifications raised the productivity of everybody who had them. This was the basis of both the "manpower forecasting" and the "human capital" approach to educational planning. This belief has been challenged by two different and to some extent contradictory claims about employers' attitudes to educated people, which have emerged partly as a result of the changing employment situation of these people.

The first is the claim that some types of education at least are positively dysfunctional as far as employment is concerned. In Britain a much-quoted passage from a representative of a major engineering firm spoke of "disenchantment with university graduates".[5] In Italy and France it is widely believed that the "liberalization" of university selection procedures which followed the events of 1968 led to a flood of students ill suited to the discipline of serious employment. A related view is that graduates, and to some extent young people in general, have excessively high expectations about the jobs that are waiting for them.[6] According to this view, therefore, being educated would increase a young person's chance of being unemployed. As mentioned earlier, there is little evidence that in the past this has been the case. In general, the probability of unemployment is higher and earnings prospects are lower the less education an individual has.

The alternative view is that employers are not interested in most educational qualifications as such but that they are interested in them as evidence of basic intellectual ability. According to this view, an employer confronted with two or more applicants for a particular job will, other things being equal, select the applicant with the best academic qualifications even if the qualification is not "required" to perform the job in question and if there is no evidence that possession of the qualification in itself increases efficiency in the job.

The reasoning underlying this attitude is presumably that there is a correlation between ability to succeed in academic examinations and ability to perform well in the labour market. The educational system is, therefore, acting as a selection mechanism for employers. A slightly different version of this view is that success in academic examinations indicates an ability to absorb instruction and, since most occupations require a certain amount of learning on the job, those with high educational qualifications will be able to absorb this training more efficiently. This is close to one of the arguments of educationalists for the teaching of subjects such as classical languages or philosophy—that they train young people to think, and hence presumably to learn. There remains the question of whether the education system *teaches* people to be able to think and learn or whether by a process of selection it merely *identifies* those who are able to learn. This is really the key issue for the future development of the economics of educational planning generally, having implications for the finance of education, for the curriculum and for selection procedures. The economics of education—for long the prodigal son of educational studies—is clearly returning to the fold.

To summarize the argument so far—we have identified five models of the relationship between education and the labour market:

1   that formal education creates "human capital" by providing young people with knowledge that is of direct value in employment;
2   that formal education helps people to develop their mental capacities so that they are more readily able to benefit from on-the-job training when they do enter the labour force;
3   that formal education helps to select people with the mental capacity to absorb on-the-job training, but does little to develop that capacity;
4   that formal education has little influence one way or the other on an individual's performance in the labour force, this being determined by such antecedent factors as social class, innate intelligence, sex and so on;
5   that formal education creates attitudes that are inimical to efficient labour-market performance.

How might we distinguish between these hypotheses in practice and what are the implications of each?

The first situation could be said to exist where there is a specific link between a particular educational qualification and a partiular occupation. If all practising physicians have a medical degree it is a reasonable inference that, even allowing for institutional restraints, an individual, during the course of obtaining his medical degree, acquires some knowledge that is useful to him in performing his job. Slightly less powerful evidence of the same type exists when individuals with a particular qualification are always more successful in a particular occupation than those with other qualifications, but are no more successful in other occupations. This hypothesis receives some support from evidence that graduates of the same level of education but with degrees in different subjects have different unemployment rates and different average level of wages.[7] In other words, employers do not treat all degrees as having the same value. However, to clinch the argument we should need to demonstrate that all students are of equal ability when they enter different courses at the same "level". This is not easy to test either way. If it were shown that educational qualifications have the effect on labour-market performance claimed by manpower-planning and human-capital theories it is legitimate to base educational and labour-market policies on estimates of future earnings and shortages and surpluses of qualified manpower. If there are adjustment problems and young people have difficulties in finding jobs, the appropriate policy is to change the mix of qualifications of young people coming on to the labour market by reforming the structure of the educational system.

Evidence that the situation is that indicated in (2) and (3) would be provided if unemployment levels were lower and earnings were higher, the higher the level of education, and if there were no differences or few differences between graduates with qualifications in different subjects. As already mentioned, it is much harder to distinguish between the two models—that is, to ascertain whether the educational system *creates* the general capacity to absorb specific training or *identifies* it.

If the principal economic role of the education system is to help identify the most able people the democratization and spread of education will necessitate the development of alternative selection procedures. It is well known that mass primary education leads to pressure for more secondary education, mass secondary education to pressure for more higher education and mass higher education, as in the United States, to pressure for postgraduate education.[8] It is possible to interpret this evolution as support for the selection hypothesis. When the large majority of the population has primary education, possession of a primary-school leaving certificate is no longer an indication of relative ability—and so on. Conversely the non-possession of the certificate is an indication of low ability and (on the assumption of this hypothesis) low labour-market potential. So long as education is provided to individuals at no direct cost, or is heavily subsidized, there is little reason why such a process should ever end. More and more education would be demanded by more and more people with no net economic benefit to the community.[9] The appropriate educational policy from a labour-market point of view would be to try to develop less costly selection procedures and to try to divorce occupational and professional qualification requirements from educational achievements. It is a major problem, however, to reconcile such policies with current democratic and egalitarian aims. The candidate's performance can always be improved by previous practice, no matter what the selection procedure adopted. If the educational system did not provide this practice, those in a position to do so could be expected to purchase the examination practice outside the formal educational system.[10]

If the educational system does not merely *identify* the ability to benefit from specific on-the-job training, but also helps to *develop* it, the implications for policy are very different. In many ways they are similar to those of the human capital hypothesis. The more education that a society

63

purchases for its members, the more efficient are its workers at all levels. The economic "optimum" expenditure would occur when the extra costs of providing further education exceeded the extra benefit obtained from the improved labour-market performance. The difference from the human-capital model is in the curriculum implications. Close links between specific types of education and specific occupations would not be necessary since education is stimulating general ability rather than inculcating specific skills.

The fourth and fifth hypotheses about mechanism linking the educational system to the labour-markets are based on claims that educational qualifications are either irrelevant to or actually inimical to the needs of employers. Although these may seem hardly worthy of consideration they are widely held outside formal economic and planning circles. It is certainly true that much of what passed for education in seventeenth-century France (see, for example, *Le Bourgeois Gentilhomme* of Molière) and nineteenth-century Britain (for example as depicted in Beerbohm's *Zuleika Dobson*) and the United States (see Veblen on *The Theory of the Leisure Class*) was directed more towards teaching young people how to consume a high income rather than how to produce it. It is possible that the increasing liberalization of secondary and higher education (which, paradoxically, occurs in large part in response to economic pressures) will lead again in this direction. In both cases policies would be based on the assumption that education is a collective consumption good, and labour-market discussions are irrelevant. If, however, it were demonstrated that this consumption expenditure had nugatory effects on the employability of school leavers and graduates (as, for example, is sometimes claimed about academic secondary-school leavers and university graduates in developing countries who refuse technician and low-level management jobs that are available), then this negative economy would need to be taken into account in deciding the appropriate size and pattern of the educational system.

THE IMPLICATIONS OF INADEQUATE INFORMATION
The economics of education have usually assumed that individual school leavers and individual employers (if not educational planners) have good information about the job opportunities available and the potential efficiency of people with particular qualifications. Much of what happens in practice when people take up their first job can be thought of as a search by employers and school leavers for information about each other.

In order to understand the implications of the proposition it is convenient to start with a rather formalized model. We assume that the individual entering the labour-market wants to maximize his expected lifetime benefits[11] and that an employer in making an appointment will seek to recruit the person who, from among those available, will make the greatest net contribution to the output of the enterprise during the period he is with it.[12] In the normal course of events not all available jobs are known to an individual at a particular point in time and not all jobs offer the same lifetime earnings prospects; it is obviously worth while for him to spend some time exploring the market. At the same time an employer is unlikely to be able to consider simultaneously all the potential contenders for a post he has to offer, so any extra time and resources he can devote to this examination will be well spent.

The optimal period of job search for an employee will depend on: (1) his reservation wage, i.e. his subjective idea of the pay level below which he will not accept a job; (2) the variability of earnings of people with qualifications similar to his; (3) the length of time he is committed to an appointment if he accepts it; and (4) the possibility he has of financing himself, at least at subsistence level, if he does not find employment. Obviously, the higher is an individual's reservation wage the longer is he likely to have to search the market before he finds suitable employment. In an extreme case, in which his reservation wage is higher than any employment available for people with his qualifications, he will never find a job. This in economic terms is the meaning of the claim that the expectations of graduates and other school leavers are too high. We would expect the reservation wage to be above the market wage when the equilibrium level of wages is falling because it is almost inevitable that people's perceptions of the labour market will lag behind actual developments. However, in the normal course of events an individual will adjust his reservation wage if, on the basis of job offers he receives, he finds that it is artificially high. The speed with which he adjusts will depend partly on the subjective characteristics of the individual but partly on the variability of earnings in the job market in which he is searching. If every job he investigates carries the same salary he will soon believe that this is the going rate for people with his qualifications. If there is variability in the wages offered he will be encouraged to search until he has been able to form an idea of the distribution of offers and until a suitable job turns up near the top of the distribution. However, he will also be influenced by the period for which he is committed once he accepts an offer. Should a particular job enable him to continue searching and also not commit him as soon as he has found a more suitable job there will be little lost in accepting such employment temporarily. Conversely if after a job is accepted, subsequent mobility is low (as it is in many developing countries[13]) it will be more important to make sure that it is the best available job. Finally the length of search an individual can envisage is limited by the extent to which he can finance himself while searching, which in general means that richer people can afford longer periods of search and therefore might be expected ultimately to find better-paying jobs than poorer people. At the same time, however, where temporary or casual employment is available individuals may choose to accept this while continuing to search for what they consider will be their permanent jobs. The subculture of juveniles at the margins of conventional employment may consist at least in part of nothing more than young people financing themselves while searching for orthodox careers.

The more closely educational courses are linked to particular occupations, the less profitable long periods of search on the part of the graduate are likely to be. For example, a teacher-training qualification leads to a profession with closely controlled salary scales and little is likely to be lost (at least financially) in accepting one teaching post rather than another. When mass secondary and higher education loosens such links, and graduates enter a wide range of jobs, the returns to search may become quite high.

Employers are in a somewhat similar position on the other side of the fence. How long an employer will search for a recruit to a particular post will depend on: (1) the salary and prospects he is willing or able to offer the appointee; (2) his idea of the ability required for the job and the extent to which a particular qualification is correlated with a particular level and type of ability; (3) the length of time to which he is committed to an employee; and (4) the costs to the firm of not making an appointment. As can be seen, the employer's considerations reflect almost exactly those of the potential recruit. If the salary he is offering is below the reservation price of all graduates with the ability he is seeking, he will have no candidates for the job he is offering. When secondary and higher education expand rapidly employers will find more applicants with what they considered previously to be suitable qualfications for particular jobs. However, an employer may well feel that a General Certificate of Education or a degree carries with it less information than previously about the abilities of a candidate. He may therefore seek additional information through supplementary examinations, personality tests, probationary periods of employment and so on. The costs to the firm of not making an appointment might make him eager to make rapid appointments to posts related to immediate production, but unwilling to offer security in such jobs. Conversely, for jobs connected with planning, policy, research and general management employers will delay making appointments until the "right" person is available but will offer him considerable security. In the first case the immediate loss to production of an unfilled post can be considerable, especially if the employee is part of a production team, and in such cases anybody is better than nobody; the employer will, however, want to protect his position against a fall in output or better-quality labour becoming available. In the latter case the loss to immediate production of an unfilled post may be quite small, whereas in the long run the "wrong" man in the job can do more harm than having nobody there at all.

This section has tried to show that, quite apart from the underlying relationships between education and the labour market discussed in the previous sections, the transition from school to work is a period in which employers and potential employees are finding out more about one another. Policies to facilitate this transition can help to smooth the adjustment process by which "shortages" or "surpluses" of people with particular qualifications are eventually absorbed by the labour market. Such policies clearly include the provision of placement services to provide information about employers and job seekers to each other, and counselling for students to provide general employment information. Other policies would link educational courses more closely to the search for jobs, which may be one of the main virtues in practice of arrangements such as sandwich courses. More radically, new graduates and school leavers might be financed through social-security schemes while they seek their first job. Of course, provision of finance will lengthen the period of search and hence of initial employment. In the long term, however, it should raise income as well as the level of contentment of workers.

NOTES

1 A recent official report paints a very gloomy picture: Department of Employment (1974).

2 Not, of course, that this is an entirely new phenomenon. "Intellectual unemployment" was a widespread and chronic problem of the 1930s. An excellent analysis of the unemployment of educated people in the 1930s is given in Kotschnig (1937).

3 Even when "educated unemployment" is a widespread and chronic phenomenon it is significant that most of the unemployment is concentrated at the point of initial entry into the labour force. See for example Blaug, Layard and Woodhall (1969).

4 In contrast, less qualified employees have a much greater chance of losing their jobs throughout their working life. There are not, therefore, the same pressures towards the concentration of the burden of adjustment on new entrants to the labour force. However, there is an increasing tendency for collective bargaining and social-security legislation to increase the security of tenure of unskilled and semi-skilled workers. At the same time redundancy of middle-aged managers and professional workers (often attributed to professional obsolescence) is becoming an issue. It is possible to interpret these trends in terms of changes in the relative availability of people with different types of qualification.

5 See House of Commons Expenditure Committee (1972).

6 See Kleijn (1973).

7 There was some such evidence in Department of Education and Science (1971) and University Grants Committee (Annual).

8 See, e.g. Organisation for Economic Co-operation and Development (1971).

9 The widespread habit among ambitious parents of purchasing practice "intelligence tests" to help their children pass the eleven plus examination is one example of such a development.

10 Though possibly with considerable cultural gain and economic gain to those providing the education.

11 He will presumably be maximizing the present discounted value of his expected lifetime money income, plus any non-pecuniary benefits such as congenial colleagues. Such complexities are ignored here because, important as they are, they do not materially affect the logic of the argument. However, it should be noted that subjective rates of discount can affect choice between jobs which pay well early but have poor long-term prospects and those with high long-term but relatively low immediate earnings.

12 In practice the employer clearly tries to maximize something more complicated than this. First, for any individual it must be the difference between his gross contribution to output and his earnings that will need to be maximized: thus someone who might be extremely productive might not be employed because, as a result of alternative opportunities, his opportunity costs are very high; second, the period over which the maximization occurs is complex: an employee (e.g. a very able but marriageable woman) who is expected to yield very high returns for a short period and then need replacing may be a worse bet than someone (e.g. a rather plodding man) who may yield rather lower returns but over a longer period. Furthermore, an individual may affect the performance of other individuals, or at least the congeniality of their working conditions, according to how well he socializes with them. Again, however, although these issues are very important in practice they do not affect the basic structure of the argument put forward.

13 See Blaug, Layard and Woodhall (1969).

REFERENCES

BLAUG, M., LAYARD, P. R. G. and WOODHALL, M. (1969) *The Causes of Graduate Unemployment in India*, Allen Lane, The Penguin Press.

CARTER, A. (1973) "The Prospects for Ph.Ds.", in M. Gordon (ed.) *Higher Education and the Labour Market*, McGraw-Hill.

CONROY, J. H. (1972) "The Private Demand for Education in New Guinea: Consumption or Investment", *Economic Record*.

DEPARTMENT OF EDUCATION AND SCIENCE (1971) *Survey of Earnings of Qualified Manpower in England and Wales*, Statistics of Education, Special Series No. 3, HMSO.

DEPARTMENT OF EMPLOYMENT (1974) *Employment Prospects for the Highly Qualified*, Manpower Paper No. 8, HMSO.

HARTNUNG, D., NUTHMANN, R. and WINTERHANGER, W. D. (1970) *Politologen in Beruf*, Ernst Klett Verlag.

HOUSE OF COMMONS EXPENDITURE COMMITTEE (1972) *Higher and Further Education*, report of Arts and Education Sub-committee, Vol. 2 Evidence, HMSO.

INTERNATIONAL LABOUR OFFICE (1971–3) *Reports of the World Employment Programme: Colombia, Ceylon, Kenya, Iran.*

KLEIJN, P. G. M. (1973) "Unemployment among Graduates", *Higher Education and Research in the Netherlands,* Vol. 17, No. 1, Netherlands Universities Foundation for International Cooperation.

KOTSCHNIG, W. M. (1937) *Unemployment in the Learned Professions,* Oxford University Press.

ORGANISATION FOR ECONOMIC CO-OPERATION AND DEVELOPMENT (1971) *Development of Higher Education 1955–56.*

UNIVERSITY GRANTS COMMITTEE (Annual) *First Employment of University Graduates,* HMSO.

1.6   U 68—A Reform Proposal for Swedish Higher Education

Gunnar Bergendal

ABSTRACT

The Swedish 1968 Educational Commission (U 68) completed its main report in 1973. The Commission recommends a very wide definition of the concept of higher education so as to include any qualified education or training for adults, whether academic or vocational in nature. Higher education should be seen in the context of an overall educational planning, with the aim of distributing educational resources to meet the needs of every citizen. As a consequence, U 68 proposes a *numerus clausus* for higher education as a whole. The geographic distribution of higher education is also being stressed, and the creation of one comprehensive institutional organisation for the main part of all higher education is proposed.

The proposals of the commission should be seen in the perspective of recurrent education. The author points to the possible development of a new educational structure, the main feature of which is the division into compulsory and post-compulsory education.

THE 1968 EDUCATIONAL COMMISSION

In the course of 1973, the Swedish Educational Commission (U 68), appointed in 1968 by the Swedish Minister of Education, has completed several reports.[1] The following discussion is intended to present the main issues of the commission's report and the debates surrounding it.

The use of Government-appointed *ad hoc* commissions for planning purposes has long traditions in Sweden. One of its essential features is the open circulation of the commission's final reports to all authorities, institutions and groups involved in the problem and the collection of their views before coming to a final decision. In the case of U 68 the deadline for this "formal" discussion was the 1st February 1974. At the time of writing, it was too early to form a comprehensive idea of the reactions to the proposals of the 1968 Educational Commission.

This openness in the decision-making procedure already existed within the commission. Thus U 68, whose members have been the Under-Secretary of State for Education (chairman), the Chancellor of the Swedish Universities, and the Directors-General of the National Board of Education and of the National Labour Market Board, has had

Source: *Higher Education* (1974) No. 3, pp. 353–64.

three adjoint Reference Groups. Through these groups, representatives of the political parties, of teachers and students, and of the various labour-market organizations, have taken part in the work of the commission.

According to the schedule suggested by the commission, Parliament should take a decision in principle on the proposals in late 1974. It is envisaged this implementation would begin in the year 1976/77.

THE BACKGROUND

Most countries have seen a rapid development of education and research in recent decades. Compared to the educational situation in most Western countries, the Swedish system thirty years ago was rather old-fashioned and relatively small. Today the level of enrolment in all forms of Swedish education (with the important exception of pre-schooling) is amongst the highest in Europe and the structure of the school has been completely remodelled. Thus, for good or ill, the changes in education in Sweden have been more profound than in many comparable countries.

In a sense, 1962 was the pivotal year of this development. Parliament introduced a *nine-year comprehensive school* (*grundskola*), compulsory for all youngsters aged 7–16. The curriculum of the comprehensive school is common to all pupils in grades 1–6. In grades 7–9 a certain specialization takes place according to the interests of the pupils, but there is no streaming with definite consequences for future choice of education or job.

A decision by Parliament in 1968 gave a more coherent organization to the *upper secondary school* (*gymnasieskola*), which has been in force since the school year 1971/72. The present capacity of the upper secondary school corresponds to about ninety per cent of the 16-year-olds. However, only three quarters of the pupils who complete the ninth grade of the comprehensive school go immediately to further studies. Many of the pupils in the upper secondary school have returned to studies after a period of work.

The upper secondary school consists of a little more than twenty branches. Five of these, representing together about one third of the intake capacity, are three- or four-year programmes that qualify, in the present organization, for university studies. The majority of the other branches, all of which are two-year programmes, have a mainly vocational goal, although all of them also give a certain amount of preparation for further studies.

Higher education is intended for adults. No description of the environment of higher education is fairly complete without inclusion of what is often called, with a rather narrow use of the term, *adult education*. Sweden has old traditions in this field through its folk high schools and voluntary educational associations. The number of participants in study circles is close to two million, a quarter of the total population. In recent years a very essential part of the country's educational effort has been labour-market training which in 1972/73 involved some 140,000 persons. The magnitude of the very extensive educational efforts within private and state enterprises is difficult to estimate.

The quantitative development of higher education in the 1950s and 1960s is illustrated in Table 1. The last few years have shown some decline in the number of entrants in post-secondary education, as is indicated in Figure 1. With some simplification which can, however, be supported by statements in government papers, it can be said that the expansion of technical, economic, medical, and other clearly professionally oriented studies with a *numerus clausus*[2] has been motivated by labour-market needs, whereas the open faculties have catered for the private demand of higher education. In practice, the line of division between *numerus clausus* and open admission has also, to a considerable extent, been a question of unit costs.

Table 1 Quantitative development of higher education in Sweden

Year	Net no. of newly enrolled students	No. of students present
1950/51	3 500	17 000
1960/61	8 000	37 000
1970/71	26 000	125 000

It is natural that practical considerations have played a predominant part in educational planning during a period of such explosive development as the 1960s. The creation of new universities and colleges and the organization of higher education so as to meet the most immediate needs of modern society are impressive results of the planning commissions of 1945, 1955 and 1963. An important part of the fundamental policy goes back to the Wicksell-Jerneman commission of the early 1930s, which considered the relationship between higher education and the labour market. Their recommendations emphasized the need for information on labour-market prospects, for educational and vocational guidance and for the development of alternatives to the traditional university education. As for the much-debated question of unrestricted admission to higher studies, the commission pointed out the disadvantages of a "mixed" system of faculties, some open to all, others with a limited intake, but turned down the idea of a general *numerus clausus* tied to manpower forecasts.

In the late 1960s, both the enormous quantitative development of higher education and the thorough change in the structure of the school system called for a review of all aspects of higher education. The 1968 Educational Commission was given the task of working out proposals for plans for the number of students, the location and the organization of basic higher education. Research and research training have not been within the domain of U 68, but the connections between basic training and research have called for obvious consideration.

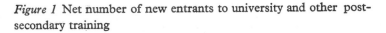

Figure 1 Net number of new entrants to university and other post-secondary training

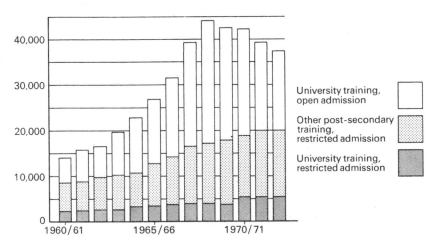

HIGHER EDUCATION FOR WHOM?

For whom is higher education intended and who participates in it? It is well known that a number of factors have an important influence on the selection of students. One is the underlying *school system* and its academic or vocational character. Another critical factor is the admissions procedure. The traditional entrance qualification in Sweden has been completion of one of the academic streams of the upper secondary school, but a decision in principle by Parliament in 1972 introduced new rules: any section of the upper secondary school, be it academic or vocational in character, will give the general qualification for higher studies. For adults with some job experience, eligibility will be determined in terms of age and the length of time spent in employment. The decision, intended for implementation in 1976, also gives new directives for the selection of students for higher studies with a *numerus clausus*.

The content and nature of higher studies also have a decisive influence on demand. The abstract, theoretical character of traditional university studies is not attractive to everyone. Those who have had an upper secondary training with a vocational bias or those with long experience of work may desire further education with a more practical emphasis. In a special report, U 68 has proposed that short-cycle technical programmes of higher education be introduced on an experimental basis to serve such needs.

The *location of higher education* and the forms for its dissemination are of great importance for the geographical and social patterns of recruitment. U 68 proposes that new provision of basic higher education should be almost entirely in locations other than the traditional university cities, with an emphasis on decentralized teaching so as to reach as many as possible of the potential students of the area. On the other hand, the commission assumes that research and research training should in the future, as now, be concentrated in seven cities (Stockholm, Göteborg, Malmö-Lund, Uppsala, Linköping, Umeå and Luleå). Thus, of the nineteen proposed higher-educational areas, twelve will have facilities only for basic types of higher education. This will require close co-operation between institutions in order to provide links between basic training and research. Other decisive factors are financial support, educational guidance and information. They are taken care of by other commissions and by regular planning activities.

The present capacity of what is generally called post-secondary education corresponds to almost one third of an age-group. The proposals of U 68 assume that higher education will expand and develop in order to fulfil the need for highly qualified training of potentially everyone. This does not mean that the commission is unaware of the constraints imposed on the development of an organization by the character of its present resources, its traditions, its "inner logic", and so on. It does mean, however, that long-term planning, and its gradual realization, should aim at a much broader and more varied concept of higher education than at present. The vision of U 68 is not mass production of higher education but an organization that serves complex educational needs, the excellence of which is to be measured along many dimensions.

Such a programme gives to overall educational planning the responsibility of distributing educational resources in accordance with the needs of every citizen, irrespective of economic and social status, sex, religion, place of residence, and, last but not least, age. The century-old tradition of open access to some of the university faculties has therefore to be questioned on grounds of equality. In fact, U 68 proposes a *numerus clausus* for higher education as a whole.

With this general outlook it is natural to use the term *higher education*[3] for a vast field of educational opportunities. In the U 68 proposals, for example, the training of ship masters, nurses, physical therapists and pre-school teachers is considered to be part of higher education. This implies an important attitude towards the future: institutions of higher education should take responsibility for a much wider spectrum of educational efforts than at present.

HIGHER EDUCATION AND THE LABOUR MARKET

The terms of reference of the U 68 commission state the principle that higher education should prepare students for their future occupational activity: this does not exclude broad educational programmes, with application in wide vocational fields. In its main report, the commission develops this theme further. Every kind of education usually has both elements that are adapted to the present state of an occupation and elements that aim at change and development. Education should train the will and ability to arrive at an overall analysis of the occupational activity and its conditions. It is also stressed that only part of the occupational preparation in basic higher education should be concerned with immediate needs. A very important task is to prepare for on-the-job training and for broader responsibility and greater independence in later years.

Against this background it was found suitable to consider the structure of higher education in *two dimensions* as illustrated in Table 2.

Table 2 Examples of the two-dimensional classification of higher education

Base fields

Occupational training sectors	physics and chemistry	chemistry and biology	behavioural sciences	social sciences	mathematics and systems sciences	linguistics	history, aesthetics, science of religion
technology	Engineer						
administration and economics				Law			
medicine and social work		Physician	Social worker				
teaching						Language teacher	
cultural work and information							Priest

Educational programmes have been divided on the one hand into five occupational training sectors and, on the other, into seven "base fields". For example, the training of physicians falls into the occupational training sector "medicine and social work" and into the base field "chemistry-biology". The two dimensions express a tension which is inherent in all education and which is reflected in the U 68 proposals. The occupational dimensions represent an exterior element in education, whereas the base fields stand for an inner structure of knowledge. There is no unique ideal for the balance between the two elements, valid for all kinds of higher education or for all times. It is, however, a firm assumption in the U 68 proposals that existing educational programmes in which one or the other dimension is lacking do not represent an ideal balance.

It has been fashionable among educational planners to frown upon *manpower forecasts*. Since they are unreliable, it is claimed that one had better neglect them totally: flexibility and generality is to be the cure of all troubles. U 68 endorses the traditional criticism of an educational planning wholly adapted to forecasts and states that planning, as far as

Figure 2 Calculated need for new recruitment and outflow: complete higher education

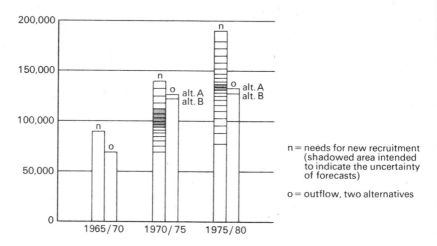

n = needs for new recruitment (shadowed area intended to indicate the uncertainty of forecasts)

o = outflow, two alternatives

the total capacity of higher education is concerned, should be guided rather by private demand and by considerations of the optimal distribution of total educational resources in order to serve the needs of all citizens.

The Forecasting Institute of the National Central Bureau of Statistics has made two extensive studies that have served as a basis, in the spirit outlined above, of the commission's proposals. These forecasts aim at covering the whole surface of contact between the labour market and the educational system. They illustrate the problems of balance at large rather than the future prospects of single occupations. Some of the results are shown in Figure 2. The shadowed areas are meant to indicate the caution necessary in interpreting the forecasts for purposes of educational planning. The reader is invited to speculate on the conclusion to be drawn for the 1980s. The proposals for quantitative planning are summarized in Table 3 below. The idea of a *numerus clausus* has been received rather favourably by most of those concerned, with the exception of the student organizations, which defend the traditional academic freedom also in this respect. When the universities accept it, they do so reluctantly. However, very few of those that accept a more conscious quantitative planning do so with the motivation given by the commission.

THE ORGANIZATION OF HIGHER EDUCATION

If higher education is potentially to serve the needs of every citizen and if one of the goals of every educational programme is preparation for a future occupation, then contacts with society become a central issue in its organization. But the organization has also to meet the demands of the inner structure of knowledge, carried by both tradition and the frontiers of fundamental research. With such points of departure, it is inevitable that any proposals, however well balanced they may seem to the commission, will be looked upon as dangerous by the defenders of the present balance of status, power and influence. A more immediate contact with society and occupational life is opposed by those whose contacts are today indirect, bureaucratic and lagging behind. The arguments very often invoke the undeniable values of freedom of learning and the training to criticize, and the democratic claims of participation in decision-making. An integration in a bigger organization, which would facilitate fruitful contacts with other kinds of education and common use of resources, is opposed on the grounds that it reduces traditional contacts with society.

The organization proposed by U 68 is more uniform in outline than the present one, but allows for considerably more freedom and variation in the content of education and in the management of institutions. The contact with society will be intensive not only in the central administration but also at local level. This is considered necessary in order to shorten the feedback cycles of educational planning.

U 68 proposes that basic higher education should normally be organized in *educational programmes,* which can be *general, local* or *individual.* General programmes should be established by the Government and local and individual programmes by the local higher-education authorities (in the case of an individual programme after application from the student). Table 3 shows the proposed capacity of the general educational programmes in the various occupational training sectors and of local and individual programmes. As a rule, an educational programme should be made up of *courses* giving credit points corresponding to estimated study time. A student may want to study only one or more separate courses of an established educational programme Sometimes a course will be given in its own right, without connection with an educational programme. The commission proposes a very considerable increase in the numbers of such *single courses,* corresponding in 1976 to about 20,000 full-time students or an equivalent greater number if some of them are part-time.

In order to facilitate combinations of courses over the whole field of higher education, a common marking system is proposed (with marks of Fail, Pass and Credit) as well as a uniform system of documentation. Certificates of basic higher education should draw the attention more to content and quality; they should not contain titles associated with the education received. The obvious aim is to concentrate the attention of students and employers on education itself and detract it from the false goal of certification.

As far as *institutional organization* is concerned, U 68 proposes a division of the country into nineteen higher-educational areas, in each of which there should be (with few exceptions) *one* joint organization of all state higher education, covering where applicable also research and research training, under a Board of Higher Education. This board should have some ten members, appointed by the Government after proposals from relevant authorities and organizations. It is proposed that the majority of the Board should represent public interests, but also representatives of students, teachers and other personnel should be included.

Instruction and research take place in the institutes. The forms of administration of these are mainly left to the local authorities. It is assumed that an institute will be able to carry through instruction within several educational programmes, and within different occupational training sectors. It is proposed that, contrary to the present situation, the classification into institutes should be a local responsibility. It can be foreseen, however, that the institutes will in many cases represent the "intrinsic" dimension of the "base fields" (Cf. Figure 2). The occupational dimension of basic higher education is represented in the proposed organization by educational committees, each responsible for the planning of one occupational training sector. Where suitable, these are

Table 3 Admission capacity of educational programmes, by occupational training sector (round numbers)

Sector		1971/72	1976/77	1983/84
Technological training	U	5 300*	7 300	10 000
	L		6 700	9 000
Administrative and economic training	U	6 500*	8 800	10 000
	L		7 700	9 000
Training in medicine, social work, etc.	U	7 500	8 800	10 500
	L		8 400	9 500
Teacher training	U	9 500	9 900	10 000
	L		9 400	9 000
Training for cultural and informative occupations	U	1 000*	2 000	3 000
	L		1 900	2 500
Local and individual educational programmes	U	—	5 000	4 500
	L		3 500	3 500
Without stated occupational aims	U	7 000*	—	—
	L			
Total	U	37 000	42 000	48 000
	L		37 000	42 000

U = Upper planning limit
L = Lower planning limit

   * The present capacity within the training sectors for administrative and economic occupations, and for cultural and informative occupations, lies partly within the free faculties, and only an approximate estimate is possible. Except as regards the training of subject teachers, training at the faculties of mathematics and natural sciences that prepares students for e.g. technical functions has been assigned to "training without stated occupational aims".

supplemented by programme committees for educational programmes or groups of programmes.

RECURRENT EDUCATION

The term "recurrent education" is of recent origin but as an individual pattern of behaviour there is nothing new in it. A more or less systematic interplay between productive work and formalized training has always been looked upon with benevolence, although the trend of the last few decades has been against recurrent education. The motives for recurrent education are threefold:

(1) better contacts between education, working life and society at large;
(2) promotion of equal educational opportunity by offering new possibilities of education for those who chose a job in their youth or who had then no other alternative;
(3) pedagogical efficiency.

None of these arguments points uniquely to one particular realization of the idea of recurrent education as the optimal solution in any single case. Moreover, it is easy to find recurrent arrangements that are pedagogically inefficient and that promote differences in educational opportunity. The point to be made is that we have to consider the problem of how to distribute educational resources over the life span of every individual rather than, as at present, concentrating them in one continuous period in youth. This holds true as much in industrialized western societies as in developing countries.

Even a short list of problems will illustrate the difficulties involved:

(1) Should school for the 16–19 year olds prepare every pupil for further studies and for an immediate period of work?
(2) In the pattern of recurrent education, what should be the balance between basic higher education and further training? What should be the division of responsibility between society, employers and the individual?
(3) How can the admission of students with work experience be encouraged? Should experience primarily be connected with and of specific value for the higher studies?
(4) How can we prevent recurrent education from developing into an even better ladder of self-development for the successful, instead of making it a means to a more even distribution of educational resources?
(5) How should financial support be designed in order to make it possible for adults to return to studies in spite of their economic responsiblities?

It is obvious that the proposals of one single planning commission cannot solve these very intricate problems. U 68 lays no claim to final solutions: the very definition of recurrent education involves so many factors that any practical decision has to be a compromise between conflicting demands. It is, however, easily seen that some features of the present Swedish reforms or reform proposals are designed to promote recurrent education. The new rules of admission to higher education, the increased capacity of single courses, the emphasis on new places and new forms of dissemination of higher education, and the short-cycle technical programmes may be mentioned. In a more general sense, the more conscious distribution of educational resources leading to the general *numerus clausus,* and the stress on contacts at all levels between higher education and society, should be seen in the same context.

When launched for discussion, the idea of recurrent education was received favourably not only by the various organizations of the labour-market but also by educationists and by the public at large. The final report has caused some concern in that it contained no proposals for *the system* of recurrent education, but the commission believes that recurrent education is not something to be introduced on a specific date or organized in parallel with existing schools and universities. It is a pattern, already existing, that has to be developed carefully, sometimes cautiously, by gradual steps and which should permeate *all* institutions of education. In the longer term, then, ideas related to recurrent education may lead to a fundamentally new structure of education. The difficult and crucial problem of the education of the 16–19-year-olds was mentioned above. It may well be that the questions of the length and content of compulsory education have to be restated in the framework of recurrent education. The traditional division of education into primary, secondary and tertiary levels seems, for example in the analysis of the Organisation for Economic Co-operation and Development (1973), to be replaced by the notions of compulsory and post-compulsory education. The function and structure, in this perspective, of what is at present called higher education is well worth a serious analysis.

NOTES

1 The summary of the main report *Högskolan (Statens Offentliga Utredningar,* 1973:2) has been translated into English and is available through the Swedish Institute under the title *Higher Education: Proposals by the Swedish 1968 Educational Commission.*
2 Limitations on numbers, in this case via the professional bodies.
3 The Commission has avoided the term "post-secondary education" because it seems to imply a formal requirement of completed (upper) secondary education. In some cases, for example, the training of ship masters, secondary education may not be the most relevant background.

REFERENCE

Organisation for Economic Co-operation and Development (1973) *Short Cycle Higher Education: A Search for Identity.*

1.7   Colleges and Governments

Walter H. Worth

In thinking about what I might say as your keynote speaker, there was a strong temptation to repeat a speech given about four months ago as part of the 1974 University of Lethbridge Seminar Series on the Politics of Higher Education entitled "From Autonomy to System: A Provincial Perspective". Doing so would have had two major advantages. It would have acquainted you with my perception of certain aspects of institutional-governmental relations in Alberta, and it would have saved me a substantial amount of time. On the other hand, while I am immodest enough to believe that what was said on that occasion has relevance beyond the borders of my own province, I felt obliged to approach this morning's presentation from a somewhat different angle. The fact that a number of you have already read my Lethbridge talk, and that many persons were outraged by what I said, obviously constitute less acceptable reasons for not repeating it.

Eventually, I decided to let you have both barrels: to make available my from "autonomy to system" talk and to offer some observations intended to be even more closely linked to the theme of this conference. My initial comments will be about the context in which we in colleges and governments find ourselves. These will be followed by some discussion about the operation of institutions in the non-university sector before a look is taken at their interaction with government. I will then conclude with a few suggestions about future roles and actions.

CURRENT CONTEXT

A very significant and positive feature of the current context is that colleges and governments throughout Western Canada appear to be in agreement about the general functions that non-university higher education institutions ought to perform. These may be defined as the development, integration and career functions.

The development function applies both to students and to the com-

---

Source: Paper presented to the opening session of the College Administration Project Conference (19 June 1974), Regina, Saskatchewan, Canada.

munity. With students it means fulfilling expectations and actually meeting their specific needs through the application of the principle of personalization. This will require more innovation and less imitation in policies governing admission, programming and evaluation. In the case of the community, it means providing leadership-service in the solution of special regional problems, and in the anticipation and direction of future events. Through such interaction with a much wider constituency each college also will establish its own special identity or mission.

Integration is concerned with the harmonious development of the total person in pursuit of the higher order needs of liberation and integrity. Character traits such as self-awareness, flexibility, openness, creativity, courage and the capacity to love may be viewed as prerequisites of personal integration and responsible citizenship. These derive from the general education efforts of the college. As in earlier phases in the educational system, the valuing aspect of learning must be a central part of college experience. Valuing is necessary, not only to establish or reinforce personal behavior standards, but also as a basis for active participation and influence in shaping the future of the wider community.

Colleges must also be involved in the education of individuals for an occupational role in society. For some they must provide first-entry occupational preparation. For others they must offer opportunities for upgrading previously acquired skills and knowledge. For still others they must provide for retraining in a different occupation. Performance of this career function requires that stress be placed upon the use of knowledge over knowledge for its own sake. In this way it will be possible to prepare persons who will be readily employable and productive within a minimum period of time. Nonetheless, care must be taken to avoid narrow prescriptions that might result in occupational obsolescence and that might restrict the awareness of the student of the broader social and personal implications of the specialized role that he may be called upon to play.

This agreement about functions comes at a time when higher education in its traditional institutional form appears to be in a steady or slow growth state because of the interaction of a variety of well-known circumstances. Less well-known—or at least less publicly acknowledged —are some of the actual and probable correlates of having a relatively modest rate of increase in revenues during the next few years.

First, and most obvious of these correlates, is the attempt on the part of those currently employed to preserve their jobs. While the phrase "feather-bedding" is probably too harsh a term, most of us have already observed efforts on the part of staff to safeguard their own positions. Tenured staff members develop even stronger arguments for the tenure system and agree that scrutiny for those aspiring to tenure be made more searching in order to limit rationally the total number of individuals permanently linked to institutions. Non-tenured staff begin to look more favorably at unionism and a negotiated contract on the assumption that a contract might well be better job security, particularly for the young, the part-time and the peripheral instructor than would an orthodox tenure system. Similarly, it can be expected that administrative officers will probably spend more time in their present posts and will be reluctant to move in the absence of quite explicit provisions for job security. All of this is likely to result in an aging teaching staff and administrative core, finding each year it is easier to espouse conventional wisdom than to withstand the physical and emotional costs of change.

Secondly, institutions experiencing competition for the clientele previously served are quite likely to embark on explorations for new mass markets which can generate increased revenue. The first step is for institutions to invade regions in which undercapacity still exists. This often gives rise to territorial disputes. The losers then search for completely new markets. This frantic pursuit of additional enrolments has led in the United States, according to a news item in the *Chronicle of Higher Education* (Magarrell, 1974), to a demand for "truth-in-education" laws to protect student interests. The era of the "education huckster" is closer than we care to admit.

A third correlate is curiously mixed in that it involves both rejection and utilization of educational technology. There are those who will eagerly embrace such things as computer-assisted learning, television, individually paced instruction, and the like, in the hope that these devices can bring about economies by reducing salary costs. Yet concurrently others will adamantly resist the application of technology except in a complementary or supportive role to the teacher. This resistance is, of course, rationalized in many ways, including the old argument of impersonality and dehumanization. But significant also is the fear that a computer, or a programmed textbook, or a television set might replace a flesh-and-blood instructor.

Traditionally within higher education, tension has existed between those who teach and those who administer. However, in a steady or slow growth state a fourth correlate is likely to be greater animosity and mutual suspicion. Staff will remain convinced that central administration has access to money which it could use to increase their salaries or add appointments if it chose to do so. Administrators or board members, on the other hand, will frequently embrace the [...] belief that staff members are inflation oriented, if not lazy, and unwilling to assume heavier work loads in order to insure the economic viability of the institution.

Another probable correlate will be a tendency for central administration or the oligarchic staff leadership to isolate itself from reality. The scenario might run something as follows: administrators who served during periods of rapid growth and acknowledged success, and who attributed or allowed others to attribute these developments to their own leadership, upon finding that the institution is experiencing difficulty may tend to blame staff, obstreperous students, or some other group.

Alternatively, they may be inclined to assume that if others would just follow their instructions, things could return to a happier norm. As these ideas persist they tend to talk more and more to their immediate associates and drift farther and farther away from the concerns of the majority of the people involved in the institution.

A sixth correlate is that institutions will be tempted to cut back on research and development activities designed ultimately to improve or terminate existing programs and to identify desirable new ones and to concentrate on business-as-usual, stressing their seemingly successful ones. As institutions try to cope with little or no increases in financial support they first cut back on physical plant maintenance, secretarial help, and library acquisitions. Then they cut back on student-related activities like counselling and health services while upping the costs of housing and food services. Eventually, they may get around to curtailing staff appointments and finally to actually terminating some existing staff. The rarely used but opposite point of view is that only through intensified research and development activities is a no-growth or declining industry likely to reverse the tide of adversity.

These six potential correlates, while understandable, are all potentially pathological, destructive, and disruptive. Job preservation, frenzied search for new markets, fear of technological change, mutual suspicion on the part of staff and administration, unwillingness to change with the times, cutbacks of expenditure on research and development, and the insulation of central administration from the actualities of changing conditions could lead some institutions into even more precarious conditions than they presently face.

At the same time, every college is being buffeted by a worldwide impulse that has promoted the development of adult education systems and the management of these systems at the national or provincial level. That impulse can be identified as follows: societies, whether modern or modernizing, are experiencing an increasing demand for access to higher education and, at the same time, an increasing requirement for trained citizens that only higher education can produce. This demand and this requirement have forced a steady expansion of colleges and universities around the world. They have also brought about growing diversity in institutions, programs and services to meet the specialized needs of students and society. No longer can one institution, or even one type of institution, hope to provide the myriad specialities that now comprise post-secondary education. Today, the total requirements of higher education are met through a system of diverse institutions and agencies. Each part of the system serves some special purpose or a particular geographic area, but collectively the system offers a fuller range of educational choice.

In an interconnected and interdependent system of institutions, programs and services, the offerings of individual institutions can no longer be left to chance. Large-scale planning is necessary to coordinate the many parts of the system, and since this is obviously beyond the capacity of any single institution, agencies for this purpose have emerged or are proposed as the newest feature on the academic landscape in virtually every country of the world.

SYSTEM OPERATION

Two of the key components in the system of adult education in Western Canada are colleges and governments. The college component consists of a number of institutions that vary in size, name, age, services, internal structure and relations to government. They are, however, quite similar in functions, clientele, and financing. Yet it is still difficult to define with precision this component, and its constituent parts, because our data base or statistics are incomplete and unnecessarily complicated.

Thus it is not surprising to find in the report on *New College Systems in Canada*, prepared by Cicely Watson (1973) of the Ontario Institute for Studies in Education, the assertion that the statistical records of colleges are of such poor quality that it is difficult to see how administrators can make rational educational policy decisions. This is a very serious weakness in the non-university sector which colleges and governments are already working in concert to overcome.

Another cause for joint concern and action identified in this same report is that the relevant legislation, regulations, staff manuals, calendars, functional descriptions of offices, and public statements of officials of this sub-system portray a picture which very often differs from that found upon visiting the various institutions. Watson and her colleagues marveled at the ingenuity with which senior officials make institutions mirror their own philosophy, reinforcing or distorting the sub-system as designed. The regulations of the CAATs in Ontario provide for no faculty or student participation in the operation of the college, yet they seem to have at least as important a consultative role as that of their counterparts in the other provinces. The Alberta public colleges provide officially for student and faculty participation, but from descriptions of procedures obtained in the institutions themselves, their consultative activities seem rather minor and their initiating power less than the actual practice in Ontario. Although formally extremely democratic, most of the CEGEPs in Quebec actually seem to be run in a quite authoritarian fashion. This state of affairs cannot be assessed other than subjectively, on the basis of the statements of administrators and the documented public stances of the faculty. Authoritarianism is a measure of the difference between one's expectation of being permitted to participate in decision-making and the degree to which one is given the opportunity to participate. Some staff and students may hold unrealistically high expectations; others are content because their expectations are humble. Generally, all of these institutions were found to be more conservative and hierarchical than was previously supposed.

At the same time, the Watson study supports the view that college administrators and associated government officers are imbued with a strong sense of mission and social cause. Those involved in the non-university sector are convinced that colleges are a liberating force, enabling students to realize ambitions they could otherwise never hope to achieve and allowing faculty to provide a service and enjoy a useful sense of purpose hitherto generally denied to teachers at this level. And there is little doubt that our colleges are serving a broader segment of society than our universities. They are indeed broadening the horizon for adults whose opportunities have hitherto been too narrowly limited. They are free from many of the constraints of academic tradition, but they are not free from the social constraints which lie beneath some of the academic selection devices. In the past, Western Canada has been able to provide considerable scope for human development to people from other countries because its rapidly expanding economy created these opportunities. Yet in many ways these were not matched with a careful cultivation, through education, of our own human resources. Our colleges can do much to redress the balance.

But the revolution in quality and quantity of adult recurrent education which they have helped to trigger has barely begun. Nor has it significantly altered college operation. Colleges have, as yet, made virtually no contribution to educational process changes. They have merely mimicked many of the most undesirable features of traditional academic studies. Their programs are fragmented, with large numbers of courses, class hours and specific assignments. There is relatively little freedom of or from study for their students. Their institutional structure is often formal and expensive, using a very large number of highly paid professional staff with considerable overlapping of administrative authority. In the rapid birth and exponential growth phases that many colleges experienced there was ample opportunity for empire building, and the duplication which these empires represent will be difficult to eliminate. Their educational process is equally expensive, characterized by a very large number of teachers and expensive machinery and material. This condition is changing as funds become scarcer. This missionary spirit of college administrators is now being put to the test as they are expected to serve many more students on proportionately fewer dollars. In such a situation, colleges might well become pioneers in reforming traditional teaching/learning processes. The OECD report concludes, however, that they lack two important ingredients to accomplish this: at the institutional level, faculty commitment to experimentation; and at the system level, administrative commitment to empirically based research and evaluation.

The apparent absence of these two ingredients or commitments may be, at least in part, a reflection of a developmental pattern which many formal organizations seem to follow. First comes the "birth" period when relationships between all staff are informal and not appreciably controlled; tasks are relatively unspecialized; routine procedures are not well established; goals and operational objectives are in the process of being developed; there is freedom to experiment in a tolerant environment. This is followed by the "youth" period when interpersonal relationships become formalized; tasks become more specialized; procedures become more routine as the number and complexity of activities increase; size increases rapidly; the environment becomes less supportive and more critical of the organization. A "productive" period then emerges in which formal interpersonal relationships become stabilized; the number and kinds of specialized tasks and standard activities are limited; the rate of size increase decreases; innovativeness is less encouraged; the amount and intensity of activities to influence a less supportive environment increase. Concluding this unfolding is the "mature" period when structures and functions become fixed; broad goals become emphasized; decentralized decision-making is encouraged; size and program changes occur slowly; some control over the environment has been obtained.

The existence and influence of such a four-fold developmental sequence in Alberta colleges was recently examined by Heron and Friesen (1973), who reported three main sets of conclusions.

In terms of levels of decision-making, as colleges grow older they tend to become more decentralized and to become more independent of their boards of governors. Though decision-making, especially for operational problems, does not necesarily become more widespread at any one level, it does seem to become distributed among more and lower levels in the college hierarchy. At the same time, a clearer distinction between operational and policy decisions appears to occur, with operational decisions being made by the chief executive officer and his staff and policy decisions by the board and the provincial government authority.

In terms of the degree to which staff behaviors are both specialized and standardized, there is a strong suggestion that increased structuring is directly related to the introduction of increasing numbers and kinds of specialized programs. Not only does specialization suggest the need for more standard types of control but it also appears to result in an increase in the number of support staff. This increase in specialization appears also to result in more decentralized decision-making.

Mechanisms for controlling and regulating employee behavior also tend to be different at different periods in the structural development of colleges. In the initial stages of growth, colleges tend to exercise control by centralizing decision-making at the level of the chief executive and the board of governors. This centralization and the wide reporting spans enjoyed by the chief executive also suggest a sensitivity to the surrounding environment to which the college is accountable, namely, the various constituencies represented on the board of governors. In the "youth" stage, colleges appear to exercise control by instituting many direct reporting relationships between subordinates and supervisors. There was a strong suggestion that control could be obtained more readily through surveillance and reporting procedures than through the establishment of more impersonal and procedural mechanisms. In the later stages these reporting relationships were either stabilized or even reduced. They became supplanted by the gradual introduction of more and more written documents to define and record the performance of employees and to communicate rules, regulations, and guidelines for standardizing procedures.

In summary, Heron and Friesen argue, as does Watson, that in the dimensions of structuring staff activities, of decentralizing decision-making and of changing hierarchical configurations, colleges exemplify the process commonly referred to as bureaucratization. In other words colleges, as has been postulated for other formal organizations, seem to move from a participative, open-climate stance in their early years to a more authoritarian, closed-climate stance in their later years. They also appear to become less influenced by community wishes as these are expressed through a board of governors or advisory committees. In addition, these progressions seem to occur independently of such factors as changes in chief executive, in legislation, in the composition of the board of governors, in location in physical plant, and in numbers and kinds of programs. Given this kind of strong internal momentum in institutions of higher education, it is litle wonder that governments sometimes resort to the use of equally strong measures to restrain or redirect it.

I am unaware of any comparable appraisals of provincial coordinating agencies—government departments or otherwise. Yet I suspect that many of you, on the basis of personal experience, would be inclined to agree with me that in Western Canada these government organizations exhibit similar characteristics. Certainly the trend seems to be more clearly toward centralization to effect greater accountability, more accurate and complete information, and more effective complementation of efforts. Closely related to this trend is growing central agency concern about issues that have often been primarily within the jurisdiction of institutions, such as faculty functions and work load. To a considerable extent this concern reflects disenchantment with traditional institutional approaches to budget justification and quality evaluation in terms of inputs rather than results. Related to accountability, effective management, centralization and internal operation is a more fundamental concern of legislators over adequate means for evaluating higher education, including its outputs in relation to societal needs. Recent controversies about surpluses of highly educated manpower in some areas and shortages in others mirror the increasing demand for more effective planning to conserve and develop human resources. There are also counter trends in every province related not to real need analysis, but to special-interest pleading and what can only be described as vested interest and local pride.

Although circumstances and means vary in British Columbia, Alberta, Saskatchewan and Manitoba, there is an obvious determination to gain the commitment to experimentation and to empirically based research and evaluation which the OECD report claimed was needed.

Currently, it seems that governments are more determined that this should occur than are the colleges. Witness the various new carrot-and-stick funding arrangements and the more rigorous program review policies and procedures appearing on the Western scene. The apparent difference in determination for reform may arise from differences in development periods between a specific college or group of colleges and a given government, including its designated coordinating agency. For example, a "mature" college is likely to be critically suspicious of a government during its "birth" period or of a coordinating agency in its aggressive "youth" stage. Similarly, a college in its "birth" and/or "youth" phases is probably going to be a source of frustration and anxiety to a "productive" and/or "mature" central authority. In either case, the resulting cross-impacts are apt to yield visible differences in externally versus internally induced initiatives for change.

FORWARD TOGETHER

Having noted the existence of some points of congruence and disparity in the intentions and behaviors of colleges and governments in a changing contextual framework, it seems appropriate to conclude with a few suggestions about what colleges and governments might do so that together they can better serve the electorate.

The first of these is that the ideal comprehensiveness by institutions should be abandoned. Instead each ought to focus on sharply delineated markets desiring specialized services. The ideal of comprehensiveness which, of course, is essential at the system level, holds that all community colleges should offer university transfer programs, technical-vocational education, general education, further education, counseling and guidance while serving as a focal point for community cultural, recreational, and intellectual interests and aspirations. Even technical institutes, vocational centres, agricultural colleges and proprietary schools are seen as offering comprehensive programs in liberal or general education. Rejecting such an ideal at the institutional level means trying to select a competitive domain in which a given institution can or does have an advantage and building upon that strength and opportunity. It means identifying a distinctive and continuing clientele through sensitive market research, and developing programs of specific interest to that group. It means assuming a "broker" role in relation to other relatively unique institutions to help facilitate the delivery of comprehensive services by the system to various regions in a province. And it also means curbing narrow faculty, administrative or community desires or aspirations so often rationalized through arguing a social or economic need. There is emerging indicative evidence that serving a specialized clientele produces stable or expanding enrolments and financial viability. When coupled with extra-institutional services arranged or purchased for specified periods for particular clients, this approach also promises to extend edu-

D

cational opportunity. Only the system can reasonably strive to be all things to all people.

A second, and closely related suggestion, is for colleges and governments to exhibit parsimony with respect to claims. Public malaise regarding higher education earlier in this decade was considerably precipitated by the grandiose claims of educators to be able to do too much too frequently during the times of expansion. The institutional question was phrased, "Is there a demonstrable social need for something?" with the answer, "If there is, the institution should attempt to do it." Such rhetoric produced rampant program proliferation. It is quite significant that researchers discovered that one of the correlates of institutions in serious financial difficulties was rapid program expansion. It is also significant that an investigator who examined the case histories of recently dead institutions discovered that all had manifested a pattern of frenzied creation of new programs during the last years before death. A better question might be, "What is the least an institution can do in order to meet its mandate and to warrant the financial support necessary to ensure institutional continuation?" Again, in order to determine a parsimonious catalog of purposes and institutionally mounted programs which will appeal to distinctive clienteles, careful market analysis to detect trends and discern likely saturation points is essential at both the local and provincial levels.

Third, increase the use of an external performance audit. Performance audits by outsiders—people who would not be representing the provincial agency or the institution—would provide a less biased appraisal of existing programs or services in terms of their stated objectives. Moreover, only an external evaluation is ever likely to question the validity of the objectives themselves. Further, the audit would assess the organization and operating efficiency of the unit in relation to the delivery mechanism, and also evaluate the extent to which effective quality was being maintained relative to the investment of resources in the unit. By providing for performance audits on the request of an institution or on its own initiative, the provincial agency would not abrogate its authority and responsibility, nor undermine institutional independence. Rather, the general overriding purpose of such an audit would be to develop a report to serve as the basis for discussion between the agency and the institution. This audit, this common ground for discussion, would provide the basis for a joint review of high-cost and/or declining enrolment programs with a view to either making them more attractive and efficient or discontinuing them.

Fourth, in setting priorities government must take responsibility for ensuring that the institutions affected both by the priorities and by the actual funding process be fully involved. Higher education budgets, because of their magnitude and potential impact, are a sensitive matter. This sensitivity extends to institutional administrators, board members and civil servants. It also extends to elected representatives, who have the responsibility for establishing priorities and eventually approving public dollars for the delivery of higher education. Apprehension and suspicion are common. Institutional administrators fear that the justifiable—even essential—items of program and service support will be deleted from their budget requests through ignorance or bias. Officials of the government agency with responsibility for the budget review of higher educational institutions are concerned that provincial priorities will not be acknowledged and given adequate consideration. In addition, members of the legislature and board members may be concerned about actions that may be detrimental to their constituents. In this kind of atmosphere it is imperative that the establishment of priorities and their translation into funding at the provincial level occurs not in isolation but rather with the full knowledge and, to the extent possible, effective involvement of all responsible parties.

A CONCLUDING OBSERVATION

These four suggestions may not be particularly startling. But they could help all of us achieve a little more satisfaction from the state of affairs projected for the immediate future. A relocalized faculty might contribute once again to the development of a feeling of community. A more parsimonious set of goals might allow time and energy to be devoted to the more effective achievement of those goals. And if understanding and acceptance of reality is the correlate of satisfying mental and organizational health, then widespread understanding and acceptance of a more realistic view of programs and services could contribute to greater tranquility on the campus and increased levels of support by government.

In such circumstances it is likely that the joint commitment of colleges and governments to an open society in which the fewest possible number of educative decisions are irrevocable will be attainable. And the concept of recurrent education is then not just a matter of rigging a safety net for those who fall, but a perpetuation of the idea of a learning community in which it is always possible to acquire knowledge and organized experience, whether for vocational reasons, for cultural reasons, for pleasure or for a combination of all these. This is a luxury which Western Canadians should be able to afford in the last quarter of the twentieth century.

REFERENCES

HERON and FRIESON (1973) "Growth and Development of College Administrative Structures", *Research in Higher Education*, Vol. 3, pp. 333–46.
MAGARRELL, J. (1974) "'Truth-in-Education' Laws Proposed to Protect Students", *Chronicle of Higher Education*, 1 April 1974, p. 2.
WATSON, C. (1973) *New College Systems in Canada*, Organisation for Economic Co-operation and Development.

1.8 A Management Scientist Looks at Education and Education Looks Back

Russell L. Ackoff

ABSTRACT[1]

First, three fundamental educational issues are identified which are usually ignored in favor of almost trivial operating problems. Secondly, a description is given of the way Management Scientists *could* contribute to the resolution or dissolution of these problems if they stopped accepting those given to them and insisted on working on the "right ones". Finally, the author describes some solutions proposed by atypical and irreverent Management Scientists.

INTRODUCTION

It is hardly necessary to say to a group of scientists and educators that no single discipline—let alone an interdiscipline such as the Management Sciences—can be spoken for by any one of its practitioners. The Management Sciences are neither monolithic nor are they always called by this name. To some, "Management Science" is synonymous with "Operations Research", or the "Policy, Organizational or Decision Sciences", to mention but a few. It is not surprising, therefore, that it is at least as hard to find a prototypical practitioner of the Management Sciences as it is to find a prototypical educator. Although I am involved in both activities the remarks that follow are made from a very personal point of view.

From where I view things educators, educational administrators and educational researchers appear to be fiddling with schools while education burns. Our educational system as a whole and every part of it is being subjected to widespread criticism.[2] The indictments against it are too numerous even to list here. It is worth noting, however, that a growing number of serious and qualified evaluators find that the primary function of schools, even primary schools, is no longer educational. Schools have become institutionalized baby-sitters, publicly supported day-care centers, low-security sleep-out detention homes and places for

---

Source: Prepared for the AAAS Symposium (1974) "Research on Decision Making—Potential for Education", San Francisco.

those between infancy and adulthood to grow up without bothering their parents or being bothered by them. Although the United States has a larger percentage of its population in school than any other nation, it is the only developed nation in the world with a declining literacy rate. Little wonder that Ivan Illich (1972) suggested "deschooling" society and that so many take his sugestion seriously.

The height of higher education has not kept it from being climbed over by its critics. It is charged with ineffectiveness, inefficiency and irrelevance; with following rather than leading cultural change; with being more an apologist for the present and past than an inventor of the future; and with failing to respond to the critical needs both of the society of which it is a part and of the young who take part in it. Those involved in higher education tend to confuse growth with life; they forget that cemeteries grow continuously.

The failure of formal education, in my opinion, derives from two sources. The first is its failure to deal with the right problems, not its failure to solve the problems with which it deals. The second is the fact that education is *not* carried out by a system but by an *antisystem*—a deliberately non-interactive set of institutions, each of which is carved up into equally non-interactive components.

Despite the need to face fundamental educational problems most Management Scientists working in this area accept less important problems posed by educators. As a result their efforts have been directed at making an ineffective system operate more efficiently. Efficiency, not effectiveness, has been at the focus of their attention.

Management Scientists have been actively engaged for many years in assisting educational administrators in solving the types of problems with which they normally occupy themselves: budgeting to and within schools; forecasting, allocating and scheduling facilities, faculty and students; trading-off between class size, teaching load and required contact hours; purchasing supplies; supplying and staffing service, administrative and academic units; locating new facilities and determining what capacity they should have; and developing automated information and budgetary control systems.[3]

The outputs of such studies have not been insignificant. They have reduced waste of valuable human and material resources, and they have led to greater efficiency of operations. There is nothing wrong with what has been done, but there is with what is *not* being done; the sins are of omission, not commission. My critique, therefore, is directed at the Management Sciences as much as it is at education.

My remarks fall into three parts. I will identify a few general educational problems which I believe are not dealt with adequately. I will say a few words how the Management Sciences *could* contribute to their solution. And finally, I will try to give you a taste of the types of solution proposed by atypical Management Scientists.

1 Education as a System

Understanding of the failure of formal education must begin with recognition of the fact that it is less effective in general than informal education. Evidence of this is plentiful. Children learn their first language at home and on the streets more easily than they learn a second at school. Most adults forget much more of what they were taught in school than of what they learned out of it. Most of the knowledge that adults use at work and play they learned at work and play. This is even true for teachers: they learn more about the subjects they teach by teaching them than by being taught about them. University professors are not exceptions; many of them are occupied with subjects they were never taught. None of the subjects I have taught since 1951 even existed when I was a student.

Informal learning takes place without formal teaching. Schools, however, are committed to teaching, not learning, because teaching, unlike learning, can be industrialized and mechanized; it is easier to control, budget, schedule, observe and measure. Educators appear to want what they can measure rather than try to measure what they want. Teaching is an input to education, not an output, but our educational institutions act as though an ounce of teaching is worth at least a pound of learning. Nothing could be further from the truth.

Therefore, the first question about education to which I believe educators and Management Scientists should address themselves is this: *how can the educational process and the institutions in which it is embedded be redesigned so that they are focused on, and organized about, the learning, not the teaching, process?*

Informal education is not organized into subjects, courses, semesters, curricula, or other discrete units. A child's learning a language, for example, is not separated from its learning many other subjects. Reading and writing, geography and history, economics and arithmetic, and philosophy and science may be taught separately, but they cannot be learned separately.

Subjects and disciplines are categories of a filing system, not of Nature. Our knowledge can be filed in many different ways. No way is more correct than another, only more useful; but no one filing system is the most useful for all purposes and none is organized in the same way as the reality it reflects. More important is the fact that, although it may be necessary to take knowledge apart in order to file or teach it, it is also necessary to reassemble it in order to use it. Formal education, like Humpty Dumpty, had a great fall but only a few educators, like all the King's men, are trying to put it together again.

What one learns informally is learned without benefit of either categories or certification by examination. This, one might argue, is only true for what one wants to learn, but schools must teach the young what they should learn regardless of whether they want to learn it or not. This argument is not only incorrect; it is also inhumane. Students should be motivated to learn whatever they ought to learn but never be forced to learn anything. To do so is to take the fun out of it and this is much more serious than is the failure to learn any particular subject. The separation of work, play and learning—a consequence of the Industrial Revolution in education—was, in my opinion, a major cultural catastrophe.

Furthermore, educators do not know what the student of today will need to know tomorrow. Most of it is not yet known. This is even true in professional schools. In a report to the Carnegie Foundation, Ireson (1959) noted that sixty per cent of graduate engineers leave their profession within ten to fifteen years after graduation. Dael Wolfle (1971) noted in *Science* that twenty per cent of American doctorates leave their fields within five years and thirty-five per cent within fifteen. And these trends are accelerating.

Therefore, the second question is: *how can we avoid organizing education around rigidly scheduled, preselected, artificially quantized units of arbitrarily bounded subject matter, and, instead promote development of both a continuous desire to learn and an ability to do so?*

Even when fine-grained filters are used to select students for admission to a school, those selected vary widely in ability, interests and knowledge. Therefore, the same input to different students does not produce the same outputs. Schools based on an industrialized model ignore or minimize the differences between students and thus require them to adapt to the educational process rather than the converse. The process should adapt to them. The individuality and creativity of the young should be preserved at all costs.

The American anthropologist Jules Henry asked what would happen "if all through school the young were provoked to question the Ten Commandments, the sanctity of revealed religion, the foundations of patriotism, the profit motive, the two-party system, the laws of incest, and so on ..." (Henry, 1963, p. 288). Dr. Ronald Laing (1967), the eminent British psychiatrist, replied, "... there would be such creativity that society would not know where to turn". Aye, there's the rub: society does not want to turn. A system that does not want to turn is more concerned with precluding disruptive inquiry than with developing the ability to inquire.

Therefore, the third and final question is: *how can we design an educational system that individualizes each student, that preserves his sense of self, and that encourages creativity rather than conformity?*

SOME METHODOLOGICAL OBSERVATIONS
We do not have answers to such basic educational questions as I have raised. Nor are they to be found, if by "answer" we mean something that disposes of a question once and for all. Social systems, their institutions and their environments change continuously. What solves an educational problem at one time or place does not necessarily do so at others. Therefore, we need an educational system that, like the students in it, can learn

and adapt quickly and efficiently. Management Scientists know enough about adaptive-learning systems to know that they cannot rely on experience to teach them. Experience is too slow, too ambiguous and too often wrong. It must be replaced by systematic and systemic experimentation.

Furthermore, such questions as I have raised are not independent of each other; hence, their solution should not be. The problems of education form a system even if education doesn't; their solutions should also. By decomposing educational problems we have obtained solutions to the parts that aggregate into what might be called an "unwholly mess". Messes cannot be cleared up by problem-solving; they require redesign of the relevant system and effective long-range planning for it. It is here that the Management Sciences can make a major contribution.

A number of Management Scientists—but far from the majority—realize that planning must replace most problem-solving. The art and science of planning are developing rapidly. The design of problem-solving and planning systems is a natural extension of the work of the Management Scientist. A still further extension, equally as "natural", is the redesign of the system being planned for, so that many of the problems with which it is engaged do not arise, and so that its overall effectiveness, not merely its efficiency, is significantly increased.[4]

When the redesign of one part of a system is undertaken independently of the redesign of the other parts, the range of alternatives which are considered to be feasible is severely limited. For example, the variety of possible changes in high schools which come to mind when we assume that no other part of the educational system is to be changed is much more constrained than it would be if we were redesigning the entire system.

There are significant benefits to be derived from considering the redesign of education as a whole. By considering combinations of changes in the parts, larger potential effects on the whole can be brought about. New possibilities are uncovered for both the parts and the whole. The focus is appropriately changed: the characteristics of the whole are not viewed as resultants of the characteristics of the parts; rather the characteristics of the parts are derived from desirable characteristics of the whole.

But even designs of and plans for a system as a whole can be severely constrained by restrictions that are perceived or assumed to exist by designers and planners. Most constraints are self-imposed. These can be removed by engaging in an *idealized* redesign of a system. This is a redesign "from scratch", with all constraints removed other than those of technological feasibility. In redesign of the educational system one would not assume, for example, direct transfer of the content of one mind to another without communication of observable symbols. Such constraints do not preclude contemplation of technological innovation but they restrict it to what is believed to be possible. On the other hand, all consideration of financial or political feasibility is removed. Therefore, an idealized redesign is an explicit formulation of the designers' conception of the system they would create if they were free to create any system they wanted.

Most system redesign and planning is *reactive*—preoccupied with identifying and removing deficiencies in the past performance of system components. Reactive planning and design moves *from* what one does not want rather than *towards* what one does. It is like driving a train from its caboose. One who walks into the future facing the past has no control over where he is going. Idealization rotates planners and designers from a retrospective to a prospective posture. It also does the following three things:

First, it facilitates involvement of a large number of those who participate and hold a stake in the relevant system. Because idealization focuses on long-range objectives and ultimate values agreement tends to emerge from apparently antagonistic participants in the system and others affected by its behavior. Most disagreements arise from consideration of means, not ends. Awareness of consensus on ends usually brings about co-operation with respect to means among those who would not otherwise be so inclined. Because the idealization process forces those engaged in it to make explicit their conception of the system's objectives, their conception is opened to examination by others. This facilitates progressive reformulation of objectives and development of consensus on them.

Secondly, idealization leads those engaged in it to become conscious of self-imposed constraints and hence makes it easier to remove them. It also forces re-examination of externally imposed constraints that are usually accepted passively and thus makes it possible to find ways of "getting around" them.

Finally, idealization reveals that system designs, all of whose elements appear to be infeasible when considered separately, are either feasible or nearly so when considered as a whole. Therefore, it leads to subsequent design and planning that is not preoccupied with doing what appears to be possible, but with making possible what initially appears to be impossible.

For example, in the recently completed idealized design of Paris carried out under the supervision of my colleague, Professor Hasan Ozbekhan, representatives of each of the many political parties in France participated and came to agreement. The design which they approved has been submitted to the French public and is now being widely discussed. The Cabinet of France and the representative body of stakeholders who served as reviewers agreed on the desirability of making Paris a global, rather than a French, city. Having agreed on this objective they subsequently accepted means that they would have rejected summarily had they been proposed separately or out of this context. For example, they have agreed to move the capital of France from Paris and to make Paris an open and multilingual city.

No formulation of an ideal should be taken as final, as an absolute. It should be revised as we approach and get a better. view of it. But equipped with an explicit ideal, however tentative, we can begin to invent efficient and effective ways of making it real.[5]

SOME ASPECTS OF POSSIBLE SOLUTIONS
At the Sixth Conference of the International Federation of Operational Research Societies held in Dublin in August of 1972, a workshop on education spent several days developing an idealized design of an educational system. Lack of time prevented completion of the effort, but the group did produce a report of some of the characteristics on which it had reached agreement. These were as follows.

A child or his parents should be able to apply for admission to any and every school in a system. Selection among applicants should be made at random. Each school should receive tuition fees from the government for each student attending. This should be the only governmental support of any school. Government should provide free transportation to any school in the system. These measures would create a competitive educational market-place.

Teachers should stop formal teaching unless requested to do so by students. They should primarily serve as resources to be used by students as they see fit in their efforts to learn, to learn how to learn, and to find good reasons for wanting to do so.

More time in early school should be spent on learning how to convert what is learned out of school into information, knowledge and understanding than in obtaining substantive inputs. Currently, the child is left on its own to convert raw material obtained in and out of school into something useful. Put another way, the emphasis of school should be on processing what is learned rather than on learning things that need to be processed.

In at least some of what are now the preschool years, parent and child should attend school together. Reading and writing, like the first language, should be learned before entering school. Schools should provide a wide variety of subjects and means of access to them. The student should be free to choose from these but he should have available continuing advice to assist him in these choices.

Students should not be assigned and confined to homogeneous age or attainment groups, but should be a part of largely self-organizing heterogeneous student groups in which the opportunity to learn from each other is maximized and the need to learn from a teacher is minimized.

Every so-called teacher at every level of the educational system should be required to be a student at some higher level of the system. This implies that there be no highest level of education.

Now for a few observations about universities.

Universities should have no entrance or exit requirements and confer no degrees. Students should come and go as they please. They should not be examined on what they have learned unless they want to be. Examinations should be conducted so as to maximize students' learning, not unlearning, and not so as to minimize the task of grading. Records of examinations should go into a file to which only the student has access. Dissemination of its content within or without the university should be completely under the student's control. Failure should not be recorded, only accomplishments. Qualifications of students should be determined outside the university. Requalification, even of professionals, should be frequent, to encourage keeping up with developments and to encourage continuous use of the university.

Selection of faculty members should be controlled by other faculty members, but their retention should depend on students as well as faculty. Faculty ranks should be eliminated because the quest for promotion currently dominates the quest for knowledge.

Finally, there must be a more effective way than tenure of protecting academic freedom and a less effective way of protecting academic incompetence.

The workshop's conclusions were considered by its members to be tentative and preliminary. We need many more, and more comprehensive and systematic, idealized educational design efforts. These should be made by educators and Management Scientists working together. Unfortunately, such efforts and the implementation of their output hardly seem imminent.

Meanwhile, there is no need to ask for whom the school bell tolls.

NOTES

1 Abstract modified by the editors from the original article.
2 For example, see Friedenberg (1971), Henry (1963), Herndon (1971), Illich (1972), Ireson (1959) and Silberman (1970).
3 An extensive bibliography and abstracts are available of studies on these and many similar subjects. See Organisation for Economic Co-operation and Development (1970) and International Federation of Operational Research Societies (1961–).
4 For discussions of system planning and design see Ackoff (1969), Ackoff (1970), Beer (1966), Beer (1972), Churchman (1968), Churchman (1971), Emery and Trist (1973), Friedman (1973), Henry (1963), Ozbekhan (1969) and Ozbekhan (1971). For an extensive bibliography on planning see Steiner (1969).
5 For an idealized design of a university see Ackoff (1968).

REFERENCES

Ackoff, R. L. (1968) "Towards an Idealized University", *Management Science*, 15, B-121 to B-131.

ACKOFF, R. L. (1969) "Towards Strategic Planning of Education", in *Efficiency of Resource Utilization in Education*, Organisation for Economic Co-operation and Development, pp. 339–80.
ACKOFF, R. L. (1970) *A Concept of Corporate Planning*, John Wiley and Sons.
BEER, STAFFORD (1966) *Decision and Control*, John Wiley and Sons.
BEER, STAFFORD (1972) *Brain of the Firm*, Allen Lane, The Penguin Press.
CHURCHMAN, C. WEST (1968) *The Systems Approach*, Delacorte Press.
CHURCHMAN, C. WEST (1971) *The Design of Inquiring Systems*, Basic Books.
EMERY, F. E. (1970) *Research and Higher Education* (mimeographed), Research School of Social Sciences, Australian National University, Canberra, 4 November 1970.
EMERY, F. E. and TRIST, E. L. (1973) *Towards a Social Ecology*, Plenum Press.
FRIEDENBERG, EDGAR Z. (1971) "How to Survive in Your Native Land" (book review), *The New York Times Book Review*, 11 April 1971.
FRIEDMAN, JOHN (1973) *Retracking America*, Anchor Press/Doubleday.
HENRY, JULES (1963) *Culture against Man*, Vintage Books.
HERNDON, JAMES (1971) *How to Survive in Your Native Land*, Simon and Shuster.
ILLICH, IVAN (1972) *Deschooling Society*, Harrow Books.
INTERNATIONAL FEDERATION OF OPERATIONAL RESEARCH SOCIETIES (1961–) *International Abstracts in Operations Research*.
IRESON, W. G. (1959) "Preparation for Business in Engineering Schools", in Pierson, F. C. *et al. The Education of American Businessmen*, McGraw-Hill Book Co.
LAING, R. D. (1967) *The Politics of Experience*, Penguin Books.
MILSTEIN, MIKE M. and BELASKO, JAMES A. (1973) *Educational Administration and the Behavioral Sciences*, Allyn and Bacon.
ORGANISATION FOR ECONOMIC CO-OPERATION AND DEVELOPMENT (1970) *List of Documents: Programme on Institutional Management in Higher Education*, Center for Educational Research and Innovation, 1 July 1970, and *Addendum 1*, 1 September 1970.
OZBEKHAN, HASAN (1969) "Toward a General Theory of Planning", in Jantsch, E. (ed.) *Perspectives of Planning*, Organisation for Economic Co-operation and Development, pp. 47–158.
OZBEKHAN, HASAN (1971) "Planning and Human Action", in Weiss, Paul A. (ed.) *Hierarchically Organized Systems in Theory and Practice*, Hafner, pp. 123–230.
SILBERMAN, CHARLES E. (1970) *Crisis in the Classroom*, Random House.
STEINER, GEORGE A. (1969) *Top Management Planning*, Collier-Macmillan.
WOLFLE, DAEL (1971) Editorial, *Science*, 173, 9 July 1971, p. 109.

2 Institutional Techniques

INTRODUCTION

Education in Britain has only gradually and recently been brought under a degree of central direction and planning, and at the same time individual schools and institutions have shown a parallel neglect of the use of management techniques in the ordering of their affairs. This has been due partly to a distrust of novel prescriptions for efficiency, and partly to genuine doubt as to whether the business of education can be systematized, measured and evaluated through the instruments of management. In this section of the Reader the problems of applying management methods to education in schools and institutions of higher education are explored and their potential value and applications for the educator are discussed.

The degree of independence enjoyed by any educational institution and the distribution of power within its organization will largely determine the extent and character of its decision-making. Graeme Moodie and Rowland Eustace in their article "The Contemporary System in Outline" illustrate this in looking at the university system, where they observe that the traditional autonomy of British universities ensures that the limitations upon it remain minimal. In both academic and financial matters their decision-making may be subject in some degree to external pressures, but not to direction. Michael Locke ("Government of Polytechnics") finds that the polytechnics have moved in recent years towards the exercise of a greater freedom in shaping policy and in decision-making. As a result of changes in their mode of government in the late 1960s the polytechnics acquired a large measure of autonomy and an enhanced prestige. But the arrangements for the government of individual polytechnics have tended to concentrate power in the hands of their directors, thus perpetuating the autocratic control of the old college principals. Locke concludes that the formation of the new polytechnics, through the amalgamation of existing colleges, was essentially a means of consolidating the resources of advanced further education.

The critical review of behavioural objectives by Michael MacDonald-Ross provides a stringent examination of what is involved in the setting of behavioural objectives in education, and in the task of measuring the extent to which they can be achieved and the relative efficacy of the methods employed in the process. The behavioural objectives scheme is open to criticisms of a fundamental kind, which are summarized by the author. But behavioural objectives are the basis of the only viable system of planning which has yet been devised for education. Innovation and change are inescapable, and since the private intuitions of individual teachers are no longer sufficient warrant for large-scale outlays in effort and cost, systems of planning and evaluation in education become indispensable. In his article "Towards an Economic Theory of Higher Education" Maurice Peston adds weight to the argument, implicit in MacDonald-Ross's critique, that "what we lack are explanatory theories either at the macro level or, more importantly, at the micro level involving the decision-making process and its outcome". Peston anatomizes university institutions according to their responsiveness to the demands of consumers and producers, and he rightly points out the difficulty of reconciling student aspirations with the objectives of individual members of academic staff. Moreover, the universities are a sub-system of the whole educational system, and the demand for places at universities is directly influenced by the activities and ambitions of those in the secondary schools. A further complication in the case of the universities is that they produce their own producers, which is a feature virtually unique in the field of education.

The universities are the most complex institutions within the educational system and therefore most likely to benefit from effective management. This is particularly evident in the context of management accounting. M. A. Sims in his article "Accounting Information in Universities" points out that decisions on resource allocation in universities have traditionally been based on principles and assumptions other than those embodied in management accounting. He suggests alternatives to conventional and simple "line item" budgeting, alternatives which would match expenditure with specific activities within a university and seek to measure not only their inputs but their outputs as well. The problem of measuring outputs in education is admittedly very far from being solved, but its investigation should continue to be pressed. The allocation of expendable resources to activities and outputs within a university can be considered as the first step towards the realization of a system akin to those known as Planning, Programming and Budgeting Systems.

PPBS is considered further in the article "Potential Economies of Scale at the University of Bradford" by John Dunworth and Anthony Bottomley. They reach the conclusion that the application of output budgeting techniques, coupled with a more intensive utilization of buildings, could enable considerable expansion in student numbers and development of activities to take place, while at the same time effecting substantial economies of scale. The quinquennial grants system provides no incentives for universities to cut costs per graduate, but the persistence of this system does not invalidate the case that such economies of scale are possible and can be made without detriment to the universities.

If we look at schools we find that today systematic planning and decision-making, based upon management techniques, are equally necessary. Peter Snape in his article "Management Problems and School Leadership" argues that the leadership of a moderately sized school now involves a degree of financial responsibility comparable with that of many industrial and business enterprises. Yet there is widespread reluctance to accept the need for management in schools. A starting point lies in organization theory; the school leadership must establish its objectives, frame a policy for their achievement and devise programmes which will allow progress to be monitored and which will measure success. To sustain such a plan communication between all those involved must be comprehensive and unfailing, and continuing incentives should be set before them in order to maximize cooperation. Snape illustrates the value of a network analysis in relation to the problem of planning for the reorganization of the secondary schools in Totnes.

Further illustrations of the value of systematic planning and analysis are given in the two articles on the construction of school timetables by John E. Brookes ("Basics of Timetabling") and Harry L. Gray ("The Secondary School Timetable: A Matrix Approach"). Gray expresses some doubts about the value of using computer methods in this process, since programming may absorb as much time as direct compilation would do, whereas meticulous planning is crucial. These routine tasks illustrate the need for management techniques which can be applied so as to ensure that administration interferes as little as possible with the essential and important activities of the school. Brookes underlines the need for optimal resource management in schools, and in the light of this the connection between timetabling and curriculum innovation is very important.

There can be little doubt that the proper management of resources in institutions of higher education and in schools now requires the precise use of complex techniques in programme planning and systems analysis. The only question is how best to apply such management procedures to the definition of objectives and the measurement of outputs in education and how to reconcile the constraints of informed decision-making with the conventional academic ways of doing things by precedent and intuition.

Lance Dobson

2.1 The Contemporary System in Outline

Graeme C. Moodie and Rowland Eustace

AUTONOMY

The universities in the United Kingdom are autonomous institutions. They are, without exception, independent corporations, able to own property, to sue and be sued, and to regulate their own affairs within the wide powers granted to them by the instruments of their incorporation. A few of the instruments are Acts of Parliament[1] whose operative part is a set of statutes, but the characteristic instrument is a Royal Charter, granted through the Privy Council, also with a set of statutes similar to those under an Act.[2] The charter proper is largely a somewhat magniloquent preamble to the statutes; and though its provisions may sometimes be of interest, it is normally to the statutes that one must turn for any detailed rules about the allocation of powers and responsibilities within the institution.

The chief formal restraints upon complete autonomy are the obligation to keep within the powers granted by these instruments; the need to obtain the permission of the Privy Council[3] for important alterations to these instruments; and the restrictions imposed by law upon the use of their endowments. Most universities are subject to visitorial enquiry and all are liable to special investigation by Royal Commissions or other similar committees;[4] they are subject to the ordinary law of the land and ultimately, of course, like all institutions and persons, to direct interference by Parliament. Some of the ancient universities, in addition, suffer direct interference by the Government in certain appointments, as to the Regius chairs.[5]

Some of these formal restraints are not inconsiderable; for example, the universities of Oxford and Cambridge have been quite extensively, and involuntarily, reformed by Parliament, and it is said that some universities have been reluctant to propose certain classes of alterations to statutes for fear that the Privy Council might attempt to impose a minimum degree of student participation.

In general, however, the formal limitations upon institutional auton-

Source: Graeme C. Moodie and Rowland Eustace (1974) *Power and Authority in British Universities,* Allen and Unwin, pp. 45–57.

omy are minimal. There is a tradition of non-interference by the State in the affairs of universities and a widespread belief in the merits of autonomy. The limitations are, in the words of most charters, "ever construed benevolently"; those in universities who know what the formal limitations amount to in practice do not (except for some of those to be mentioned) appear to find them irksome or important. This is in large measure because these formal limitations are indirect.[6] In any case, apart from the appointments mentioned, external control is of the legal basis —charters and statutes—rather than of the actual administration.[7] Within these instruments, in their internal government, universities have a very wide degree of autonomy, financial and academic, especially in contrast to universities in many systems abroad.[8]

This formal autonomy is affected in various ways by other restraints, some of which may today exercise so direct a control on purely academic decisions, or be so extensive in their appearance[9] as to raise reasonable questions about the reality of autonomy.[10] But this is not a study of institutional autonomy, and it will be sufficient to say here that however powerful the external pressures on universities may be, they remain for the most part pressures rather than directions. The universities are still today required to make up their own minds, individually, on a great range of their activities; even where the choice may be strictly limited, it still has to be made.[11] Moreover, because new funds have been so much more available, the range of their activities and the options open to universities are today enormously greater than before the last war; thus both the amount and the importance of their internal and autonomous decision-making has at the least kept up with diminutions due to outside pressures.[12] Even the sharp reduction in the availability of new funds for some purposes since the late 1960s has of itself presented universities with very serious decisions that they must take for themselves. It is part of the conventional wisdom to believe that he who pays the piper calls the tune. But there are limitations. To start with, it is no use calling outside the piper's repertoire, and there are things some pipers will not play.[13] But in any event universities are not only pipers: they are also composers. Thus a study of internal government in isolation would still be as possible now as it ever has been, even if the worst fears now being expressed were found to be justified. Universities are in no way to be compared, governmentally, with the state secondary schools.

TYPES OF UNIVERSITY

By the criterion of internal governmental structure British universities may be grouped in three categories: Oxford and Cambridge; the federal universities of London and Wales; and the rest, including the constituent university colleges in Wales and the dozen or so major non-medical schools which help make up the University of London.

The first groups are governed through structures which are peculiar to themselves and unlikely to be copied elsewhere. In any discussion of university government it is imposible to avoid reference to, especially, Oxford and Cambridge, but we have not attempted to make a detailed or comprehensive study of any of them.[14] A brief indication of some of their distinctive characteristics may nevertheless be useful at this stage.

Oxford and Cambridge, apart from being the oldest of the English universities, are distinguished by the governmental role of the general body of staff and the continuing importance of their colleges. The colleges still play a major role in teaching, in the appointment of staff, and the admission of students, though that of the universities has considerably increased in the first two respects during the past fifty years. They also elect representatives to the main governing bodies of the university and, in Cambridge but not Oxford, the vice-chancellor is drawn (for a limited term of office) from the college heads. The continuing importance of the colleges is buttressed by their financial independence and their legal status as independent self-governing corporations.[15] The most important governmental characteristic of these two universities, however, is that the ultimate authority still lies with the legislative assembly of all the resident masters (the vast majority of whom are members of the academic staff, the remainder consisting of senior university and college officials). And, though some distinction is drawn between professorial and other academic staff in academic decision-making (especially in the natural science departments), the tradition has tended to greater egalitarianism than is generally found in other universities. Nevertheless, much that we have to say about the general features of university government applies also to Oxford and Cambridge and the differences in structure seem steadily to be lessening.[16]

The federal group today contains two institutions.[17] The older of these federations, Wales (formed in 1893), consists of widely scattered and highly autonomous institutions with poor communications between them. (The Council meets in Bloomsbury.) It probably would not continue in being if purely academic considerations were paramount,[18] and it might be regarded as a confederation. Until the Charter of 1967 was granted the point of chief interest to this study was the virtual exclusion of the academic staff from the "executive body of the University", the Council,[19] an exclusion which was by then unique in these islands.

The larger of the federations, London, was formed in 1900.[20] It is large,[21] and has a uniquely wide variety of constituent units, ranging from very specialized research institutes, to the large colleges or schools which closely resemble autonomous universities.[22] Constitutionally, it represents various rather uneasy compromises, mainly between the claims of rationalization and specialization on a unitary basis and those of the individual units for independence. In addition, however, the position of external students and the great power of the graduates have complicated the issues. The resulting constitution is highly particular and is of limited general interest except, potentially, in one respect. (It is also, 1973, in process of reform.)

This respect is that the University of London now provides, in effect, a regional Grants Committee (the Court) and a very extensive system of service and specialist support for its autonomous units. This has been built up, despite the strong centrifugal tendencies of some of the major units, partly because most of them cluster so close together geographically. Elsewhere in the country the need for similar support is being felt, and common services are slowly emerging.[23] The appearance of second universities in some towns, the formation of the polytechnics, and the likely up-grading of other institutions, will create many more clusters of important units which will have the same opportunities and needs as the London institutions. It is therefore possible that the London federation will, in time, become of immediate practical interest to others.[24]

What we have labelled the "unitary" group is by far the largest, consisting as it does of some sixty institutions. Since the bulk of our whole study is devoted to it, the outline of its system of government will be postponed until the next section. Here we will merely offer a brief account of our reasons for treating so many institutions as a single group.

Obviously there are immense differences between the various members of the unitary group in terms of, for example, their size, social and geographical environment, age, history, research activity, emphasis on different kinds of subject (arts, applied science, medicine and so on), or percentage of students in residence.[25] To most university people, moreover, the usual categories of Scottish, civic, major and minor redbrick, and technological convey information, if only a set of impressionistic messages about atmosphere and status. It is also meaningful to group certain charters together on a rough chronological basis, but, as we have seen, the differences between contemporary constitutions may be as significant as the similarities. [...] However, particular developments may affect all institutions in some degree, regardless of their age, and not always through formal amendment to constitutions. Today all universities seem to be subject to a new wave of change in a broadly liberal direction, and few are not (or have not recently been) engaged in a process of constitutional creation or review. As a result universities are tending to converge on a single broad governmental ideal. But, even if one were to discount this recent trend, the other differences between universities within the unitary group do not coincide with the difference in their constitutions. (Perhaps, more modestly, we should merely say that we have been unable to detect a consistent coincidence of significant governmental variations with any of the other bases of classification.)

There are, of course, many detailed differences in the systems of government to be found in the unitary group, many of which we mention in the following chapters. But the further our study progressed the more impressed we became by the broad similarities. In large and significant measure, we believe, the vast majority of university staff and students in this country are subject only to variations on a single type of internal government. To its elements we will now turn.

GOVERNMENT IN THE UNITARY GROUP

Even within this group there are immense variations of detail, some of it important, and of nomenclature. Many of the variations of substance are noted in the relevant sections of this book, but for the remainder of our discussion we will adopt a standard terminology to refer to the main organs of government. In the "Note on Terminology" at the end of this chapter we list a virtual glossary of titles and indicate the principal referents of our labels. But, in this section and in the subsequent discussion of the system in action, we will not complicate our account by listing on each occasion the range of bodies to which terms like "council" or "senate" refer. They should, therefore, be taken to mean either bodies with those names or the bodies which fill the same essential roles as council or senate. Where the context demands it we use the label in inverted commas to indicate that we are using it in this latter, functional, sense. Our choice of titles is based on those used in Owens College, Manchester, in its 1880 Charter and adopted, since then, by the great majority of English and Welsh unitary universities.

The characteristic structure of government in the unitary universities has five levels, and we use them to organize our outline exposition. Right away, however, it should be emphasized that too much should not be read into the notion of a hierarchy of levels. At least in this stage of the argument "level" should be understood to refer to something like a "level of formal competence". Thus, to say that a body forms, or is at, the lowest level is to signify nothing more than that it is competent to decide only for a small section of the university, which is to say, for a relatively small number of people and/or for a relatively small span of activities. It should not, in particular, be assumed that the "higher" levels necessarily carry more authority than the "lower" in every area of their jurisdiction, nor that decisions are necessarily taken at "higher" levels in any sense other than mere ratification or formal endorsement. Just what the relations are between the various levels is, of course, a major theme of this study; they cannot, therefore, be explored at all fully in this initial description of the machinery of government. Our initial reference to levels is therefore in part a matter of convenience and otherwise signifies only that different bodies have a wider or narrower range within which, legally, they take the official decisions for the university.

In most universities the "supreme governing body" is still the court.[26] The top level (in the sense mentioned) therefore consists of a large court[27] consisting of local notables, local government nominees, and representatives of various local bodies and institutions of religious, professional, and other organizations, of trade unions (recently, e.g. at Leeds and Warwick), and also of graduates, staff and, increasingly, students (and, less frequently, of non-academic staff). In size they range from the unusually small court of Newcastle or York, around fifty to sixty, to the unusually large 600-odd at Sheffield; 250 is probably the average size with more modern instruments providing for the small bodies. Court thus provides a means by which usually local society may be associated with the government of the university. Court meets rarely (commonly once a year) and few attend from any distance. Even the traditional courts, though their powers are magniloquently stated ("the Supreme Governing Body . . . shall have absolute power within the University"), can usually only exercise their powers indirectly. Typically, "control over the Senate [must be] through Council and not otherwise".[28]

The senior executive body, however, is council; it too has a predominantly lay membership, but it is both smaller and more active than court. The Robbins Committee's (1963) investigations revealed that the numbers of members of councils in 1961–2 ranged from sixty-three at Aberystwyth and fifty-five at Sheffield to twenty-nine at Manchester and fourteen at the London School of Economics, with nine councils having a membership in the forties. The old Scottish equivalent, court, was much smaller, St Andrews being the largest at eighteen.[29] The new charters of the 1960s usually prescribe numbers in the middle thirties, with only Loughborough over forty, but with Newcastle, York, Lancaster, and Heriot-Watt below thirty. Thus English councils have been getting rather smaller.

The academic share of membership [. . .] is rising from around one-fifth of the membership at the unreformed older civics to over two-fifths provided by some recent charters. Councils meet frequently enough (usually between six and ten times a year) for members to be kept informed about the main issues; even so, they work very largely through their committees. Each council has powers of legislative initiative, and usually of veto, as well as having access to the bureaucracy through its secretary. As we have seen, however, its legislative powers are increasingly hedged about by requirements that it take senate advice. Council's main effective role lies in its responsibility for finance and the management of the university's physical assets. This has traditionally been very much its exclusive province, and remains so despite the requirement, in some newer instruments, that senate be consulted on academic budgeting.

The third major body is senate. Its chairman is the vice-chancellor and its membership almost wholly academic.[30] It varies immensely in size, from under fifty members to over 200, as also in the extent of non-professional staff representation. There is a clear tendency, however, to move away from the virtually standard senate, to which all professors belonged *ex officio* and a few others were selected, to a body in which all staff grades are represented, but not in proportion to their numbers, and in which only the holders of certain offices (not ranks) are *ex officio* members.[31] Even where the charter does not make explicit legislative reference to the fact, senate is generally regarded as the supreme authority on academic questions other, usually, than the making of appointments. Like council it usually makes extensive use of committees in exercising its authority.

The next level consists, typically, of the faculties. These groupings of related subjects usually comprise all the teachers in those subjects. As a body each faculty meets for advisory discussions, but its direct powers are usually limited to the election of the dean (e.g. at Birmingham, where the deans sit on council) or of representatives to council or senate (e.g. at Liverpool; S. 24). The executive of the faculty is the faculty board, which normally includes a substantial proportion of non-professional staff. The powers of the faculty boards are formally advisory to senate or delegated by it and extend mainly to matters affecting the courses and examinations in the faculty, including the appointment of examiners. A few, however, may also advise on staff appointments (e.g. at Liverpool; S. 27:7) or elect members of senate (e.g. at Newcastle; S. 25:16). There may also be similar sub-faculty bodies within a faculty, usually set up by ordinance.

Traditionally, the next step beyond the sub-faculty has been to the department, a body very seldom legislated for at all, and left wholly to the discretion of its professor, who was responsible for the development and conduct of all teaching and research in his subject. This is still the case in most, and especially in the older institutions, but the situation is changing and difficult to categorize. ·

In many of the newest universities the organization of teaching and curricula is left, below the senate level, to bodies with labels like "school" and "board of studies" rather than faculties and departments. No standard usage for these labels has yet developed. The purpose behind these changes seems to be, first, to break down the barriers which have developed between the traditional subjects and faculties by setting up new combinations and, second, to legislate for greater non-professorial participation at the lowest level of government.[32] It is not yet clear, however, how far these new institutions in fact constitute governmental innovations when compared with some of the older faculties and departments (and especially with those which have also provided for wider participation in taking their decisions).

Beyond, or beside, these "levels" we have three university-wide organizations. The first of these, traditionally, is the convocation, the organization of alumni (or graduates as they mostly are today). It is sufficient to say here that the graduates have little organizational significance in the unitary sector.[33] It is, however, worth remarking, in the light of the development of the assembly which we discuss below, that in many places staff in all grades have for long been heavily represented on convocation, and could probably have dominated its proceedings had they wished.

Next there is the student organization, usually the union or students' representative council, whose role is increasing. Despite the immense amount written about the student movement, little of it concerns government, and less of it concerns the actual practice of student involvement,[34] but it is increasingly common to find students represented on council, many committees, and senate.

Finally, an essentially modern development, found chiefly at the newer universities, is the assembly of all staff. This may be said to symbolize the transition towards a view of the staff as a group of equals, a view which has already been mentioned in our historical chapter. Its functions are very limited (it may have some electoral rights[35]) but the analogy with the Oxford Congregation is obvious enough. [. . .]

NOTE ON TERMINOLOGY

As we have already warned, we have adopted a uniform terminology for our account of university government despite the fact that no such uniformity is to be found among the sixty and more institutions with which we are concerned. In this Note we set out the terms we use along with their close or approximate equivalents. The list of equivalents includes the major examples but is not necessarily exhaustive.

1 *Constitutions. Charters* is used to refer to all the main documentary constitutions or instruments of government. It is normally used to denote both the charters themselves and the associated statutes. Under this heading are also included, when appropriate, Acts of Parliament (for example, in the cases of the universities of Durham and London) and the Statutes at Oxford and Cambridge. Specific reference will be made, where necessary, to subsidiary rules like ordinances and regulations.[36]

2 *Organs of government. Court* corresponds to Convocation at Aston and Heriot-Watt, Conference at Stirling, and General Convocation at Strathclyde. In certain respects parallel functions are performed by, for example, the Governors of Bedford College, Imperial College, and the London School of Economics (all of them schools of the University of London), and by the General Councils at the ancient Scottish universities.

Council corresponds to Court at the Scottish universities and the Senate at Queen's University, Belfast. It approximates, functionally, to Hebdomadal Council at Oxford, Council of the Senate at Cambridge, Standing Committee at the London School of Economics, and Court at the federal universities of London and Wales.

Senate corresponds to the Academic Council at Belfast and Stirling and to the Professorial and General Academic Boards at York. It approximates to the General Board at Oxford and Cambridge, Academic Council at the University of London and, at the London School of Economics, to the Professorial and Academic Boards.

Faculty and faculty board refer, respectively, to the whole body of staff and to the executive committees within each faculty. Where we wish to refer also to the "new" *schools* and *boards of study,* etc., we refer, where appropriate, to *faculty-level* bodies; and similarly with *departments* and *subject-level* bodies.

Assembly (of most or all academic staff) corresponds to Academic Congress at Strathclyde, Heriot-Watt, and Salford, to Academic Council at Dundee, and to the Academic Staff Association at City. It is the approximate counterpart of General Board at Manchester, Academic Board at the London School of Economics (but see also under "senate" above), Congregation at Oxford, and Regent House at Cambridge.

Convocation (of graduates and some or all staff) is used to refer collectively to bodies which are only roughly similar, but which are sufficiently unimportant, governmentally, for the differences to be of small consequence in this context. The bodies include Convocation at Oxford, Senate at Cambridge, the Graduates Council at Dundee, the Graduates and Former Students Association at Strathclyde, and General Council at the ancient Scottish universities (but see, also, under "court" above).[37]

3 *Officers and Officials.* *Chancellor* is equivalent to the President at the University of Manchester Institute of Science and Technology and to the Patron at Birkbeck College.

Chairman of council is the equivalent of the President at Reading and Liverpool and, until 1927, of the Vice-Chancellor at Birmingham.

Vice-chancellor is the equivalent of the President and Vice-Chancellor at Belfast; the Vice-Chancellor and Principal at Birmingham since 1927 (Principal until 1927); the Principal and Vice-Chancellor at the ancient Scottish universities, Dundee, and Heriot-Watt; Principal at the other Scottish universities and many of the London schools (colleges); and to the Rector, Director, Provost, and Master at, respectively, Imperial College, the London School of Economics, University College, and Birkbeck College, London.

Assistant vice-chancellor approximates to the Deputy Principal at Birmingham and the Vice-Principal at Bradford. These are full-time administrative posts which should be distinguished from that of *deputy-* or *pro-vice-chancellor*, a post filled, part-time and for a limited period, by a member of the academic staff elected by "senate".

The bureaucracy is the professional full-time administrative staff normally headed by the *registrar* (sometimes, secretary) or jointly by him and the *bursar*, the senior financial official. We refer to all members of the bureaucracy as *officials*. None of these should be confused with the *administration*, a term used to include all those who administer the affairs of the university; it therefore includes certain lay members of "council", the "vice-chancellor", and many academics as well as the bureaucracy.

NOTES

1 e.g. London, Durham, Newcastle and the older Scottish universities.
2 Oxbridge have neither an Act of Parliament nor a charter, but do have a body of statutes, changes to the more important of which require the authority of the Privy Council, and which, for our pur-

poses, are similar to the statutes of other institutions. The incor-corporated colleges of London University (University and King's) have statutes made by the federal senate, but other colleges (and units of the University of Wales) have their own charters.

3 Or, where appropriate, as in Durham and the ancient Scottish universities, of Parliament. (Parliamentary authority is in any case required for transfers of property, so that amalgamations and transformations require an Act.)

4 Of which the most recent example is the Robbins Committee on Higher Education 1961–3. See its report (Robbins Committee, 1963).

5 And to certain administrative appointments, notably to principalships in some ancient Scottish universities or the mastership of Trinity College, Cambridge.

6 In Scotland, however, the Royal Commissions in the nineteenth century interfered not only by statute but also directly in curricular matters. See, e.g. Davie (1961) and Rait (1898).

7 *Ad hoc* interference, as by commissions, has at times involved control of administration, e.g. by requiring statements of accounts in stated forms.

8 International Association of Universities (1965a and 1965b).

9 e.g. notably, the activity of the Comptroller and Auditor General's office. This is not, however, supposed to issue in directives, nor is the office an arm of the Government, but of Parliament. Another, new, form of external pressure comes from the local planning authorities, who are not always sympathetic and who, it is sometimes feared, can be prejudiced by, e.g. student demonstrations. We have been told by members of staff that they have been asked by their vice-chancellor to moderate their political activities for this reason.

10 See, for example, Beloff (1967). A list of forms of interference is given in Caine (1969).

11 "Because external circumstances, including government action, stimulated the growth of universities generally Aberdeen expanded. . . . Nevertheless the initiative in the choice of rate and direction of expansion has rested with the university". See Angus (1967).

12 Sir William Mansfield Cooper has asked: "How far was the almost unique pre-war freedom of the British universities a function of their poverty . . . ? How far was their freedom a freedom *not* to do things because they did not have the means . . . ?" Donors' wishes have often been more restrictive than those of the University Grants Committee.

13 "Today no university is interested in an offer to endow a Chair unless such Chair forms an integral part of its academic development programme. . . ." University of London (1967–8).

14 We could not hope, in any case, to add anything of significance to the studies of the Franks Commission of Inquiry into the University

of Oxford which reported in 1966 nor of the Murray Committee of Enquiry into the Governance of the University of London which reported in 1972.

15 In none of these respects do the colleges at Durham, Kent, Lancaster, and York play as significant a role.

16 For example: the Oxford vice-chancellorship is now more powerful than it was, the power of laymen elsewhere is still declining, and the department or institute at Oxford and Cambridge is steadily assuming greater significance in all faculties.

17 There were, until recently, federal situations at Durham/Newcastle and at St Andrews/Dundee.

18 The University of Wales Commission of 1964 produced a majority in favour of independence for the constituent colleges, but the report was rejected by the overwhelmingly lay University Court.

19 The Council was composed of a majority of laymen (or co-opted persons). The minority were appointed by the University Court, on which staff were in a small minority. The Court appointed the heads of the constituent units but not teaching staff.

20 On the basis of an Act of 1898. The functions of the examining board known until then as the University of London were continued by the new body.

21 In 1968–9 it listed some 44 units and an overall enrolment of 31,500 full-time students, not to mention the 33,847 registered external students.

22 Considerable semantic confusion is caused by the fact that London and Oxford and Cambridge are often described as "collegiate". But there is no useful basis of comparison between them. The Oxbridge colleges today are primarily tutorial and social units, to which, certainly since the women's colleges admitted men, London has no counterpart. The major London colleges (technically called "schools") have, for instance, various degrees of direct access to the Vice-Chancellors' Committee, their own laboratories, and their own specialized institutes and units. More important, perhaps, the London schools can have substantial control of their own first degree examinations, while they have an organization, of boards, etc., and above all of subject departments, that is recognizably appropriate to a university. The remaining smaller units of London correspond much more nearly to the specialist institutes and departments of Oxbridge, than to any college except, perhaps, to one or two specialized institutions like Nuffield or St Anthony's.

23 Organization and methods units have been set up in several areas by the joint action of the universities within each region.

24 There is a close, but not federal, link between the University of Manchester and the University of Manchester Institute of Science and Technology. They are financially separate, but academically united by cross-representation on the appropriate governing bodies.

There is no "superior" body ruling over both units. This relationship provides another possible model for regional co-operation elsewhere.

25 See, for example, the interesting analysis in John King: "The Typology of Universities", *Higher Education Review*, Summer 1970, pp. 52–61.

26 In many of the post-Sussex charters it has been relegated to a purely advisory status, and this was proposed for Birmingham by the Grimond Committee in 1972.

27 But not, for example, in Durham or the ancient Scottish universities, where the body of graduates (supplemented by current members of staff), has the analogous, but advisory, role. The right to express an opinion is more frequently expressed by the Scottish General Councils than is usual in the Durham Convocation partly, perhaps, because they also elect several members to the Scottish courts (equivalent to the English councils; see below).

28 See, for example, the Sheffield Charter, S. 9, and S. 12:5.

29 See the Robbins *Report*, cited above, Appendix IV, tables 5, 7, 10, and 12.

30 The librarian is normally a member, and occasionally an official (as at Exeter and Lancaster).

31 The *ex officio* members are likely to include, normally, the deputy or pro-vice-chancellor(s), deans, and heads of departments.

32 But at one large traditional university we were assured that the term "school" had been adopted mainly for its cosmetic effect in the prospectus.

33 They often have power to elect to council and court, however.

34 But for an authoritative history see Ashby and Anderson (1970), pp. 51–6. See also Dennis (1969) and Eustace (1970).

35 e.g. at Aston, where the Assembly elect four members of Council, and at Warwick, where the election is to six seats on Senate.

36 Ordinances may normally be made by council only, regulations by any authorized body, but usually by senate.

37 In many universities the label of *congregation* is applied to a wholly formal body convened for the conferment of degrees. (The term seems to have been taken from the Ancient House of Congregation at Oxford.)

REFERENCES

ANGUS, W. S. (1967) "Growth of the University of Aberdeen", *University of Aberdeen Record*, p. 110.

ASHBY, E. and ANDERSON, M. (1970) *The Rise of the Student Estate in Britain*, Macmillan, pp. 51–6.

BELOFF, M. (1967) "British Universities and the Public Purse", *Minerva*, Summer 1967.

CAINE, S. (1969) *British Universities: Purpose and Prospects*, Bodley Head, pp. 186–7.

DAVIE, G. E. (1961) *The Democratic Intellect*, Edinburgh University Press.

DENNIS, A. (1969) *The Changing Role of Students*, University of London Ph.D. Thesis.

EUSTACE, R. B. (1970) "Student Participation" in Shattock, M. L. (ed.) Franks Commission of Inquiry (1966) *University Administration in a Period of Expansion*, British Council.

FRANKS COMMISSION OF INQUIRY INTO THE UNIVERSITY OF OXFORD (1966).

INTERNATIONAL ASSOCIATION OF UNIVERSITIES (1965a) *University Autonomy—its Meaning Today*.

INTERNATIONAL ASSOCIATION OF UNIVERSITIES (1965b) Report of the IAU meeting in Tokyo, *IAU Bulletin*, Vol. XIII (Supp.), No. 4, Nov. 1965.

MANSFIELD COOPER, W. (1972) "A Private University in Britain?" (book review), *Minerva* X, 2, pp. 333–4.

MURRAY COMMITTEE OF ENQUIRY INTO THE GOVERNANCE OF THE UNIVERSITY OF LONDON (1972).

RAIT, R. S. (1898) *The Universities Commission 1889–97, A Review*, Aberdeen.

ROBBINS COMMITTEE (1963) *Higher Education*, report of the Committee (Chairman: Lord Robbins) appointed by the Prime Minister, Cmnd 2154, HMSO.

UNIVERSITY OF LONDON (1967–8) Principal's *Report*, p. 13.

2.2 Government of Polytechnics

Michael Locke

THE IMPORTANCE OF GOVERNMENT

When the Secretary of State [for Education] announced to the House of Commons on 5 April 1967 the list of 30 proposed polytechnics, he presented at the same time his Notes for Guidance (Department of Education and Science, 1967) to the local authorities. The Notes advised the local authorities involved how to submit schemes for polytechnics and how to draw up the instruments and articles of government so as to win ministerial approval: "the Secretary of State is sure that the authorities will agree that the arrangements for the government and academic organisation of polytechnics are of great importance for their full development as major institutions of higher education complementary to the universities". From then on the educational aspects of their "full development" were pushed into the background. The negotiations over the next couple of years between the Department and the local authorities—the meetings at Curzon Street, the protracted telephone calls—were not about student numbers, building plans or curricula, but about the instruments and articles of government. The 1966 White Paper (Department of Education and Science, 1966) and subsequent statements may not have been explicit about the intentions for the polytechnics in educational terms. Local authorities may have had to scrabble around in ministerial speeches to discover the real purpose of the operation. But in one area ministers were definite: they knew what system of government they wanted for the polytechnics.

From the very beginning, when officials first introduced the idea of "polytechnic institutes" to the Prentice Committee, they had regarded it as basic that these new institutions of higher education should be as autonomous as possible under local education authority responsibility. The academic staff were to have a large measure of self-government, and the colleges were to be free from detailed local authority control, having their own secure constitutions. When the polytechnics were being established the Department insisted that local authorities followed closely the form of government suggested in the Notes for Guidance, and made sure that

---

Source: *Polytechnics: A Report by John Pratt and Tyrrell Burgess* (1974), Pitman, pp. 149–71.

everything was well-ordered, before it would formally designate a polytechnic.

But why did Ministers and their officials emphasize government so, and what did they hope to achieve by the system of government proposed?

One answer is simple: the Department put government first because, in administrative terms, that is the logical way to do things. As one official described it: "government was the skeleton, all else was merely the flesh". Until the system of government was fixed there was nothing tangible to deal with. The governmental and hence administrative system was an entity with which the professional administrator and bureaucracy could deal. No real academic plans could be made until the government was organized and the director appointed; a polytechnic would not be designated until its director was in office. It was a reflex action, just as it had been ten years before when the CATs were formed.

This administrative logic was not only a reflex action, particularly in one aspect of the development of polytechnics. They were to be combinations of colleges, and in some cases more than that, combinations of colleges maintained by different local authorities. In the original conception there would have been four kinds of polytechnics: single colleges; colleges from one authority combined; a central college in one authority associated with satellite colleges in other authorities; colleges of equal standing in different authorities combined. The last two possibilities seemed fraught with difficulties to the Department, wary as ever of local authorities. It would have to bring LEAs together and to make sure they stayed together. A well-defined system of government was therefore needed to prevent squabbling and break-up later. One possibility, a joint board of governors, would have been inadequate because the authorities would have retained statutory control over the colleges which were to combine. The preferred alternative was the Joint Education Committee. A JEC could become the maintaining authority of a polytechnic. The statutory basis for this system—though it was needed for only five polytechnics—was already available in the 1944 Act. Though it was not envisaged originally as an expedient for polytechnics, there was a history of this sort of exercise in further education; the CAT at Salford was initially run by a JEC of three authorities. Nonetheless, the polytechnic would still need its own board of governors. For all the other polytechnics, those that were to be combinations of colleges from one authority, the authority would set up a board of governors and include on it minority representation of those neighbouring LEAs whose students would make particular use of the polytechnic. Here also a firm constitution was thought to be needed if factional jealousies were not to break out among the authorities, or indeed among the colleges.

There was, however, a third factor, and that was the structure of government and its relationship to the efficiency and status of colleges. The Department had been having a difficult time with local authorities on the issue of college government for a number of years, and there was an important issue of principle involved which became more urgent during the negotiations about polytechnics. Ten years before the polytechnic White Paper the Department had urged in its White Paper *Technical Education* (Ministry of Education, 1956) that colleges of advanced technology be given "independence appropriate to the level of their work". It extended its encouragement in Circular 7/59 (Ministry of Education, 1959). Nonetheless, many local authorities—and a common view was that it was nearly all of them—were loath to loosen the reins on the colleges. The authorities had responsibilities for the financial affairs and the operation of the colleges, took pride in them or even enjoyed their power over them, and were not prepared to pass over control to the governors or to the teachers. Yet local authority procedures were held to be obstructing the work of the colleges and causing resentment among staff. The nature of the complaints was reported in anecdotes rather than in detailed studies. They suggested that some LEAs and their committees made arbitrary decisions on matters beyond their understanding and these damaged educational development or frustrated the teachers. They suggested that local authority procedures restricted opportunities for development and acted illogically on the college: it was, for example, harder to get approval for new non-academic posts than academic because non-academic appointments were regulated by procedures for county or town hall staff. They accused local authorities of being overly bureaucratic and, in relations with teachers, authoritarian.

The Robbins Committee, reporting in 1963, supported the staff's cause and recommended that colleges doing advanced work be freed of detailed local authority control and that teachers be given the opportunity to turn their colleges into academic communities approaching the university model. The Robbins Report also appealed to the aspirations of the colleges of education with the recommendation that they move from LEA to university control. The local authorities were not amenable to this proposal. The DES was left in an awkward position between the colleges, which resented not getting the freedom and university association Robbins had recommended, and the local authorities, which insisted on retaining their influence over higher education.

The best the DES could do was to set up the Weaver Committee to investigate the government of colleges of education. The Weaver Report, published in 1966, duly recommended greater autonomy for the colleges in the use of their resources and greater teacher participation in their government. In autumn 1967 the DES introduced what became the Education (No. 2) Act 1968, and which required both further education colleges and colleges of education to have autonomous governing bodies with articles of government approved by the Secretary of State. This bill was toughened up with a late amendment which made in the case of colleges of education the instruments of government also subject to the approval of the Secretary of State. The instruments for colleges of further education were judged to be more dependent on the local situation and not subject to central government approval. The reform of the colleges of education then went ahead, hurried along by Circular 22/68 (Department of Education and Science, 1968). The tenacity of the local authorities can be seen in that it was two years before Circular 7/70 (Department of Education and Science, 1970) was able to describe the Secretary of State's requirements—having consulted the LEAs—for the government of the colleges of further education.

The issue of polytechnic government became mixed up with the post-Weaver debates. Discussion about the government of polytechnics had been held back until the publication of the Weaver Report, and that report became the guiding light. The experience of ministers in dealing with LEAs over the implementation of the Weaver recommendations made them all the more insistent about structures of polytechnic government. Their reasoning was much the same as that of Robbins and Weaver: it was essential to the self-respect and efficiency of a college doing advanced work that it be allowed to make up its own mind on academic matters. Thus the arguments began to centre on teacher participation. The Notes for Guidance demanded that teachers "share fully in [the polytechnics'] government and management as academic communities". The status of the polytechnics as institutions of higher education would depend, it seemed, on their imitation of the academic communities which universities were presumed to be. The opportunity to share in government would also attract well-qualified teachers who, it was alleged, had been driven out of further education colleges by the frustration of coping with local authority procedures and interference. It was this philosophy that led the Department and its ministers to stress teacher participation and, in the context of the battle with the LEAs, a properly defined system of government. When, later, students put so forcefully their demands to be represented in government, this also emphasized the need for staff representation.

A further factor also developed student demands for representation: 1968 was the first year of the student troubles, and it was the year when polytechnic government was negotiated. Some of the problems in setting up the polytechnics arose from the changing nature of student thinking and action between 1967 and 1969 and we shall be looking at that later, but it is enough here to point out how the urgency of dealing with student demands for representation pressed upon the issue of polytechnic government. Ministers believed that the polytechnics should not begin life with the antagonism of their students; perhaps the polytechnics would even be able to show the way forward for the universities. The sit-ins and the dissent all went to prove just how important the issue of government was. Moreover, those two greatest disturbances in the public sector colleges, at Hornsey and Guildford Schools of Art, both could be related to this issue. Hornsey, of course, had had its first taste of protest action in 1967 over its proposed amalgamation into the Middlesex (then called the North London) Polytechnic but, more significantly, by November 1968 part of the turmoil of summer 1968 had resolved itself into arguments about the government machinery of the college and about student representation. Likewise at Guildford, the trouble had been sparked off by an attempt to amalgamate it with Farnham (into a larger art college, however, not a polytechnic). During 1968 the Minister responsible was Mrs Shirley Williams, who had great sympathy for the student case and beavered away making sure that polytechnic instruments and articles matched her convictions about democracy. Her concern was shared by other Ministers: Mr Anthony Crosland, the progenitor of it all, was insistently liberal, and Mr Edward Short would always believe in teachers and was sympathetic to student demands.

For these reasons government was brought to the fore—almost to the exclusion of everything else. The whole build-up of issues involved is impressive; one can easily appreciate its significance, (although not the neglect of polytechnic development). It explains much of what the DES hoped to achieve. For the civil service there was the administrative logic, for ministers social justice and the support of students and teachers, and overall there was a belief that the status of the polytechnics would depend on a large measure of autonomy and on their being self-respecting academic communities, the justification for which stems in part from a distrust of local authorities and in part from Robbins and the university creed.

It is true that part of the submission for a polytechnic from a local authority included facts and figures about the number of students, the courses, the land available, development plans and the opportunities for expansion. It might not be quite accurate to say that gathering this information was a waste of the local authority's time—it might have found such statistics useful for its own purposes—but it is hard to see what the Department of Education and Science got out of them. It was not at this stage of the proceedings considering whether colleges fitted together and had the right potential; that had been settled by the regional advisory councils working over the names the Prentice Committee put forward. The facts and figures in the submission could only give the Department some idea of the size of the ball they had already pushed down the hill, and were probably out of date too quickly to do even that adequately. What the Department was concerned with, what its officials pored over and what Ministers took home for intricate study at the weekend, were the instruments and articles of government.

THE NOTES FOR GUIDANCE

Before the Notes for Guidance were issued the DES had been non-committal about the government of polytechnics. The 1966 White Paper had noted, when discussing the conditions under which polytechnics would be designated: "[the Secretary of State] will also need to be satisfied that the government of the polytechnics will be on acceptable lines". It referred its readers to paragraph 25, but this talked only of "separate consideration" of the issue and of consultation. The Prentice Committee had not produced firm recommendations on the subject and generally it was felt best to wait for the publication of the Weaver Report.

The Notes for Guidance described a system of government and included details on the structure and substance of instruments. and articles. The Notes were presented as an administrative memorandum, which is a form of communication not usually carrying such weight, but it was stated that it would be "a condition of the designation that the arrangements for the government and academic organisation are consistent with those recommended by the Secretary of State". It was from the Notes for Guidance that the local authorities learnt the Secretary of State's requirements, though informal channels of communication were open and most local authorities involved visited the Department. In May 1968 further advice was given in a letter about the financial arrangements, advice much the same as that given in Circular 7/70 (Department of Education and Science, 1970). At various times after that more advice was filtered through about student representation and discipline, amongst which was a commendation of the NUS–local authorities statement on the subject.

The Notes for Guidance hammered out the message :

The system of government must be suitable for institutions offering courses of higher education in a wide range of disciplines and serving national as well as regional and local needs. It must be such as to attract into the service of the polytechnics the highly qualified academic staff who will be essential and to enable them to share fully in their government and management as academic communities.

There had to be governing bodies:

The Secretary of State believes that these objectives can only be achieved by delegating the main responsibilities for conducting the affairs of the polytechnics to suitably constituted governing bodies with a large measure of autonomy. . . .

There had to be freedom from LEA financial control:

It is important ... that, within the limits necessitated by national policy and their dependence on public funds for financial support, they shall be given all possible freedom in managing themselves with the minimum of detailed control by the maintaining authorities.

There had to be devolution of responsibility:

It should be made clear in the articles of government that the governing body and the academic board should provide for the devolution of responsibility which will be essential in both academic and administrative matters.

The instruments of government were to provide for a governing body, "balanced and broadly based" and including representatives of the maintaining LEA, and of other LEAs within the polytechnic's catchment area for part-time students, "strong representation" of industry, commerce and the professions, the director of the polytechnic and at least six members of the teaching staff, plus co-opted members from universities, schools, and so on.

The articles were to provide for a governing body with specific responsibilities, and defined the message of the preliminary notes quoted above:

> There should be a clear statement of the responsibilities which will be reserved to the local education authority and of those which will be assigned to respectively the governing body, the Director, and the academic board.

The powers of the governors should be stated:

> The governing body should be responsible for the general direction of the polytechnic.
> The governing body should be responsible for submitting the estimates of the polytechnic to the authority, and within the estimates as approved should be free to incur expenditure without further reference to the authority.

And the role of the director:

> Under the general direction of the governing body the director should be responsible for the internal organisation, management and discipline of the polytechnic.

And of the academic board:

> The functions of the academic board should be specified. Within the general policy of the polytechnic and subject to the ultimate responsibility of the governing body, the responsibilities which are delegated to the board should cover planning, co-ordination, development, and oversight of all the academic work of the polytechnic, including the admission and examination of students. It should have powers of devolution to subcommittees and otherwise, and should be required to make arrangements for the delegation of faculties (if any) and departments as far as practicable of matters (such as design of courses, examinations, and admission of students)

not directly affecting other departments or the polytechnic as a whole.

What does all this amount to? Through a governing body with teacher representation the Secretary of State hoped to provide freedom from LEA control and to help form the academic community. Clearly power is meant to devolve from LEAs to the governing bodies, and from governing bodies to committees and departments. The suggestions, however, do not say as much as the Department meant, certainly not as much as Circular 7/70, in this respect. The Notes do not say that local authority representatives are expected to be in a minority, nor do they specify the arrangements for removing detailed local authority financial control, as Circular 7/70 does. In fact the polytechnic government was expected to conform roughly to Circular 7/70's requirements and possibly to go further than them in matters of teacher and student representation, and advice about financial arrangements was issued in May 1968. The Notes for Guidance are more precise about teachers. Where local authorities get "representatives" and industry "strong representation", the teachers get "normally ... at least five academic members in addition to the director, and ... at least one other member of the teaching staff elected [by the] teaching staff as a whole". Students were mentioned only superficially in the Notes and not included as members of the governing body.

The articles of government would, according to the Notes, provide for autonomous powers for a governing body, and by the Education (No. 2) Act (1968) governing bodies ceased to be subcommittees of the education committees and became bodies with their own original powers. The articles would also provide roles for the director and for the academic board. In retrospect the powers and roles provided are not as clearly defined as was thought at the time, and the resolution of which body undertakes which task can depend on local circumstances, which perhaps could have been anticipated (Locke, 1972a). It is also questionable how far the articles coped with the actual situation of the new colleges and with the criticisms of previous structures of government. The proposed arrangements called into question the role of the LEA. Its role between central government and the college was almost entirely limited to financial matters and here it had a very limited function. Its role as an institution representing public interest—against the demands of the academic community—was almost entirely eliminated. But what had never been clear was the exact nature of the complaints about detailed local authority control. The Weaver Report in discussing "the broad issues" emphasized that its "starting point (was) that it should be possible for colleges of education to enjoy academic, even if not financial, freedom". Nowhere did the report identify or discuss the problems that the colleges were facing, relying presumably on the anecdotes about procedures. Its recommendations simply allocated to the governing body a number of the powers previously held by the local authority, such as the determination of total numbers of teaching staff and proportions in grades, within the approved estimates of the colleges; it proposed to give the governing body power to spend money within the approved estimates, with virement, and so on. It was not clear on paper how far these measures would be appropriate to deal with the problems of the colleges of education or how far the proposed structure of government of polytechnics would be suitable for their situation. We look at the issues and some of the consequences of these developments for polytechnics later in this section.

PROGRESS TOWARDS DESIGNATION

The Notes for Guidance were issued and invitations to submit schemes sent to the thirty-one local authorities involved in April 1967. The majority of local authorities were fairly fast off the mark and submitted schemes during the autumn of that year, some hoping their polytechnic would be designated for September 1968. There was official silence for the rest of 1967 about the fate of these schemes whilst they were considered and commented on first by DES officials and then, in the New Year, by ministers. It wasn't until March that the then Secretary of State, Patrick Gordon Walker, chose Manchester University as the place for a major speech about the future of the polytechnics. Unfortunately the students were more interested in their grants—a proposed increase had been halved in the January 1968 cuts—and Mr Gordon Walker was shouted off the stage and reduced to delivering his speech in the Manchester BBC studios. The import of it was that he would shortly be announcing his approval of a number of polytechnic schemes. It was, however, his successor Edward Short who had this privilege when on 28 May 1968 he gave the names of sixteen schemes which had been approved subject to certain modifications. Four others had been received but not yet approved. Those modifications, the further advice the DES then put out and the May statement proved to give no green light for the polytechnics, scarcely even a cautious amber. All sixteen had to come up again for fresh approval and some were not designated until two years later (Table 1).

The first scheme to win full approval was that of Newcastle in September 1968. Hard on its heels were Sheffield, Sunderland and Wolverhampton, with Hatfield and Leicester being approved in December. The first designations were of Hatfield, Sheffield and Sunderland on 1 January 1969, twenty months after the Notes for Guidance were issued. At that time, the Department's statement anticipated that several more would be designated on 1 April and most of the rest on 1 September. It was over-optimistic. Only Leicester was approved that spring and only Bristol, Newcastle, Portsmouth and Wolverhampton in September. The rest were designated in batches during 1970, though Birmingham had to wait until January 1971, Middlesex until January 1973 and central Lancashire is outstanding at the time of writing.

The delays were over the instruments and articles of government. The

Department insisted that local authorities followed the formulae of the Notes for Guidance closely and where these proved to be unclear, further advice was issued. The Department became more rigorous during the period and its requirements for the independence of the institutions became hard for the local authorities to bear (Locke, 1972b). When it came to the crunch, the local conditions referred to deferentially in the Notes for Guidance were of small significance. The Minister responsible for higher education, Mrs Shirley Williams, studied the instruments and articles intimately, checking them especially on teacher and student representation and rights. Under her influence local authorities had to revise and revise their submissions, especially the parts about students, which had to become more and more liberal as the months passed.

In their nervousness the ministers and the Department took meticulous account of the letter of the instruments and articles—the spirit alone might fail in later days. Local authorities were annoyed to find the DES doing what they described as dotting the Is and crossing the Ts, polishing out blemishes, suggesting gently but unstoppably that such a word would be preferable to that one. An irritating episode was the Department's confusion over whether "a friend" who could accompany a student or teacher before a disciplinary committee might be a "legal adviser" or whether both species should be spelt out.

A larger problem was concerned with local authority control over the governing body. Several authorities resisted strongly the proposal that the clerk to the governors should be the chief administrative officer of the college and not their chief education officer: the issue was whether through the CEO the administration of the polytechnic and its LEA should be formally linked. Others had to be persuaded that they had weighted the committee which would select the polytechnics' director too heavily in their own favour and there might possibly be a danger of appointing a stooge.

The negotiations over these matters took the form of visits by most authorities to the DES and interchanges of letters on how the instruments and articles could be improved or brought into line. After the submissions and the notes had flown back and forth a few times there were long telephone calls between LEA and DES officials. When the difference of opinion was concentrated on just a few points, the submission could come back from the Department with just a curt try-again note. The Department could always threaten to delay the scheme, let it get lost in its files or in the Minister's bedroom. It could even threaten to refuse to designate. The threats worked better with some authorities than others: the Middlesex authorities, one would presume, were not moved by them, whilst an authority to whom the prestige of a polytechnic mattered would respond.

The two principal stumbling blocks were finance (with regard to the extent of local authority control) and students. Finance was the subject of

Table 1 Progress to designation

Situation in May 1968 statement	Designation	Authority	Number of colleges	Director's previous job
Approved	*January–April 1969*			
	Hatfield	county	1	same
	Sheffield	cb	1 + art	same
	Sunderland	cb	1 + art	same
	Leicester	cb	1 + art	same
	September 1969			
	Bristol	cb	3	university
	Newcastle	cb	3	industry
	Portsmouth	cb	1 + art	same
	Wolverhampton	cb	1 + art	same
	January 1970			
	Kingston	lb	1 + art	same
	Manchester	cb	3	industry
	Plymouth	cb	1	same
	North Staffs	jec	3	further education
	Later 1970			
	Glamorgan	county	1	same
	Oxford	cb	1	university and Chairman of Governors
	Teesside	cb	1	same
	North East London	jec	3	further education
Submitted but not approved	*January 1970*			
	Leeds	cb	4	university
	Later 1970			
	Brighton	cb	1 + art	university
	Huddersfield	cb	2	industry
	1971			
	Birmingham	cb	5	polytechnic
Not submitted	*January 1970*			
	Lanchester	jec	3	same
	Later 1970			
	Liverpool	cb	4	further education
	Trent	jec	1 + art	dep dir of educ Nottingham
	South Bank	ilea	5	same
	City of London	ilea	3	same
	Central London	ilea	2	same
	Thames	ilea	2	same

Table 1 Progress to designation   (*Continued*)

1971			
North London	ilea	2	university
1973			
Middlesex	jec	3	university

Abbreviations: cb: county borough; lb: London borough; ilea: Inner London Education Authority (the polytechnics of which are established under the Companies Act in order to accommodate the voluntary aided colleges); jec: joint education committee.

the advisory letter distributed in May 1968 and was the main area where local authorities had to modify their plans. The requirements for student representation and discipline developed during the negotiations.

The Notes for Guidance referred deferentially to the financial accountability of the local authority and to their "important responsibilities" but advice was limited to a paragraph in the articles:

> The governing body should be responsible for submitting the estimates of the polytechnic to the authority, and within the estimates as approved should be free to incur expenditure without further reference to the authority. In order to give the governing body the necessary freedom of action, the main subheads should be drawn widely and there should be provision for virement within them. In submitting schemes authorities should give particulars of the subheads and arrangements for virement which are proposed.

LEAs were referred to the Weaver Report's suggested headings for virement. These were fifteen which, as the Notes said, might not be appropriate for polytechnics. Some authorities drew up fewer heads—according to some anecdotes, because they misread the list—thus giving their polytechnic considerably more freedom; others resisted the whole concept.

The Department had to explain further, it had to make explicit the financial set-up that would support the autonomy and devolution of powers and it had to insist on it. It issued advice similar to that which was to be promulgated in Circular 7/70 for other colleges of further education and colleges of education:

> It is in particular important that there shall be no doubt about the relationship between authorities and polytechnics in financial matters. In the Secretary of State's view the following are the minimum powers in financial matters that should be delegated to a polytechnic in its Articles of Government: —
> (i) The annual financial estimates of the polytechnic should be pre-

pared under the direction of the Director and in the form laid down by the local education authority, for submission by the governors to the authority by such a date and with such supporting data as the authority may require.

(ii) Within the estimates, as approved by the authority, the governors should be entitled to incur expenditure without further reference to the authority and should be empowered:

(a) to exercise virement within stated headings (which might conveniently be listed in an appendix to the Articles);

(b) to determine (subject to the provisions of the Burnham Report) the numbers and grades of teaching staff;

(c) to carry out repairs, maintenance and minor alterations up to a figure of at least £500 per job by what they judge, having regard to economical management, as the best means; and

(d) to place orders for supplies (including equipment) and services at their discretion, subject, above a reasonable sum, to their making use of the authority's central arrangements where this would be more economical.

The battle was a very straightforward one. Several local authorities were not prepared to allow the governors spending power of up to £500 on maintenance and small building works, nor up to £100 on equipment, though some were prepared to allow the latter to go up to £500. The idea offended the traditions of local authority budgeting and financial control. Nor were other authorities happy with the principle of virement, that a polytechnic having been granted money in the budget for one item should be able to spend that money on something else under the same head.

Students and the rise of their power are a subject in themselves, but the time scale of their new awareness and new demands coincided with the negotiations about polytechnic government and the issues are entangled. The Weaver Committee, which was so influential on teacher representation and autonomy, neither included representatives of students nor took evidence from them. When in the autumn of 1966 the NUS conference debated that report it deplored this absence but concentrated on the report's failure to make recommendations about student discipline and students' rights in disciplinary actions. The Notes for Guidance merely required provision to be made for independent students' unions in polytechnics with arrangements to "enable representations on matters of proper concern to students to be made on their behalf to the governing body, the Director or the academic board as may be appropriate". There should, the Notes said, be a procedure for suspending a student for misconduct and the right of a hearing for the student concerned accompanied by a friend or legal adviser. In May 1968 this was still the Department's requirement though it was insisting that provision on these topics should be made specifically in the articles of government. Ministers, however, in public speeches were leaving open the possibility that there should be student representatives actually on the governing body and academic board. The ministers, particularly Mrs Williams, were going to say there must be student representatives, not just channels of representation. Pressure from students increased during 1967 and 1968. NUS conference resolutions demanding representation attracted public notice whilst the NUS gained the influence and power to push its demands to a conclusion. The official NUS policy was that one-third of the governing body should be students though in fact the NUS leadership never pushed it as far as this. The tenor of the demands changed too, from an emphasis on "communication" to "participation". During 1968 sit-in followed sit-in, university after university was disrupted. A moderates' philosophy developed that student participation in government was not only just and sensible but practical in that it would take the wind out of the militants' sails. Not only were the student demands escalating, so too was the sympathy with which they were held by ministers and other influential forces. By the summer of 1969 the Secretary of State, Mr Edward Short, was telling the parliamentary select committee which had begun investigating student unrest the previous autumn that the colleges and universities worst hit by student troubles were those "where the rules were excessive and students had not shared in making them".

Local authorities were hard put, even when they were willing, to keep pace with students' demands and their acceptance by ministers. It is a measure of the ministers' suspicion of local authorities as much as of their democratic convictions that they were so willing to hear and argue the student case. Students, both in their national union and in local unions were able to gain direct access to the Minister. One union was able to enter into discussion with Mrs Williams about the proposed polytechnic without the local authority being informed and indeed only finding out later from the students themselves. (Legitimately one might ask why this should cause surprise because after all the students' union was an independent body entitled to be heard. But the established attitude was that a students' union would be an item of a local authority's concern and could only be reached with its knowledge.) Local authorities found that they would agree what was an acceptable phrasing of student rights at one meeting with the Department and then when they resubmitted their scheme they would discover that they were expected to be more liberal now. This annoyed them.

In the late summer of 1968 the NUS leadership—which had until then stressed its "responsibility" and its role as mediator between its militant brethren (who baffled it as much as anyone) and the establishment—produced an uncharacteristically forceful ten-point plan for campus peace. The NUS negotiated with the Committee of Vice-Chancellors and Principals on the basis of this statement and in November produced an agreement. The Vice-Chancellors had accepted that "the machinery of student participation can and should be extended and improved". There was nothing in the agreement that could be seen as a plan or blueprint, but it did define three areas in university government and the appropriate amount of student involvement: student welfare—"varying degrees of participation in the decision-making process"; academic matters—students' view "properly taken into account"; and staff matters—nothing except "opportunities to discuss the general principles".

These three areas were taken up by the joint agreement between the NUS and the local authority associations published at the beginning of December 1968. The agreement was commended to the local authorities by the Department—as well it might, for the Department had had a large hand in formulating it. The polytechnics were expected to subscribe to it. As an agreement it had the advantage over the universities' one in being slightly more specific about the proportions of student representation. It failed to mention student representation on the governing body, in much the same way as Circular 7/70 was later to suggest that "consideration" be given to student governors. The polytechnics, as were other advanced further education colleges later, were expected to go beyond the agreement and have student governors. It is significant that only one polytechnic—Sunderland—had no student governor and that it was one of the first approved. It was later to be updated, but it indicates how demands for student representation increased. One cannot leave the NUS-LEAs agreement without noting that it was revoked at the National Union of Students conference the following spring, but it proved nonetheless useful for all that.

The crowning irony after all this attention to students and their place in government was that during the winter 1970-71 the whole thing came perilously close to collapse. The London borough of Kingston-upon-Thames discovered in the course of resisting an increase in per capita fees from the students' union in their polytechnic that local authorities were probably acting *ultra vires* in paying union fees as an element in student grants. Without fees from LEAs, students' unions would have collapsed and with them their role in college democracy. Fortunately Mrs Thatcher, the Secretary of State for Education and Science in the Conservative Government, stepped in to change the wording of the regulations so that local authorities could pay up. What had happened was that the 1970 grants regulations (Statutory Instruments No. 497, 1970) had qualified the standing regulation that union fees were payable where membership of the union was obligatory by the phrase "obligatory by reason of any provision of the instrument regulating the conduct of the establishment"—and that was something the polytechnics' instruments and articles of government didn't mention.

Before a polytechnic was designated a director had to be appointed, and this too created tensions between the Department and the LEA. Ministers and officials insisted that the appointments committee should not be weighted too heavily in LEA representation in order to secure this—and hence the college's independence. In the event, as Table 1 shows, the polytechnics which appointed the principal of the major constituent college as director tended to be among the earlier designations. Overall, the appointments did not diverge much from traditional technical college pattern. Over half retained a principal as director, whilst six appointed from university and three from industry.

THE CONSEQUENCES OF THE POLICY

The issue of government became the single most important factor in the establishment of the polytechnics. What were the consequences of this policy? They can be considered in two parts, first the efforts of the way the policy was implemented and secondly the problems posed by the measures themselves.

The means by which the Department of Education and Science carried out its policy was to make the drawing up of satisfactory instruments and articles of government a condition of the designation of the polytechnics. It did not enforce a common set of instruments and articles, but gave the initiative to local authorities to prepare the schemes in the light of the guidance given in the Notes for Guidance and other communications. In taking this course of action the DES was working in the accepted style of a "national system locally administered" and respecting the autonomy of the local education authorities. The Department, as previous sections of this chapter have shown, used its ability to persuade and ultimately to approve or not the instruments and articles in order to influence both their substance and wording. Every polytechnic has different instruments and articles but there are many similarities and some standard components. Study of the instruments and articles reveals two characteristics: an imprecise chronological development and a confusing combination of uniformity and variety (Locke, 1972b).

The standard which the DES set for the instruments and articles changed during the period of the negotiations. Certain of the changes can be fixed—the May 1968 letter of the financial arrangements and the December 1968 statement on student representation and discipline—but there is a less specific progression also. These developments are characterized by a greater precision in the Department's requirements and by an increasing progressiveness in terms of academic control, limitations upon LEA powers, devolution of responsibility, disciplinary procedures for students. The most important developments after the Notes for Guidance are those which also caused the most problems between the Department and the local authorities, financial arrangements and student matters. The new standards were introduced by the Department in time to be included in nearly all the articles, although in the first group of designations Hatfield, for example, did not have the standard wording on student disciplinary procedures nor the detailed statement of the functions of the academic board. Sunderland did not include a student representative on the governing body. Articles of government approved later are more likely to show the effects of the Department's pressure to have the academic board involved in the preparation of estimates, to have statements of delegation to committees, to include students on the academic board. A detailed study of the instruments and articles shows, however, that the most progressive were not the last designated, which indicates both that their LEAs resisted some of the progressive features and that more compliant LEAs gained approval for their schemes more quickly.

The most important requirements set by the Department are common to nearly all the polytechnics: the composition of the governing body; an academic board with decision-making powers; the chief administrative officer as clerk to the governors; staff and student representation. Many other features of the articles vary. For example, academic boards are randomly given responsibilities to "regulate" or to "make arrangements" on topics like examinations or research.

It seems unlikely that most of these variations in instruments and articles can be significant, if they are either random or a product of the time when they were written. Few of the variations are significant in operational terms. An academic board could work differently if its functions included, as Bristol's does, "preparation of annual estimates affecting academic matters" than if they did not, as Hatfield's, Kingston's and North East London's do not. But it could not make any difference that in addition to a common phrase about "planning, co-ordination, development and oversight" of academic work, North East London's articles included "the regulation of the teaching work", or Huddersfield's "to consider and decide questions relating to courses of study". It could be argued that the introduction of the instruments and articles for polytechnics was a successful operation of the partnership of the Department with the LEAs in that local initiative and variations were fostered whilst achieving national standards on major issues. On the other hand most of these local variations are of small or no significance and many of the national standards were not guidance from the Department but effectively instructions. The introduction of the instruments and articles could be interpreted therefore as a charade, but the playing of it delayed the development of the polytechnics by periods ranging from a few months to two years or more.

As for the measures themselves, what did they achieve? As we saw earlier, the problems they might have set out to solve were vaguely formulated. As a consequence, we must look at what has been left out of the structure of polytechnic government, and the most ignored factors prove to be among the largest. These included the role of the Department of Education and Science and the role of the local education authority beyond the once-a-year session on the estimates. Both factors are likely to be the dominating influence in the educational development of the polytechnics. To see how the ministers viewed those we must return to the text of the Notes for Guidance, particularly to paragraph 6:

The polytechnics must of course operate within national policies and within limits set by the financial and legal responsibilities of the local education authority. It must rest with the Secretary of State, for example, to determine the number of polytechnics and to co-ordinate developments throughout the system as a whole through his control of building programmes and the approval of courses. He must continue to set and enforce minimum standards. Salary and grading structures for the academic staff will also continue to be settled under national arrangements. A number of important responsibilities must similarly be discharged by the local education authorities. Within national policies they must settle the broad range of courses to be provided, and the polytechnics must continue to be subject to controls in financial and administrative matters such as the approval of estimates, capital development and the level of fees. It is important, however, that within the limits necessitated by national policy and their dependence on public funds for financial support they shall be given all possible freedom in managing them-selves with the minimum of detailed control by the maintaining authorities.

It is questionable what this paragraph is saying. First, with regard to the Secretary of State's powers it might be doing no more than restating his statutory controls over further education, but it might be saying that he would be prepared to use these powers as sanctions and to gain a greater influence on the educational development, for example, in the approval of courses. It could be that the DES had a conception of what the polytechnics should be about and was prepared to press its influence with these sanctions. But if it did this it would be dealing not with the poly-technic itself but in most respects with its local education authority, which has the statutory responsibilities for building programmes, sub-mission of courses and finance. There might be informal meetings between, for example, HMIs and the polytechnic staff, but the formal negotiations take place removed from the polytechnic. The polytechnic has no formal means to argue its case for new buildings directly with the DES and has to send its new courses for approval through a circuitous procedure of local authority, regional advisory council, examination body and Secretary of State. This raises the questions of how the DES can exercise control to promote its national policies—it can only pull its level at one end of the process and wait to see if it has the desired effect in the college—and of what sort of independence the polytechnics have if these major decisions are made between other bodies. The vital passage in the notes does nothing to resolve the situation. It prefers to confuse the situation and offend no one.

Similarly the relationship between the LEA and the polytechnic is muddied over. What are "important responsibilities"? What is settling "the broad range of courses"? The definite statement refers to known statutory responsibilities whilst the overall impression could imply either that a creative LEA has "important responsibilities" to work with the college's academic development, or that the LEA is left only with mean-minded (legal) sanctions. The truth, of course, is between: the LEA must be expected to have an influence educationally, for it has such responsibilities under the Education Act (1944) and the Further Regulations [. . .]. Presumably between this responsibility and the protection from interference in the academic matters of the college given in the instruments and articles, there is a line to be drawn locally according to political circumstances. The main question relates to the way the local authority can exercise its influence through its minority representation on the governing body and financial power over the estimates. But power to approve or disapprove estimates, and certainly to pick and choose items in a list of expenditures, is a drastic power, the use of which will lead to antagonism between the parties. It is in the interests of both sides to avoid such a confrontation. It is furthermore in the polytechnic's interest to behave itself *vis-à-vis* the education office and the borough treasurer to lend credence to its estimates next year. Its powers of virement must be limited by concern not to damage the credibility of next year's estimates. Its spending powers are effectively reduced.

One of the aims of the new system of government for polytechnics was to free these institutions of meddling by local authorities, of having to subscribe to the local authorities' financial standards, of decisons made in the arbitrary fashion of bargaining between those with the money and those who want it. The avoidance of these two issues—the DES role and the LEA educational role—has failed to change the situation as much as the Notes for Guidance might have suggested. The lack of structures in these areas means that bargaining, with its irrationalities and frustrations to academic staff, is bound to continue. The inadequacy of formal LEA-polytechnic links puts a great deal of pressure upon informal contacts; they are the only way the education committee and education office have of influencing the educational development of the polytechnic. If informal contacts are the principal means of external government control or influence, the polytechnics are likely to be subjected to the same kind of pressures as their system of government was intended to free them from. Inconsistencies and meddling by an LEA are likely to be encouraged because decisions are the outcome of bargaining and *ad hoc* situations rather than justified or made as part of defined policy.

The structures of government may even reinforce these effects. The emphasis on teacher representation and the academic community tends to close off the influence of those who have power over the resources. The academic staff can decide their own destiny but must do it in committees which lack full knowledge or power over resources. They have a somewhat alarming choice between academic purity in the committees and joining in the bargaining. The emphasis on teacher representation has had another effect. By sticking to the formula for academic boards in the Notes for Guidance it was possible for a minister to force upon a polytechnic an academic board of unmanageable proportions in the name of democracy. When this board, or indeed a smaller one, needs to create subcommittees to discharge some of its duties, it does at the same time lengthen the decision-making process. If decisions cannot be made on time inside committees, they will be made arbitrarily outside it. As for the governing body, it is open to it to be variously a post-box between academic board and education committee, a tool of the college or a body of disguised local authority men (Locke, 1972a). It may feel it lacks the expert knowledge to project the future of the polytechnic even in such general terms as student numbers. Its powers, though autonomous, are not clearly defined, and its role depends on the local situation.

The committee structure of the board of governors and academic board plus their subcommittees was the foundation of the scheme of government proposed by the DES. The board of governors was the assurance of the autonomy of the college; the academic board of teacher participation. It is questionable, however, whether the system will work as intended. Certain important functions of government—notably those relating to the Department's role and to LEA educational influence— have been neglected, and this must force consideration of issues and taking of decisons on these matters into routes outside those constituted in the instruments and articles. But even within the formal structure the governing body is liable to be squeezed out between an academic board which exercises its academic powers to the full and an LEA which keeps its hold on the purse-strings. As for the academic boards, early experience suggests that the number of their sub-committees multiplies to consider issues which require more thought or less committee members than the board itself can provide. Nor can the academic board take full consideration of an issue, being deprived of both financial and political power. The emphasis on committees—whilst neglecting certain functions of government—may perpetuate delays and time-procedures as frustrating as and often very similar to those which the schemes were intended to overcome. Some of the procedures have simply been moved out of the education office and into the polytechnic.

When such delays occur the weaknesses of this elaborate structure become apparent. If decisions cannot be taken in time by the academic board then they will be rushed through by the administration. The director, whose appointment was a major factor in the designation of the polytechnics, thus becomes a key figure in their administration. His strength relies not only on his personal characteristics, but also on the method of his appointment and his situation alongside complicated committee structure. When he arrived on the scene he found some sketchy plans from the local authority in their submission to the Department which nobody was very interested in. He found too an interim academic board making plans about, perhaps, the distribution of faculties. This board was largely a hang-over from the constituent colleges and the director could, and sometimes did, disregard it. There was as yet no senior staff nor academic board for the new college. He was to have a formidable say in appointing the first and in forming the second. Possibly the polytechnic was months from its actual designation, as its instruments and articles were straightened out. During the negotiations between the local authority and the DES the local authority had to start making plans for its new polytechnic and had to operate informally in advance of the Department's formal requirements. The director slotted into these arrangements and as the polytechnic got going he continued to use them. He is at the crucial position of power between academic board and governors, teachers and local authority; he alone has full access to academic and resource planning, and holds sway over academic and administrative staff. It even depends on his largeness of spirit to allow the academic board and its sub-committees to function as the concepts of academic democracy intended. He is in an autocratic position and, more than that, the development of the polytechnic had to depend upon his vision, for no one else had the power to implement one. The academic community may be formed out of committees, but it is the director who runs it. Small wonder that Terence Miller described his role as director of the North London Polytechnic as "helmsman", "pyramidal point", "ideas pool", "reservoir of ideas", "conductor", and "tin-opener". But all this means that many of the powers delegated from the authority to the academic board in practice have fallen into the hands of the directors. Again, rather than giving staff in the institutions control over their academic development, the new arrangements for polytechnic government have tended to perpetuate the autocratic control of the old college principal. And since more often than not local authorities appointed existing principals as directors, they obviously got the right man for the job.

GOVERNMENT AS AN INSTRUMENT

We have looked at the reasons why the government of the polytechnics became such an important issue, and at some of the problems and effects of the measures. We can look also at government as an instrument of the polytechnic policy. Is the structure of government an essential part of polytechnic development? Does it tell us anything about ministers' and the Department's intentions for the polytechnics?

We saw that there were a number of factors behind the emphasis on government, administrative and political. Arguments for greater teacher representation and for more independence from local education authorities were based on notions of professional self-management, of prestige and of democracy, and these were very much interrelated. Arguments based on democracy or the social justice of giving people greater control over their own affairs were implicit rather than stated and also owed much of their inspiration to the demands of students. It is hard, without a much longer and more detailed analysis of social movements, to say more than that they caught the spirit of the times, that they became associated with popular demands for participation in many other areas of society and that ministers in paying meticulous attention to the instruments and articles of government appeared to perceive them as a means of achieving greater democracy in higher education. But this was a political conviction rather than a polytechnic philosophy, and the same exercise was carried out with other further education colleges with Circular 7/70. Arguments based on professional self-management were concerned with allegations of LEA interference in academic matters and of bureaucratic procedures. These were related to arguments about the prestige of the institutions, partly because the universities were believed not to labour under such difficulties and partly because the abolition of these difficulties would be intended to attract more high-level staff.

Teachers were to be given more self-management by means of representation, devolution and the greater independence of the colleges from LEAs. It is not clear, however, how this could be intended to provide a specifically polytechnic educational development. Is it reasonable to expect that simply setting teachers free—if indeed they had been —would produce a specific kind of educational development, a polytechnic policy? It could, for example, be argued that teachers would seek to protect their own interests rather than to promote those of their institutions or of society. But if ministers had any educational philosophy for the polytechnics they must have been relying on self-management by teachers as a progressive force. If ministers had a specific philosophy for the polytechnics, they must have been relying on those teachers receiving a common inspiration not only of that philosophy but of how to implement it. It seems unlikely.

Alternatively, we may consider that the greater degree of teacher self-management was justified not by any assumed educational development of the polytechnics, but by other aspects of a polytechnic policy, those relating to their status and administration. The precedent for the careful construction of committees into an academic community is, in fact, that of the universities. If we trace the Department's actions back, we arrive at the Weaver Committee's response to the Robbins Report. Robbins was about universities, and universities have traditionally claimed to be academic communities and have functioned through committees and subcommittees of the greatest academic committee, the senate. If we accept this as the model of the polytechnic system, much else that is confusing falls into place, not least the occasional references to the academic board as the polytechnic senate. There is no evidence, however, that this system of government adopted from the universities was meant to produce a distinctive educational development in the polytechnics. Indeed, if the system of government is seen in terms of its educational effects, it seems hardly logical to take the same system of government to produce different effects. It seems more likely that it was a question of status, both to attract teachers and to impress the public, that polytechnics were required to imitate the university system of government.

The schemes of government for the polytechnics do not define an educational development but seek to establish the status of the institutions. This is more closely related to one of the other reasons we discussed for emphasizing government, the amalgamation of the colleges into the polytechnics, the administrative exercise. We are brought back to the primary justification for the polytechnics in the White Paper (Department of Education and Science, 1966):

> This will enable staff and students to enjoy the advantages of belonging to institutions offering a wide variety of disciplines and it will concentrate expensive resources in fewer centres.

The polytechnics were basically a means of consolidating the resources of advanced further education. Their schemes of government are an instrument of this administrative exercise, though the exercise was coloured up with the associations of better days at university.

REFERENCES

DEPARTMENT OF EDUCATION AND SCIENCE (1966) *Higher Education in the Further Education System*, Plan for Polytechnics and Other Colleges, Cmnd 3006, HMSO.

DEPARTMENT OF EDUCATION AND SCIENCE (1967) Notes for Guidance, Administrative Memorandum 8/67, HMSO.

DEPARTMENT OF EDUCATION AND SCIENCE (1968) Circular 22/68, HMSO.

DEPARTMENT OF EDUCATION AND SCIENCE (1970) Circular 7/70, HMSO.

EDUCATION ACT (1944) Ch. 31, HMSO.

EDUCATION (No. 2) ACT (1968) Ch. 17, HMSO.

LOCKE, M. (1972a) "College Government: the Law and the Issues", Coombe Lodge Report, Vol. 5, No. 3.

LOCKE, M. (1972b) "The Instruments and Articles of Government of Polytechnics", Coombe Lodge Report, Vol. 5, No. 15.

MINISTRY OF EDUCATION (1956) *Technical Education*, Cmnd 9703, HMSO.

MINISTRY OF EDUCATION (1959) Circular 7/59, HMSO.

ROBBINS COMMITTEE (1963) *Higher Education*, report of the Committee (Chairman: Lord Robbins) appointed by the Prime Minister, Cmnd 2154, HMSO.

WEAVER COMMITTEE (1966) Report of the Study Group on the Government of Colleges of Education, HMSO.

2.3 Behavioural Objectives — A Critical Review

Michael MacDonald-Ross

ABSTRACT

Behavioural objectives lay the foundations for a thoroughgoing attempt to improve the effectiveness of educational systems. By specifying what the student should be able to do after the learning experience, the hope is that the outcomes of education can be brought in line with the intentions of the educator. To achieve this goal, it would be minimally necessary to ensure that the objectives were relevant, and that they could be used to prescribe fairly exactly the design of the educational process and the evaluation which would follow. The object of this paper is to assess such claims.

The paper starts by placing behavioural objectives in the context of the systematic approach to education, a particular kind of rational planning. A distinction is drawn between two kinds of systematic approach—the feedforward prescriptive mode and the feedback cyclical mode. The feedforward mode is ambitious, placing great stress on objectives, and insisting upon explicit procedures both for deriving objectives and for the subsequent process of design. The cyclical mode is less ambitious, but less vulnerable to attack. It accepts a downgraded role for objectives (they are seen just as part of an interconnected system) and it accepts that success will only be achieved by a process of testing and recycling. The cyclical mode puts less stress on the need to be explicit, and relies more on the intuitive skills of the individual educator.

The cases for and against behavioural objectives are then discussed in considerable detail. At the end of this analysis it is clear that the strongest claims made for behavioural objectives cannot stand as they were. For example, it seems certain that objectives do not prescribe the design of the educational system, or the validity of test items. And there are not satisfactory principles for deriving relevant objectives. These, and other criticisms, arise from deep-seated deficiencies inherent in the conceptual framework of the systematic approach. In particular it is claimed that the system is based on a poverty-stricken model of student-teacher interaction, that lists of behaviours can never adequately represent the struc-

Source: *Instructional Science* (1973), No. 2, pp. 1–52.

ture of knowledge, and that the whole schema suffers from the weaknesses of operationalism.

These conclusions appear to demolish the stronger feedforward prescriptions, and weaken somewhat the softer cyclical approach. The arguments on which these conclusions are based were tested on one of the standard and best-known defences of behavioural objectives, and it seems fair to conclude that this particular defence does not meet the criticisms raised.

It is unlikely that the deficiencies of behavioural objectives can ever be fully repaired, no matter how much time or effort is expended. A certain mileage can be expected of any conceptual schema, and the behavioural objective/systematic approach, as practised by the best consultants, seems close to its limits. This paper suggests that radical improvements depend upon constructing a less limited framework which allows progress in directions denied to the systematic approach. No such framework is proposed in the paper, though some hints are given.

For the present, behavioural objectives provide a well-worked-out tool for rational planning in education. They have made possible certain improvements in the technique of curriculum design; and should not be discarded in disgust just because they fail to meet more exacting standards. But the application of these objectives should be tempered by a deep understanding of their limitations. This paper attempts to promote this understanding.

INTRODUCTION

Behavioural objectives have been, for at least a decade, one of the central concepts of programmed learning and educational technology. They have now been incorporated into the theory of curriculum design, and so assume even greater significance. The recent flood of publications on behavioural objectives reflects the number of curriculum design courses which adopt this approach (in addition to the works of Mager and Popham, to be discussed later, Block, 1971; Davies, 1971; Hauenstein, 1972; Hartley, 1972; Kemp, 1970; McAshan, 1970; Sund and Picard, 1972; and Vargas, 1972 all bear directly on the subject). Also, the development of elementary management control systems in education (such as *performance contracting, mastery learning, 90–90–90 criteria, payment by results*), depends critically on behavioural objectives.

So, much rests on whether the idea of behavioural objectives stands up to critical examination. Can the idea bear the weight that is now put upon it? This paper is an attempt to answer that question in a fairly thoroughgoing fashion. But before starting the main investigation we should ask a prior question: why should rational planning in education be interesting in *any* form? The reason is quite straightforward. Individual teachers of genius have always been able to rely on their personal hunches and intuition; but as long as intuition is private others cannot easily learn its basis. So, for as long as anyone can recall, the outcomes of education have been at variance with the idealised pretensions of the educator. Systems of rational planning attempt to realise in practice the aims set in theory: and behavioural objectives form the basis of the only well-worked-out system of planning in education. That is their importance.

PART I: RATIONAL PLANNING IN EDUCATION
Begin at the beginning and go on until you come to the end: then stop. (King of Hearts to White Rabbit)

To state educational aims in behavioural terms is to say what you expect the student to do after the learning experience that he could not do before. Such a prescription only makes sense within a certain context— inside a particular world-view, if you like. In this case the context is a group of procedures bearing a close family resemblance one to another, and known collectively as "the systematic approach to education". The systematic approach is, in its turn, a member of an even more extended club which includes all sorts of rational planning and design procedures.

1 The nature of planning
Planning is a typically human activity. By planning ahead we aim to regulate the disturbances that occur in our environment, anticipate and avoid forseeable difficulties, and act upon the world so as to turn it gradually into a more favourable place to live in. Our species has done this quite comprehensively, yet until recently the processes of planning have received little serious attention. Planning has been justified (above) as being necessary if results are ever to match intentions. This goal is now more difficult to achieve than ever before, because of the rapid developments in our society and in our knowledge of the world. We have the (correct) impression that we live in a dynamic world system which is complex and highly interconnected, and which we are not yet much good at regulating. The various well-known problems facing us result from our lack of true (regulatory) control mechanisms.

There is now, fortunately, some recognition of the need for an adequate account of the planning process (see especially Alexander, 1964; Churchman, 1968a, 1968b, 1972; Ozbekhan, 1969, 1971; Vickers, 1959, 1965, 1967, 1968, 1970; Braybrooke and Lindblom, 1963). Although influenced by their work, the account which follows does not attempt to summarise their views in detail. It does, however, outline some of the features required of a successful system of planning so that the systematic approach to education can be seen in perspective.

Any system of planning may be called *rational* insofar as satisfactory relationships exist between ends and means (this is a criterion of internal coherence); and may be called *successful* insofar as relevant problems are actually solved (a criterion of pragmatic effectiveness). This raises the question of the relationship between ends/means analysis and problem-solving. One account of the problem goes like this: when both ends and means are well-defined the problem becomes just a matter of putting the right procedure into effect (procedural). Other problems start life with either ends or means ill-defined; in this case solution depends first upon resolving the ill-defined dimension. But the most interesting (and the most common) human problems have both dimensions ill-defined. There is then a choice of routes towards a solution, as shown in Figure 1:

Figure 1 The ends/means approach to problem-solving. An ill-defined problem may be converted into soluble form via either of two routes (from an idea of Brian Lewis)

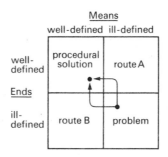

Route A, the conceptual route, clarifies ends before means are selected. This puts emphasis upon definition of objectives and on a prescriptive, feedforward mode of planning. Many recent kinds of rational decision-making procedures use this route; for example, systems analysis, PPBS, management by objectives, etc. (see Ansoff, 1965; Churchman, 1968b; Odiorne, 1965; Quade, 1967). But despite the publicity given to these new methods most problems are solved by route B, the expedient route, which uses the information about means to restrict the goals that are aimed for. Route B is closer to the form of traditional evolution, for it stresses feedback, successive adjustment, cycling procedures of design. It is the standard mode for the political animal, and has been called piecemeal social engineering (Popper, 1945, 1957) or the art of the possible (Butler, 1971) or planned muddling through (Kahn, 1972) or the strategy of disjointed incrementalism (!—Braybrooke and Lindblom, 1973).[1] Often temporal constraints force planners along this route in practice even though they may express preference for route A in theory.

Now although the pros and cons of these two approaches are fiercely debated by their respective advocates, the alternatives are not mutually exclusive. Most real acts of planning use a mixed strategy by alternating the two extremes or even pursuing both routes at the same time. But the distinction does mark a real difference of attitude, and has practical consequences, as we shall see when we contrast hard- and soft-line approaches to deriving behavioural objectives.

What might be expected of a successful theory of planning? If this were clear there would at least be some basis for judging behavioural objectives and the systematic approach as an example of planning in education. Below some criteria are suggested with special reference to the role of objectives in planning.

Objectives lie at the heart of the planning process, though they are far more crucial wherever route A is chosen. So it should be possible to get some further mileage from the ends/means distinction by dissecting the notion of *an end*. We can entertain all sorts of goals or objectives. How are they related one to another? Are they mutually exclusive, or causally or temporally related? Where do they come from, and how can we choose between conflicting alternatives? Such questions are susceptible to various lines of attack, most of which recognise that short-term operational goals only make sense if selected as steps towards longer-term strategic or normative goals. Thus, in Ozbekhan's scheme planning objectives are arrayed in a hierarchy (Ozbekhan, 1971):

1 NORMATIVE PLANNING

Here what *ought* to be achieved is decided according to the prevailing value system (for more extensive discussions of norms see Vickers and also von Wright 1963; and Ross 1968). The decision to fight a war, or to shift budgets from tertiary to primary education are essentially normative decisions.

2 STRATEGIC PLANNING

Here is determined what *can* be done—given a certain time and situation. Military strategy is the original example; nowadays we talk of aims being broken down into a plexus of sub-goals. That plexus is the strategy.

3 OPERATIONAL PLANNING

No goal can be attained unless the appropriate sequence of operations is chosen and put into effect. Thus the use is similar to military tactics. More generally, operational planning is "instrumental", dealing with inputs from the environment, and taking action to attain the goals.

Ideally we should expect (i) clear rules or principles governing the origin of objectives, (ii) clear rules governing the transition from one level to another, and (iii) clear rules governing the relationship between objectives at any one level. So far as I know, no existing planning systems meet such exacting requirements.

Systems of rational planning can often be characterised as favouring one or other of these three levels. For example, when Rapoport (1964) says, "Conscience, by its very nature, compels people to act on other than pragmatic grounds" he is putting emphasis on the normative level of decision-making in contrast to Kahn (1962), whose essay on "Thinking about the Unthinkable" is primarily concerned with strategic considerations. We shall find that the systematic approach to education is an operationalist scheme which very seldom considers the normative and strategic levels.

There are other expectations we might reasonably entertain of a system of planning. For example, it is important for the criteria for decision-making to be explicit rather than implicit. Only when criteria become public can they be examined, criticised, tested and improved. So, although no system of human action can hope to be fully explicit, the general intention is to shift decision-making from the private into the public arena.

Another expectation concerns the relation between the planning system and the environment it is trying to influence. This amounts to asking whether the planning system has an adequate model of the domain on which it intends to operate. A successful model of the *domain* enables accurate prediction; that is, enables the planning to be right, or nearly right, first time around. (And a successful model of the *environment* enables constraints to be correctly allowed for.) Later it will be argued that the lack of an adequate model of learning is one of the particular weaknesses of the systematic approach.

These are just the most obvious requirements of a system of planning. There are plenty more; but at least we can see that a system of planning is unlikely to be wholly successful in practice unless it satisfies adequately each of the criteria discussed above. And this is especially true if the domain of application is complex, which it certainly is in education.

2   *The systematic approach to education*

First, a comment on the word "systematic". Throughout this essay the approach is called systematic, and never "the systems approach". There is a good reason for this choice. The word "systems" is best reserved for those cases where a true systems theory is used. General systems theory and cybernetics are two closely related attempts to provide such a systems theory. The behavioural objectives approach to education rests in no sense whatsoever on any such systems theory. It simply relies upon the systematic application of common sense to the problems of education. This is a worthwhile end in itself, and does not need the pretentious conceit so often found, where the mere linking of boxes by arrows is held to be sufficient justification for using the word "systems".

The systematic approach is an attempt at rational planning in education which claims wide validity. It can be applied (so it is said) at any educational level or to any subject-matter. And its advocates claim success where the approach has been properly applied. These are important claims, and justify attention. A distinction needs first to be drawn between the two extreme styles of the systematic approach, namely, the feedforward and feedback modes.

a Feedforward mode

Feedforward systems are predictive; the firing of a space ship from Earth orbit into Moon orbit is a feedforward exercise, if we disregard minor route corrections (which are often not required). Such a system needs to have (in advance) an extremely effective model of the world, if right actions are to be predicted with a high degree of success.

In its feedforward mode the systematic approach conforms as closely as it is able to the King of Hearts's prescription. Objectives are decided upon, then the system is designed, then put into operation. Finally its success is evaluated using the objectives as criteria. So, in the strongest formulation, objectives are held to be completely sufficient for the purpose of designing educational systems (providing due allowance is made for external constraints). Such a scheme, depicted in Figure 2, corresponds to the route A strategy discussed above, since ends are decided before means are chosen.

Figure 2 The systematic approach, feedforward mode

Objectives———→Design———→Execution———→Evaluation

b Feedback mode

Feedback systems use the results of initial action to alter their own behaviour. They fall into two classes: goal-attaining systems which cease functioning once a goal is achieved, and regulatory systems (like thermostats) which maintain constant relationships. Typically, feedback systems attain success by a process of successive adjustment. They need not (initially) have an especially accurate model of the domain they are attempting to control.

Since educational situations are very complex, success is rarely attained the first time off. So the feedback mode seems the natural model to use. The results of the first trial can be used to improve the system the next time around, and so on, as long as the system is operational. Thus in practice the systematic approach is usually *cyclical,* and has many features associated with route B.

A feedforward scheme is ambitious, but dangerous. If successful it would virtually solve at a stroke the problems of designing educational systems—that is the extent of the ambition. The danger comes in the likelihood of failure. It will later be shown that the stronger claims made for behavioural objectives do not stand up to critical examination. Since the feedforward systematic approach to education rests so clearly on behavioural objectives, the consequence is clear.

On the other hand, the cyclical systematic approach is safer, but less ambitious and so less interesting. Success may eventually be achieved, but often after the objectives have themselves been revised. Or, it may not be possible to wait for success. Sometimes things do need to work first time. Clearly there are costs associated with this mode of operation, too. And since both extremes, or styles, have benefits and costs, the various advocates of the systematic approach have taken up their individual positions somewhere along the spectrum.

Some problems plague the systematic approach whichever style is adopted. For instance, insofar as the systematic approach rests on behavioural objectives (and it does in all the formulations we shall consider), it can be characterised as being almost entirely operational in nature, truncating the normative and strategic levels. This leads as we shall see to certain insoluble difficulties, or rather, difficulties that can only be solved by importing individual hunch and intuition rather than explicit formulation. So when it is asked, "Where do objectives come from?", no really satisfactory answer emerges.

Another problem is the view taken by the systematic approach of the domain (environment) it is trying to influence. We ask: what view does it take of the learner? Of the teacher? Of the interaction between the two? Of the structure of the knowledge, skills and attitudes it hopes the learner will develop? Of the relation between the goals of the learning situation and broader societal needs? We shall see that the systematic approach does indeed have a view on these questions, amounting to a model of the learning situation which will later be described, rather unkindly, as "impoverished".

But, whatever its deficiencies might be, the systematic approach is already in action—indeed it is by far the most influential style of rational planning in education today. Earlier the approach was described as "a group of procedures bearing a family resemblance". That group includes *performance contracting, mastery learning, 90–90–90 criteria, payment by results,* and various other ideas, each one differing slightly from its neighbours. All these schemes depend quite fundamentally on the idea of behavioural objectives, which will now be examined in detail. Devotees of the systematic approach believe their prescriptions are perfectly adequate, and of wide (or even universal) applicability, not bounded by subject-matter or by the type of objective aimed for. To what extent is their confidence justified?

PART II: THE CASE FOR BEHAVIOURAL OBJECTIVES
Once objectives have been defined, there is no step in curriculum design that can legitimately be entitled "selecting content". (Gagné, 1967)

Any system of rational planning must place emphasis on the definition of objectives; and to this rule the systematic approach to education is no exception. By developing in detail the idea of behavioural objectives it has been possible for advocates to claim that a strongly prescriptive basis exists for designing educational systems.

1   The form in which objectives should be stated

The primacy of objectives in curriculum design has been advocated, off and on, for many years (Bobbitt, 1924; Charters and Waples, 1929; Dale, 1967; Tyler, 1950). But only recently has there been a coherent account of the *behavioural* objective (Mager, 1961). Mager's famous little work has had a widespread effect on training and education during the last decade. Originally meant as a training manual for programmed learning writers (and itself a program), it has now gained a much wider currency. The book's message is simple: it proposes that objectives should state what the student should be able to do after the learning experience that he could not do before. So, Mager makes a distinction between prerequisites, course description and objectives, as follows:

Prerequisites	*Course description*	*Objectives*
What a learner has to be able to do to qualify for a course.	What the course is about.	What a successful learner is able to do at the end of a course.

Now, since prerequisites have essentially the same *structure* as objectives (they may be the objectives of previous instruction), the critical distinction is between course descriptions and objectives. An example of a course description would be:

> The course will include: an extended study of the social, political and economic changes, and a critical examination of these changes, and the applicability of the term "revolution". (Part of course description for the Open University course A202, the Age of Revolutions)

An example of an objective is:

> Students will be able to give, or select from a given list, examples of the dependence of modern industry on basic science. [One of the objectives of the Open University Science Foundation course S100. It is fairly typical of its kind, even to the extent of not satisfying all Mager's criteria as set out in the following paragraph.]

Mager's prescription requires objectives to have three characteristics. The first is that they should be relatively *unambiguous*. This is achieved by selecting verbs which describe observable actions rather than verbs describing mental states or achievements. It seems clear that such verbs as to write, to construct, to list, to mark, etc., are open to fewer interpretations than such verbs as to know, to understand, to appreciate, etc. For example, suppose someone claims to know how a car engine works. What does this mean? Perhaps he can answer questions about the four-stroke cycle of the internal combustion engine. Or maybe he can mend an engine when it goes wrong. Who can say? They are quite distinct types of performance (labelled by Ryle, 1948, as *knowing that* and *knowing how*) and would require different kinds of training. So the problem is overcome by stating the objective in terms of what the man should be able to *do*, not what he will know.

This kind of distinction (between, for instance, the different performances that might count as "knowing") is conceptually sound and practically useful. To draw attention to it has probably been the major contribution of behavioural objectives to the improvement of education and training, if only because the distinction encourages people to *think what they mean* when they plan a course. If there are limits to the transfer of learning (and there are) then it becomes crucially important to decide what, precisely, we expect the student to do afterwards.

The second characteristic of a well-defined objective is that the *conditions of performance* should be stated. Mager points out (correctly) that to say the student should "be able to solve problems in algebra" would hardly be adequate. Instead, by clarifying the conditions of performance we arrive at some such formulation as:

> Given a linear algebraic equation with one unknown the student must be able to solve for the unknown without the aid of references, tables or calculating devices. (Mager, 1962)

So, to amplify the car engine example, we should need to say what type of engine was to be mended, what faults might be included, what tools and reference manuals would be available, and what time would be allowed for repair. Or if an essay on the car engine was required, we should need to say how many types of engine were to be included, how long could be spent on the essay, whether references would be allowed, and so on. Now since such conditions can be specified ever more fully, how far should the process be taken? Far enough, says Mager, "so that others understand your intent as *you* understand it". That seems a sensible, if ambitious, criterion but it does have limitations, as we shall see later.

The third characteristic of a behavioural objective is that the *standard* of the student's expected performance should be indicated. If he is to mend car engines, then he must correct n faults in a given time; or he may score points for corrected faults on a scale of importance. If he answers an essay question, then a skeleton marking schedule would show the intended standard (as would a model answer); and for objective tests the percentage correct acts as a standard.

So Mager emphasized the *structure* of objectives: the way they should be stated. In doing so he omitted some vital considerations, especially the question of the origin of objectives (where do objectives come from?). For present purposes all that needs be said is that there is one more characteristic of a satisfactory objective, namely, that it should bear some meaningful relationship with the general educational aims of a course.

That is, the objective must be relevant and meaningful in its context. No rules are given for achieving this criterion—which is actually the most difficult to achieve, yet the most important of all.

So, to summarise, the characteristics of an adequate objective are, in order of importance:

1 The objective (somehow) relates properly to the general educational aims.
2 The objective states what the student will be able to *do* after the learning experience (that he could not do before).
3 The objective is brought to the appropriate level of detail by specifying the conditions relevant to the performance.
4 A standard of performance is indicated.

2 Benefits claimed for behavioural objectives

One of the undoubted advantages of the behavioural objective approach is that it alone has been worked out in sufficient detail to be of use in practice (no other rational approach to education has got so far). The system thus wins by default, since no one can imagine another or a better way of doing things without incurring the penalties (as well as the benefits) of relying heavily on individual experience and intuition. But advocates of the dogma claim more than this, naturally. They claim that the use of behavioural objectives, and the systematic approach of which the objectives are an integral part, leads to the following kinds of benefit.

a Stimulus to clear thinking

The detailed, explicit form of the objectives certainly forces the teacher to come down from the clouds and think in specific terms, not in vague ambiguities. That is good in itself (it would be a prerequisite for *any* system of design or planning) and has the additional benefit of revealing value judgments that might otherwise remain hidden. So one can see, for example, just what a teacher does mean by "teaching science" or "inculcating a sense of moral values" or whatever. And, once externalised, such plans can be subjected to the rational processes of discussion, criticism and testing, and so may be improved.

b Aids to design

One important design problem is knowing what will count as a valid evaluation. Anyone designing or planning a system needs to ask: what would a successful solution look like? What criteria must it satisfy? It is claimed that behavioural objectives answer this by providing the only possible rational basis for evaluating the success of a learning experience (this is the strongest formulation). So the course is successful if, and only if, the student can perform as the objectives predict. The terminal test items are predetermined by the objectives, in an obvious way—i.e. can he or can't he mend the car engine? This contrasts favourably with most traditional educational situations, where the examinations may have no obvious connection with the vaguely stated aims.

A second important design problem is knowing how to construct the system, given the objectives. Objectives supposedly make clear how the process of teaching should be executed, that is, they assist in the selection and design of instructional activities. This is especially crucial for those workers who intend to build a full-blooded behavioural technology of education (e.g. Gilbert, 1962; Gagné, 1965). Gagné (1965) says:

> What various authors have attempted to show . . . is that there seem to be classes of behaviour, the members of which have a *formal identity,* irrespective of their particular content. . . . The question can then be asked, with respect to each of them, what conditions are necessary to bring about their learning?

The idea is, then, that classes of behaviour, such as multiple discrimination, behaviour chains, concept learning, etc., each need a distinct kind of instructional treatment. This is an attempt to provide a strong prescription for designing an educational system. Gagné's most distinctive contribution follows on by suggesting how different learning goals may be interrelated. His idea is that any complex subject-matter can be regarded as a "psychological learning hierarchy" where the ultimate terminal goal is a high-level principle dependent on various lower-level principles or concepts (enabling objectives).

Though there are now good reasons for thinking that this is not a completely adequate account of the structure of knowledge, for present purposes Gagné's idea can be taken at its face value. He did present empirical data showing that mastery of highest-level principles depended on mastery of lower-level principles. This suggested that there were only a limited number of ways that teaching could be arranged if the terminal objectives were to be efficiently attained, an implication that was fully understood by programmed learning writers.

c   As part of an integrated system

The attempt to use objectives to prescribe design and evaluation is to use them in a feedforward manner. But since only a *perfect* scheme could solve such complex problems first time around, most practical workers take a more lenient view. Although in *theory* objectives come first and everything else afterwards, in *practice* all parts of the system can be mutually adjusted until a satisfactory "fit" is found. This means that the design procedure is really cyclical, with various activities carried on in parallel, and many feedback loops in action. Not only does the finished product get tested and revised, but it is widely conceded that even the objectives themselves should be subject to revision in the light of experience. It can on occasion be dangerous to fix objectives too early. Of course, if you allow this, then you do undermine the more extreme claims made for behavioural objectives. But it seems the only sensible way to proceed. As an example, when I introduced my colleagues at the Open University to the systematic approach to course design, this rider was cautiously added:

> We have placed the sections on objectives, assessment and activities in the order which seemed to us to be the most sensible: this does not imply that the author must go through these stages in that order, completing each one before he moves on to the next. That would be altogether too mechanical a view of the procedure we advocate. Rather we would suggest that the author did the best he could with objectives, then moved on to a consideration of the end-of-unit test, and then moved on to some sample activities. At this stage he would be well advised to return to the objectives and revise them in the light of his work on tests and activities; and to carry on with this procedure until he felt that each of the three stages had been specified as exactly as was possible at this stage. That having been done, he would be in a position to try a first draft; and naturally in the course of writing the first draft he would think up activities and possibly change some of the objectives. But he would of course be doing this upon a soundly structured basis instead of a vaguely thought out, rather haphazard, off-the-cuff scheme (MacDonald-Ross, 1970).

So we ought to bear in mind that although objectives are supposed to prescribe course structure and evaluation, all sorts of subtle adjustments are made in practice. This is a point scored for common sense, though it does make the role of objectives somewhat less dominating. The advantage of such a cyclical design system is that it enables the system to continue improving over a period of time.

The first consequence of cycling is that the objectives, course content and tests may eventually form parts of an interlocking system, a coherent whole, where changes in any part will require adjustments in all other parts. This amounts to saying that educational systems should exhibit the property of internal consistency or coherence. This has value as a diagnostic feature, for if inconsistencies exist the student is sure to be in trouble. The following example (from the Open University course TS 282/2 Electromagnetics and Electronics) illustrates the point:

Extracts from the unit	*Comments*
A *General aims* The aims of this unit are: ... 2. To give a physical and mathematical understanding of flux and	Bear in mind, as you consider the objectives and test items, that they are supposed to index "understanding".

F

magnetic fields and their relationships to the flow of electric current.

B *Behavioural objectives*
When you have finished this unit you should be able to:
... 3. Sketch the H-field lines associated with a current carrying wire, coil and solenoid, and a bar of soft iron in an H-field.
... 4. Sketch the B-field lines associated with a current carrying wire, coil and solenoid, and a bar of soft iron in an H-field.
... 5. Calculate the flux density at the centre of a current carrying loop and a solenoid in air.

Sounds all very innocent, just two sketches and a calculation. Can the student rely on these objectives describing all he will need to do at the end? Alas, the answer is probably no. Notice the mismatch with the aims in A and C, with the actual teaching material (not shown here) and with the assessment questions.

C *Aims mentioned in text*
In this and the next few sections of the unit, I want to try and establish certain ideas and results; namely
1   why we need to introduce the H-field
2   how it is related to the B-field
3   how the magnitude of the H-field can be calculated
4   how the H-field is related to the concept of a magnetic circuit.

This is quite a shock. These aims are very far-reaching. What *are* the authors' intentions, and what *will* the students be expected to do?

D *The text*
The actual teaching material cannot be reproduced for space reasons.

But even when read carefully does not resolve the problems (though it does tell us that B-field ≡ flux density, and H-field ≡ magnetic field).

E *Self-assessment questions*
There are several calculations of B-fields (flux density) and some worked examples (but no questions) on H-fields.

The flux density calculations relate directly to objective B.5., and the H-field calculations relate directly to aim C.3. Is this what the author's aims really amount to?

F *Examination question*
Not possible to display.

Would be difficult to predict. Probably a calculation. So much for the grand aims.

Now this example has been introduced for one reason only: to show what results when the principle of internal consistency is not followed, and to make clear the problems students face when they are presented with conflicting clues as to the teacher's intent. The great merit of the cyclical systematic approach is that it pinpoints such inconsistencies, and allows them to be eliminated by a process of adjustment. There is no doubt that the revised version of this unit can take advantage of these criticisms and present a better face to the student the next time round. This contrasts favourably with some traditional teaching situations where the same mistakes tend to be repeated *ad infinitum*.

The second consequence claimed for the cyclical design approach is, that eventually the aims set in theory can be realised in practice. To appreciate what an attraction this is one must recognise how often the actual outcomes of learning are at variance with the idealised pretensions of the educator. Much credit is due to those programmed learning writers who, by defining objectives, writing frames, testing and revising, showed conclusively that the outcomes of learning *could* be brought in line with prestated objectives. This, the replicability of instructional outcomes, is held by some to be the most important of all advantages offered by the systematic approach.

d   As an operational aid

Objectives serve usefully as operational aids, principally because they are formulated in terms of action. For instance, they can act as a medium of communication or, as Lewis would have it, a mechanism for telling (Lewis and Cook, 1969). Curriculum design is almost always carried out by teams, and these days there can be division of labour even in class-room teaching. How shall each member of the team know what is being asked of him? Only by having highly definite, well-specified guidelines, in the form of behavioural objectives.

The need for this communication has been made dramatically clear at the Open University, where a course unit author must tell his colleagues on the course team what he intends to do. This is partly because they have the right to criticise and influence his teaching scheme; but even more so because their units are expected to fit in with his. If they are not clear as to what it is that he is trying to teach, there is little hope of an integrated course resulting. So this is a process of consultation and adjustment between members of a team who are equals. Then there is the process whereby the author's ideas are executed with the assistance of visual designers, typographers, television and radio producers, etc. It is easy to see that clear specification of intentions is of critical importance to the success of such a complex process.

Objectives can also be useful as a medium of communication between the author (or teacher) and the student. In other words, if students benefit from knowing where they are going, then it is suggested that they be shown the list of behaviours they will be expected to exhibit. Thus (so it is said) there can be no doubt that the students know what is expected of them. This is related to Ausubel's idea of the "advance organiser".

The other operational benefit claimed for behavioural objectives is less obvious and more controversial. The objectives may be used, it is claimed, to provide individual treatment for students. That is, because *outcomes* are replicated, *treatment* can be individualised. But it is not clear what is being meant by "individualisation" in this context. It clearly doesn't mean that students work for different objectives, though bright students will achieve more objectives and so have a greater range of personal choice. It may mean that students with different entry characteristics are catered for, and that remedial support is provided appropriate to the nature of the student's deficiency. This presupposes that the teacher has considerable diagnostic capability at his command, a condition that may be realised if an adequate network of tests has been based on the objectives.

Or perhaps individualisation means that the student can choose his own way to reach the objectives. Thus, he might *contract* with the teacher to reach the goal using various facilities to do so. In either sense, we know it is *possible* to build individualised instruction around a framework of behavioural objectives: there are successful projects to prove it. But is this the only way to individualise? Here the evidence is less clear. Bishop (1971) and Esbenson (1968) believe that behavioural objectives play an essential role; Noar (1972) obviously does not, for her book concentrates on process, with only glimpses of the role that objectives might play. Perhaps the range of new problems caused by individualising instruction is so considerable that no author feels competent to present a complete synthesis at present (see also the essays in Howes, 1970; and Weisgerber 1971a, 1971b). Or, more likely, the usual conceptual schemes are not adequate to support an effective indivdualisation of instruction (for a fresh look see Pask, 1972a; Pask and Scott, 1972).

The advantages claimed for behavioural objectives are, then:

1   They form the only well-worked-out method of rational planning in education.
2   They encourage educators to think and plan in detailed, specific terms.
3   They encourage educators to make explicit previously concealed values.
4   They provide a rational basis for the evaluation.
5   They prescribe the choice of instructional means.
6   They form the basis of a self-improving system.
7   The system eventually achieves internal consistency.
8   The system eventually realises in practice the aims set in theory.
9   Objectives serve as a medium of communication.
10 Objectives can be made the basis of individual instruction.

This list does have some overlap between items and hence some redundancy. Nevertheless, it shows clearly what an attractive case can be made for behavioural objectives. Alas, most of these strongly worded claims will need to be watered down or even negated in the light of the following criticisms.

PART III: THE CASE AGAINST BEHAVIOURAL OBJECTIVES
Any of the objections given by teachers to instructional objectives seem to be predicated upon inadequate conceptions of education, curriculum, or instruction. (L. Tyler, 1969)

In the writings of the advocates of behavioural objectives one often senses a certain lack of patience with those who do not entirely concur with their dogma. Opposition from educators is often interpreted as symptomatic of laziness, ignorance, self-interest or general incompetence. Of course, this will be true of some individuals. But it is worth considering another interpretation, i.e. perhaps teachers sense that at the very basis of the dogma lie certain crucial difficulties—difficulties so fundamental that they cannot be entirely eradicated no matter what effort is applied, difficulties that arise from the very conceptual framework upon which the behavioural objective/systematic approach is constructed.

The central message of this paper is that such difficulties do exist, they are real and cannot be avoided. The purpose of this section is to document and analyse these difficulties in such a way that their implications are clear and cannot be easily evaded. Most of the examples have been developed from my experience of using the systematic approach at the Open University and elsewhere, though some have appeared in the literature previously in one form or another.

1 Where do objectives come from?
The first and most natural question for teachers to ask after hearing about the behavioural objective dogma is, where do objectives come from, and how are they derived? This immediately uncovers the serious and deep-seated problem of *origins*, which has never been solved by advocates of the systematic approach, though various unsatisfactory attempts have been made.

a Avoiding the issue
Quite a few people have discovered to their surprise that some leading advocates go out of their way to avoid this problem altogether, as Mager (1962) did in his preface:

This book is NOT about the philosophy of education, nor is it about *who* should select objectives, nor is it about *which* objectives should be selected.

Now, an author is perfectly entitled to limit his area of discussion if he so wishes. But the problem does not go away, and Mager's subsequent books have not brought the solution much closer. Two of them have been mainly concerned with training for skills, which as we shall see allows the problem of origins to be deflected (Mager and Beach, 1967; Mager and Pipe, 1970). The third book is concerned with reinterpreting the students' attitudes towards learning as a matter of approach or avoidance behaviours—an interesting, but limited viewpoint (Mager, 1968). Mager's latest work (1972) does face the problem more directly, though not, in my opinion, successfully. (If this volume had arrived earlier in England, I would have discussed it in more detail.)

Gilbert's (1962) attempt to construct a technology of education, which he called "mathetics", also foundered on the same rock. He says of mathetics that "its techniques do not extend with any authority to the problems of human value" (and what, then, is education supposed to be about?), and goes on to explain:

> The responsibility of those who design the teaching materials does not extend to determining the constituents of mastery; technical knowledge of the learning process does not supply special wisdom about what *should* be taught. The matheticist, *as a technical person*, has no alternative but to assume that the repertories of synthetic behaviour prescribed by the public school authorities represent the best available account of the public's educational objectives.

This evasion amounts to a truncation of the process of planning—chopping off the normative and strategic levels, and concentrating on operational issues. The adoption of a "technical person" disclaimer would only be appropriate if there existed fairly widespread and detailed agreement about the desired nature of education. Otherwise, the technical person would be avoiding the most important issues, and perhaps applying his energies in a quite misconceived direction. Does a widespread agreement exist about what constitutes a relevant and worthwhile education these days? There is plenty of evidence that it does not—not among teachers, certainly not among students, and probably not in the public at large (who often complain, and maybe justifiably, at the products of our educational system). A whole body of literature has now arisen to articulate this discontent, sufficient, one would imagine, to demolish naive faith in the "public school authorities" (Goodman, 1962; Holt, 1964; Illich, 1971; Kozol, 1967; Neill, 1962; Postman and Weingartner, 1969; Reimer, 1971).

There is one possible defence of Gilbert's position, namely the defence provided by the behaviour therapist Bandura (1969, see Chapter 2, "Value issues and objectives"). He makes the avoidance of normative judgment by the therapist a virtue, as follows:

Behavioural objectives are frequently [left] unspecified in order to avoid acknowledging the value judgments and social influences involved in the modification of behaviour.... The choice of behavioural objectives is rightfully the *client's*.

This style of argument may be translated into educational terms rather like this: a teacher is entitled to teach (or "shape the behaviour of") a student *if and only if* that student agrees to the list of behavioural objectives that represent the goals of the transaction. This is, at first sight, quite a good defence; for a start it eliminates many of the deschooling critics mentioned earlier, since they, too, believe the "client" should exert a controlling influence. Alas, the defence is not completely adequate, though it has much to commend it. (No mention will be made here of the counter-arguments a psychoanalyst might make; discussion is confined to the educational issues.) The key weakness lies in the differences between the educational enterprise and the enterprise of behaviour modification. For instance, if I compulsively wash my hands several hundred times a day, or if I have a morbid fear of cats, then I will probably be only too keen to agree that such behaviours should be "extinguished". No problems of morals would seem to arise, and even if they did only two people would need to agree—myself and my therapist.

But many factors would militate against such a simple procedure in education. Some (many?) students genuinely do not know what they wish to learn and expect the teacher to provide guidance and leadership. Even if a student *agrees* that he wishes to learn, say, chemistry, then he is bound to be ignorant of the *meaning* of the terminal goals (whereas the patient knows only too well what compulsions or phobias mean). And then, the detailed goals may be independent of both the teacher and the learner, in the sense of Popper's (1972) "third world" of objective knowledge. It would not be possible for a student to agree to learn chemistry and at the same time not agree to learn about chemical reactions. That is part of chemistry whether he likes it or not. Finally we should note that teacher and learner are not alone in this transaction: many others have a right and a duty to influence the nature of education, just as they must assist its execution (even if only by paying taxes). So no *simple* contractual situation exists, though the needs and wishes of the student might well be allowed to exert more influence than they do at present.

If Bandura's defence is not sufficient, then the problem of origins must be faced. We need to know, in some detail, how objectives can be derived. What would a solution to this problem look like? Minimally, objectives must be *justified* (by considerations at the strategic and normative levels) and explicitly stated selection *procedures* must be provided. To their credit, most experts have paid attention to methods of deriving objectives; we shall now see whether their prescriptions are satisfactory. Two schools of thought have emerged. One set of authorities attempt to provide explicit rules for converting observable human action into behavioural objectives. These, the "hardliners", tend to minimise or deny the distinctions between knowledge and skills and consequently between education and training. The other group, the "softliners", acknowledges the distinction between education and training, and concentrates on trying to justify the objectives.

This latter group usually presents no explicit rules for moving from the normative to the operational level, thus leaving much to individual hunch or intuition. As a consequence of their positions, the hardliners stress the feedforward role of the systematic approach, whereas the softliners emphasise the need for cycling and successive adjustment. Each of these prescriptions will now be examined.

b   The hardliners
The basis of the hardliners' case was laid during and after the Second World War, when great advances were made in the theory and practice of military and industrial training. The strongest set of procedures (task analysis) owes its origin to R. B. Miller, working on the problems of the American Air Force. Like other armed forces, the AAF found itself able to develop new equipment faster than trained personnel. The object of Miller's (1962) research was to find how to reduce the lag (sometimes amounting to several years) between the introduction of new equipment and the availability of trained personnel to operate and maintain it. Though the details of Miller's scheme will not be presented here (since it is really geared to man-machine systems training), the first of his "major classes of training decisions" is worth noting, namely: *what are the criterion performance requirements?* This shows how the results of task analysis lead naturally to a behavioural specification of objectives.

The criteria for man-machine systems can be deduced before they are operational from the predicted machine and system performance characteristics. But more usually, task analysis descriptions are taken from actual observations of experienced workers or "master performers". The most extreme formulation of this idea was contained in Seymour's (1968) skills analysis:

> Starting from the detailed breakdown provided by work study, the skills analyst proceeds to identify and to record in detail each movement made by an experienced worker. . . .

There might seem to be no insuperable obstacle to deriving behavioural objectives if the intention is to train people to do things. What else, it may be asked, should be the criterion of a skill except the ability to perform? Actually, this kind of specification of training by the exhaustive description of behaviours has quite severe limitations, even in the industrial training context for which it was created. Jobs change and new jobs arise (in which case there is no "experienced worker" available); and the list of behaviours exhibited by a master performer may be so long that a training programme designed to cover them all would be most costly. The critical incident technique of Flanagan (1954) is an attempt to face this problem by identifying those performances which are *most critical* for the job; and in the last resort the objectives of training must contribute significantly to the objectives of the whole organisation (Odiorne, 1970). Unfortunately the problem of relevance is even less tractable in the field of education.

Another typical problem of industrial training occurs when personnel need to think and use their own initiative rather than follow set procedures. The mere mention of the word "think" is enough to make a training analyst shiver, yet its use seems inescapable. For example, the United Kingdom Atomic Energy Authority (UKAEA) have a whole training film devoted to the necessity of thinking. Apparently technicians using high energy electrical equipment are taught the acronym SIDET meaning:

1 Switch off,
2 Isolate,
3 Dump
4 Earth
And *think*

Why should thinking be necessary if the procedure is adequate? In short, because all sorts of alarming accidents may occur if the procedure is followed blindly. Thinking about the principles underlying the procedure of earthing is the surest (and most economical) safeguard against unforeseen occurrences.

But still, it may be conceded that task analysis is a valuable tool for training analysts.[2] It is possible to transfer the technique, using it as a strong procedure for deriving *educational* objectives? This is what the hardliners propose.

For this purpose it is necessary to deny that any real distinction exists between education and training, so that the technique which worked for training would automatically work for education. Duncan (1972), for instance, talks about avoiding "the arbitrary distinction between skill and knowledge". But this is a pretty uncomfortable stand to adopt, as I have said elsewhere:

The distinction between knowledge and skills is actually quite valuable, as a little reflection will show. We can ask about an idea (expressed, for example, as a statement): is it true or false? how did we come to know it? how can it be justified? And we can then note that knowledge consists of meaningful ideas linked together to form a coherent view of the world (notice that you can say "skills" but not "knowledges"). The notions of truth and coherence aren't directly applicable to skills; they are the identifying features of knowledge.

On the other hand, skills are usually useful and are performed to given standards. They become refined, repeatable, routinised, predictable and eventually may come to be performed subconsciously. In any event, it is easy to find types of educational experience which have nothing to do with skills—learning for learning's sake, for instance. The distinction between knowledge and skills is deeply embedded in our ordinary language for the excellent reason that it is meaningful and functionally necessary. To have a skill is to have the ability to execute useful tasks to publicly agreed standards of performance. This clearly implies that a task analysis procedure might be effective for skills but inadequate for general education (MacDonald-Ross, 1972c).[3]

If this type of argument is accepted then the hardline approach must fail, for it does not show what extra must be added to task analysis to make it suitable for education. Look at it this way: where observable actions really are an end in themselves, and are supported by mimimal knowledge or understanding, then task analysis procedures are appropriate. But to specify the objectives for a course on economics by going along to observe a "master performer" would be quite fruitless unless you were also willing to take seriously the huge network of knowledge and understanding that lay behind his actions. And these are the very notions that were initially supposed to be rejected.

The merit of the task analysis approach is to draw attention to the performatory aspects of education. Students do have to pass exams, and will be expected to operate in the outside world.

The question is, how should these performances be related to the objectives? One prescription is that given by Evans (1968) who comments on the difficulty of constructing good objectives ("nobody in the world but Bob Mager and myself knows how to write behavioural objectives and sometimes I wonder about Mager"), and suggests that test items could usefully do service in place of objectives. This makes a good deal of sense; students often do take tests and examinations to be the real objectives of a course, and with some justification. But it would take rather a lot of test items to specify a whole course—too many for easy comprehension. And where, pray, do the test items come from?

The hardline case thus seems to fail. It is not sufficient to use observations of action (whether of action at work, or during examinations) for a prescription of educational objectives, if one takes the meaning of the word "education" at all seriously. This is a blow to the hopes of a straightforward no-nonsense prescriptive approach to education

c   The softliners
In contrast, softliners fully accept that educational objectives need to be derived in a way which does justice to the difference between education and training. This makes their approach safer, though this gain is

achieved at the price of being less explicit than the hardliners about the mechanism of derivation. Typical of this school are the works of R. W. Tyler and Popham (Tyler, 1950; Popham and Baker, 1970a, 1970b—see especially diagram on page 96 of the latter). Tyler's suggestion, which Popham endorses, is that objectives are derived from three major sources of data—the *learner,* the *society* and the *subject-matter.* Most people would have to think hard to imagine any *other* sources—but *how* should the derivation be made? No answer is given, except that the philosophy of education and the psychology of learning should act as filters. Now the notion that philosophy and psychology can be used to turn "tentative general objectives" into "precise instructional objectives" is frankly hilarious—one cannot believe the authors are seriously suggesting this as an operational procedure. All the critical decisions seem to be left to the intuition and common sense of the teacher, a strange position for a systematic approach to be in. And the situation is not much improved by providing behavioural objective banks—on what basis should the teacher make his selection?

How should the softline approach be rated? This depends on what claims are initially made for the systematic approach. If it is supposed to provide successful, predictive solutions to the problems of education, then it is not sufficient to provide weak rules for deriving objectives that leave so much to the intuition of the individual. On the other hand, if the systematic approach is seen as a fairly weak crutch, better than nothing but not leading to powerful prescriptions, then perhaps the softline approach does all that is required. But it is not my impression that the advocates of behavioural objectives wish to be driven into such a corner; that is their dilemma. Weak versions of the systematic approach cannot support such ambitious and demanding schemes as, for instance, payment by results or mastery learning. More important, it is not clear whether weak procedures can deliver the goods: that is, whether the outcomes of education can be brought in line with the initial aims. And that, surely, was the purpose of the whole enterprise.

2 Design

Now assume that the list of behaviours is *agreed.* If the dogma is correct then such a list should show how the learning situation should be designed (strongly prescriptive), or at any rate be extremely helpful in the design process (a weaker formulation). That is, from the list of behaviours can be derived, by a rigorously logical procedure, both the strategy and the tactics of the many educational experiences which are to be presented to the student. This ambition, very prominent in the writings of Gagné for instance, runs into some serious snags.

a Voyages of exploration

We sometimes find it useful at the Open University to distinguish between those course units which represent a voyage of exploration by the author, and those which are simply a mechanical repetition of a task often performed before. On the one hand the author struggles with ideas he may never have fully worked out before, let alone taught. Or he tries to present familiar ideas in an entirely new light. In the second case he will have run such courses many times before, set and marked examinations on the course, written papers and text books, and so on.

Now it is a sad fact that on voyages of exploration people most need guidance, and are least likely to get it. Only while actually creating and running the course will the author solve his conceptual problems. In a very real sense he does not really know where he is going until he gets there. That doesn't mean he lacks purpose, but it does make the detailed prespecification of goals rather pointless. In exploratory situations authors are (rightly) reluctant to close their options too early, and if browbeaten into writing behavioural objectives will face the uncomfortable option of having their creative choices constrained, or else constantly changing the objectives. In the latter case, of course, the hope of using the objectives prescriptively fades.

In contrast, it is rather easier for an author to produce and use behavioural objectives for courses whose conceptual problems he has already faced and solved. In general, he has worked out a reasonably effective teaching procedure for getting students through the kinds of tests or examinations he wishes to set. But this amounts to saying that the objectives are descriptive rather than prescriptive, or at any rate, that they have only a marginal influence on the design process.

b The anti-planner

The kind of teacher who is often criticised by systematic theorists is the one who lays great stress on flexibility and the need to adapt to take advantage of the opportunities that occur in the classroom. This is a classic stance for an anti-planner (see Churchman, 1968b) and is so often encountered that it deserves mention here. Popham responds, quite reasonably, by saying that adaptation should take place within the context of planned objectives. This would be adequate, if it did not lead to another problem: if the teacher has just a short list of aims, he can remember them, but they are rather general; whereas if he has a fully specified list of behavioural objectives they are too unwieldy to use in a classroom. This is the level of specificity problem, discussed later.

Should teachers consult their protocol of behaviours before deciding how to adapt? Is there a procedure which works and can be suggested as a response to the anti-planner?

c Instructional sequence

Is there one best sequence for all students, or one optimal pathway through the subject-matter? It used to be thought by linear programmed learning enthusiasts that the answer to this question ought to be yes. The reasoning was that whatever terminal behaviour required could be shaped by applying an appropriate schedule of reinforcement. And the word "schedule" entails the notion of sequence.

The relationship between goals was investigated by Gagné (1965) who concluded that the psychological organisation of knowledge could be represented as a hierarchy of principles. This has the consequence of strongly constraining the order in which principles may be learnt, since "the learning of higher-level principles was dependent on the mastery of prerequisite lower-level principles in a highly predictable fashion".

But it is possible to mount a radical attack on the notion of such strongly constrained options on the instructional sequence. Strangely enough, Mager (1961) himself showed how this might be done. Over ten years ago he carried out experiments on learner-controlled sequencing. In the first of these experiments students were given neither teaching material nor objectives but simply allowed access to instructors who would answer any question on the subject of electronics. The questions asked and the sequences followed were noted. It was found that the students' chosen sequences varied greatly one from another and, what is more, bore little relationship to sequences in formal courses designed by experts.

In subsequent experiments students were given a 24-page statement of objectives and access to instructors (Mager and McCann, 1962). In this case sequences varied *and* the learning time was 65% shorter than the length of the formal course. These results are supported and extended by recent experiments conducted by Pask to explore his notion of human learning as a form of information processing (Pask, 1972a, 1972b; Pask and Scott, 1972). The realisation of the huge variety of pathways available to a learner is quite discomforting for believers in the systematic approach, and none have so far offered to explain how it may be encompassed in their scheme. Perhaps it is no surprise that a traditional course (badly constructed as so many are) should prove inefficient, but the variety of successful alternative pathways chosen by students is difficult to explain on the presuppositions outlined earlier. Apparently, no matter how well objectives are specified initially, major design problems remain which cannot be solved inside the conceptual framework of the systematic approach. If true, this is a serious objection. All the old problems of teaching return, perhaps ameliorated somewhat by the initial specification of objectives.

It may well be possible to cope with these problems under an alternative conceptual framework—a framework which takes account of the structure of knowledge, views the interaction between teacher and student as a defined type of conversational dialogue, and which admits (indeed insists) on the meaningfulness of knowledge, understanding and explanation. But to present this scheme in full would require an article at least as long again as the present.

d Subject-matter differences

One of the prime claims of the systematic approach is to apply to all subjects at whatever level they may be taught. This presupposes that behavioural goals are appropriate for all subjects, a claim that has brought most complaints from the humanities and the arts (Eisner, 1967a, 1967b, 1969; Stenhouse, 1971).

The typical argument runs like this: Arts subjects are concerned, not to reach goals once and for all, but to develop standards of judgment, taste and criticism. Often these aims stay the same year after year, but the student is expected to become even more effective in their application. If this amounts to saying that process is more important than content then the argument may apply to all subject areas. For example, a scientist might well believe that the process of scientific problem-solving is more significant than the particular results of the process. Such "manner of behaving" objectives are dealt with later under "attacks on goal-directed models of education". Typically, it is possible to apply standards after the event, but extraordinarily difficult to predict correct behaviour in advance—that is, to use the feedforward mode.

Now, a lot depends on whether the behavioural advocate regards his list of objectives as *just instances* of acceptable behaviour or whether he regards the process skills as *nothing but* the list of objectives. The first position is weak but safe—weak because he gives no rules for generating further instances and safe because he avoids "nothing-buttery". The second position is strong but vulnerable—strong because if the student can exhibit these behaviours then he must (by definition) be well-educated, and vulnerable since there are so many correct behaviours that can mask understanding.

The second style of attack is to point to the occasions where a personal response to a work of art is required. Since both the observer and the work of art are, in some senses, unique individuals, if the student is expected to exhibit predictable behaviour, a self-defeating situation arises. But if the objectives just say "principles of critical judgment should be applied", is this not just the kind of "imprecise" formulation that was supposed to be eschewed? Similar considerations hold for creative activities where the systematic advocate is reduced to such spineless formulations as noting whether or not a response had been made previously (as if that was what was meant by creativity).

Another argument points to the paradox involved in the use of ordinary language for encoding objectives relating to other art forms. Although language can be used to *refer* to the meaning of non-linguistic arts, the reference can never convey the same meaning as the original:

> ... the notion that any kind of commentary will even explain any kind of poetry is of course vulgar. Even if there is a hidden meaning, the poem which contains no more than what an explanation of that

meaning can translate should have been written in the form of the explanation in the first place (Northrop Frye, 1947).

And doubly so for the visual and musical arts. It is difficult to know whether this fundamentally prevents the use of behavioural objectives in such subject areas. Probably it does not, though one is bound to notice that the systematic approach has rarely been successful in the fine arts.

This section has raised several difficulties whose significance is difficult to judge. First, humanities were held to be exceptions because they entailed "manner of behaving" or process objectives. Though it is clear that most subject-matters could make such a claim, it was agreed that such objectives were difficult to use in prescriptive mode. The second and third points claimed that responses to works of art were of necessity individual, and in any event non-linguistic objectives could not be adequately coded in linguistic form. It is difficult to gauge the weight of these objections. There is little in the behavioural objectives literature on these matters, and not much practical experience of applying the method to these subjects.

It seems possible to have objectives relating to standards for judgment that can be applied *after the event*. Such objectives are of little use for prescriptive design purposes, though they could be invaluable if one cycles a number of times round the same system. This allows the weaker (cyclical) formulation some scope; even so a lot depends on the extent to which presuppositions underpinning the judgmental process can be made public—an exceedingly difficult task.

3 Problems of evaluation

According to the theory, objectives determine the test items. Test constructors who justify items on any other grounds suffer the stinging rebuke of "arranging the target after the shot has been fired". This shows quite clearly how the advocates of behavioural objectives see the systematic approach as (in theory) a feedforward process, though in practice they are forced to adopt a cyclical design procedure.

Now, the claim that behavioural objectives provide the only objective basis for evaluation must be taken seriously, for if true it would quite alter the traditional theory and practice of educational assessment. It might be difficult to justify those systems where the pattern of marks approximates a normal distribution. Instead, criterion-based tests would put the emphasis on absolute standards and mastery learning. Many would regard such a shift of emphasis as beneficial. Also, the need for complicated and tortuous discussions about content validity or construct validity (Cronbach, 1971) would be by-passed, for by definition such matters would be settled in advance by the selection of objectives. This would be a great and welcome simplification—if it were possible.

Unfortunately it turns out that objectives do not in practice, and cannot even in principle, determine by themselves the validity of test items. Three principle reasons are adduced to support this opinion: first, that the significance of a test item depends in part upon the nature of the learning experiences the student has been engaged in. Second, that objectives are inherently ambiguous, and so, typically, various items can be written for each objective. Third, it seems impossible in principle even to relate objectives and test results in a simple fashion whenever the student's behaviour change may be assigned to causes outside the learning situation. Finally, attempts to reduce ambiguity by specifying objectives even more finely run up against the level of specificity problem. These issues will now be discussed in detail.

a   Interactions within the learning system
Seemingly excellent objectives and test items depend in part for their validity upon the integrity of the teaching process. Obviously, students can be "crammed" for exams, thus turning the items into measures of role learning. So objectives cannot by themselves determine the validity of test items *unless* the objectives also specify in detail the nature of the designed learning situation. And we have just seen that objectives leave a lot to be desired as prescriptors of design, so that defence is not available. How close *should* test items be to the examples given by the teacher? No one has *ever* solved this problem (except intuitively), and it seems the solution is not brought much closer by adopting behavioural objectives.

b   Interactions outside the learning system
Consider the evaluation of complex or long-term aims. Imagine a management education course lasting a month whose aim is to improve the performance of the managers when they return to their operational positions. Now some of the component goals can be evaluated at the end of the month; but no evaluation which did not consider the managers' performances on the job would be regarded as complete. Let us suppose that it is possible (having regard to his span of discretion) to assess the manager once a year. So a year later, assuming a management by objectives system has been installed (and that has snags, too), we get the first measure of the manager's improved performance. Suppose he improves by $X\%$. What does this mean? Can we assign the improvement to the course? Or has he got insights from other sources? Or perhaps his environment has ameliorated. How would the systematic paradigm help to disentangle these factors? At any rate it is clear that no protocol of behaviours could be *sufficient* for a full evaluation in these circumstances.

Similar considerations apply to many complex, long-term aims in schools, for instance high-level affective and cognitive objectives. Months or years may elapse before students' behaviour changes appreciably, by which time other factors will be candidates for responsibility. Popham (Popham and Baker, 1970a) says, sensibly enough, that difficulty in measuring such elusive attributes as "a scientific attitude" should not discourage a teacher's efforts to get at them. Quite right; but in the first place this admits that theoretical constructs are valuable (more of this later), and in the second place it does damage the claim of behavioural objectives as *prescriptive* (it amounts to saying that you only know when an instance of behaviour is an example of scientific attitude after the event).

c   Ambiguity of behavioural objectives

If objectives did unambiguously specify observable actions, then of course they would specify the test items. But unless the objectives are actually identical (synonymous) with the test items, some degree of ambiguity must and does remain. In brief, it is easy to "fix" tests, and if the learning situation is "fixed" as well, then any performance criteria can be guaranteed in advance. It has been common knowledge among programmed learning experts for some time that the pass rate for a programme can be improved by the simple strategy of revising the test items. This is a good deal cheaper than revising the programme and not easily detected, since both sets of test items can be seen to relate to the same set of behavioural objectives. So when administrators install 90–90–90 criteria, accountability and payment by results, you can guess how crafty teachers will react.

If indeed verbs did divide cleanly into verbs of state (to know, to understand, etc.) and verbs of action (to cut, to cover, etc.) then naturally a great reduction in ambiguity would be achieved by using only verbs of action, as Mager advocated. We have already gladly conceded that "to know how a car engine works" is an imprecise formulation, and have no intention of retreating from that position. But, alas, not all cases are so clear-cut. Actually, *most* verbs do not fit comfortably in either category, for reasons that only a sophisticated linguistic analysis would reveal. An interesting experiment by Deno and Jenkins (1969) showed just how difficult it is for people to decide whether a verb describes an observable behaviour or not. Eleven teachers were asked to place verbs on a five-point scale from one (clearly observable action, e.g. to bite) to five (clearly unobservable states, e.g. to believe). Table 1 shows their results.

Notice that nearly half the verbs are placed between 2.0 and 4.0. This group contained many of the verbs teachers value and use most frequently. (Why is that? Interesting question). Many of these verbs also had large variances, indicating lack of agreement among the teachers. The prize example is "to solve" at 4.2—a verb Mager lists as "open to fewer interpretations"! Of course, the meaning of *any* word, verb or not, is essentially ambiguous. Not infinitely flexible, just ambiguous. The ambiguity can be resolved by taking the semantic and syntactic context into account; but sometimes a great deal of context is necessary, more than is provided by even a well-specified behavioural objective.

All this militates against any simple-minded classification of objectives into dichotomous observable/non-observable categories, and ensures that

Table 1 Rank-order distribution of means and variances for 99 verb ratings (Deno and Jenkins, 1969)

Terms	Means	Variances	Terms	Means	Variances
to cover with a card	1.0	0.0	*to add	3.0	1.3
to lever press	1.0	0.0	*to supply	3.0	1.3
to line-draw	1.0	0.0	*to demonstrate	3.1	0.8
to mark	1.0	0.0	*to regroup	3.1	1.0
to point to	1.0	0.0	*to multiply	3.1	1.2
to cross out	1.1	0.3	*to round off	3.1	1.4
to underline	1.1	0.3	*to group	3.2	0.5
to walk	1.1	0.3	*to complete	3.2	0.9
*to circle	1.2	0.3	*to respond to	3.3	0.6
to repeat orally	1.2	0.3	*to average	3.3	1.1
*to count orally	1.2	0.7	to summarize	3.3	1.1
*to say	1.2	0.7	to inquire	3.5	0.8
*to write	1.3	0.4	to utilize	3.5	1.0
*to put on	1.4	0.4	*to borrow	3.5	0.4
*to read orally	1.5	0.4	to acknowledge	3.5	1.1
*to shade	1.5	0.8	*to find	3.6	1.6
to number	1.5	0.4	*to identify	3.8	0.8
*to name	1.5	0.8	to see	3.8	2.3
*to fill in	1.6	0.9	*to convert	3.9	1.3
to label	1.7	1.1	to distinguish	4.1	0.8
*to state	1.7	1.4	*to solve	4.2	0.9
*to remove	1.9	0.6	*to apply	4.2	1.1
*to place	1.9	0.9	to develop	4.3	0.4
to tell what	1.9	1.1	*to test	4.3	0.4
*to draw	2.0	0.9	*to determine	4.3	0.6
*to identify in writing	2.1	1.4	to generate	4.3	0.7
*to check	2.2	1.2	*to create	4.3	1.1
*to construct	2.2	1.2	to discriminate	4.5	0.6
*to match	2.3	0.7	*to recognize	4.5	0.4
*to take away	2.3	1.1	to discover	4.7	0.2
*to make	2.4	0.9	to become competent	4.7	0.3
*to arrange	2.5	0.6	to infer	4.7	0.3
to finish	2.5	0.6	to like	4.7	0.3
*to read	2.5	0.8	to analyse	4.8	0.1
*to play	2.5	1.7	to be curious	4.8	0.1
*to locate	2.6	0.6	to conclude	4.8	0.1
*to connect	2.6	1.1	*to deduce	4.8	0.1
*to give	2.6	1.3	to feel	4.8	0.1
*to reject	2.7	1.1	to concentrate	4.8	0.3
*to select	2.7	1.4	to perceive	4.8	0.3
to choose	2.8	0.5	to think	4.8	0.3
*to partition	2.9	0.4	to think critically	4.8	0.3
*to change	2.9	0.9	to learn	4.8	0.3
*to use	2.9	1.1	to appreciate	4.9	0.0
			to be aware	4.9	0.0

Table 1 (*Continued*)

Terms	Means	Variances	Terms	Means	Variances
*to subtract	2.9	1.3	to know	4.9	0.0
*to perform	3.0	1.8	to wonder	4.9	0.0
*to total	3.0	1.8	to realize fully	5.0	0.0
*to divide	3.0	0.8	to understand	5.0	0.0
*to order	3.0	0.9			
*to measure	3.0	1.1			

  * Denotes verbs extracted from the objectives of a "behavioristic" curriculum.

some essential ambiguity remains with any objective. Even if tests were not deliberately fixed, the problem would remain.

d   Ambiguity of test items
Philosophers often make the distinction between behaviours (movements or muscle twitches) and actions (which must meet various *criteria*). This is what MacMillan and McClellan (1968) allude to when they say:

> But the curious thing about the acceptable objectives is that they do not give descriptions of behaviour, but rather specify criteria of correctness of *results* of behaviour ... the behavioural objectives, then, are not behavioural.

That this is not just a matter of terminology is shown by this example (from Evans, 1960): "Objective: to solve quadratic equations. Test: solve $X^2 + 5x + 6 = 0$."
The equation can be solved by factoring or by completing the square or by using the quadratic formula. But we have not said which method should be used, and it may be (for all one knows) a matter of educational consequence. To that extent the test item is ambiguous, as indeed is the objective, as indeed is any description of an action which can be performed in various ways. This relates to an earlier comment about making right responses for wrong reasons.

e   Level of specificity
The natural defence to the ambiguity of objectives and test items is to suggest that objectives should be specified ever more finely. This defence does not hold water; indeed it raises one of the most critical defects of behavioural objectives—the absence of suitable rules for deciding at which level of specificity objectives should be pitched.
The level of specificity problem is the most cruel dilemma faced by the advocate of behavioural objects. It runs like this: if you have only a few general objectives they are easy to remember and handle, but too vague and ambiguous. But if you try to eliminate ambiguity by splitting down

171

the objectives and qualifying the conditions of performance, then the list becomes impossibly long.

Here are two examples, taken from a text on behavioural objectives, which show how the advocates of the systematic approach have no rules for deciding the level of specificity:

> Objective: the student should *apply* the principle that plants are dependent on animals and animals are dependent upon plants and both are dependent on the environment.
> 1   The fish in which tank would survive the longest? Why?
> 2   In what tank would the plants survive the longest? Why?
> 3   If you were going to alter tank 1, what would you do and why?
> (Sund and Picard, 1972. A diagram of the three tanks accompanies the test items.)

This objective is so general that an almost *infinite* number of items could be legitimately generated. There is no sense in which such objectives can be said to prescribe the test items, but you wouldn't need many to cover a whole biology course.

> Objective: The student should *explain* why the retrograde motion of Mars occurs.
> Item: The diagram below shows the movement of the planet Mars. How would you explain why it appears to move the way it does? (Sund and Picard, 1972).

Now this objective is quite specific and only a limited number of test items could validly follow. (Note, though, that it is not so clear what kind of behaviour is going to count as an explanation.) But the cost of moving even to this level of specificity is quite serious: if all the objectives in a physics course were at this level they would run into thousands and fill a small book. This is no exaggeration, incidentally. In a review of a recent book on objectives in educational psychology (Stones and Anderson, 1972) I estimated that if the authors had followed Mager's rules strictly they would need to produce 10,000 objectives—a volume of 150,000 words at least, probably more. At this juncture it is worth remembering Eisner's (1969) comment:

> In retrospect it is not difficult to understand why this (the objectives) movement in curriculum collapsed under its own weight in the 1930s. Teachers could not manage fifty highly specified objectives, let alone hundreds.

Every time behavioural objectives have been constructed on a large scale this problem of specificity has proved quite fearsomely difficult. No satisfactory rules have emerged though prominent advocates have long been aware of the need (for instance, both Gagné and Mager worked on Project Plan). Suggestions have ranged from extreme specificity (replacing objectives by test items [Evans 1960]) to the generality of Tyler's (1954, 1960) objectives. Perhaps the problem is insoluble in principle.

4 Objectives as instruments of communication

Objectives can certainly be useful instruments whereby a teacher can show his colleagues and students what he expects the outcome of learning to be. But there are certain limits to this communication, limits which are rarely discussed in the literature.

Earlier we saw how objectives can be used to assist co-ordination between members of a design team or curriculum reform group. Each person must know where his contribution lies, and what he can safely rely on others to do. The chief limitation is, of course, the extent to which different people will make different interpretations of the same objective.

Objectives are, as we have seen, always capable of being interpreted in various ways, even of being misinterpreted. This is because they are ambiguous, to some extent, and it is not practicable (even if it were possible) to eliminate all possible misunderstanding by ever finer specification. There is a limit to the extent to which any human can understand the intention of another no matter what, though in practice and in certain circumstances the risk of serious error can be minimised. (Much depends on the structure of the universe of discourse, that is, whether key terms, rules, etc., have publicly agreed meanings or not.)

So it would be foolish to suppose that agreement on a list of objectives constitutes a general understanding of intent. Several other heuristics are necessary to reduce the possibility of misunderstanding, of which the most powerful makes use of the insight that every person's world-view is unique to the extent to which his unrevealed *presuppositions* are unique. So, as a minimal procedure, designers can attempt to explain their presuppositions to each other, thus revealing how some objectives rather than others are chosen. Such presuppositions contain, as it were, routines for interpreting objectives so as to reduce their ambiguity.

Objectives are also supposed to be a vital kind of "advance organiser" for the student's learning. Students should be given objectives so they can appreciate the nature of the goal they are working towards. And the experiments where students are given just goal statements and allowed to organise their own learning show that this claim has some validity (Mager and McCann, 1962). But our experience at the Open University has shown the limitations of this idea. Teachers understand what objectives mean because they have already attained the goal. They have been there, experienced the terminal behaviour, if you wish, and this personal experience gives the words meaning for them. But the student does not have this experience.

This dilemma is seen quite forcibly whenever a subject has a vocabulary of technical terms (and many subjects in higher or technical education do). If the objectives are written using the technical terms, then the list can be kept reasonably manageable, and ambiguities kept to a minimum. Such objectives are useless for the student who doesn't know what the terms mean, though they might be helpful during revision to direct his attention to the crucial parts of the course. But if the technical terms are described in ordinary language the list becomes impossibly unwieldy, virtually as long as the teaching material itself. Objectives are a useful but deficient tool of communication. They need to be supplemented by the teacher revealing his *presuppositions* and his reasons for believing the education to be *relevant*. In such a discussion the student should gain some interpretive routines which will help him make sense of the objectives.

So behavioural objectives are not a foolproof system of communication. More realistically they are useful, but rather weak, needing to be buttressed by extensive in-depth discussions between the concerned parties.

5   *Other objections*

a   Triviality
The complaint is often heard that the most trivial aims are the easiest to operationalise. This much, everyone agrees on. Advocates usually try to turn this to their advantage by pointing out that trivial objectives can be weeded out as being unworthy of educational effort. (This is the response Popham gives; see later.) But this assumes that the problems of operationalising "worthwhile" aims has been solved, or what shall we do if *none* of the objectives are worthwhile? We should have nothing left. Thus, this complaint (of triviality) is real, but may be subsumed under the broader problems of origins. It is also strongly connected with the question of operationalism, discussed below.

b   Attacks on goal-directed models of education
Sometimes behavioural objectives have come under fire from those who wish to make a radical assault on the central notion of goal-directed behaviour as a suitable model for education. For instance, Vickers (1968) says "most human regulatory behaviour is norm-seeking and, as such, cannot be resolved into goal-seeking". Oakeshott (1962) puts it elegantly like this:

It is asked: why travel if there is no prefigured and final destination? But it may be replied: why suppose that the analogy of a journey towards a prefigured destination is relevant? It is clearly irrelevant in science, in art, in poetry, and in human life in general, none of which have prefigured final destinations and none of which are (on that account) considered to be "pointless" activities. . . . To describe the enterprise as "keeping afloat and on an even keel" is to assign it an office neither to be overrated nor despised.

This line of argument, which enjoys quite a vogue amongst philosophers of education, is a more general case of one of the difficulties raised above (p. 166) under "Subject-matter differences". It is puzzling to know what would count as an adequate answer to this objection, but there is one defence that might be tried. Cyberneticians usually distinguish between two kinds of goal-directed systems: the ones which cease functioning once a specific goal is reached (for instance, once an insect lays its eggs the ovipositor is retracted, and the whole system is then out of action), and the ones which continually act so as to keep some parameter within set limits (for example, a thermostat). It is possible to imagine objectives so worded that they would count as members of the second (regulative) class of goal-directed systems. But, as discussed previously, this type of regulation occurs after the event, and its value in prescription is limited.

c Costs of feedback cyclical design systems
The costs of designing systems which do not initially work well can be quite considerable. For example, at the Open University our courses are designed to last basically for four years. If the initial design is unsatisfactory then thousands of students may suffer, and considerable sums of money spent in remedying defects. There are times when one *does* want to get design as near right as possible the first time round. So the retreat from the ambitious, but untenable, feedforward prescriptive mode to the less demanding cyclical mode is a significant, and at times costly, retreat.

d Lists do not adequately represent the structure of knowledge
Many of the surface difficulties experienced by those trying to apply the systematic approach are caused by deep underlying problems which are rarely if ever articulated. One of these deep issues concerns the structure of knowledge. Since knowledge or understanding presupposes a coherence amongst ideas—a fitting together or interlocking of parts to form a meaningful whole—it is difficult to see why advocates of the systematic approach are so addicted to list structures. For behavioural objectives *are* presented in lists, lists which virtually demolish any structure that might once have existed.

Some lists reveal structure when surrounded by well-specified interpretive routines (e.g. computer programs). But lists of behavioural objectives are more like heaps—they show little of the complex manner in which ideas are interrelated, and so have no higher-level structure. This is important in itself, and must be taken seriously as soon as it is realised that some of the intransigent problems raised earlier are primarily due to this lack of structure. For example, it has been shown how there exist no procedures for justifying the inclusion or exclusion of a given objective unless (a) it relates to an obviously necessary task, or (b) hunch or intuition is resorted to. This arises from the absence of a way of representing the whole structure so that the interrelation of parts can be seen in manipulable terms.

Once more, apologies must be made for arbitrarily truncating the discussion. Pask and I have raised this topic before, and will do so again (MacDonald-Ross, 1972a, 1972b; Pask, 1972a, 1972b).

e Model of teacher-learner interaction

It is actually true, but not easy to explain, that the use of behavioural objectives implies a poverty-stricken model of student-teacher interaction. This point was made by Pask and Lewis (private communication) when they analysed the systemic implications of various curriculum schemes. The following Table 2 contrasts the main features of a behaviour-shaping curriculum with the theoretical approach favoured by Pask, Lewis and myself (which envisages the teacher and learner as general learning systems and the interaction as "conversational learning").

Since it would take a paper at least as long again as the present one to explore fully all the ideas contained in Table 2, we must be content to realise that the existence (even by implication) of the primitive behaviour-shaping model sets limits to what can be achieved by a behavioural objectives approach.

Table 2 Contrast of behaviour-shaping with conversational-learning models*

	Behaviour shaping	*Conversational learning*
View of teacher:	Simple regulator	General learning system
View of student:	Simple adaptive machine	General learning system
View of subject-matter:	List of target behaviours and list of reinforcements	Knowledge of entailment structure and associated descriptions and tasks
Communication restrictions (form of transactions allowed):	Stimuli (which or whether questions) and assertions (cues, prompts)	Assertions: problems (including how and why questions) with explanations as solutions
	Schedules of reinforcing events	Goal or subgoal statements; evaluative statements; pupil's selection of strategy and description of this state; teacher's instructions about how to learn, etc.
	Responses (answers to which or whether questions)	

* Meaning of technical terms regrettably beyond scope of present paper.

f   Operationalism

The notion of behavioural objectives is strongly related to the philo-sophical position of *operationalism*. This is an embarrassing relationship, to say the least, for it is now clear that operationalism suffers from some severe defects and is generally regarded by philosophers of science to be in a mortally wounded condition. At first sight, however, it does seem an attractive proposition, as shown in this extract from Bridgeman's (1927) original account:

> To find the length of an object, we have to perform certain physical operations. The concept of length is therefore fixed when the oper-ations by which the length is measured are fixed: that is, the concept of length involves as much as and nothing more than the set of operations by which length is determined. In general, we mean by any concept nothing more than a set of operations; the concept is synonymous with the corresponding set of operations.

Such a prescription appears to free the scientist from the need to deal with "occult qualities" (theoretical constructs, in this context knowing, understanding, etc.). But closer examination reveals critical problems. For instance, what exactly counts as an operation? What happens to the concepts when we are not performing operations? What happens if we cannot physically perform operations or if we have not yet learnt how to perform them? Do we wish to say, in these circumstances, that no kind of scientific discourse is possible? Hempel (1958) says:

> Scientific systematisation is ultimately aimed at establishing explanatory and predictive order among the bewilderingly complex "data" of our experience, the phenomena that can be "directly observed" by us. It is a remarkable fact, therefore, that the greatest advances in scientific systematisation have not been accomplished by means of laws referring explicitly to *observables,* i.e. to things and events which are ascertainable by direct observation, but rather by means of laws that speak of various *hypothetical* or *theoretical entities* i.e. presumptive objects, events, and attributes which cannot be perceived or otherwise directly oberved by us.

Now it is sufficient for present purposes to realise what implications follow from the demand that terms such as "know" and "understand" should always be fully reinterpreted as lists of observable actions. These implications have never been faced by the protagonists of behavioural objectives. As Cronbach (1971) wrote recently:

> The writers on curriculum and evaluation who insist that objectives must be "defined in terms of behaviour" are taking an ultra operationalist position, though they have not offered a scholarly

177

philosophical analysis of the issue. A person who insists on "behavioural" objectives is denying the appropriateness and usefulness of constructs (=theoretical terms). The educator who states objectives in terms of constructs (e.g. self-confidence, scientific attitude, a habit of suiting one's writing style to one's purpose) regards observables as indicators from which the presence of the characteristics described by the construct can be inferred. But he will not for example *substitute* "volunteers ideas and answers in class" for "self-confidence". From the construct point of view behaviour such as this is an indicator of confidence but not a definer. Indeed no list of specific responses-to-situations, however lengthy, can define the construct, since the construct is intended to apply to situations that will arise in the future and cannot be specified now.

This short discussion of operationalism shows how some of the problems encountered in the behavioural objective domain are extensions of the basic problems faced by operationalism. For instance, it explains why trivial aims are easiest to state in behavioural terms: they are always close to their empirical basis, whereas long-term or complex higher-level aims may be quite abstract or far removed from empirical indicators. Again, we can see why lists of objectives get so long and are so tedious to prepare, for it is possible to operationalise a theoretical concept in almost limitless detail. The decisions about levels of specificity and the meaning of key terms are also problems to operationalism and in the context of behavioural objectives.

6   Summary of objections
These are the objections that have been raised to behavioural objectives. In some cases the items are interconnected, and it is possible to slice the pie in various fashions. But this would not greatly alter the points that have been made:

1   No consistent view exists as to the origin of objectives.
2   In the educational domain no well-defined prescriptions are available for deriving objectives.
3   Defining objectives before the event conflicts with voyages of exploration.
4   Advocates do not show how teachers can use objectives to guide unpredicted classroom events.
5   There is an extremely large number of paths through any body of knowledge, thus reducing the effectiveness of objectives in design.
6   In some disciplines criteria can only be applied after the event.
7   Objectives do *not* prescribe the validity of test items.
8   Objectives are inherently ambiguous.
9   The level of specificity problem has never been solved.

10 Objectives do not communicate intent unambiguously, especially to students.
11 Trivial objectives *are* the easiest to operationalise, and this *is* a problem.
12 The relevance of goal-referenced models of education can be questioned.
13 Weak prescriptions lead to cycling. This can be costly.
14 Lists of behaviours do not adequately represent the structure of knowledge.
15 The use of behavioural objectives implies a poverty-stricken model of student-teacher interaction.
16 The behavioural objectives scheme suffers from many of the weaknesses of any operationalist dogma.

The most important items, in this author's opinion, are 1, 2, 7, 9, and 13 to 16 inclusive. The difficulty of writing objectives, often mentioned in the literature, has not been listed here. It seems most likely to arise from some combination of the above list of intractable problems. Many of the more detailed objections can be traced back to the three really fundamental problems: 14, 15 and 16. Such problems are hardly soluble within the conceptual framework of behavioural objectives and the systematic approach. This opinion contrasts sharply with the view of advocates of the systematic approach who, though admitting problems, believe they are soluble simply by applying more effort in the same direction.

PART IV: A REASSESSMENT OF POPHAM'S DEFENCE
Yet, as a partisan in the controversy (about behavioural objectives) I would prefer unanimous support of the position to which I subscribe. You see, the other people are wrong. . . . Moreover, their particular form of sin . . . will probably harm more people than the most exotic forms of pornography (Popham, 1968)

Under the magnificent title of "Probing the Validity of Arguments Against Behavioural Goals", Dr. James Popham presented in 1967 his own response to "most of the arguments used to resist the implementation of precise instructional objectives". It is now necessary to re-examine this defence. The necessity arises because Popham's defence is so widely regarded by systematic advocates as a complete answer to criticisms of behavioural objectives; it is often quoted, and has been reprinted at least three times since the original conference (originally presented at conferences in California in 1967 and Chicago in 1968; reprinted in Popham *et al.*, 1969; Kibler *et al.*, 1970; and Stones and Anderson, 1972). There is only one way to approach this task—which is to take each objection and rebuttal one by one and examine them, making use of the framework established earlier in this paper.

*Reason one: Trivial learner behaviours are the easiest to operationalise,
hence the really important outcomes of education will be
underemphasised.*

This has already been discussed above (Part III, Section 5a, p. 174).
We there noted that Popham's response (that trivial objectives can be
weeded out once revealed) is true, but not sufficient since it ducks the
huge problems of origins and operationalism (which have also been discussed above).

So we are bound to conclude that the problem of triviality is still a
problem. Presumably this objection should have been phrased thus:
"What are your (explicit) procedures for generating worthwhile objectives?" Since Popham's procedures are safe but weak, as discussed above
under "origins", (Part III, Section 1c, p. 162) it is not clear that he could
answer such a question adequately.

*Reason two: Prespecification of explicit goals prevents the teacher from
taking advantage of instructional opportunities unexpectedly occurring in
the classroom.*

This we have also briefly discussed (Part III, Section 2b, p. 164).
Popham's response (that "serendipity in the classroom . . . should always
be justified in terms of its contribution to the learner's attainment of
worthwhile objectives") is perfectly reasonable, but again does not raise
the underlying problem, which is, how can teachers do it? This is the
level of specificity problem in yet another guise, for if the teacher has a
set of very detailed objectives he surely cannot use them in real-time
action, but if "the lesson plan is written at a level of generality upon
which the teacher can function" (Popham and Baker, 1970a) then few of
the benefits of precise objectives will be reaped. You can't have it both
ways.

*Reason three: Besides pupil behaviour changes, there are other types of
educational outcomes which are important, such as changes in parental
attitudes, the professional staff, community values, etc.*

This objection comes as something of a surprise, since it is so weak and
so obviously asking for the treatment which it deservedly gets from Dr.
Popham (". . . the school's primary responsibility is to its pupils"). This
is the first of the straw men. (By using the term "straw men" I do not
wish to imply that Dr. Popham invented the objection. But some objections are so lame that their reproduction in a professional paper and
subsequent destruction give the behavioural objective schema a repu-
tation which it hardly deserves.)

*Reason four: Measurability implies behaviour which can be objectively,
mechanistically measured, hence there must be something dehumanizing
about the approach.*

It's difficult to know how to respond to an objection which itself is so full of confusions. Measurement is not the same as observation; what is said to be "implied" is not actually implied; what does "something dehumanizing" mean?—and so on. I suppose what lies behind this muddle is a concern with the validity of evaluation procedures based on behavioural objectives. If this *is* the case then we have already seen what a considerable problem this presents (Part III, Section 3, p. 167). Popham's excellent example (of how human judges can accurately score springboard divers) shows that valid assessment of complex behaviours can be obtained, but does not show how this may generally be achieved by a systematic procedure.

Reason five: It is somehow undemocratic to plan in advance precisely how the learner should behave after instruction.

This is the old chestnut raised by Arnstine (1964) about programmed learning. The rebuttal (described by Popham as "a brilliant refutation") came from Komisar and McClellan (1965) who said that instruction is by its very nature undemocratic, and to pretend that classrooms are democratic places would be untruthful. This is a good start, but more could be said. For instance, the use of "democracy" in this context is rather odd; it is not clear that this concept can rightfully be used, or if it is used then what, exactly, would count as being "democratic"? Perhaps we are really talking about the need for *justification,* which is part of the problem of origins. If so, then the problem is a good deal more deep-seated than the question of where control resides in a classroom.

Reason six: That isn't really the way teaching is; teachers rarely specify their goals in terms of measurable learner behaviours; so let's set realistic expectations of teachers.

This invertebrate specimen is the second straw man. It gets the treatment it deserves (maybe teachers do not, but they ought to).

Reason seven: In certain subject areas, e.g. fine arts and humanities, it is more difficult to identify measurable pupil behaviours.

This has already been discussed (Part III, Section 2d, p. 166) as an objection whose validity is difficult to assess. Popham rightly says that arts and humanities teachers do have standards, and do make judgments. He advises them to put their evaluative criteria "on the line", good advice, but not absolutely sufficient. Behavioural objectives are supposed to be prescriptive (before the event) tools, and when criteria of judgment are applied, say, to works of art, they are applied *after the event.* (Because you know a good painting when you see one does not mean you can predict all the good paintings that might ever be created, nor even need you be able to specify how to create a good painting.) So in these cases the prescriptive benefits of objectives are weakened.

Reason eight: While loose general statements of objectives may appear worthwhile to an outsider, if most educational goals were stated precisely, they would be revealed as generally innocuous.

This is the third straw man. In such circumstances (where worthless education is the rule) the explicit nature of objectives is of positive benefit—so it is perverse to raise this as an objection, as Popham shows in no uncertain fashion: "We must abandon the ploy of 'obfuscation by generality' and make clear exactly what we are doing."

Reason nine: Measurability implies accountability; teachers might be judged on their ability to produce results in learners rather than on the many bases now used as indices of competence.

Should teachers be accountable for securing behaviour changes? Popham believes they should be, and goes on to say that a teacher "should not be judged on the particular instructional *means* he uses to bring about desirable *ends*". This response is no surprise, for advocates are prone to claim for the systematic approach that it lays an objective basis for accountability. But all systems of accountability depend on (1) agreement as to what ends are desirable, and (2) valid and reliable methods of evaluation. And we have already seen that the problems of origins and evaluation are quite intractable inside the world-view of the systematic approach. It is *this* which causes opposition to accountability, not love of incompetence or "mysticism".

Reason ten: It is far more difficult to generate such precise objectives than to talk about objectives in our customarily vague terms.

Interestingly, Popham says this is "a very significant objection to the development of precise goals". This may not be entirely unconnected with the idea of a behavioural objectives bank, one of which he organises, and which allow teachers to select objectives and so short-cut the hard work of specification. However, the question arises as to whether difficulty in generating objectives is due to psychological factors (i.e. teachers are incompetent, or, only a few of us are skilled in writing objectives) or due to basic logical deficiencies embedded deep inside the systematic approach. In other words, it is no surprise people find it difficult to write objectives *if* there are no rules for generating them, for deciding their specificity, for deciding how their attainment may be assessed, and so on. In these circumstances one might begin to suspect anyone who *did* find objectives easy to generate. Now suppose (by magic, as it were) there were a complete bank of objectives, numbering tens of millions. On what criteria should teachers select?

Reason eleven: In evaluating the worth of instructional schemes it is often the unanticipated results which are really important, but pre-specified goals may make the evaluator inattentive to the unforseen.

This objection contains the assumption that the prespecified goals are not the most important ones. We were supposed to have been protected from this sort of thing by the prespecification of design, and undoubtedly a "hardliner" would have responded by advising you to improve your task analysis. Popham (following the "softliner" strategy, as you will remember) cannot give this rebuke, and is bound to admit tacitly that such an occurrence is possible. The advice given ("keep your eyes open") is both weak (as he acknowledges) and an admission of failure.

Of Popham's eleven objections, three are straw men which provide him with targets which are altogether too easy. The other eight contain indications of serious, deeper problems though these are not precisely articulated. In virtually every case Dr. Popham has chosen to give a superficially convincing answer to the surface problem, but has neither uncovered nor answered the deeper issues.

CONCLUSIONS

Most of the claims made for behavioural objectives need to be weakened or even negated as a result of the criticisms raised in Part III. There appear to be no reliable and explicit principles for generating relevant objectives: the various suggestions made fall short in one respect or another. There are no clear rules even for deciding on the specificity of objectives. And once objectives have been specified they do not prescribe the choice of instructional means, nor ensure the content validity of test items. These objections were tried out on one of the best-known defences of behavioural objectives (in Part IV). The fair conclusion to draw from this analysis is that the defence was not sufficient. This means that the case against behavioural objectives must be taken seriously.

The original ambition of the systematic approach was to make education more effective and to bring the outcomes of learning in line with the intentions of the educator. This ambition is now in some danger of falling short of its goal. The stronger feedforward version of the systematic approach rested heavily on behavioural objectives laying the foundation for explicit, adequate and well-justified procedures which would work when applied by anyone who understood them. This position is now undermined; the prescriptive approach fails—unless in practice it is buttressed by unspecified and unformulated intuitive skills imported *ad hoc* to support the design system. This reliance on intuitive skills was just what the "hardliners" hoped to avoid.

The cyclical versions of the systematic approach are still viable, though weakened. Advocates of this approach never did expect objectives to be sufficient for prescriptive purposes. They are willing to settle for a final internal coherence reached after repeated trial and revision. A sensible attitude, adopted by many successful consultants when operating in the field. But this approach has costs attached, for example the cost of cycling, that is, of not getting the design right the first time around. Successes are certainly recorded by people working within the cyclical framework. But—are the successes due to the procedures of the systematic approach, or are they due to the unformulated personal skills of the consultant, teacher or design group?

This article has *not* argued that behavioural objectives are worthless, nor is it doubted that the systematic approach represents an advance on purely intuitive methods of curriculum design. The criticisms of traditional methods were entirely justified—no one wishes to put the clock back. But the application of behavioural objectives and the systematic approach needs to be tempered with an understanding of its inherent deficiencies. The chief function of this paper has been to identify these deficiencies so that they may be allowed for in some way.

The question arises: can these defects be repaired, or are there limits which the systematic approach can never transcend? Insofar as they admit any such defects, advocates of behavioural objectives have always believed they could be overcome by experience and hard work. My view is quite different. I think that behavioural objectives will never achieve all that their supporters hope, for they are limited by the very presuppositions on which they are based. The defects of operationalism, the poverty-stricken model of learning and the assumption that lists can represent the structure of knowledge: these are embedded deep inside the behavioural objective schema, and cannot be transcended. The discussion in Part I showed how the systematic approach was a system of design with "the normative and strategic levels truncated". This is caused by the aforementioned presuppositions.

Behavioural objectives provide a framework which has led to some progress in the design of educational systems. The conceptual framework which provided the basis also sets certain absolute limitations. If we are close to those limitations then improvements are likely to be of marginal importance. In my opinion a new and potentially more fruitful conceptualisation is needed; meanwhile the strengths and weaknesses of the behavioural objectives paradigm can at least be seen in sharper focus.

NOTES

1 These concepts are not exactly co-extensive; but they are closely related.
2 See Ammerman and Melching (1966) and Chapanis (1959) for further references on task analysis and methods of direct observation.
3 The fact that the right answer can be given for the wrong reason is a further argument for retaining concepts such as knowledge and understanding.

REFERENCES

ALEXANDER, C. (1964) *Notes on the Synthesis of Form*, Harvard University Press.

AMMERMAN, H. L. and MELCHING, W. H. (1966) "The Derivation, Analysis and Classification of Instructional Objectives", *Technical Report* 66—4, *Task INGO*, HumRRO, George Washington University.

ANSOFF, H. I. (1965) *Corporate Strategy*, McGraw-Hill.

ARNSTINE, D. G. (1964) "The Language and Values of Programmed Instruction, Part 2", *The Educational Forum*.

BANDURA, A. (1969) *Principles of Behaviour Modification*, Holt, Rinehart and Winston.

BISHOP, L. K. (1970) *Individualising Instructional Systems*, Harper Row.

BLOCK, J. H. (ed.) (1971) *Mastery Learning*, Holt, Rinehart and Winston.

BOBBITT, F. (1924) *How to Make a Curriculum*, Houghton Mifflin.

BRAYBROOKE, D. and LINDBLOM, C. E. (1963) *A Strategy of Decision*, Free press.

BRIDGEMAN, P. W. (1927) *The Logic of Modern Physics*, Macmillan.

BUTLER, LORD R. A. (1971) *The Art of the Possible*, Hamish Hamilton.

CHAPANIS, A. (1959) *Research Techniques in Human Engineering*, Johns Hopkins Press.

CHARTERS, W. W. and WAPLES, D. (1929) *The Commonwealth Teacher-Training Study*, Chicago University Press.

CHURCHMAN, C. W. (1968a) *Challenge to Reason*, McGraw-Hill.

CHURCHMAN, C. W. (1968b) *The Systems Approach*, Dell.

CRONBACH, L. J. (1971) "Test Validation", in Thorndike, R. L. (ed.) *Educational Measurement*, American Council on Education.

DALE, E. (1967) "Historical Setting of Programmed Instruction", in Lange, P. (ed.) *Programmed Instruction*, National Society for the Study of Education, Washington DC.

DAVIES, I. K. (1971) *The Management of Learning*, McGraw-Hill.

DAVIES, I. K. and HARTLEY, J. (1972) *Contributions to an Educational Technology*, Butterworths.

DENO, S. L. and JENKINS, J. R. (1969) "On the Behaviourality of Behavioural Objectives", *Psychology in the Schools*, 6, pp. 18–24.

DUNCAN, K. (1972) "Strategies for Analysis of the Task", in Hartley, J. (ed.) *Strategies for Programmed Instruction: An Educational Technology*, Butterworths.

EISNER, E. W. (1967a) "Educational Objectives: Help or Hindrance?" *School Review*, 75, pp. 250–60.

EISNER, E. W. (1967b) "A Response to my Critics", *School Review*, 75, pp. 227–82.

EISNER, E. W. (1969) "Instructional and Expressive Educational Objectives: Their Formulation and Use in Curriculum", in Popham *et al. Instructional Objectives*, AERA Monograph No. 3, Rand McNally.

ESBENSON, T. (1968) *Working with Individualised Instruction*, Fearon.

EVANS, J. (1968) "Behavioural Objectives are no Damn Good", in *Technology and Innovation in Education*, Praeger.

185

FLANAGAN, J. C. (1954) "The Critical Incident Technique", *Psychological Bulletin*, 51, pp. 327–58.

GAGNÉ, R. (1965) *The Conditions of Learning*, Holt, Rinehart and Winston.

GAGNÉ, R. (1967) "Curriculum Research and the Promotion of Learning", in *Perspectives of Curriculum Evaluation*, AERA Monograph 1, Rand McNally.

GILBERT, T. F. (1962) "Mathetics: the Technology of Education", reprinted in *RECALL Supplement No. 1*, Longmac, 1969.

GOODMAN, P. (1962) *Compulsory Miseducation*, Horizon Press.

HAUENSTEIN, A. D. (1972) *Curriculum Planning for Behavioural Development*, Charles Jones.

HARTLEY, J. (ed.) (1972) *Strategies for Programmed Instruction: an Educational Technology*, Butterworths.

HEMPEL, C. G. (1965) "The Theoretician's Dilemma: A Study in the Logic of Theory Construction", in Hempel, C. G. *Aspects of Scientific Explanation*, Free Press.

HOLT, J. (1964) *How Children Fail*, Pitman.

HOWES, V. M. (1970) *Individualisation of Instruction*, Macmillan.

ILLICH, I. D. (1971) *Deschooling Society*, Harper and Row.

KAHN, H. (1962) *Thinking about the Unthinkable*, Horizon Press.

KAHN, H. (1972) *The Prospects for Mankind*, Hudson Institute Report H1-1648/4-D.

KEMP, J. E. (1971) *Instructional Design*, Fearon.

KIBLER, R. J., Barker, L. L. and Miles, D. T. (1970) *Behavioural Objectives and Instruction*, Allyn and Bacon.

KOMISAR, O. B. and MCCLELLAN, J. E. (1965) "Professor Arnstine and Programmed Instruction", *The Educational Forum*.

KOZOL, J. (1967) *Death at an Early Age*, Houghton Mifflin.

LEWIS, B. N. and COOK, J. A. (1969) "Toward a Theory of Telling", *International Journal of Man-Machine Studies*, 1, pp. 129–76.

McASHAN, H. H. (1970) *Writing Behavioural Objectives*, Harper and Row.

MACDONALD-ROSS, M. (1970) "Introductory Notes on Objectives, Assessment and Activities", *IET working paper No. 2*, The Open University.

MACDONALD-ROSS, M. (1972a) "Behavioural Objectives and the Structure of Knowledge", in Austwick, K. and Harris, N. D. C. (eds.) *Aspects of Educational Technology VI*, Pitmans.

MACDONALD-ROSS, M. (1972b) "The Problem of Representing Knowledge", paper presented to Structural Learning Conference, Philadelphia.

MACDONALD-ROSS, M. (1972c) Review of Hartley (ed.) "Strategies for Programmed Instruction: An Educational Technology" (Butterworths, 1972), in *British Journal of Educational Technology*, 3:3, pp. 246–9.

MACMILLAN, C. J. B. and MCCLELLAN, J. E. (1968) "Can and Should Means-Ends Reasoning be Used in Teaching?" in Macmillan and

Nelson (eds.) *Concepts of Teaching: Philosophical Essays*, Rand McNally.

MAGER, R. F. (1961) "On the Sequencing of Instructional Content", *Psychological Reports*, IX, pp. 405–13.

MAGER, R. F. (1962) *Preparing Instructional Objectives*, Fearon.

MAGER, R. F. (1968) *Developing Attitude toward Learning*, Fearon.

MAGER, R. F. (1972) *Goal Analysis*, Fearon.

MAGER, R. F. and McCANN, J. (1962) *Learner-Controlled Instruction*, Varian Associates.

MAGER, R. F. and BEACH, K. M. (1967) *Developing Vocational Instruction*, Fearon.

MAGER, R. F. and PIPE,. P. (1970) *Analysing Performance Problems*, Fearon.

MILLER, R. B. (1962) "Analysis and Specification of Behaviour for Training", in Glaser, R. *Training Research and Education*, Science edition, Wiley.

NEILL, A. S. (1962) *Summerhill*, Gollancz.

NOAR, G. (1972) *Individualised Instruction: Every Child a Winner*, Wiley.

OAKESHOTT, M. (1962) "Political Education", in Oakeshott, M. *Rationalism in Politics*, Methuen.

ODIORNE, G. S. (1965) *Management by Objectives*, Pitman.

ODIORNE, G. S. (1970) *Training by Objectives*, Macmillan.

OZBEKHAN, H. (1969) "Toward a General Theory of Planning", in Jantsch, E. (ed.) *Perspectives of Planning*, Organisation for Economic Co-operation and Development.

OZBEKHAN, H. (1971) "Planning and Human Action", in Weiss, P. (ed.) *Hierarchically Organised Systems in Theory and Practice*, Hafner.

PASK, G. (1972a) "A Fresh Look at Cognition and the Individual", *International Journal of Man-Machine Studies*, 4, pp. 211–16.

PASK, G. (1972b) "CASTE: A System for Exhibiting Learning Strategies and Regulating Uncertainty", *International Journal of Man-Machine Studies*.

PASK, G. and SCOTT, B. C. E. (1972) "Learning Strategies and Individual Competence", *International Journal of Man-Machine Studies*, 4, pp. 217–53.

POPHAM, W. J. and BAKER, E. L. (1970a) *Systematic Instruction*, Prentice-Hall.

POPHAM, W. J. and BAKER, E. L. (1970b) *Establishing Instructional Goals*, Prentice-Hall.

POPHAM, W. J., EISNER, E. W., SULLIVAN, H. J. and TYLER, L. L. (1969) *Instructional Objectives*, AERA Monographs on curriculum evaluation No. 3, Rand McNally.

POPPER, SIR K. R. (1945) *The Open Society and its Enemies*, Vol. I, *Plato*, Vol. II, *Hegel and Marx*, Routledge and Kegan Paul.

POPPER, SIR K. R. (1957) *The Poverty of Historicism*, Routledge and Kegan Paul.

187

POPPER, SIR K. R. (1972) "Epistemology without a Knowing Subject", in *Objective Knowledge*, Oxford University Press.

POSTMAN, N. and WEINGARTNER, C. (1969) *Teaching as a Subversive Activity*, Delacorte.

QUADE, E. S. (ed.) (1967) *Analysis for Military Decisions*, Rand McNally.

RAPOPORT, A. (1964) *Strategy and Conscience*, Harper and Row.

REIMER, E. (1971) *School is Dead*, Penguin.

ROSS, A. (1968) *Directives and Norms*, Routledge and Kegan Paul.

RYLE, G. (1949) *The Concept of Mind*, Hutchinson.

SEYMOUR, W. D. (1968) *Skills Analysis Training*, Pitman.

STENHOUSE, L. (1971) "Some Limitations of the Use of Objectives in Curriculum Research and Planning", *Paedagogica Europaea*.

STONES, E. and ANDERSON, D. (1972) *Educational Objectives and the Teaching of Educational Psychology*, Methuen.

SUND, R. S. and PICARD, A. J. (1972) *Behavioural Objectives and Evaluational Measures: Science and Mathematics*, Merrill.

TYLER, L. L. (1969) "A Case History: Formulation of Objectives from a Psychoanalytic Framework", in Popham, W. J. *et al. Instructional Objectives*, AFRA Monograph No. 3, Rand McNally.

TYLER, R. W. (1950) *Basic Principles of Curriculum and Instruction*, Chicago University Press.

TYLER, R. W. (1964) "Some Persistent Questions on the Defining of Objectives", in Lindvall, C. M. (ed.) *Defining Educational Objectives*, Pittsburgh University Press.

VARGAS, J. S. (1972) *Writing Worthwhile Behavioural Objectives*, Harper and Row.

VICKERS, SIR G. (1959) *The Undirected Society*, University of Toronto Press.

VICKERS, SIR G. (1965) *The Art of Judgment*, Chapman and Hall.

VICKERS, SIR G. (1967) *Towards a Sociology of Management*, Chapman and Hall.

VICKERS, SIR G. (1968) *Value Systems and Social Process*, Tavistock.

VICKERS, SIR G. (1970) *Freedom in a Rocking Boat*, Penguin.

WEISGERBER, R. A. (ed.) (1971a) *Developmental Efforts in Individualised Learning*, Peacock.

WEISGERBER, R. A. (1971b) *Perspectives in Individualised Learning*, Peacock.

VON WRIGHT, G. H. (1963) *Norm and Action*, Routledge and Kegan Paul.

2.4 Towards an Economic Theory of Higher Education

Maurice Peston

Although a great deal of empirical work concerning the British education system has been carried out during the past ten years, it is remarkable how little research has been carried out into the way individual institutions work and of how they are interrelated. It is also remarkable how few attempts there have been at analysis or at the provision of a pure theory of educational behaviour. We have a great deal of macro information concerning such things as social class and education, or national income and total expenditure on education. What we lack are explanatory theories either at the macro level or, more importantly, at the micro level involving the decision-making process and its outcome.

This is especially apparent to the economist because of the emphasis he places in micro-economics on the individual decision-maker, on his preferences and the constraints on his choices, on the existence of equilibrium and on the forces that bring equilibrium about. What I am offering here are the first steps of an attempt at a micro-analysis of the education system (or rather, more narrowly, of higher education) in the spirit, so to speak, of the normal methods of micro-economic theory. I am not, of course, asserting that the theories which the economist has developed to account for household and business behaviour carry over directly to other institutions and organizations. I am also not arguing that what happens in education is the product of economic forces, crudely understood. It is my view that the economist's questions are the relevant ones, and that the way he organizes his thinking is helpful in answering them. At the very least they offer a cockshy to be demolished by other forms of theorizing and with a different emphasis.

There are two preliminary points of a methodological nature that I must make. The first concerns terminology, and is much misunderstood by non-economists. The economist's language, although made up of ordinary words, is very much his own and is much more abstract than ordinary language. He uses words like "output" and "product" to refer to whatever it is that is being generated by an organization, and not simply to refer to goods and services produced by manufacturing businesses and

---

Source: *Higher Education Review* (1969), Vol. 1, No. 3, pp. 44–54.

similar institutions. Similarly, "demand" is not restricted in its applicability to any particular "outputs". Above all "price" and "cost" apply to the rate at which any things are substituted one for the other, and not just to what is expressible in money terms. In other words, economics, and especially micro-economics, is not merely about the economy as viewed by the inexpert layman, but applies to a much broader range of systems. It follows that in comparing one system with another or in analysing them jointly at an appropriate level of abstraction, I am not saying that they are very much alike at a lower level of abstraction or according to other criteria. A university can be like a firm in that it pursues certain objectives subject to various constraints, but it may differ from the firm in terms of its actual objectives or constraints or in all sorts of other detailed characteristics.

My second methodological point is that my emphasis is on discovering a positive, explanatory theory of behaviour rather than on presenting a normative evaluation of institutions. It is my opinion that too much work in this field is normative and pays excessive attention to schemes, policies, reforms, saying what is good or bad. While one's ultimate objective may be normative, it is unlikely to be achieved except on a solid foundation of positive analysis and research. (I have also noticed that many economists who make a great fuss about the value-free nature of their contributions to this field seem to lapse even the more readily into social criticism and recommendation of what ought to be done. I hope for once that this is a danger which I have avoided.)

In interpreting institutions we may first of all classify them in terms of their responsiveness to change. Institutions which are non-responsive or minimally responsive we call traditional. Institutions which are responsive we divide into two sorts, those responsive to consumer demands (or interests or preferences) and those responsive to producer demands (or interests or preferences). In the case of universities, for a long time in the past they are best interpreted as having been traditional. For most of their recent history they have been producer dominated. Increasingly they are becoming subjected to consumer demands. Producer domination is made up of two parts, the university teachers and the university administrators. As far as the United Kingdom is concerned one of the gaps in our knowledge relates to this division, namely, we do not know what the roles of teachers and administrators are in the decision-making process nor do we know their relative power. As a result we are unable to test such hypotheses as "the power of the administrators increases relative to that of the professors as the university gets larger and as its rate of growth increases".

The consumer demand is also made up of two parts. First, there are the direct beneficiaries of university education, the students themselves. Second, there is a wide spectrum of indirect beneficiaries ranging from the students' parents, at the one extreme, to the general taxpayer at the other. All of these are beneficiaries in the sense that the benefits of university education spill over to them in a variety of ways, and this, indeed, is one justification of state intervention and subsidy in higher education. Responsiveness to consumer demand may mean, therefore, either responsiveness to student demands or responsiveness to the broad demands of society, where the latter is presumably represented by the Department of Education and Science, the University Grants Committee (UGC), and other relevant public bodies.

In analysing responsiveness, a useful analogy can be drawn with some recent work of Kenneth Galbraith. He has endeavoured to account for the behaviour of some large business firms in terms of producer power to which consumers have to adapt or are made to adapt. The products of these firms are not devised simply to meet an externally given consumer demand, but are selected according to the preferences or needs of the producers.

Although it is an open question how far this analysis is applicable to businesses in the real world, it is not too far-fetched to say that it does seem a fair description of the behaviour of universities. The product (or product structure) is higher education in its various forms, and its nature and extent is determined by the producers, that is, the university teachers and administrators. The consumers may be thought of as comprising partly the direct beneficiaries of the education, the students, and partly the indirect beneficiaries, the remaining inhabitants of society. The producers have monopoly power based on their intrinsic ability to provide higher education, and on society's willingness to restrict the supply of university places below what would be demanded at existing prices.

Of course, this monopoly power is not unlimited, and varies between subjects and institutions. Even in the extreme interpretation of the Galbraith model there are limits to the extent to which the consumer can be manipulated, or his underlying preferences, if they exist, ignored. Galbraith himself has analysed the concept of "countervailing power" (represented in this case by the UGC and, perhaps, the National Union of Students). Apart from this universities do compete with each other in their desire to attract so-called good students. Nonetheless, it is difficult to reject the view that where university institutions are non-traditional, their response mechanism is geared as much to producer demand and authority as to consumer demand. It is important, therefore, to go into the question of what are the preferences of university teachers.

The obvious point to make about them is that they are multi-dimensional. Academic staff have some interest in teaching, in writing, in research, and in a wide variety of outside activities. (It is worth noting how many voluntary activities they engage in as a result of their university position.) Given complete freedom to choose they will allocate their time in an optimal way as far as they are concerned individually. This would probably lead to very great differences in the structure of activities between teachers. Also insofar as teaching for most people becomes irksome after very few hours the result would be to minimize the amount of teaching undertaken. Because the financial viability of the institution depends to a large extent on (publicly provided) funds for teaching, and because there are obvious institutional benefits in providing appropriate teaching, teachers are made to teach more than they would freely choose to do. In addition, if most teachers find their marginal teaching irksome, they will share out this burden using some type of internal social criterion of the sort that everybody teaches to the same extent or that reductions in teaching hours must be offset by increases in something equally irksome, namely, administration. I make the assumption in all my analysis that most teachers are teaching more than they would freely choose to do, in other words that the marginal utility of teaching is negative, and explore the consequences of that. It is perfectly possible for somebody else to analyse the consequences of the assumption that teaching is pleasurable at the margin, and even that people are generally being made to teach less than they want to.

If the flow of funds to a university depends to a considerable extent on the number of people it teaches and on the demand by students to come to it, the institution will respond even though teaching is irksome. Teaching is the price paid for the other benefits of being a university teacher or administrator. If it is true that good students are easier or more pleasurabe to teach than bad ones, universities will try and adapt by attracting such students. They will also be interested in growth. The reason for this is partly that there are economies of scale in teaching and research, so that the academic staff will expect to gain from growth. The administrator will expect to gain partly for reasons of prestige and partly because he may expect his promotion and salary prospects to be an increasing function of the size of organization to which he belongs.

There is not a great deal of evidence on what determines student demand to attend a particular department or a particular university or on what determines the UGC allocation of funds. Assume, however, that demand is a function of the quality of teaching, the prestige of the institution, the economic value of its degrees and so on. Assume also that in the long run the UGC allocates its funds according to the excess demand for places (that is, the number of students wishing to attend a particular department of a university relative to the existing number of places), and according to cost. If now any institution has any advantage compared with others it may expect an excess demand for places and in the short run be able to attract better students. Given the assumed response mechanism of the UGC it will expand, and if there are economies of scale its expansion will lead to further improvements. This will generate an even greater demand for places and enable even better students to be enrolled. It follows that up to a point and in the long run the postulated response mechanism of the UGC coupled with economies of scale leads to a situation of accelerated growth. At the same time it must also lead to a comparative decline in other institutions. This process could be halted, first, if according to some notions of balance or equity the UGC response mechanism was much more attenuated. Second, it could be halted if great size did not suit the preferences of administrators and academic staff. Third, it would be halted if after a point diminishing returns to scale occurred. My own view is that some halt to expansion derives from the activities of the UGC; but without a detailed study of the behaviour of that organization it is impossible to pronounce with any confidence on how important a factor that is. More important, as a restraint, are eventual diseconomies of scale and rising costs.

A few remarks are in order about economies of large scale in university teaching. The concept as economists have used it refers to costs varying less than proportionately to the scale of output, the quality of the commodity remaining constant. Not all commodities are producible under conditions of increasing returns to scale, and certain commodities, while exhibiting increasing returns up to a particular scale of output, may then show diminishing returns for larger scale. It may also be the case that while a particular commodity may not be producible under conditions of increasing returns to scale, a similar (perhaps, rather simplified) close substitute is.

I have argued already that universities must be regarded as multi-product institutions. Some of these products may be generated more cheaply in large departments than in small. This is obviously true of a great deal of research. Researchers able to specialize more narrowly but being a part of a group of people with similar and related interests may be expected to do better work than teachers having to cover a broad range of frequently dissimilar topics. As teachers these same people will show a greater mastery of their narrow fields to the benefit of the student interested in the coverage of these fields in depth. At the same time, almost by definition, their ability to provide a broader view will decline.

More obvious examples of the efficiency of large-scale operations lie in lectures, examination setting, and libraries. Over a very large range it makes no difference how many people listen to an individual lecture. Any number of students can sit the same examination. To guarantee a specific level of availability of any book means that the stock of books can vary less than proportionately to the number of students (a large department can have fewer books per student than a smaller one and yet its students will experience no greater degree of unavailability of books).

At the other extreme, just as activities in the economy at large geared precisely to the individual do not exhibit unlimited economies of scale, so much the same sort of thing may be expected in parts of higher education. Let me emphasize immediately that the point at issue is "unlimited" economies of scale. There are very few activities indeed which are uniformly more efficient the smaller the scale they are carried on. The bespoke tailor, the bespoke hairdresser, the bespoke dressmaker, etc., all increase in efficiency up to some scale of operation, especially up to the point where they can hire enough ancillary staff in order to concentrate on what they do best. Even the greatest surgeon works with a team.

It follows that even with education based on individual tuition it is possible for a department to be too small, so that expansion may lower costs without any decline in the attention paid to the personal requirements of each student. Indeed, it is by no means obvious that up to a large scale of operation diseconomies of scale need occur at all. If not all student needs are entirely personal, it is quite likely that departments can expand, achieving considerable economies connected with standardization and specialization, while still catering to individual requirements.

There is, however, one major source of diseconomy which although encompassed by economics is of a social kind, namely, that within any location the environment changes as the mass of activity within it increases. Whether the external impact of the mass on the individual (call it congestion, if you like) is regarded as a major social disutility depends on taste. To some people the mass university (just as the mass city) is a source of pleasure. To others it is a source of pain. Clearly, those who emphasize the existence of scale diseconomies within the field of higher education have this point in mind above all others.

In other words, the major diseconomy of large size is large size itself. If, however, it is university teachers who are the chief decision-makers here, the other disadvantage of large size is a change in product mix, and this is a state of affairs that is chosen to be brought about rather than what must inevitably happen. If some activities, lectures, classes, programmed learning and so on exhibit economies of scale these may be expanded relative to other activities, the *quantity* of teaching received by the student remaining the same while the number of teaching hours put in by the staff diminishes. This substitution effect may be at the expense of bespoke teaching and in favour of the research and other activities of the staff. The staff are not obliged to arrange their activities in this way. All the benefits of economies of scale could be placed on teaching either in terms of broader coverage, or greater depth, or increase in student numbers. Whether or not they are depends initially on the motivation of teachers and on the constraints of their activities.

Consider, therefore, the response of universities to any technical advance in teaching. Assume this is of a sort which enables some teaching activity to be undertaken using fewer hours of labour, and that whatever extra capital expense is increased is, at the social rate of discount, more than offset, by the lower labour cost (we are able to substitute physical capital for human capital). Universities will introduce this technical change if they have access to whatever funds are needed to finance it, and if these funds do not have to be taken from other activities which are more valuable still. In principle they might do this by reducing staff numbers. Alternatively, they may change the use of staff time, that is, they may change some of the teaching activities of the staff reducing the extent of teaching and adding to research time. Teachers who decide the quantity of their teaching according to their enjoyment of teaching will find in this new circumstance no reason to teach less. Other teachers who are teaching "for institutional reasons" more than they like will endeavour to take up as much as possible of the new available time for non-teaching activities. Teacher preference will be, therefore, to favour the technical advance insofar as it leaves them extra time for other things they would like to do.

Is this offset by competitive pressure between universities? The nature of competition as we have outlined it suggests that it is not. The nature and extent of competition between universities is, perhaps, the most important subject which comes into our field of interest, and yet it is at the same time the most neglected. There are a number of interesting normative questions concerning the desirability of competition in general or in any particular form, but this is not what I wish to discuss here. Instead, I want to look at the competitive or non-competitive situation as it actually exists.

Let us start by listing the ways in which universities might compete. Typically, in economics a distinction is made between price competition and non-price competition, between what commodity is offered and the terms on which it is offered. In addition, some economists have attempted to distinguish between the commodity itself and the general advertising and persuasion that go with it.

There is little, if any, explicit price competition between universities. Fees are nugatory and fall on virtually no students. Grants vary only moderately with respect to universities and are mainly determined by the parental situation. *Implicitly* the price charged may not be the same in all universities. The cost of living is not constant throughout the country and, therefore, the *real* value of grants will vary between universities. Some universites may subsidize their student accomodation and student meals more than others, and the greater provision of textbooks in libraries is also a subsidy as far as the student is concerned. Without further detailed research it is impossible to tell how important these differences are, whether they represent policies consciously pursued by universities, and whether students, in fact, respond to them.

Quality differences are, of course, enormous. (At least they appear to be enormous to the casual observer. I know of no published detailed study of such differences, not even for a single subject.) These differences occur in the structure of degrees, in what is taught, how it is taught, who teaches, how students are examined and evaluated, the environment in which teaching occurs, discipline, enjoyment, extra-curricular activities, staff-student mixing, and every other dimension of student life.

Universities in general and some of their departments in particular have "brand images" in the minds of students and of their employers. There are differences in the vocational impact between subjects and, given the subjects, between universities. The economic advantage of different degrees and of different universities is not the same. (There is an interesting problem that arises in connection with the economic value of education that is worth mentioning *en passant* at this point. One would guess that the immediate economic value of a degree varies widely by subject and by university. In my day it was generally believed, for example, that Oxbridge graduates got a disproportionately large share of the best job opportunities. What is not clear is whether those differences persist through time, or whether the exigencies of the economy lead gradually to choice in terms of the superficial biased image being cast aside in favour of the "real products" that lie behind. It may even be that the differences persist in some occupations and sectors of the economy but not in others.)

In a world of excess demand for university places and where existing universities possess great monopoly power these differences will reflect to some extent the preferences of the staff. Producer power, however, is not unlimited and, therefore, to some extent what is offered must correspond to consumer demand, and effort must be made to make consumers want what is offered. In addition, those institutions whose inherent advantages are less (they possess less monopoly power) will compete by responding relatively more to student demands. (In the short run this will obviously be the case with the polytechnics.)

Consider now what happens if students' preferences change so that they would like relatively more teaching. If universities act in concert (and there is no other competition from the polytechnics) there need be no response at all. University administrators meet together a great deal both formally and informally so that a considerable amount of collusive activity is to be expected; but it is unlikely they collude on all matters and the larger the number of universities and polytechnics the more difficult collusion becomes. In that case a university would be able to improve the quality of its applications by responding to the change in students' preferences. In particular, colleges and faculties closer to the competitive margin which are relatively less popular will respond more strongly while others with greater monopoly power will not respond at all. It cannot be argued for these reasons that there will be no response at all.

Consider also what happens if students' preferences between subjects change. This is an extremely complicated problem and another aspect of it is dealt with towards the end of this essay. Here I wish merely to mention how departments, the demand for whose facilities is falling, may respond. In the short run the capacity of these departments is given, and the long run in which this capacity can be reduced may be very long indeed. This means that one likely response is an increase in the marketing activities of these departments. By advertising in various ways, by the issue of elaborate brochures, by organizing conferences of school-children, they will endeavour to create a demand so as to justify their existing staff, equipment and building. In other words, the response is not so much to an externally given demand, but in order to generate a demand.

What obviously limits universities' responsiveness even under competitive conditions are the objectives and market position of the staff. Response to student demands for interesting and enjoyable teaching at the university, which also has economic and non-economic value later on, may benefit the institution in general and in the long run by raising the quality of entrants; but it is much less likely to benefit the individual university teacher, especially in the shorter·run which he may find more relevant to his career. The reason is very simple that teaching ability and responsiveness to demands is not a marketable commodity for the individual in the same way and to the extent that research ability coupled with publications is. This means that even where a university wishes to emphasize and reward non-research activities, it will find it hard to do so, just as universities wishing to recruit appropriate staff for those purposes will equally find it difficult. It follows from this that if student demands to read a particular subject or to attend a particular university fall relatively, the optimum response for the individual teacher may not be to adapt to these changes. Instead, his own personal position may be enhanced by responding in the other direction, concentrating more on his own market value with a view eventually to moving elsewhere. (A possible prediction here is that staff nearing the end of their careers will not respond to student demands because the adverse consequences will occur only when they have retired. Similarly, very junior staff will be less responsive because of their greater mobility. Maximum responsiveness may be expected from established staff in the middle of their careers.)

Let us consider finally how the universities might respond to some change in the economy. Suppose the demand for engineers rises. This will reflect itself in higher salaries for engineers, accelerated promotion, improved facilities and a general increase in their lifetime earnings and conditions of work. This may be met in the short run by a transfer into engineering from related occupations, but, subject to the delays in interpreting the new trend and of the relevant information filtering through, an increase in demand for engineering places will eventually result.

This demand may possibly be met by expanding the number of engineering places. (If we were to suppose that the demand for all sorts of places were growing with supply expanding also, then what we are talking about is the expansion of the rate of expansion of engineering places. In either case we are discussing expansion relative to what would otherwise be the case.) It is by no means clear, however, that the UGC and the universities respond to demand in this way, at least in time periods less than two quinquennia. Instead their response in the shorter run may be qualitative rather than quantitative. This means that engineering faculties will start to take in superior students and the quality of engineering graduates will rise over time.

But what of the behaviour of university teachers of engineering in this new situation? It is at least possible that with an improved quality of undergraduate they will change their teaching somewhat, making it more academic, and thereby gaining greater personal satisfaction from their day-to-day activities. In other words, there will be a second quality change towards more academic and fundamental engineering.

The extra demand for engineering places will be partly a net addition to the aggregate demand for university places, but much of it may be expected to be a transfer of demand from related disciplines, competitive with engineering. The consequences of the switch of demand away from the natural sciences and possibly even from the social sciences must also be analysed, therefore.

It is tempting to argue that the consequences of a fall in demand are likely to be the converse of an increase in demand. It is worth noting, however, that a possible asymmetry may exist here, namely that while the major response to an increase in demand is qualitative, over the same time horizon a decrease in demand may be met chiefly by not filling available places. In other words, if an increase in demand for engineering places went hand in hand with a decrease in demand for physics places, there might be some tendency to lower the quality of entry to physics departments; but there would be a significant tendency to admit fewer students, the staff-student ratio improving and possibly the quality of the education of the remaining students being enhanced. (Incidentally, if it is the less academic students who switch from science to engineering the academic quality of the science graduates will also increase!)

Thus, the outcome of a change in one part of the economic system, via the short-term response mechanism of universities, may be a qualitative improvement in engineering graduates and a quantitative decline in science graduates. For it to occur at all requires that the demand for places be influenced by the economic factors under consideration. If demand is not influenced by the changing value of various qualifications in the economic system then there will be no adaptation by the universities at all. But what must be emphasized is that the adaptation, if it occurs, will be in terms of a qualitative response (desirable or otherwise) to what may be a quantitative demand. (It may also be noted that any faculty which is quite happy with the quality of its entry will not respond at all.)

In conclusion, I must emphasize once again that it has not been my intention in this article to provide a complete theory of the behaviour of the higher education system of this or any other country. There is obviously a great deal more to be said about the University Grants Committee and the Department of Education and Science. Equally the competitive and complementary relationships of the polytechnics to the established universities needs further exploration. It is also not a trivial point that the higher-education system is a sub-system of the whole of education, the demand for places at universities being strongly influenced by the activities of the secondary schools. In addition the universities are noteworthy in that they produce their own producers.

These and many other subjects await further exploration. I hope, however, that the examples I have given make clear the kind of theorizing I have in mind, its strengths and weaknesses, and the sort of questions which it is intended to answer. Some of them do have important policy consequences related to the future activities of the UGC and the DES. Of these I would most want to stress the rather peculiar, almost paradoxical responses to external forces that seem to emerge as quite distinct possibilities from the analysis as presented, and the significance here, as in other fields, of the speed of the response mechanism.

2.5 Accounting Information in Universities

M. A. Sims

At a time when Universities are increasingly being called upon to account to society for the vast amount of resources that they consume, and to justify more vigorously than ever before the continuance of their current standards of living, it is appropriate to examine the methods adopted for the presentation of financial information, and the extent to which format may influence major decisions regarding resource allocation within universities. The intention is to encourage efficiency in the use of resources in order that the amount of satisfaction gained can be maximised.

STEWARDSHIP VERSUS MANAGEMENT ACCOUNTING
University financial information systems are rarely sophisticated, for the reason that the "stewardship" function of university finance still tends to dominate any "management accounting" contribution to decision-making. But the recent quinquennial settlement indicates that universities may be placed in the position of having to continue existing activities on a level of financial support lower in real terms than that to which they have been accustomed. One consequence may be that finance officers will be increasingly concerned with problems of resource re-allocation under conditions of financial stringency such that expansion of innovation can only be financed by the contraction of existing activity. The stewardship function that finance officers have traditionally carried out will remain very important, but more attention will need to be given to the management accounting type of financial information that will become of increasing importance in the decision-making processes of universities.

FORMATS AND INFLUENCE
Before considering ways in which the information input to the decision-making process can be improved, it is appropriate to comment on existing practice. Almost all university budgets are currently produced in a "line-item" format, based on the grouping of aggregated transactions by subject of expenditure (e.g. academic salaries, technical salaries,

Source: *Higher Education Review* (1973), Vol. 5, No. 3, pp. 3–23.

materials, etc.) in a manner which facilitates and was originally inspired by concern for the stewardship function. Such financial statements provide few clues about the activities that are actually being carried on within the university, or the extent to which they are funded, and consequently attempts at effective planning of the balance of disposition of resources are conducted in an informational vacuum. Decision-makers' perceptions tend to be concentrated on items of expenditure rather than activities, and this influences the path which subsequent discussion of the available alternatives tends to follow. The subject of expenditure format may facilitate decision-making, since it is easier to gain agreement to a cut of £5,000 in expenditure on technical salaries than for a proposal to discontinue an activity such as the biophysics course. Subject of expenditure formats discourage discussion about whether or not particular "activities" should be developed or restrained and encourages concern with items most amenable to economy. The budgetary process is usually incremental in that provision is first made for the continuance of existing activities, and discussion then centres on the disposition of the remaining resources.

The format adopted by universities for their published annual accounts is largely determined by the classifications of expenditure required in the annual returns which must be made to the University Grants Committee (UGC). University accounting systems are geared to meet UGC requirements and internal needs of the university tend to be met by adaptation of that information, although the uses to which the information will be put in the two institutions are quite different.

THE IMPACT OF ALTERNATIVE FORMATS

Since they concentrate on subjects of expenditure rather than activities, traditional accounting formats offer little information as to the activities carried on within an institution. It should be possible in most universities to amend accounting routines so that in addition to cost control reports based on subjects of expenditure, descriptive statements identifying expenditure with activities are produced. Such descriptive statements should improve decision-makers' perceptions and encourage concentration on informed discussion of the level of resources devoted to each particular activity. Of course, the priorities attached to the various activities in competition for resources are discussed at present—but in most cases without any relevant information.

A suitable structure on which an activity accounting system could be based is shown in Table 1.

The intention is that objects of direct expenditure arising from "primary activities" should be allocated to those activities by school or department, with further analysis of expenditure between "sub-activities" where appropriate. Similarly, the "secondary activities" would be individually costed, but not allocated to school or department. Sug-

Table 1 University activity structure

Primary activities			
1 Undergraduate teaching	2 Postgraduate teaching	3 Research	4 Public service

Which can be divided into the following "sub-activities":

(a) Lecture courses	(a) Lecture courses	(a) Action research	—
(b) Tutorials	(b) Tutorials	(b) Mission-oriented research	—
(c) Practical classes	(c) Practical classes	(c) Curiosity-oriented research	—

Secondary activities			
1 Student Support Services	2 Community Services	3 Library	4 Computing

Which can be divided into the following "sub-activities":

(a) Health service	(a) Site amenities	(a) Under-graduate texts	—
(b) Appointments service	(b) Sport and recreation	(b) Other texts	—
(c) Chaplaincy	(c) Catering	(c) Journals	—
		(d) Other	

gested bases on which expenditure heads might be allocated between activities are given in Appendix 1 (p. 212).

A simple illustration (using fictitious figures) of an activity format is shown below (Table 2). The figures will include expenditure from all sources, i.e. UGC grant, research grants and contracts, and Research Council training support grants.

The treatment of capital expenditure is considered in Appendix 1.

Such statements would complement the existing cost control statements, not replace them.

Activity accounting would invite explicit consideration of the allocation of resources between teaching and research. Most British universities allocate resources on the basis of staff/student ratios, without distinction between proportions allocated to teaching and research. It therefore follows that an increase in student numbers in a particular subject attracts resources which not only enable those students to be taught, but also facilitates a proportionate increase in research in that subject—without any discussion of the relative merits of increasing research in other subjects. This practice of non-discrimination between the research orientation of different subjects when allocating resources is supported by the traditional argument that teaching and research are complementary activities, and that any attempt to distinguish the resources spent on each of them is not only meaningless, but even harmful, in that it gives the impression that they are distinct activities in competition for resources. The tradition is reinforced by the practice of the UGC of not specifying the purposes for which the annual grant to each university is given, or the basis of its calculation.

It is acknowledged that the allocation of costs between teaching, research and other activities presents significant difficulties, particularly with regard to staff time. The problem of accounting for the allocation of an academic's time over major activities is well known, but it is desirable that the attempt should be made. Academic salary costs represent about 75 per cent of total academic expenditure, so that the result of any analysis is likely to be indicative of orders of magnitude rather than definitive as to avoidable costs. The Committee of Vice-Chancellors and Principals (CVCP) have recognised the importance of trying to identify the amount of time that academics spend on major activities by instituting their "Enquiry into the use of academic time", the results of which were published in February 1972. In the intro-

Table 2 Department of Physics financial year ended 31 July 1972: actual recurrent expenditure

£000s

Subject of expenditure	Primary activity Under-graduate teaching	Post-graduate teaching	Research	Public service
Academic salaries	37.6	5.4	110.0	18.2
Technical salaries	10.4	1.0	90.3	—
Secretarial salaries	3.5	0.5	7.5	—
Other recurrent expenses	5.0	1.0	60.0	—
Buildings maintenance	3.0	0.1	12.0	—
Direct administration	5.5	—	8.2	—
Total	65.0	8.0	288.0	18.2

Subactivity

Lecture courses	20.0	4.0	—	
Tutorials	30.0	4.0	—	
Practical classes	15.0	—	—	
Action-oriented research	—	—	80.0	
Mission-oriented research	—	—	120.0	
Curiosity-oriented research	—	—	88.0	
Total	65.0	8.0	288.0	

duction to the report of the enquiry it is stated that "though we feel a reasonable degree of confidence in the results here presented, we are also confirmed in our belief that there can be no clear cut division between teaching and research activities", indicating that the problem of "jointness" was fully recognised but that it was not felt to be detrimental to the overall results of the exercise.

The preferred operation of an activity accounting system requires that diary exercises such as that instituted by the CVCP would periodically be carried out (probably only every two or three years) in order to check whether there have been any significant changes in the distribution of time in particular categories of staff. Each staff category could be dealt with on a rota basis so that the burden of providing the information would not fall on academics regularly.

The results of exercises such as that of the CVCP make possible the allocation of salary costs over the broad areas of activity of undergraduate teaching, personal research, etc, but a practical difficulty may be encountered when trying to subdivide those costs over subsidiary activities like lecture courses or tutorials. In order to accomplish this latter objective either a more detailed diary of information would be required, including such items as time spent on preparation, marking, etc, or arbitrary assumptions would have to be made about the allocation of, say, the total sum for undergraduate teaching, between its various components. The former method is preferable provided that the benefit to be gained from the information outweighs the cost of collecting it.

Non-salary items of expenditure are more amenable to accurate analysis, and where a computer accounting system is operated the technical difficulties of organising the routine analysis of expenditure should not be great.

OBJECTIVES AND EVALUATION

Having established a system for the routine identification of resource inputs with activities, the logical next step is to relate those inputs to the respective outputs, but we run into a difficulty which is characteristic of the education system, namely the as yet unsolved problem of the measurement of output. It is easy enough to describe how many students have graduated each year and the class of their degrees, but can we measure change in the quality of a degree between one year and another? What measure shall we use to evaluate research: the number of papers published? the success with which external research funds are attracted? the number of research studentships awarded? Each of these factors offers some evidence about the general state of health of research activity within a university, but equally they are of little help in valuing outputs.

It is often argued that rational evaluation of activities demands prior specification of the objectives which are sought by those activities. For example, in a commercial organisation activities are usually judged by reference to the extent to which they contribute towards the maximisation of profits. In a university context the specification of objectives is a most difficult task. Because of the conflicting and changing values of faculty and students any statement of aims that was widely accepted would by definition be so vague and generalised as to be operationally useless for the purpose of evaluating performance.

If one accepts that the meaningful specification of objectives in a university is an almost impossible task, is it a necessary corollary that attempts to evaluate activities are doomed to failure? The absence of clearly defined objectives need not hinder evaluation if the problem is approached from a different viewpoint. By accurately describing the existing state ("what is"), and seeking to move incrementally towards a state offering greater utility ("what will result") by choosing from an identified set of feasible alternatives, it is possible to assess subjectively the extent to which the improved state has been achieved.

In the absence of any acceptable method of measuring educational outputs, it is suggested that information on inputs and outputs should be marshalled so as to assist rather than determine the basis of subjective evaluations. Information relating to periods of (say) five years should be displayed so that trends are illuminated and questions begged rather than answered. For example, an apparent decrease in the wastage rate of undergraduate students might link in with information that the median A level results of new intakes had not altered over the period, and that an increasing proportion of resources had been devoted to undergraduate teaching. The initial and intuitive conclusion might be drawn that a policy of diverting more resources into undergraduate teaching had been repaid by an increasing proportion of students benefitting from a university education (as measured by their examination results). But that same information ought on reflection to beg the question—have examination standards fallen during the period? In this way the subjective evaluation of activities is encouraged and facilitated without measuring the extent to which they contribute towards the achievement of predetermined objectives. An example of the information that could usefully be gathered together in respect of departments, faculties or schools is shown in Appendix 2 (p. 217).

MARGINAL COSTS
While acknowledging that financial information presented in activity accounting formats would represent a worthwhile addition to the aids for decision-makers, it is clear that such information is not necessarily relevant to the whole range of problems that face them. An activity accounting statement will usually be based on historic costs, and although this is useful for relating the overall distribution of resources between activities, and for comparing the costs of faculties and subject groups, it is not of much help in assessing, for example, the resource implications of introducing a new major subject which implies an expansion of student intakes. For this purpose the decision-maker is interested not in historic

average costs but the costs necessarily incurred on the project, including the extent to which currently under-used resources can be absorbed. Because there will often be under-used resources available such as faculty time and teaching space, and because new faculty members tend to be appointed towards the bottom of a salary scale, the "marginal" cost of teaching additional students will often be lower than average cost, and it would therefore be misleading to use historic average cost information for decisions of this type. In order to present meaningful information on marginal costs it is necessary to have available information on staff teaching loads, space utilisation patterns, etc. An appropriate procedure for the identification of marginal costs would be for an administrator with knowledge of the required staff and facility inputs to prepare a preliminary version of the costs involved in an expansion proposal, and, using this as a basis for discussion, to work through the various expense categories with the department head and thus achieve an agreed statement of the likely costs involved.[1]

An activity accounting system can, however, have a significant impact on the ease with which information about marginal costs can be gathered, particularly if sub-activities such as major subjects or lecture courses are used, since the routine allocation of costs to such activities will facilitate and make more accurate the estimates of costs associated with new developments. Similarly, the assessment of resources released by the cessation of an activity is aided by this system.

One consideration which distorts the accuracy of costing development proposals in teaching is that when a university lecturer is engaged he expects, and is expected, to devote a significant proportion of his time to research, and the decision to hire a lecturer to teach a new course automatically implies that a proportionate input to the research of that subject is acquired whether or not it is deemed to be the most appropriate area for development. This is one of the problems arising from the "jointness" of roles of a lecturer.

OTHER POSSIBLE DEVELOPMENTS

The reference to allocation of expenditure to activities could be construed as a first step towards the introduction of a system akin to PPBS (Planning, Programming and Budgeting System), and although this is not strictly the intention, it is the case that the recommended changes in information presentation do prepare the way for adoption of some of the principles inherent in PPBS. By focusing accounting information on activities it is hoped to improve the perceptions and the perspective of decision-makers so that they concentrate on the relative distribution of resources between activities, and also be more concerned than at present with the overall pattern of activities. Given the difficulty of specifying university objectives as previously described, a full PPBS system would be inappropriate since it requires that objectives and activities should be related. But one of the other planks of the PPBS system can and should be adopted, that is, the identification and vigorous analysis of substitutive and alternative courses of action and their consequences, the difference being that instead of seeing these alternatives in the light of ultimate objectives we regard them in relation to an incremental improvement in the stock of activities. Perhaps the greatest difficulty in introducing even a modified form of PPBS would be the structural change needed in the organisation in order that it become "activity"-oriented and evaluation conscious. An activity-based structure would very much cut across the existing school or departmental boundaries, and the traditional departmental control of budgets might perhaps be replaced by a system whereby a budget for "science undergraduate teaching" would be administered by a "dean of science undergraduate teaching" who would have responsibility for the co-ordination, integration and development of undergraduate curricula and teaching methods. Such a redistribution of power would almost certainly meet with opposition, but is by no means inconceivable.

PPBS in its "text book" form does involve a significant realignment of political influence, and since universities are political institutions, any attempt to introduce PPBS or any of its precepts should be approached with caution. The traumatic effects resulting from the sudden (rather than phased) introduction of radical organisational changes threaten the unity of an institution. Such a system should be introduced stage by stage, *after* the political climate has been prepared to accept the change. Certainly, at a time when the organisational and decision-making structures within universities are being closely scrutinised by both internal and external observers, it would seem inappropriate even to consider the introduction of such a system without first testing all shades of opinion. Hyneman's reference to changes in governmental structures at national level can be applied admirably to the university scene (the words in brackets are introduced by the present writer):

A nation (university) that is devoted to democratic government should, to the extent possible, forgo revolutionary change in favour of gradual adaptation; ... a quick installation of fundamental changes, even when we are caught flat-footed by the deficiencies of existing arrangements, is likely to defeat the very purposes which caused it to be advocated. The people (students, faculty, other university workers, the general public), who must ultimately indicate their satisfaction or discontent with the way things are going, can only do so with confidence if they feel at home among the institutions available to them for exerting influence. If fundamental understanding about the forms and methods are upset, the people will flounder in their efforts to participate in political life [Hyneman (1950)].

The adaptation of PPBS to the higher education sector is claimed to help faculty, students and administrators by improving understanding of their organisation, providing better estimates of the impacts of various decisions, organising and systematising institutional information, and encouraging a more comprehensive view of the institution. The major requirement of PPBS which requires modification in order that the system can be considered for application to higher education is the specification of institutional objectives. One of the factors contributing to the past stability of higher education institutions may be that the absence of articulation of objectives has enabled members of those institutions to aim for personal goals without feeling that they were in conflict with institutional objectives. And since the responsible management of such an institution rests on the ability to maintain a balance between the personal contribution required from each participant and the climate within which he feels he can work towards his personal goals, any attempt to define specific objectives might result in the alienation from effective participation of those members who felt their own goals to be at odds with those of the university.

ADMINISTRATIVE NEUTRALITY AND ROLE CONFLICT

If it is accepted that the information available can significantly influence the actions of decision-makers,[2] it follows that the compiler of information is in a potentially powerful position insofar as he could attempt to influence matters by presenting information in a manner calculated to encourage decisions matching his own preferences. In a university context the overt exercise of that kind of influence is unusual because university administrators are traditionally expected to adopt a 'civil servant' role in policy formation processes, and are usually only involved in an advisory capacity. The acceptance of this role implies that information presented to decision-making forums be strictly neutral, in the sense that it is not selected to favour one particular course of action and that the various alternatives open to decision-makers are equally and exhaustively described. However, even within this defined role the financial administrator·must inevitably exercise his judgement and bring his perceptions to bear in deciding what information is relevant and how it is to be presented. Since it is typically impossible to describe all the various alternative courses of action available in respect of a given problem the administrator must select those which in his judgement are most feasible in the circumstances. Similarly, he cannot describe all the consequences of the alternatives that he has selected, and consequently limits description to those that he considers most relevant. It can be seen that by this process of selection the administrator inevitably influences decision-making.

It must also be acknowledged that there is an element of role conflict in the jobs to be performed by most university administrators and not least by finance officers. On the one hand, they should be the providers of objective and unbiased information (within the constraints mentioned above), and on the other are often required to give specialist advice as to which course is most wise to follow, given knowledge of external financial systems. The demand for specialist advice in the fields of finance, data processing, planning, etc., has led to the employment by universities of professional administrators who are expected to take the initiative in the resolution of problems falling within their specialisms. This development may have been expected to change the traditional "civil servant" stance adopted by administrators in favour of one of overt involvement in general policy formulation, with a consequent reduction in the influence of the academic body in this area. This has not come about because the academic body has challenged the advice of its specialist advisers from time to time, and because the influence of the university council has waned following the transfer of the function of giving specialist advice from its lay members to professional administrators employed by the university, thereby increasing the relative influence of the supreme academic body, the senate.

CONFIDENCE

People will only allow information to influence their actions if they have faith in its reliability and the objectivity of the person who prepared it. This emphasises the importance of the efficiency with which routine accounting functions are seen to operate. If academics regularly experience irritating deficiencies in basic procedures, they may be less inclined to be influenced by information prepared by persons they associate with inefficient systems. Further, if an administrator is seen to be a politically active person, always striving to bring his own views to bear in matters of policy formulation, it is unlikely that any information introduced by him into the decision-making process will be accepted as being impartial. It will be thought to be biased towards his own preference in a given situation, and is therefore liable to be rejected by decision-makers who do not agree with that point of view!

It is essential that administrators should be sensitive to the factors which affect the usefulness of their reports, and that they should foster the conditions within which that usefulness can be maximised.

It does seem that the dual pressure on universities to be more efficient in the management of their resources, and to exercise more selectivity in the activities which they finance, can only mean that financial administrators will become increasingly involved in top level policy discussions. Of particular importance in this respect is the need to ensure that the users' perception of the "message" contained in financial statements will be the same as that of the person who prepared them.

WHAT IS "RELEVANT" INFORMATION?

An approach to the relevance of information is proposed by Sterling (1972) who suggests that information should be relevant to a "rational decision model" rather than to the needs of the decision-makers. He says

> The accounting system cannot supply all the information desired by all the decision-makers and, therefore, we must decide to exclude some kinds of information and to include other kinds. Restricting the decision models to rational ones permits the exclusion of a raft of data based upon the whims of decision-makers. It permits us to concentrate on those models that have been demonstrated to be effective in achieving the decision-makers' goals. Information specified by decision models may be classified as alternatives, consequences and preferences. Excluding information about preferences, on the grounds that the decision-makers already possess this information, permits us to concentrate on supplying information concerning the definition of feasible alternatives and the prediction of consequences.

This statement when applied in a university context raises the questions of what is a rational decision model and who are the decision-makers.

The unique nature of the university as an institution is characterised by the fact that in its decision-making process economic rationality is, properly, subordinated to political rationality. That is, in comparison with commercial organisations, the objectives of a university cannot be compressed into a brief economic statement such as "the maximisation of profits": rather, its objective is the preservation of a slowly changing pattern of values in which competing preferences collide in political debate to produce policy. In seeking to introduce more meaningful accounting information into such a politically rational decision-making process, so that more efficient use may be made of available resources, a "rational decision model" can be regarded as one which will enable decision-makers to achieve their goals by aiming for the congruence of political and economic rationality.

The question of the decision-makers is a vexed one in universities today. Traditionally, professors and heads of departments have been the decision-makers, since they have generally dominated the committee system through which most of the major decisions affecting a university are made. There is, however, a definite contemporary shift towards a broadening of the power base within the committee system, following demands from students and junior members of faculty, and even in some cases from technical and other support staffs. These demands appear to originate from fairly specific issues, for example, the provision of residential accommodation or the contents of confidential files, but once the issue is settled the process by which the disputed decision was taken is called into question, and the previous distribution of power is threatened. The rallying call of those who wish to see a wider and more effective participation in decision-making is that the people who are affected by a decision should be involved in the process by which that decision is reached. This attractive proposition invites rejection by conservatism inherent in the governmental structures of a university, which would not approve a scheme which by definition would admit students to active participation in all decision-making forums (because all decisions in a university could be said to affect students). But reasonable consideration of the consequences of implementation of the tenet in certain spheres of a university's activity might be repaid by a realisation of the useful role that students can play therein.

Increasing acknowledgement is being given to the right of students to be involved in decisions relating to community services such as catering, student residences and so on, but that acknowledgement rarely extends to the detail of academic matters. Students are increasingly involved in discussions about curriculum development, assessment methods and other academic affairs, and sometimes have minor representation on academic committees, but the final decisions in these matters are invariably reserved to their academic peers.

IDENTIFYING ECONOMICALLY RATIONAL DECISIONS WHICH ACCORD WITH POLITICALLY DETERMINED POLICY

The "rational model" into which our relevant information is to be introduced is, therefore, one in which it is necessary to acknowledge that in order for the most economic use to be made of resources, the political forces influencing such an exercise must be recognised, accepted and kept in mind in deciding the content and format of the information to be introduced. The information will be concerned with alternatives and their consequences, and, in seeking to achieve the most economic use of resources, it is suggested that administrators should include among those alternatives some solutions which aim at reconciling the needs of economic and political rationality. For example, in conditions of unfilled capacity and increasing applications for undergraduate places in a university, the economically rational reaction would be to admit students until the spare capacity is filled. Now, if it is suspected that in the distribution of the quinquennial settlement the UGC will rely heavily on existing average unit costs, the admission of further students would be detrimental in the politically rational sense since it would potentially reduce the portion of the quinquennial cake that the university would receive. Among the alternatives presented in this case the administrator should include one which would reconcile the conflicting views, perhaps by suggesting that some additional students could be taken, but only in those subjects where the institutional unit costs are much higher than the national level.

CONCLUSION

Our opinion is that increased emphasis must be given to the management accounting aspect of financial information, and that one way to achieve this is by accounting for activities. The anticipated changes in attitudes of decision-makers arising from "activity accounting" should pave the way for subsequent introduction of some of the elements of PPBS which can be adapted for use in institutions of higher education. By giving increased attention to activities and the pattern of resource allocation between them, and by the analysis of alternatives and their consequences, it is possible to create a capacity for improved resource allocation decisions.

In summary it is asserted that universities are institutions in which there is a proper and constant collision and conversion of values (in the philosophical sense), such that it is impracticable to specify corporate objectives as a preliminary to attempts to evaluate "performance" which in any case is not susceptible to valuation (in the economic sense). That does not excuse lack of attempt to exercise judgement and informed discrimination. Quantification is not the opposite of subjectivity. Even without quantification it is possible, indeed inevitable, that subjective judgements will be facilitated by a flow of objective information.

By acting upon the relevance and accuracy of information flowing to decision-makers it is possible to create a capacity for improved economic rationality in decisions, but it is not possible to guarantee that decisions will be more economically rational. That is what is meant by asserting that a university is a politically rational institution in which economic rationality is properly subordinated to a political policy-making process.

APPENDIX 1

The allocation of expenditure to activities
The allocation of expenditure over activities is a difficult task in the university setting because there are no clear cut boundaries between the interdependent activities of teaching and research. However, sufficient differentiation exists to enable a worthwhile attempt at allocation to be made. The secondary activities, listed in Table 1 are quite discrete, and the allocation of expenditure to them can be achieved with some accuracy.

The definition of the secondary activities is self evident, but the primary activities are based on the descriptions used in the CVCP Report (1972).

The activity structure shown in the paper includes suggested headings over which the costs allocated to primary and secondary activities could be further subdivided. It should be noted, however, that the necessary degree of "arbitrariness" involved in the allocation of expenditure to main activities will be compounded in further sub-division, and any results obtained should be used with due caution. This applies particularly to the sub-activities of undergraduate and postgraduate teaching where the main cost component is faculty time.

A scheme by which the various heads of expenditure can be allocated over expenditure is as follows:

1 Academic salaries

These costs comprise more than 75 per cent of academic recurrent expenditure, but in many ways are the most difficult to allocate. The results of the CVCP Report, to be repeated on a five-yearly basis, are the most convenient data to use for expenditure allocation purposes. Each university is advised of the proportion of total time and the actual number of hours spent on each of five activities, broken down according to UGC-defined subject groups. The five activities are: undergraduate teaching, graduate course work, graduate research, personal research, and external professional, with a separate category for unallocable internal time, such as background reading, etc. This information can be used to make initial allocations to activities, but is not of much help in subdividing the activity costs to sub-activities.

With regard to the undergraduate sub-activities it is possible to build up the salary costs attributable to lecture courses, tutorials and practical classes by using course schedules, which give details of the frequency and length of lectures, tutorials, etc., and hourly rates of salary expenditure derived either as an overall rate for each subject group, or an individual rate for the lecturer concerned with each course. In calculating these hourly rates it should be remembered that part of the salary bill will have been put down to "unallocable internal time" and that a grossing-up adjustment should be made in order that the full cost is recovered in the hourly rate. The total time associated with each lecture or tutorial should be not only for that delivery but also preparation and essay marking, etc. These additions to basic delivery time should preferably be determined on the basis of observation rather than guess work.

The aggregation of salary costs attributable to undergraduate sub-activities will not total to the sum allocated for the undergraduate "main" activity since this will have included elements of examining, committee work, admissions work, etc., for which separate sub-activities will not have been established. The difference between the two must be assumed to refer to these other uncosted items.

Those universities which prefer to improve upon the quinquennial CVCP time survey will presumably conduct intermediate surveys of their own, possibly on a selective basis, and possibly with the intention of obtaining greater analysis in order that activities such as examining, committee work and so on can be separately identified. Such an exercise will be necessary if the accurate identification of the costs attributable to sub-activities is required.

The subdivision of that part of salary costs applicable to research over the sub-activities listed in the chart presents perhaps the greatest difficulty so far encountered. If the figures are to have any relation to reality it seems inescapable that a register of all research projects in progress will have to be maintained. It should not be too difficult to classify externally financed grants over the headings of action, mission and curiosity-oriented research, and the direct costs associated with each project can be easily identified since they are usually recorded separately in order that expenditure can be reclaimed from the grant awarding body. It is not usual to isolate the costs in respect of internally financed projects, but if accurate information is required then an extension of the system that already exists for externally financed projects will be required. Assuming that the identification and classification of all projects can be achieved it still remains for each faculty member to state how much of his research time is spent on each of the projects, and in this way the meaningful allocation of costs to sub-activities can be arranged.

As with undergraduate expenditure, the aggregation of research sub-activity costs will not total to research "main" activity costs, since there will have been other background items included in the main activity costs.

2   Technical salaries

The salaries of technical staff are more amenable to precise allocation over activities than those of academic staff. For the undergraduate activities the main component will be the salaries of those technicians who man the teaching laboratories and those who provide ancillary services exclusively for the teaching function. In most cases it should be possible to identify the individuals concerned and allocate their salaries accordingly.

Similarly with research: the individuals concerned can be specifically identified as working in research laboratories and ancillary services, but the difficulty will come with allocation to sub-activities. Externally financed technicians usually work on specific contracts and can therefore easily be slotted into one of the sub-activities, but UGC financed technicians may well work on a number of projects and it would therefore be necessary to analyse the time of each individual in order to make accurate subdivisions.

There will also be some technicians who provide central services such as glass blowing, photography, etc., and in these cases it will be necessary for individual analyses of their time to be made.

A recent development which will assist the allocation of technical staff costs over activities is the restructuring exercise carried out in respect of technicians' pay, grading and conditions of service. The Manual of Implementation in respect of the scheme describes fifty or so "benchmark" job specifications which are intended to cover the majority of jobs undertaken by technicians, and by attention being focused on job content in the future this will presumably assist the exercise of allocating costs to activities.

3   Secretarial clerical staff

There will be certain secretarial staff associated with schools or departments whose range of duties will be sufficiently restricted to enable the easy allocation of their salaries. Most staff in this category will however probably be associated with the work of one or two members of faculty, and the most reasonable basis on which to allocate their salaries is in the same proportions as that of the members of faculty for whom they work.

4 Other recurrent expenditure

Included under this heading are purchases of materials, chemicals, books, etc., travelling expenses, equipment maintenance and so on. With a computerised system each purchase order or expense claim form can be coded according to the activity and sub-activity to which it refers, and most items should be susceptible to straightforward classification in this way. The only difficulty arising in this category may be in the bulk purchase of materials or chemicals for a science store, which are subsequently issued for use over a period of time. The normal practice here would be for the initial purchase to be charged to the relevant store, and for individual issues to be recharged to the appropriate activity by means of a journal entry.

5 Building maintenance

This heading includes expenditure on repairs and maintenance of buildings and the wages of porters and cleaners. Allocation of this expenditure over activities can be achieved by using the space register which records the spatial details and use made of each room in a building. A total square footage can be attributed to each activity by analysing the room usage, and the expenditure can reasonably be allocated in the same proportions.

Lecture theatres and teaching laboratories will be automatically classified as undergraduate teaching space, and research laboratories as research space. Faculty rooms, and the rooms of the secretaries working for them, will be classified according to the individual time distributions of the faculty members concerned. Seminar rooms can be accurately allocated to activities by determining the pattern of usage from room time-tables. Other rooms which do not lend themselves to easy classification such as those housing typing pools or photocopying equipment must be allocated to activities on some arbitrary basis determined in the light of the particular circumstances of each case.

6 Direct administration

In those universities which have an administrative organisation based on devolution it is possible to apportion accurately the costs to activities. Faculty school or area-based administrative offices will usually carry out specific functions with which individual administrators and clerks can be identified, and cost allocation is therefore simplified.

A computerised accounting system will facilitate the month by month analysis of most of the costs described above. The distribution of academic, technical and secretarial salary costs on the above bases can be arranged by means of the computer programme for salaries. Other recurrent expenses are allocated on the occasion of each purchase. Sufficient information should also exist to enable the distribution of building and direct administration expenses to be determined in advance.

The secondary activities indicated in Table 1 are discrete entities and the direct costs associated with them are easily identified. A further sophistication can be achieved by re-allocating the costs associated with computing and the library to primary activities. On the assumption that computing work is carried out on the basis of a job scheduling system, it should not be difficult to ask users to indicate the activity category within which their jobs fall and thereby to build up a basis upon which the total costs of the computing centre can be allocated to primary activities. The accurate distribution of library costs presents more difficulty, and the method adopted will be somewhat arbitrary, since book purchases cannot be associated exclusively with the needs of one particular class of reader. A scheme is described by Khanna and Bottomley (1970) whereby points are allocated to staff and students in accordance with their assumed use of library services, and the point totals for each category are used for the purposes of cost allocation.

This Appendix has been concerned with the allocation of recurrent expenditure, but a significant portion of a university's total expenditure goes to provide buildings and equipment, and it may be helpful to include in financial statements such as that suggested on page 201 an item for the imputed rentals arising from the use of these facilities. It has been suggested that the "social opportunity cost" should be used for this purpose, that is, the cost of investing resources in universities rather than the next preferred alternative use (Bottomley et al., 1973). The intention of including such information is to bring home to users the social cost of the facilities at their disposal, in the hope that increased efficiency in the use of those facilities will be encouraged.

NOTES

1 A method of estimating the extent to which under-utilised resources are absorbed by expansion proposals is described in Bottomley et al. (1973).

2 For examples to support this assumption see Bruns and Coster (1969).

REFERENCES

BOTTOMLEY, J. A. et al. (1973) Costs and Potential Economies, Organisation for Economic Co-operation and Development.

BOTTOMLEY, J. A. and KHANNA, R. K. (1970) "Costs and Returns on Graduates of the University of Bradford", Accounting and Business Research, No. 1, Winter 1970.

BRUNS, W. J., Jnr. and DE COSTER, D. T. (1972) Accounting and Business Research, No. 7, Summer 1972.

COMMITTEE OF VICE–CHANCELLORS AND PRINCIPALS OF UNIVERSITIES OF THE UNITED KINGDOM (1972) Report of an Enquiry into the Use of Academic Staff Time.

HYNEMAN, C. S. (1950) Bureaucracy in a Democracy, Harper and Bros.

STERLING, R. S. (1972) "Decision Oriented Financial Accounting", Accounting and Business Research, No. 7, Summer 1972.

APPENDIX 2 *Annual record of activities for the Department of* .... (*period of return 5 years ended 31 July 1972*)

	1967–8	1968–9	1969–70	1970–1	1971–2
1 (a) Students—Undergraduate					
Applications					
% of total UCCA applications					
Actual intake					
Intake target					
Intake as % of applications					
Level of standard offer					
Median A levels of intake					
Transfers					
Net intake					
Graduates					
Wastage					
Other transfers					
Net intake 3 years ago					
Total population at 31 December					
(b) Students—Postgraduate					
Intake—course					
research					
Output—doctorates					
masters					
wastage					
Total population at 31 December					
Research Council studentships awarded					
(c) Students—Undergraduate and Postgraduate					
Total population at 31 December					
Student load (with P/Gs unweighted)					
Student load (with P/Gs weighted)					

217

Appendix 2 (continued)

	1967–8		1968–9		1969–70		1970–1		1971–2	
	U	O	U	O	U	O	U	O	U	O
2 Staff	*									
Academic staff at 31 December										
Staff who left in the year										
New staff taken on in the year										
Technical staff at 31 December										
Leavers in the year										
Starters in the year										
Clerical/secretarial staff										
Leavers in the year										
Starters in the year										
3 Student/Staff Ratio										
(Ratio of student load figures to UGC financed academic staff)										
With student load weighted										
With student load unweighted										

	1967–8		1968–9		1969–70		1970–1		1971–2	
	£	%	£	%	£	%	£	%	£	%
4 Finance	*									
(a) Recurrent										
Expenditure in each year on:										
Academic staff salaries										
Technical salaries										

Other academic expenses

Porters, cleaners and minor alterations

Total recurrent expenditure — 100 100 100 100 100 100 100 100 100 100 100

Annual percentages of total recurrent expenditure financed from UGC and non-UGC sources — — — — — — — — — — —

Balance in hand (overspent) on 31 July (UGC and PG support fund only) —

Total recurrent expenditure as above analysed by activity:
Undergraduate teaching
Postgraduate teaching
Research
External service 100 100 100 100 100 100 100 100 100 100 100

(b) *Capital*
UGC Capital grant
Balance as at 1 August — — — — — —
Annual allocation — — — — — —
Annual expenditure
Balance as at 31 July

Capital expenditure from other sources — — — — —

% of capital expenditure from other sources to total capital expenditure

* U = UGC grant; O = finance from other sources, e.g. research grants, etc.

2.6 Potential Economies of Scale at the University of Bradford

John Dunworth and Anthony Bottomley[1]

ABSTRACT

The paper applies output budgeting techniques to the "production" of graduates at a British University. The cost per student graduated in 18 different disciplines is first divided between: (1) capital and maintenance costs, (2) teaching costs, and (3) administrative and general expenditures. Techniques are devised so as to allocate expenditures under these heads to individual students. Examples are given to show that: (1) academic staff costs per student can be cut by about 30 per cent with a doubling of enrolment, and that (2) total costs per student in scientific disciplines can be reduced by up to 25 per cent through a more intensive use of laboratories with little or no deterioration in the quality of instruction or in staff workloads. By contrast, more efficient use of classroom hours and seats available shows much lower potential economies, as do changes in student contact hours, size of teaching group and range of optional subjects. The article is directed towards those concerned with planning university resource use.

INTRODUCTION

The rate of increase of student numbers in higher education has been remarkably steady since the beginning of the century in both England and Wales and the USA, with a doubling every 15 and 17 years respectively. However, there are now indications that the rate of increase is becoming greater. It has been calculated that in 15 West European and North American countries, the doubling period of total student enrolments in higher education in the period immediately prior to 1966 was, with only one exception, between 6–10 years (Edwards, 1971).

Thus there is nothing revolutionary in projections made by the UK Department of Education and Science which show the student population of British universities doubling to an estimated 394,000 in 1981. (DES, 1970, p. 22). Nevertheless, taxpayers may be startled by the absolute size of the financial commitment that this expansion would

Source: *Socio-economic Planning Sciences* (Feb. 1974), Vol. 8, No. 1, Pergamon Press, pp. 47–55.

involve—a rise in real expenditure in 1971–1972 from £300 million (including capital and current items and student maintenance), to an estimated £573 million (DES, 1970, p. 33). These same taxpayers may insist upon the possibility of a university education for their burgeoning families, but do they need to pay on this projected scale? Our work at Bradford seems to reveal that they do not.

To get this answer we have used the techniques of Output Budgeting; part of what the Americans call Planning Programming Budgeting Systems (PPBS). The methodology involves attributing the total cost of university operation to the units of the various outputs produced—first degree graduates by discipline, post-graduates and research. In this paper, however, we are concerned only with first degree graduates.

Any approach to attributing costs to particular courses is unavoidably complicated and open to criticism at every stage. In practice, virtually every resource used by the university contributes to more than one course and nearly all costs are, in one way or another, joint costs. Academic staff teach and pursue research; technical staff service teaching and research laboratories; classrooms, laboratories and items of equipment are used by students on different courses; materials are purchased on behalf of Schools of Studies and it is difficult to find the course for which they are ultimately used, and so on.

Nevertheless, we have tried to discover how each of these components contributes to the expense of producing each student in each discipline at the University of Bradford and to enumerate the potential economies which we believe are revealed.

We deal with: (1) the components of these costs per student (2) potential economies in academic staff costs and (3) potential economies in teaching accommodation costs.

COMPONENTS OF COST PER STUDENT

These components we classify as:

1 Capital and maintenance costs; 2 Teaching costs; 3 Administrative, library, student facility, general and miscellaneous costs.

Table 1 illustrates the way in which total cost per student for the various courses at Bradford is divided between the three classes of components.

Capital and maintenance costs represent an imputed rent for the use of classrooms, laboratories, libraries, office and student facility space, such as refectories and social facilities. The rent comprises annual interest at 7 per cent and amortization payments[2] over 50 years on the insured value of buildings and non-teaching equipment, together with maintenance costs. The annual cost of each building in the University is then allocated to the different kinds of room (classrooms, laboratories, offices, etc.) in proportion to the area that each type constitutes of the

Table 1 Total cost per student at the University of Bradford (1969–70)

Course	Capital and maintenance costs		Teaching costs		Administrative, library, student facility, general and misc. expenditure		Total cost per student
	£	% of total	£	% of total	£	% of total	£
Laboratory based courses							
Chemical engineering	908	35	1089	43	560	22	2557
Civil engineering	1030	41	956	38	523	21	2509
Electrical engineering	1278	36	1769	49	556	15	3603
Mechanical engineering	1768	44	1679	42	544	14	3991
Applied biology	849	27	1639	53	622	20	3110
Pharmacy	1446	44	1329	40	519	16	3294
Chemistry	1915	49	1332	34	627	17	3874
Colour chemistry	1888	48	1517	39	513	13	3918
Materials science	1134	31	1874	51	672	18	3680
Ophthalmic optics	1011	34	1484	49	504	17	2999
Applied physics	1375	36	1635	46	672	18	3682
Textile science	1245	40	1290	41	621	19	3156
Classroom-based courses							
Business studies	710	34	693	32	711	34	2114
Modern languages	818	34	748	32	820	34	2386
Social sciences	548	34	475	30	609	36	1632
Applied social studies	676	36	419	22	812	42	1907
Mathematics	907	39	744	33	656	28	2307
Statistics	563	31	613	35	599	34	1775

total usable area of the building, but with a weighting factor to allow for the greater cost of constructing laboratory space.

The annual cost of laboratories and classrooms was distributed over different undergraduates following different courses in proportion to their use by each of these students. This involved a detailed study of the timetables of teaching rooms and took full account of the use of space in one School of Studies by students from other Schools.

The cost of academic staff offices was distributed in direct proportion to the relative amounts of time devoted to various activities by members of staff. The division of staff time between undergraduate teaching and other activities, such as post-graduate teaching and personal research, was based on the results of a survey carried out in 1968 in which staff kept a diary of their activities for a term-time week.[3] The subsequent division between courses was based on a study of teaching timetables.

The cost of administrative offices and student facility space was divided equally over all students except those on "thin-sandwich" courses[4] who were weighted one half. The cost of library space was also divided equally over all students, but with post-graduates weighted two.

Teaching costs comprise academic and technical staff salaries, super-annuation and insurance, the annual value of teaching equipment, and expenditure on materials used in teaching. The cost of academic staff was divided in the way already described. The cost of technical staff was attributed to different courses in proportion to the relative areas of teaching and research laboratories, and of their use by different courses, since it was found that their number correlated closely with laboratory area per discipline.

Similar techiniques were employed with respect to the cost per student of staff, stock and equipment in the university administration, library, students' union, and so on.[5]

The results of the foregoing calculations for the academic year 1969–70 varied widely between different courses at the University of Bradford. Laboratory-based courses in science and engineering were considerably more expensive than classroom-based courses in social sciences (see Table 1). The cost of educating an undergraduate to first degree level in science or engineering ranged from £2509 in the lowest discipline to £3991 in the highest, as against £1632 to £2386 in different social science disciplines.

Annual capital and maintenance costs varied between 27–49 per cent of the cost of educating a student to first degree level, depending upon the course involved. Teaching costs were between 22–53 per cent of the total, while residual and miscellaneous expenditures ranged from 13–22 per cent of costs per student for laboratory-based courses, and 28–42 per cent for classroom-based courses.

The comparisons between laboratory-based and classroom-based courses were even more marked when overhead administration and other costs, which apply to all the University's students regardless of discipline,

Table 2 Directs costs per student at the University of Bradford (1969–70)

Course	Teaching space (1)		Academic staff (2)		Technical staff (3)		Secretarial staff plus offices (4)		Equipment and materials (5)		Total direct costs (6)	% of total cost (7)
	£	%	£	%	£	%	£	%	£	%	£	%
Laboratory-based courses												
Chem. eng.	580	32	617	34	204	11	128	7	268	15	1797	70
Civil eng.	613	37	458	28	240	14	93	6	258	15	1662	66
Elect. eng.	882	32	1073	38	352	14	144	4	344	12	2795	77
Mech. eng.	1388	44	981	31	452	14	120	3	240	8	3187	79
App. biology	416	19	946	43	339	15	145	7	354	16	2200	70
Pharmacy	1026	42	549	22	474	19	114	5	306	12	2469	75
Chemistry	1482	49	600	20	432	14	187	6	300	10	3001	77
Colour chem.	1465	47	785	25	432	14	156	5	300	9	3138	80
Mat. sci.	618	23	982	37	472	18	164	6	420	16	2656	70
Ophth. opt.	624	28	815	37	354	16	123	5	315	14	2231	74
App. physics	859	32	743	28	472	18	164	6	420	16	2658	72
Textile sci.	777	34	696	30	468	20	224	11	126	5	2291	73
Classroom-based courses												
Bus. studies	284	24	486	41	42	4	204	17	165	14	1181	56
Mod. lang.	258	22	624	53	64	5	176	15	60	5	1182	50
Soc. sci.	188	24	406	52	18	2	114	15	51	6	777	47
App. soc. stud.	116	17	327	49	24	4	136	20	68	10	671	35
Mathematics	339	27	652	52	0	0	172	14	92	7	1255	55
Statistics	126	14	544	62	0	0	144	16	69	8	883	50

were taken out of the calculations. Then direct costs per student in classroom-based courses ranged from only £671 to £1255 in the different social and mathematical sciences as against £1662 to £3187 in science and engineering. Table 2 shows the total direct cost per student for each course, and its principal components. The percentage figures measure the proportion which each component forms of total direct cost.

2 STAFF COST ECONOMIES

(a) *With increased enrolment*
It seems difficult to make economies in the foregoing cost components with present levels of student enrolment. Greater promise appears to lie in the possibility of reduced costs per student with the projected expansion in numbers over the next decade.

We, therefore, made detailed studies of the teaching structure of nine courses. This involved analysing for each course: (a) the annual contact hours, i.e. the number of hours teaching that a student receives each year; (b) the number of optional subjects embodied in the course, from which students may select a limited number; (c) the size of teaching groups regarded as educationally acceptable by the School of Studies; (d) the relative balance of lectures, classes, laboratory sessions and tutorials within the total contact hours.

From this data we calculated the total number of teaching meetings that must be provided at the present enrolment. We then postulated for each of nine courses successive increases in enrolment, by one student at a time, up to more than twice the present number, calculating the number of teaching meetings that must be provided at each level of enrolment on each course, if the appropriate professor's maxima regarding student numbers per type of meeting were observed. Assuming a constant staff teaching load, then the number of academic staff required, and therefore the total academic staff cost of the course, is directly related to the number of meetings. We next divided the number of meetings at each level of enrolment by the number of students to obtain the number of meetings provided per student and therefore the academic staff cost per student.

Figure 1 shows the proportionate change in academic staff cost per student as enrolment increases on the Civil Engineering course from its present annual intake of 66. For convenience it is expressed in index form with the value at the present enrolment equal to 100. We term this the Staff Cost Index.

For all the nine courses studied the Staff Cost Index exhibits the same form—falling as enrolment increases, but with periodic upward jumps corresponding to those levels of enrolment at which a series of teaching meetings must be duplicated because a laboratory class, seminar or tutorial reaches the maxima designated by the professors involved. The rate of fall, the points at which the jumps occur and the size of the jumps,

225

Figure 1 Academic staff cost per student

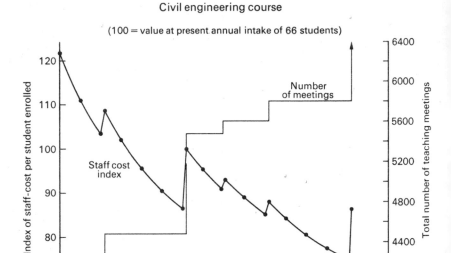

Civil engineering course

(100 = value at present annual intake of 66 students)

vary from course to course, but the pattern is similar. The moral is clear—if expansion is to occur it should be to a level of enrolment corresponding to a "trough" rather than a "peak" on the Staff Cost Index.

It seems that, for nine courses examined, the per student cost of providing teaching staff falls by a minimum of 18 per cent and a maximum of 48 per cent when enrolment is increased to the "trough" nearest to twice the present number. This saving in staff cost may be achieved without increasing the number of hours per week which each staff member teaches, or reducing the number of hours of instruction which each student receives. This may be done in spite of the fact that the size of seminars, tutorials and laboratory classes are held at a level which professors or their representatives think reasonable. In other words, these economies arise from expanding numbers in lectures where direct student–teacher exchanges do not normally take place. The average saving in total cost per student achieved by a carefully chosen approximate doubling of numbers, whilst maintaining existing course structures is 7.7 per cent through savings in staff costs alone. This implies that the overall UK weighted staff : student ratio could fall from its recent level of 1 : 11 to 1 : 16 without any apparent increase in teaching duties per staff member or deterioration in quality of instruction if the situation at Bradford is representative.[6]

We believe that serious study should be given to assessing the staff requirements for the proposed increase in student numbers on the basis of the number of additional teaching meetings generated, instead of by using a staff: student ratio. It would appear from our research that expansion, accompanied by a constant staff: student ratio and unchanged course structures, would mean a *reduction* in the average weekly teaching load of staff.

(b) *With existing enrolment and alternative course teaching structures*
By way of comparison, we calculated the total number of teaching meetings that would have to be provided for each of the nine courses at their present enrolments as the values of the parameters listed in Table 3 were varied. From the number of teaching meetings we calculated the number, and therefore the cost, of academic staff required and the consequent effect on total cost per student.

Taking the nine courses together and using the costs outlined in the previous section as a base, the following results were obtained. A 20 per cent reduction in contact hours per student caused average cost reductions per graduate of 5.1 per cent. A reduction by two in the range of optional subjects offered per degree course saved between 1 and 4.8 per cent of cost per graduate. Yet increasing the maximum size of teaching groups by 60 per cent did not reduce per student costs by more than 1.7 per cent on any but one of the courses examined. Similarly, replace-

Table 3 Changes in cost per student in Social Sciences in relation to changed course structures

Change in total contact hours (%)

	+40	+20	Present number	−20	−40	−60
Change in cost per student (%) (− = saving)	+11.4	+ 5.7	0	− 5.7	−11.4	−17.0

Number of optional subjects

	2 more	1 more	Present number	1 less	2 less	
Change in cost per student (%) (− = saving)	+ 3.7	+ 1.7	0	− 2.0	− 4.8	

Change in size of teaching group (%)

	−40	−20	0	+20	+40	+60
Change in cost per student (%) (− = saving)	+10.5	+ 5.0	0	− 3.7	− 4.5	− 5.7

ment of small tutorials by lectures and classes produced an average saving of only 2.7 per cent.

As an illustration, Table 3 represents some of the results obtained for the undergraduate course in Social Sciences.

It may be seen that the savings from any reasonable alteration in course structures at the present level of enrolment are considerably less than 7.7 per cent saving expected from a doubling of the number of students.

3   ECONOMIES IN TEACHING ACCOMMODATION COSTS

Space cost economies of scale exist as a result of what appears to have been a good deal of overbuilding at the University of Bradford in recent years. This probably also applies to a greater or lesser degree to the British university system as a whole.

The current situation in the courses we examined at Bradford is that teaching is taking place in laboratories for only 41 per cent of a 32-hr basic teaching week, and classrooms are in use for only 52 per cent of the time. Furthermore, in most Schools of Studies the teaching week consists of only 33 weeks a year.

(a) *Laboratories*

The cost of laboratories forms between 11–35 per cent of the total cost per student on science and engineering courses. Any economy of scale in this factor is to lead to a significant saving in total cost.

In the majority of the Schools studied, an increase in enrolment sufficient to bring laboratory use up to 80 per cent of a 32-hour week would reduce total costs per student by between 7–19 per cent. If this 80 per cent utilization were extended to a 60-hour week, the total cost per student could be reduced by 10–34 per cent of the present cost. Table 4 shows the reduction in cost per student with successive increases in laboratory utilization in each of five courses investigated.

However, there are a good many practical problems involved here in time tabling, setting up experiments and inducing academic staff to work outside the normal working week, even though the objections of the latter might be met by some supplement to salary provided out of productivity savings.

Furthermore, the increases in student numbers required to achieve 80 per cent or even 60 per cent frequency of use are considerably in excess of anything at present envisaged for the University of Bradford, or of the likely availability of suitable students.

The University is conscious of the apparent under-utilization of laboratories, and is at present conducting a large scale survey of laboratories in all Schools of Studies. This is attempting to measure the capacity of laboratories (the maximum number of students that could reasonably be accommodated at one time) their frequency of use, the number of students present when the laboratories are in use, and the

Table 4 Reduction in total cost-per-student in relation to increased laboratory utilization*

% Laboratory utilization and length of teaching week	Pharmacy Total cost per student £	% of existing cost	Colour chemistry £	%	Electrical eng. £	%	Applied biology £	%	Applied physics £	%
Existing	3294		3918		3703		3110		3682	
60% at 32 hr	2957	90	2802	71	3151	87	2999	96	3275	89
70% at 32 hr	2777	84	2737	70	3054	85	2917	94	3215	87
80% at 32 hr	2671	81	2694	69	2994	83	2885	93	3131	85
80% at 40 hr	2593	79	2649	68	2938	81	2837	91	3083	84
80% at 50 hr	2536	77	2613	67	2898	80	2816	90	3039	82
80% at 60 hr	2497	76	2586	66	2878	80	2801	90	3023	82

* This relates to greater frequency of use only. No account is taken in these figures of the proportion of places that are unoccupied when the laboratories are in use.

factors inhibiting improvements in their utilization. Preliminary results suggest that the frequency of use may be rather lower than the 41 per cent quoted above and indicate occupancy factors of 60–70 per cent when the laboratories are actually in use.

(b) *Classrooms and lecture theatres*

We went on to analyse the use of classrooms and lecture theatres in the main building of the university in terms of the frequency and occupancy factors.[7] This building is the University's largest and the level of its utilization is greater than that for the University's buildings as a whole. Nevertheless, its classrooms and lecture theatres were only used on average for 55.3 per cent of a 32-hour week. Even when rooms were in use, only 52.0 per cent of the available seats were occupied.

It is evident that considerable economies in cost per student year could be obtained if building design and timing were to be more closely related to academic plans. For example, Figure 2 shows the discrepancy between the size of rooms required and the capacity of the rooms available in the main building. Of a total of 619 meetings scheduled each week during the academic year 1971–72, 423 (69 per cent) were held in rooms within a

Figure 2 Room-hours available and meeting-hours occurring per week, analysed by size of room/meeting, 1971-2

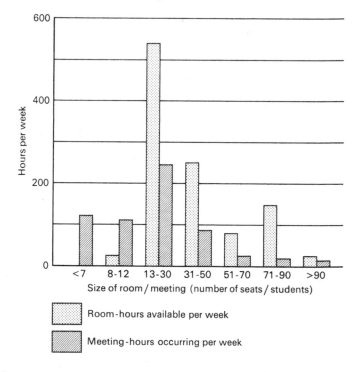

Table 5 Room requirements in the main building

Range of meeting size (No. of students)	No. of meetings of this size scheduled per week	No. of rooms required (with 66.7% frequency of use)	No. of rooms available
≤7	125	6	—
8–12	110	6	1
13–30	252	12	17
31–50	71	4	8
51–70	28	2	2
71–90	24	2	5
>90	9	1	1
Total	619	33*	34

* The total of 33 rooms required is an overestimate, as it is obtained after all the elements of the total have been rounded up to the nearest integer. If the elements are added to two decimal places, and the total rounded up, a figure of 29 is obtained. (Applying the 66.7 per cent directly to the 619 meetings also gives 29 rooms.)

greater size range than was actually required. More detailed analysis showed that 334 meetings (54 per cent) were held in rooms of more than twice the required size, including 142 (23 per cent) where the rooms were at least four times too big.

Table 5 shows the number of rooms of each size which are actually required assuming the 66.7 per cent frequency factor regarded as normal by the UK University Grants Committee (UGC) within our 32-hr week. A comparison of the last two columns shows the differences between the rooms actually available in the main building and those which were really required during the academic year 1971–72. As a result of this study, some of these surplus classrooms are being altered during the present vacation. Two of the 31–50 seat rooms and four of the 13–30 seat rooms are being converted into a total of seven 12-seat classrooms, five 7-seat tutorial rooms and seven staff offices. By rescheduling the small meetings in the new small rooms it is hoped to release a further three classrooms in the 13–50 seat ranges during the 1972–3 session for non-teaching uses.

Figure 3 further demonstrates how the aggravating factor of low seat-occupancy compounds the overall under-utilization arising from the low frequency of classroom usage. The situation varies widely at different hours of the day. Considerable potential economies of scale would there-fore exist with increases in enrolment which used classrooms and seats in accordance with the varying percentages of capacity detailed in Table 6 (p. 234), and which follows the pattern for potential laboratory use out-lined in Table 4 (p. 229).

It is again clear from Table 6 that costs per student-year at Bradford

Figure 3 Room and seat utilization in the main building by hour of day—1971–2

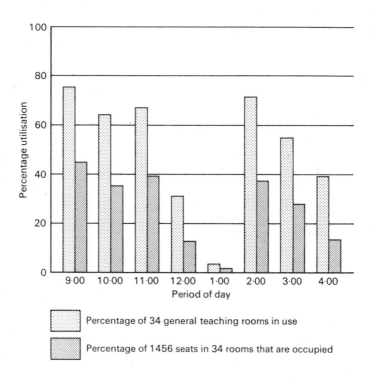

Percentage of 34 general teaching rooms in use

Percentage of 1456 seats in 34 rooms that are occupied

could be substantially reduced given the various postulated room *x* seat-occupancy factors. This might be achieved either by expanding enrolment on existing courses, or by transferring the surplus teaching accommodation to other uses or to new courses. It might, however, be difficult to get the precise required increment in student numbers in this respect or to time-table in accordance with the exigencies of an 80 per cent utilization factor. In any event, the reader may choose whatever percentage of capacity he thinks reasonable when identifying potential economies per student year from Table 6.

It might be argued that the 33-week working year is not sacrosanct, and it is clear that further economy would lie in using the buildings for 48, rather than 33 weeks per year. This could permit an intake of two groups of students per year. This is already done on several of the "thin-sandwich" courses at the University of Bradford, and doubling the throughput of students per year goes a long way towards cutting the cost.

We calculated the savings per student year in this respect with a conversion of what are now 33-week courses to two intakes over a 48-week year. The possible cost reductions range from 4–12 per cent with the pessimistic assumption that all costs other than for accommodation increase pro rata with the increase in student numbers. The greatest savings are, of course, in the laboratory-based courses. If, on the other hand, we optimistically assume that there will be no increase in library expenditures and student facility space and only a 50 per cent increase in technical staff expenditure, equipment and material costs, costs per student fall by between 18–24 per cent for laboratory-based and 15–19 per cent for classroom-based courses.

The savings from greater utilization of buildings either more intensively, or for more hours per week, or more weeks per year, are thus substantial. On the other hand, our investigations showed that any "reasonable" reduction in building standards and costs could not be expected to yield more than a small fraction of these sorts of savings. A 10 per cent reduction in the capital cost of buildings and non-teaching equipment, for instance, would result in reductions in total cost per student of only 1.7–3.1 per cent.

4 QUINQUENNIAL EXPANSION PLANS

Current expansion plans within the University confirm our view that considerable economies of scale exist. This was seen to be so when we costed the plans for six existing courses during the 1972–77 quinquennium. These costings were based on estimates of staff and other resource requirements made by professors or their representatives, and were in no way influenced by any of the potential economies identified by the research reported on above. It was calculated that, taken together, professors' proposals for a 66 per cent increase in student numbers on the six courses could be met with an increase in total costs of only 14 per cent. The cost of each additional student (the incremental cost) would be only 22 per cent of the present average cost, with the result that the average cost per student on these courses would fall by 31 per cent over the quinquennium. Figure 4 shows for each of the six proposals, the cost per student in 1969–70, and after expansion in 1976–77; and the incremental cost for each of the additional students. It is assumed that surplus accommodation is brought into use during the existing teaching hours and years, and that course structures remain the same. (Figure 4 p. 235.)

CONCLUSIONS

It seems that considerable potential economies of scale exist in higher education if the University of Bradford is in any way representative. If enrolment is doubled or thereabouts with present accommodation surpluses and course structures, then average costs per student may fall by between 11–38 per cent, depending upon the course involved and the

Table 6 Percentage saving in total cost per student in relation to improved utilization of classrooms

Percentage saving in total cost

Course	60% Freq.	32 hr week 70% Freq.	80% Freq.	40 hr week 80% Freq.	50 hr week 80% Freq.	60 hr week 80% Freq.
Chem. eng.	1.9	2.3	2.6	3.4	3.7	3.9
Civil eng.	3.8	4.1	4.4	5.0	5.2	5.3
Elec. eng.	1.7	2.0	2.2	2.7	2.9	3.0
Mech. eng.	1.3	1.6	1.9	2.8	3.0	3.2
Biology	0.9	1.2	1.3	1.8	1.9	2.0
Pharmacy	0.7	0.9	1.1	1.7	1.8	1.9
Chemistry	0.9	1.3	1.6	2.5	2.7	2.9
Colour chem.	1.8	2.1	2.2	2.6	2.7	2.8
Materials sci.	3.2	3.4	3.5	3.9	4.0	4.1
Oph. optics	0.5	0.9	1.1	1.8	2.0	2.2
App. physics	3.2	3.8	4.2	5.3	5.6	5.8
Mod. langs.	2.2	2.8	3.3	4.6	4.9	5.2
Social sci.	4.0	4.6	5.0	6.1	6.5	6.7
App. soc. stu.	2.3	2.8	3.2	4.4	4.7	4.9
Maths.	2.6	3.7	4.6	7.1	7.8	8.3
Statistics	1.7	2.5	3.0	4.7	5.2	5.5

An occupancy factor of 75% (i.e. the UGC norm) is assumed in all cases.

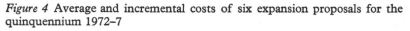

Figure 4 Average and incremental costs of six expansion proposals for the quinquennium 1972–7

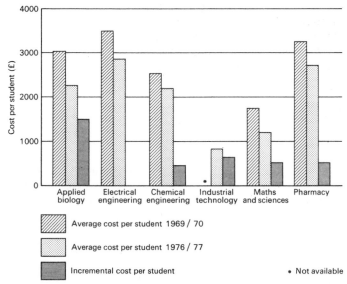

assumptions made. Further substantial cost reductions would arise with a course structure which handled two intakes a year.

It is evident that building plans have been sanctioned in a manner which fits university requirements more like a *sack* than a *glove*. Architects and academic planners should now be joined in providing tailor-made building programmes over time. Unfortunately, the universities themselves cannot be relied upon to do this. They have no incentive to economize on space-use where buildings are construed as free goods and no interest or amortization charges need to be carried by the individual institution.

We became increasingly aware during our research of such absence of built-in incentives to use resources efficiently. It was most obvious with buildings, but it was also the case in respect of current items of expenditure. Under the present system of British university financing and planning, universities know in advance, subject to certain specific exceptions, their income for a five-year period and the approximate number and type of students they will enrol. Thus cost per student over the quinquennium has been determined before the students enter. Once the quinquennium has begun, there are few real ways to effect economies, since revenue, and therefore expenditure, have already been determined. Nor is there any incentive for universities to cut costs per graduate. The critical time to achieve economies is therefore before quinquennial recurrent grants are fixed, and the power to do this lies with the University Grants Committee and the Department of Education and Science, not with individual universities. Thereafter, universities would need to react to such economies by implementing them as painlessly as possible.

Finally, we would emphasize that the nation would be getting the worst of both worlds if it reduced the projected rates of expansion mentioned at the outset, while roughly maintaining the present grant per student year. Fortunately, there are signs that this will not happen and the considerable economies of scale which we have here identified may, perforce, become of interest throughout the British university system.

NOTES

1 We are indebted to the following post-graduate students at the University of Bradford, upon whose work we here report: R. K. Khanna, R. M. Dasey, M. Pickford, R. E. Cooley and C. Barton. Abdul Khan and Aiden Duggan have also contributed to our work, but the usual disclaimers apply. The study was financed by the UK Department of Education and Science and the Organisation for Economic Co-operation and Development (OECD) and is published in English and French by the OECD (Dunworth and Bottomley, 1972). *Studies in Institutional Management in Higher Education—Costs and Potential Economies,* Centre for Educational Research and Innovation, Paris (1972).

2 Interest only is charged on the land upon which the building stands as it is assumed that it will not depreciate in value.

3 The allocation of staff vacation time was based upon the relevant section of the Robbins Report (1963).

4 A "thin-sandwich" course is one with two entries of students per year, arranged so that at any one time only half the students are present in the university, the remainder receiving practical training in industry.

5 For a detailed description of this methodology as applied to the earlier academic session of 1966–7, see Khanna and Bottomley (1970).

6 These conclusions are supported by the fact that on existing courses at the University of Bradford, teaching costs per student are inversely correlated with student numbers.

7 The frequency factor is the number of hours a room is used expressed as a proportion of the total hours available in the normal teaching week. The occupancy factor is the proportion of seats in a room that are occupied when the room is in use. For the University as a whole the frequency factor is 52.0 per cent, and the occupancy 46.6 per cent meaning that on average seats are occupied for only 7.75 hr of a 32-hr teaching week.

REFERENCES

DEPARTMENT OF EDUCATION AND SCIENCE (1970) *Student Numbers in Higher Education in England and Wales*, Educational Planning Paper No. 2, Table 10, HMSO.

DUNWORTH, J. and BOTTOMLEY, A. (1972) "Potential Economies of Scale at the University of Bradford", in *Studies in Institutional Management in Higher Education—Costs and Potential Economies*, Centre for Educational Research and Innovation, Organisation for Economic Co-operation and Development.

EDWARDS, E. G. (1971) in *History of Education Society, The Changing Curriculum*, p. 91, Methuen.

KHANNA, R. K. and BOTTOMLEY, A. (1970) "Costs and Returns on Graduates of the University of Bradford", *Accounting and Business Review*, 1.

ROBBINS COMMITTEE (1963) *Higher Education*, report of the Committee (Chairman: Lord Robbins) appointed by the Prime Minister, Cmnd 2154, HMSO, Appendix III, pp. 60–61.

2.7 Management Problems and School Leadership

Peter Snape
(With an appendix on Network Planning by Tony Gear)

INTRODUCTION

Everyone would agree that schools are not what they were; the wide-ranging changes that have occurred have brought new pressures, many, though not all, associated with increased size. Schools have doubled and even trebled in size in the past ten or fifteen years. With this has come an increasing complexity of organization, so that stresses and anxieties of choice have been added to those of dimension. Reorganization and the assumption of a greater welfare role have both brought about a disturbing diffusion and obscuring of purpose, and all these changes coincide with a major rescrutiny of curriculum and methodology. These direct pressures, arising from political and educational decisions, intensify the other less deliberate ones. Most parents now accept the formerly middle-class view of schools as the major instruments of social mobility, which makes them the focus of tensions rising from high unemployment and a general shortage of post-school educational opportunity; the generation gap has rarely been wider, and there is frequently a cultural hostility which is more explicit than in the past. Teachers have adopted the militancy fashionable with all groups of workers, and the whole army of ancillaries and other staff in schools nowadays pose additional if similar problems. This goes on against a background of increased national expenditure on education which gives the leadership of a moderately sized school a financial responsibility similar to that of the management of many industrial and commercial enterprises; there may be plant and equipment worth millions and annual budgets, not including salaries, running into tens of thousands of pounds. Given all this, there would seem to be an obvious need for management advice.

Nevertheless, the idea seems to arouse immediate and widespread

---

Sources: Snape, P. (1971) "A Management Approach to School Leadership", *Journal of the Association of Education Committees*, Dec. 1971; and edited extracts fom The Open University (1974) E221 *Decision-making in British Education Systems*, Unit 15 *Introduction to Planning and Decision Models*.

hostility. Perhaps people cling affectionately to inaccurate stereotypes of teachers developed in their own less complex schooldays, and resent the substitution of "managers" for the charismatic father-figures of their own childhood. Management has had a bad press, too, so that corporate figures and organization men are both disliked and feared. For years, school leadership has had more affinity with the laying on of hands than with leadership in any other field, so that requirements of qualifications and training have been reserved for such key personnel as cooks and caretakers. It is nevertheless true that many highly effective school leaders learn with surprise they have been acting for years on sound management principles. They, and their pupils, have learned from their mistakes. Learning by doing, however, as most teachers know, has its limitations, and a systematic approach to school management is as relevant as it is to other modern enterprises. After all, education generally is the biggest business there is nowadays.

MANAGEMENT IN SCHOOLS

A management approach would involve two areas of theoretical study and an analysis of practical tasks. The starting point is organizational theory. Despite the variety of interpretations there is some agreement on the nature of formal organizations like schools, hospitals and factories, and on the various constraints that operate on those working within them, such as formal and informal authority structures and the varieties of job satisfaction. Such information is essential for those who have to work within these constraints. An allied field is that of social psychology, interpersonal relationships and group dynamics, which seeks to study concepts of leadership and how groups work together. Skills exist, and can be taught. Interviewing, for example, has the most enormous importance on the education service, but very little formal training is available to schools. Teachers may like to cultivate their reputations as shrewd judges of character, but a little specific psychology might be more to the point. The same is true for large and small group management, which forms a major part of the school leader's day.

These essential studies are the preliminaries to the determination of the professional tasks of school leadership, as opposed to the (not inessential) "administrivia" that can legitimately be left to less well qualified staff. They can be classified under nine headings, as detailed below; in addition to these, the school leader has a continuing role to act as general repair man when parts of the organization begin to disintegrate.

1 *Goal identification*

The identification of goals is probably the most difficult task. Society determines fairly intelligible extrinsic goals when accreditation is a major factor in recruitment at all levels of skill. Intrinsic goals which maintain the school as an organization and support goals of a non-academic nature might be more important to some teachers. Not all schools have identical goals, which will vary with both catchment area and educational philosophy. However, if goals are not defined by the school leadership, the organization will provide its own, not necessarily acceptable ones. The general progress here is from philosophy to policy to programmes for attainment.

2   Establishing measurement criteria
Simultaneously with this should come the establishment of measurement criteria. This is done at present in the field of examination success, but techniques exist nowadays to measure attainment of other kinds. Shifts of attitude can be measured as well as "O" level passes. Measurement criteria can also be established for teacher performance and for administrative effectiveness.

3   Organization of staff and students
This must be relevant to the school's stated goals, and a rigid hierarchy is not the only effective system for teachers. Student time can be the subject of quantitative analysis, so that the leadership can face choices realistically. Time-tabling itself, a major constraint on organizing, deserves more space than is available here.

4   Staff selection and development
Staff selection is not always in the hands of the head or his senior colleagues; where it is not, the techniques of job specification and man description can at least give the appointing body a sense of accountability. Existing staff deserve the same kind of care of their professional development that they would get in other enterprises. A school that does not provide potential leaders with appropriate experience is failing in an important aspect of its management.

5   Forward planning
Schools spend a good deal of time in planning for the coming September, since programmes are planned for a year at a time. A longer time scale might be more appropriate. Forward planning is really decision-making on the allocation of scarce resources of money and manpower, and numerate cases should be made out for any increase in the share-out. Innovation in curriculum or method needs at least two years' preparation, with associated retraining, and a three- or five-year plan would result in purposive development.

6   Finance
Financing is closely related to forward planning and here again planning, programming and budgeting of the not inconsiderable revenue over a similar period will result in effective spending.

7   Internal and external communications
One of the most crucial areas of management is the establishment of

communications both within the organization and with the environment. Parents need to know what is happening and the media are part and parcel of the school's method in this task. It is important, too, to involve staff and pupils in the general life of the community to encourage support for the school's purposes. The establishment of schools as community colleges can help here. Communications within schools, often on split sites, need special attention and techniques. Certainly the secrecy that often attends communications with parents and administrators is misplaced.

8 Major reorganization

Occasionally a school or group of schools in an area has to plan major changes. Recent examples are the introduction of comprehensive schools, the raising of the school-leaving age and the development of lower and middle schools coupled with sixth-form colleges of further education. Sophisticated management techniques, particularly network planning, decision-tree diagramming and mathematical programming, would appear to have a part to play. The first of these techniques is designed to aid the scheduling of a complex set of interrelated tasks; the latter two seek to *optimize* decisions concerned with the allocation of resources between competing options in conditions of resource scarcity. A network-based plan used during the reorganization of secondary schools in Totnes is given below, while an explanation of the basic principles of network planning appears in the Appendix to this chapter (p. 248).

9 Motivation of staff and students

Finally, the leadership must provide continuing incentives for everyone in the school. The task is more straightforward for the students than it is for others. Their stay in the school is limited and progress afterwards will depend to a large extent on achievements there. Schools are fairly strong, too, in providing normative factors of motivation such as the various group feelings. The pattern of teacher motivation is far more complex, but in an effective school job satisfaction at least ought to be high, and the varieties of staff motives should be provided for.

THE TOTNES REORGANIZATION

The reorganization involved the amalgamation of three schools into a single comprehensive system. Decisions to reorganize the shape of secondary education in an area stem from more than one source; political issues are not always the dominant ones, either at local or at national level. In this respect the advent of a Labour government in 1964 was only indirectly a factor in Totnes, and the decision to reorganize was arrived at quite separately from central government action. Thus, the reorganization in Totnes was not a result of the famous circular 10/65, but of other changes which had exposed the Totnes schools to very severe pressures. The town has some 5,500 inhabitants, a figure which has not changed very much during the past fifty years. The educational provision was therefore lavish: in 1965 there was one secondary modern school (built in 1937) with 400 pupils, one girls' grammar school (opened in 1928) with 275 pupils, and one boys' grammar school of very long standing with some 300 boys. About 75 of the grammar-school pupils of both sexes were boarders.

These schools served an area very much larger than the town itself; pupils came from considerable distances in the rural district, up to a radius of about ten miles. The main source for the two selective schools, however, was the neighbouring town of Paignton which, for a variety of reasons, did not have its own grammar school until 1962. The opening of Paignton's selective school quickly brought crisis to Totnes. Numbers entering the town's two grammar schools dropped very rapidly from a peak of about 66 each year (small by most standards) to less than 30 and, in the case of the boys' school, to 18 in 1965.

The opportunity for reorganization came when it appeared that the resignation of the headmasters of the grammar school and the secondary modern school might coincide with the inclusion of Totnes in a Department of Education and Science building programme. The Local Education Authority decided firmly that any new building should be for a comprehensive school, rather than a reinforcement of the selective arrangements. The discussions which led to these decisions were all based on the assumption that a substantial new building would be available before the reorganization took place; and indeed, most of the advantage claimed for the non-selective system as far as the selective children were concerned stemmed from the age and unsuitability of the existing boys' grammar school (a converted regency mansion in the centre of the town), and the smallness of the separate units which, it was said, led to inadequate provision of courses and the restriction of public choice.

The situation abounded with considerable problems, the major one being the nature of the buildings. The girls' grammar school and the mixed secondary modern stood side by side on the outskirts of the town. They were divided by a main road which, at the height of the tourist season, carried as much traffic as any dual carriageway in the London suburbs. The boys' grammar school, on the other hand, occupied a restricted site about a mile away in the town centre, with extremely limited facilities and space. All three buildings would have to be used and, clearly, any large degree of commuting between the centre of the town and the outskirts would be out of the question. The way the students were to be distributed between the existing buildings was therefore of major importance; equally important, however, were curriculum issues. The reorganization was to be of the "instant" variety, with no gradual absorption of pupils year by year into an existing school. It would be unacceptable therefore if the programmes or general atmosphere for those completing O and A Level GCE courses were subject to any significant disturbance. In this connection the contributing grammar schools operated different systems, one being streamed with limited choice in the fifth form, the other being unstreamed with significant choices taken up after the third year. The modern school had no examination programme to worry about, since CSE was in its infancy in Totnes, but had its own problems of staffing and curriculum.

The first tentative network (shown in Figure 1) was sketched out after the first decisions had been made, and among them the most important— the decision to "go"—had already been taken. But the networking of subsidiary decisions gradually became both an aid to action and to communication, particularly with the planning group that eventually evolved. The route marked in bold in Figure 1 was found to be the "critical path", and therefore concentrated attention on the most important activities.

As can be seen from the Totnes network, there were three crucial points in the reorganization. The first was the decision to reorganize, the last was the day the new school opened and in between was the date when the curricula and syllabuses of the contributing schools were standardized. It was felt that it would be important from the start for all the pupils in the new school to be working in the same system, e.g. classes of hitherto separate sexes would have to be mixed; and yet at the same time, work towards the external examinations would have to continue without interruption. It would be of little use, for instance, combining together two O level history sets who were each preparing different parts of the syllabus. The key date for standardization of curricula and syllabuses was therefore about one year before the date of reorganization. Fourth-year courses beginning examination work then could be standardized to enable them to combine on amalgamation. A further six months would be needed to agree on the details. Before this process of deliberation could be even started, it would be necessary to nominate the key personnel to lead the discussions, and ultimately to make the decisions for all the schools. These issues emerged during the period of reflection that followed the decision to change the schools, and the network was drawn up in the first few weeks. At first, the roughest sketch sufficed, with merely a few points on it (2-4, 2-3, 4-6, 3-5, etc., of Figure 1), but gradually the details filled themselves in as the usefulness of the plan became clear.

One problem in the networking of a reorganization plan is that few of the activities concerned are measurable specifically in days or weeks, or even months—for instance, network estimates of two weeks as the time to write the curriculum. In fact, an experienced headmaster might be able to do that job in the space of a morning; but the expertise which enabled him to do this would have been acquired over the years. In the case of Totnes, there were several difficult curriculum issues which bedevilled the situation.

One constraint was that no adjustment could be made to the staff involved, who are guaranteed both status and tenure; if the contributing schools by any chance have a large number of foreign-language teachers who teach only a few students (in consequently small classes) economies of scale can lead to empty timetables for some of them. In our case this

2 Institutional Techniques

Figure 1

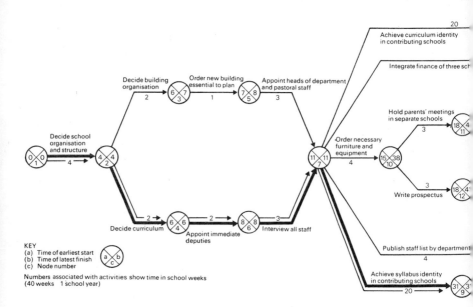

KEY
(a) Time of earliest start
(b) Time of latest finish
(c) Node number

Numbers associated with activities show time in school weeks
(40 weeks 1 school year)

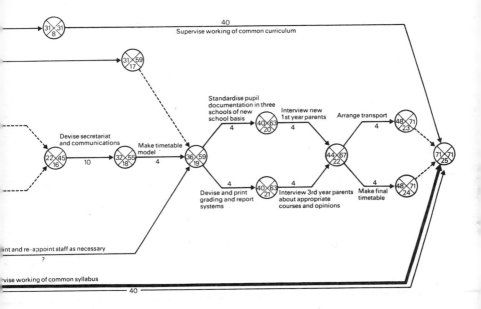

40
Supervise working of common curriculum

Standardise pupil
documentation in three
schools of new
school basis

Interview new
1st year parents

Arrange transport

Devise secretariat
and communications

Make timetable
model

Devise and print
grading and report
systems

Interview 3rd year parents
about appropriate
courses and opinions

Make final
timetable

nt and re-appoint staff as necessary

?

vise working of common syllabus

40

problem was severe and led to difficulties later. The resolution of problems like this may take a long time, or alternatively, it can happen very quickly; a member of staff may leave the school at an opportune moment, for example, or a sudden surge in the number of students may make a great difference to the situation. Estimates of timings in the network are therefore very approximate, and more in the realms of clairvoyance than calculation. Certain points in our plan, however, were clear and critical. These were activities 7-8, 8-25, 7-9 and 9-25; achieving completion of these on time was essential as otherwise the whole acceptance of the reorganization by the parents and students might have been jeopardized. This part of the plan is similarly crucial for most school reorganization and our experience would suggest that in order to achieve a smooth transition for students concerned in an amalgamation, sixty school weeks (eighteen months) are needed—some twenty for the working out of common curricula and forty for syllabuses and curricula to become operational.

In devising the plan, account was taken of possible bottlenecks and delays over which there was no possible control. For instance, an early activity (3–5) was to order new buildings essential to the plan. From the head's point of view the problem is fairly complex in that he must decide on the priorities of what he wants. It is easy to make up one's mind that boys' lavatories are needed in what was previously a girls' school. It is less easy to decide whether it will be possible to work without a further physics laboratory, or a new workshop, or technical facilities for girls of one sort or another.

During the working out of the reorganization, the network provided the main control instrument and monitor of progress. Its use was mainly in seeing how far along the road progress had been made, and in this it was not only a basis for action, but also a boost for morale. During a complex operation it proved useful to have some visual symbol of progress, and as one moves from left to right along the network there is a reassuring feeling that stages of a journey have been covered and will not have to be done again.

This is not to say that the network was not revised in the light of experience. Step 10–11 (hold parents' meetings), for example, were added as it became clear that the original single public meeting of all parents to discuss plans was inadequate to allay the natural disquiet of those with children at school, and it would be necessary to hold separate sessions in each school in order to deal with specific problems at length. Activity 11–14 (decide on uniform with Parent-Teacher Association (PTA)), came out of one of these parents' meetings. In those days it was not as customary as it is now to have parents' associations, and of the three contributing schools only one already maintained a PTA. Parents' meetings in each school revealed a need for some sort of association in the new school, which could help to take domestic decisions about uniform, school rules and so on. Similarly, revisions in the timing had to be accepted in the plan. Step 18–19 (make timetable model), for which four weeks had been allowed, in fact took more than this: fortunately there was a good deal of float in the network. This network shows the order of doing things rather than the time taken. For example, step 10–11 (hold parents' meetings), was planned to take three weeks. However, one could accomplish this step in three evenings if wished, and the time taken for the operation is less important than the fact that it must take place before 11–14 (decide on PTA, etc.,), since the parents must be involved in these decisions.

Compared to an industrial process, organization of a comprehensive school system makes very little use of critical timing. The important processes are consultations (essential if the plan is to work smoothly and be acceptable to the people most concerned) and decisions (which cannot be related to any length of time). The network's importance is therefore to show relationship of consultations and decisions to each other, and what must be done in one area before decisions are taken in another. Here, for instance, step 16–18 (devise secretariat and communications) was a crucial operation, which could contribute enormously to the success of the plan. That decision must obviously depend on 1–2 (decide building organization and structure), and 4–6 (appoint immediate deputies) since they were very much involved in the secretariat. In turn, the standardization of pupil documentation (19–20) awaited decision on the nature and number of the secretariat staff.

The network was not allowed to be too dominant a master, encouraging too slavish an obedience to its instructions. In any operations involving skilled and imaginative people, ample scope must be allowed for creative leadership from many sources, and for sudden improvisation which the leader's flair may tell him is absolutely right.

One must bear in mind, too, that in any operation involving large numbers of people (and their daily jobs and life styles), our kind of society demands that we devise means to achieve an agreed way of going about things, acceptable to everyone concerned. The staff to be reorganized have the right to know what is supposed to happen, and they will co-operate more readily if they feel they are participating in the processes. It follows from this that, once the plan is agreed, it should have some stability and should not be changed whimsically or capriciously to suit only one person's ideas. On the other hand, extreme inertia (a powerful and common force) can prevent the plan from being altered whenever it seems necessary; the fact that events may throw the whole thing out, so that modifications to the original are essential, is probably advantageous. In this respect, networking a single (though complex) operation that has never been done before differs radically from an operation like servicing an aero-engine, where each step is familiar and fairly cut and dried.

LEADERSHIP

In addition to the management tasks outlined in this paper the leadership has also a more traditional role as counsellor and ultimate arbiter of difficult disputes. In this work there are few precedents and no rules of thumb, but school leaders are probably no less wise here than the next man. The major wisdom, after all, is to make sure that other and more tractable management tasks are given no priority over this one. The purpose of managing a school well is to preserve its personal, humane and caring character.

These are the specific tasks of school leadership that emerge from a management view of the job. It is not claimed that the analysis reveals anything new, but that it helps to make the running of large schools comprehensible, even less alarming. In our times, "headmastering" is for heroes; ordinary people need management techniques!

APPENDIX: NETWORK PLANNING

(Prepared by Tony Gear from The Open University (1974) E221 *Decision-making in British Education Systems*, Unit 15. *Introduction to Planning and Decision Models*.)

In the last decade or so a group of network-based techniques to aid the planning and control of projects has been developed and is extensively applied to operations such as: construction and building projects; maintenance and periodic shutdown of plant; advertising campaigns; applied research and development work; complex administrative procedures and routines. A number of alternative versions of network analysis exist: Critical Path Method (CPM), Critical Path Scheduling (CPS), Programme Evaluation and Review Technique (PERT). However, the basis of all the techniques is essentially the same.

Network analysis may be applied to a project (or operation) with the following characteristics:

1   The project can be broken down into a number of *separate* activities (or tasks).
2   The time required (duration) of each activity can be estimated.
3   To complete the project certain activities must *precede* others, while some activities may be carried out in *parallel*.
4   Each activity requires some combination of resources in terms of men of various skills, facilities, materials or money. (There may be more than one feasible combination of resources for an activity, and each combination is likely to result in a different estimate of activity duration.)

Drawing networks

The project is represented by a figure consisting of two building blocks, i.e. lines to represent activities; and circles, known as events, to represent points in time. An activity consumes time and/or resources, while an event is a stage in the life of the project when defined preceding activities will all have been completed and succeeding activities can start. All the activities and events associated with the project are joined together to form a single network diagram which illustrates the logical sequence of activities and events. An example is shown below:

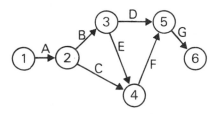

In this case six activities, labelled A to G, are involved. A short description would be attached to each activity in practice. The usual convention is to construct networks from left to right, and to attach a reference number to each node (event) as shown. Thus activity C, for example, is uniquely defined by its preceding and succeeding event numbers as activity 2–4. The above network embodies the following relationships:

1 Event 1 is the starting point of the project.
2 Activities B and C cannot start until A is completed.
3 Activities D and E cannot start until B is completed.
4 Activity F cannot start until E and C are completed.
5 Activity G cannot start until D and F are completed.
6 Event 6 is the end of the project.

All that is needed to construct a network diagram of a project is a large sheet of paper, a pencil and rubber! It is not often that one succeeds in drawing a satisfactory network first time because one's preconceptions often have to be revised as the construction of the network brings to light planning problems which were previously hidden. The network, once drawn, provides a framework for all those involved in the project, enabling individuals to see how their activities fit into the overall plan. Network diagrams differ in size and complexity from ten activities to perhaps thousands, depending on:

1 The inherent size and nature of the project.
2 The degree of detail which the people involved in its construction feel it necessary to represent for the purposes of planning and control. Network construction is still very much an art born of experience.

I

2.8 Basics of Timetabling

John E. Brookes

A curious feature of timetabling is the lack of communication between timetablers; during the timetabling "season" those heads, deputies and other staff involved in constructing a manual timetable tend to isolate themselves as much as possible from the hurly burly of school affairs and from each other, to emerge at the end of the day feeling they never want to see another timetable as long as they live. It is not surprising then that during the "off-season" timetabling matters are pushed very much into the background.

As a result of this lack of communication each school tends to feel that it has timetabling problems which are not only unique, but are also more complex than those of other schools. But the examination of many time-tables from schools of varying shapes and sizes, and experience in making timetables for these schools, has shown that there are many common problems. After all, however differently schools express their objectives, and however different these objectives may be, the elements which make a timetable are basically the same in all cases—teachers, pupils, rooms, units of time and educational content. Although it is possible to impose many types of constraint on the ways in which these basic resources are put together, it seems reasonable to suppose that there are common laws governing the timetabling problem. And although the task of formulating these basic principles of timetabling has barely begun, it is already clear that much is to be gained from the interchange of ideas and experience between timetablers, and from formulating what usually amounts to implicit understanding and "feel" into explicit rules.

Perhaps another effect of the isolation of timetablers has been the scant attention paid to timetabling as a subject for systematic study. Far more attention has been concentrated on curriculum innovation, almost always without serious consideration of timetabling implications. From the time-tabling point of view, and from the wider viewpoint of resource manage-ment in schools, the link between curriculum innovation and timetabling cannot be forged too strongly. To ignore the practical implications of

Source: Commissioned for this volume by The Open University.

educational ideas and theories is to risk poor or unbalanced use of resources in the school as a whole.

I am often asked what makes a school difficult to timetable and many people seem to expect a quantitative answer such as "schools with more than 150 pupils in the sixth form" or "schools where there are complex option structures". To such people the answer I give must seem intolerably vague. It is that the hard schools are generally those where little or no planning and forethought have been done. Complexity, numbers and restrictions on particular resources—specialist rooms, part-time staff, etc., can of course make for greater difficulty. But if a school has paid scant attention to planning its timetable and to thinking through its educational ambitions in terms of practical feasibility, then the task of producing a timetable is made very much more difficult, and can become impossible.

Departmental freedom versus central control

Schools vary considerably in the extent to which the timetabler accommodates the wishes of the various departments. On one hand there are schools in which the heads of department are given almost total freedom to determine their own requirements, and in which the timetabler slavishly attempts to reconcile the inevitable conflicts between "rival" departments. On the other hand there are schools in which the timetabler dictates to the departments, who have very little say in timetabling matters or control over their own areas of responsibility.

Undoubtedly some measure of departmental freedom is desirable for purely educational reasons. Yet unless there is some central control and co-ordination it is easy to reach a situation in which one department—or even one individual—dominates the entire timetable, either by force of personality or strength of numbers.

The timetabler is therefore in a key position when it comes to translating the educational requirements of the departments into a workable and balanced timetable. While he should always be aware that his job must put education first, not ease of timetabling, he must have sufficient authority to act as arbiter and decision-maker. His basic problem is thus to reconcile conflicts in such a way that the final timetable is unbiased and is acceptable to all concerned.

An example of departmental conflict

The following example shows very simply how different departments can be in conflict even though their requests, when taken in isolation, can seem quite reasonable.

In the fourth year of a school there is an option pattern as follows:

Option 1 craft/French/chemistry, etc	8 periods/40
Option 2 physics/German, etc	8 „ „
Option 3 biology/history, etc	8 „ „
English	5 „ „
Maths	5 „ „
P.E., games, R.E.	6 „ „
Total	40 periods

In Option 1 we have, among other things, craft and French. The head of craft wants his eight periods to be formed by two triple periods and one double period, while the head of French wants his eight periods to be formed by three doubles and two singles. It is clear that, since the entire week of forty periods is taken up by the curriculum (i.e. there is no "slack"), the craft and the French in Option 1 must take place during *the same eight periods*.

Considering next the requests made by the two heads of department, we can show very easily that craft and French are conflicting in their wishes. The following schematic diagram illustrates the point: to accommodate both French and craft in the same option would need ten periods where only eight are available.

There are, of course, a number of ways in which such problems can be resolved. The important point is that this kind of situation should be resolved as early as possible in the timetabling process and certainly before the task of putting the timetable together is begun. Time spent in co-ordinating departmental requests and in resolving conflicts *before* timetabling—whether by hand or by computer—will pay great dividends not only in time saved but also in the acceptability of the finished product.

THE PRINCIPLE OF COMPATIBILITY

A common feature of most modern timetables is the option structure, in which pupils are offered a choice of subject. Where option structures extend from the fourth year to the sixth and seventh years, planning becomes even more important. More problems are encountered because of the poor planning of options than for any other reason.

We have already seen how departmental requests can lead to conflict situations in an option structure. In addition to such simple, almost trivial, cases, there is the problem of compatibility of resources in the more general sense of the term. Examination of many timetables has suggested that the more closely the arrangement of resources follows what we have called the principle of compatibility, the easier the task of making a timetable becomes. The principle of compatibility is as follows: "subsets of a universal set of resources should be disjoint". To illustrate this rather abstract principle a further example will be helpful.

An example of compatibility of teacher teams
Let us suppose that the English department of a school consists of six teachers, A, B, C, D, E and F. Each of the five years in the school is divided into two groups of pupils, each group to be taught English by a team of three teachers, for five periods in a forty-period week. We thus have $5 \times 2 \times 5 = 50$ periods of English to timetable.

Consider now two different ways in which the six members of the English department can be allocated to these fifty periods.

1 Disjoint (non-overlapping) sets of teachers (obeying the principle of compatibility)

Year 1a	teachers	A, B, C
Year 1b	„	D, E, F
Year 2a	„	A, B, C
Year 2b	„	D, E, F

and so on. Notice that from the total team of six teachers, two subsets —A, B, C and D, E, F—are used consistently. We can timetable two half-year groups simultaneously since the two teams of teachers do not contain a common number. In other words the subsets A, B, C and D, E, F are disjoint subsets of the universal set A, B, C, D, E, F.

In this situation there is considerable scope for lateral movement and the timetabling possibilities are therefore large. A minimum of 25 periods would be needed to timetable the English requirements in this example.

2 Overlapping sets of teachers (contrary to the principle of compatibility)

Year 1a	teachers	A, B, C
Year 1b	„	C, D, E
Year 2a	„	B, D, F
Year 2b	„	A, C, F
Year 3a	„	A, D, E
Year 3b	„	B, C, D
Year 4a	„	C, E, F
Year 4b	„	A, B, E
Year 5a	„	B, E, F
Year 5b	„	A, D, F

Notice that this arrangement of teachers gives each member of the English department the same number of teaching periods as the first case, but that whereas previously we could timetable groups simultaneously we can no longer do so. This is because each team of three teachers has at least one member in common with each other team of three teachers. In this case we would need fifty periods to timetable the English!

The second example shows an extreme case of overlapping teacher teams and the conclusion from the timetabling point of view is self-evident—the nearer one can come to non-overlapping teacher teams (or any other resource team) the better.

COMPATIBILITY BETWEEN OPTIONS

The example of teacher teams in the English department was again a simple one, although cases like this and like our first example are far from uncommon in real timetabling situations. But to get the full flavour of the timetabling problem, consider the difficulties inherent in an average option structure extending from fourth year to upper sixth and involving in each year a dozen or more teachers. Clearly the principle of compatibility cannot always be followed to the letter without violating important educational criteria; all the same, it is important to appreciate the consequences in timetabling terms of overlapping teams of resources.

In planning an option structure it is quite common to find that, while compatibility of teacher teams is taken account of, compatibility of time itself is largely ignored. In the following example you will see that, for the options in fourth, fifth and sixth years to "fit", it is necessary for each option block to be compatible with at least *two* option blocks in each other year. This arises because the block size is variable—eight periods in the upper sixth, six or seven in the lower sixth, and so on.

Upper 6th	Option 1 (8)		Option 2 (8)		Option 3 (8)		Option 4 (8)		Games, etc. (8)
Lower 6th	Option 2 (6)	Option 3 (6)	Option 1 (6)		Option 4 (7)		Option 5 (7)		Games, etc. (8)
5th	Option 3 (8)		Option 1 (8)		Option 2 (8)		Games, etc. (6)		English & Maths (10)
4th	English & Maths (10)		Games, etc. (6)	Option 3 (6)		Option 2 (6)		Option 1 (6)	Option 4 (6)

As an alternative, consider the pattern shown below. Here there is a common block size of eight periods. In this case, compatibility of teacher teams need only be considered for each block with *one* other block in every other year.

Upper 6th	Option 1 (8)	Option 2 (8)	Option 3 (8)	Option 4 (8)	Games, etc. (8)
Lower 6th	Option 2 (8)	Option 3 (8)	Option 4 (8)	Option 1 (8)	Games, etc. (8)
5th	Option 3 (8)	Option 4 (8)	Option 2 (8)	Games, etc. (8)	English & Maths (8)
4th	English & Maths (8)	Games, etc. (8)	Option 1 (8)	Option 2 (8)	Option 3 (8)

But even in this case it is important to consider how the eight periods of each block are to be split into doubles, triples and singles. For example, if Option 1 in the upper sixth requires two triples and two singles, and Option 2 in the lower sixth—against which the upper sixth will fit when teaching resources are considered—requires four doubles, then there is bound to be some overlapping between more than one option block in each year, as shown below: the periods marked 'x' must be used by other options.

Upper 6th Option 1

Lower 6th Option 2

Space does not permit a full treatment of the commoner problems of timetabling, but the examples described should give some insight into the nature of the timetabling process and particularly should indicate the kind of things of which a good timetabler should be aware during the planning stages.

2.9 The Secondary School Timetable: A Matrix Approach

Harry L. Gray

It is generally agreed that the secondary-school timetable has just about reached the limits of complexity. Though some teachers actually enjoy compiling the timetable as a kind of mental exercise, many find it a chore and, furthermore, most find it a restrictive and frustrating instrument. Some schools use computers to help compile the timetable, but since the results are never completely satisfactory and programming may take as long as compiling one with pencil, paper and rubber it is doubtful if computerised timetables are worth their considerable cost. There seems, therefore, to be the need for another approach to timetabling and some work done recently on a course attended by a group of Heads and deputies of comprehensive schools in Glamorgan would appear to point the direction of a new approach.

The secondary-school timetable is essentially an instrument, a means to a complexity of ends, but a mere tool nevertheless. It is an administrative device and as such its purpose is to make life easier for everyone and not more difficult. Once the timetable becomes irritatingly restrictive it is failing in its purpose. Though it must impose some restraint, these restraints must be generally acceptable and, above all, lead to a creative response, not a frustrated one. The criteria for a school timetable which applied in this paper are that it should:

1 be simple: expressing general principles rather than detail;
2 be facilitative and amenable to amendment with minimum disruption;
3 be creative and open up possibilities;
4 push detailed decision-making and responsibility as far away from central administration as possible;
5 provide for planning and administration.

Inevitably the timetable imposes limitations, but these should be

---

Source: North East London Polytechnic and Anglian Regional Management Centre (1974), Occasional Papers in Education Management, No. 1.

minimal. It is concerned with regulating or allocating three variables—time, place and people—in that order of priority. In essence, the time-table is concerned with the allocation of time in order that places may be put at the disposal of people. Conventionally, the time allocated in the school day is from 9 am until 4 pm, but it would not be unreasonable for other time use to be allocated, such as time after school devoted to games, rehearsals, meetings and administration. For the most part, however, the school timetable is concerned only with teaching/learning time. The focal period of time so far as the school is concerned would appear to be the week—though the day and the year are also important in a slightly different way. Most teachers think about their job in terms of what happens in the school week rather than the day or year.

If we are to simplify the school timetable, we need to look for key time periods within the school week as our starting point. Since there are five days in the week (and five years before "O" level in the average secondary school) we can take five as the base figure for some arithmetical calculations about time usage. The basic timetable, then, consists of an arbitrary number of time blocks (in our case five) which can be most conveniently manipulated to give minimum interference with the primary tasks of the school—those related to teaching. In other words, we use an explicitly mechanical approach but reduce its implications to the minimum required to facilitate the work of the school. We require blocks of time which will enable a specified number of people to meet in specified places for predetermined maximum time spans. We can express the allocation of time in the form of a matrix, thus:

Figure 1

Day

School year	1	2	3	4	5
I	A	E	D	C	B
II	B	A	E	D	C
III	C	B	A	E	D
IV	D	C	B	A	E
V	E	D	C	B	A

VI / VII	A	B	C	D	E

The sixth form, treated as one unit, shares time-block designations with the main school in a way to be described below.

Clearly time blocks are meaningless in themselves and each must represent some part of the curriculum. Being clear, however, that the structure of the timetable is concerned with time blocks, people and places, and not with what happens during these time blocks, we can allocate a curriculum area to each block. For simplicity's sake, each time block can now be allocated a curriculum area designated by the same letter—the content as yet being undefined. The basic timetable is now complete. We have allocated throughout the school people to places for certain durations of time and this permits very considerable variation in how that time is used. For instance, block A on Day 1 for Year 1 may consist of 150 pupils with 7 teachers in 6 places—and how they distribute themselves is not indicated, nor does it need to be so far as the timetabling is concerned. The problems for this group of people are now curricular and pedagogic—not timetabling problems.

When the timetable compiler has written down the places where the specified people will be he has completed the purely mechanical parts of his task. From now on his considerations are of quite a different quality since they concern the real jobs of teaching. What is now important to notice is that the determining of what is taught and how is open to discussion, trial and development by all the teachers in the curriculum area/time block. Of course there are some restraints—this group will not be together until the next time Day 1 comes round—but there is more freedom of a different kind. What has happened is that decision-making in the areas that most concern the teacher is now possible by his working in his curriculum team. Since he is not timetabled for a "subject" for specific brief periods spread randomly throughout the week he can begin to examine the implications of what he teaches. We have made administration a minimal interference with behaviour and hopefully released energies for more highly valued activities.

We can conveniently call the curriculum areas (which have been allocated time blocks) Faculty areas (using Faculty somewhat in the American sense). Faculties are arbitrary divisions of learning and it is up to each school to determine what a Faculty consists of in "subject" terms. In fact, five time blocks may or may not have five related Faculties. In practice there will be more than five subject groupings but together they add up to five as, for example, in the following:

Maths	1
Science	1
Humanities	1
Creative Activities	1
Languages	$\frac{1}{2}$
Recreation	$\frac{1}{2}$

Here (arbitrary) subject areas or groupings have been given weightings that add up to five; they can be further varied so long as they relate to the time blocks on the timetable. Faculties may be paired in practice, which will give smaller time blocks and permit further dividing up of day, locations and people.

Figure 2

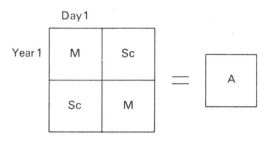

It is important to keep the time blocks as large as possible or the flexibility of the matrix timetable is lost, and in practice most matrix timetables will use the half-day as a time division.

In the model used for Figure 1, the Faculty/curriculum areas for the sixth form relate to those in the main school, though this need not be so. As described, however, it indicates that sixth form teaching is done by withdrawing staff as required from one team each day; but equally, withdrawal from five (or fewer) teams would be possible.

All teachers are timetabled continually but this does not mean that they teach all the time. Time off is by arrangement since the whole Faculty will work as a team. There is no time allocated for team meetings, though all Faculty members can be together at the same time; in any case, a Faculty may consist of several teams. On the other hand, a 6 time-block timetable (Figure 4 p. 261) makes allowance for weekly team Faculty meetings. Weightings can be altered to suit the requirements of students of different ages and this may involve changes in the curriculum content of Faculties.

Schools may make divisions according to physical provision. Schools with two or three sites may divide at a year boundary, as is convenient. Years 1 and 2 may have different Faculty groupings from Years 3 to 7 and the model might be as in Figure 3, (p. 260).

Additionally, years may be divided into two groups of equal (or unequal) size.

There would seem to be many theoretical advantages to the matrix timetable and in Figure 5 an example of how it could be applied to an actual school is given. Although there will be adjustment for given situations, there is no reason why these should not remain minor adjustments. In practice many schools already "block" time and in many cases

Figure 3

		Day			
	1	2	3	4	5
School year I	P(A)	Q(B)	X(C)	Y(D)	Z(E)
II	Q(B)	P(A)	Z(E)	X(C)	Y(D)

III	A	E	D	C	B
IV	B	A	E	D	C
V	C	B	A	E	D
VI	D	C	B	A	E
VII	E	D	C	B	A

curriculum or Faculty areas virtually exist already. Furthermore the implementation of the matrix timetable need take no longer than two years—just as long as it takes to work through the current fourth- and fifth-year options. New "options" in the matrix timetable present no logistic problems at all. Another advantage of the matrix timetable is that long-blocking can be provided when an intensive course is required—say a saturation course in a foreign language—because the large basic time units can be easily displaced. Additionally, the matrix blocks make possible a more realistic appraisal to the actual teaching time available and a "modular" approach to teaching programmes is facilitated.

Matrix timetabling highlights the need for the whole year to be considered in thinking about "time available". If special activities such as examinations, school plays, Christmas activities, etc., can be concentrated into time blocks, the remaining time is a realistic allocation of teaching time. Displacement can be dealt with either by transposing days or half-days (since days need not be tied to weekday names) or by compensating by omitting selected blocks as appropriate. Furthermore, the matrix timetable allows for radical variations each term. Thus the summer term could be composed of quite different programmes and curriculum areas from the first two terms.

Of course, the matrix timetable does not solve all problems. It will be a matter of personal values as to whether it is helpful or not in teaching certain subjects. Obviously it does not allow languages to be taught/learned in small doses each day and some teachers will object to a "subject" occurring only once a week. But the matrix concept forces us to rethink the whole idea of subjects and disciplines. The matrix timetable will facilitate a rethinking of the curriculum in terms of skills and skill areas which generally cut across traditional subject boundaries. For instance "communication skills" may represent a Faculty area or a thread across several areas. At least a real, active debate about curriculum content becomes characteristic of the school adopting a matrix approach and the challenging of educational assumptions is not the least of the advantages of the approach. Once a school begins to work on the matrix concept, its versatility and usefulness become increasingly apparent, not least because it allows teaching staff an important share in determining the content of the curriculum.

Figure 4 An example of a 6 time-block matrix

School year	Day									
	1		2		3		4		5	
I	A	B	C	D	E	F	C	D	E	F
II	B	C	D	E	F	A	D	E	F	C
III	C	D	E	F	A	B	E	F	C	D
IV	D	E	F	A	B	C	F	C	D	E
V	E	F	A	B	C	D	A	B	A	B
VI / VII	F	A	B	C	D	E	B	A	B	A

Constant   Variable

Each time block has equal weighting throughout.
[1] Some subjects can be taught more intensively at certain times
  (e.g. more basic mathematics in the first year).
[2] Long-block teaching of, say, languages (crash course) is facilitated.
  Teams teaching Year 6/7 can be programmed to take a team meeting and
  Year 6/7 is taught on a simple A–F pattern or separately timetabled.
A and B curriculum areas may be specific (e.g. mathematics and English).
C–F may be composite or open areas.
A 6-day 6-block matrix is a possibility, but it involves uncertainty over which day of the week is which: the kind of complication the matrix timetable aims to avoid.

2 Institutional Techniques

Figure 5

	MATRIX 1	MATRIX 2	MATRIX 3
1ST YEAR	**A** STAFF 1 2 3 4 / ROOMS 1 2 3 4 **B** STAFF 12 13 14 15 / ROOMS 19 20 5 6	**B** STAFF 12 13 14 15 / ROOMS 19 20 5 6 **A** STAFF 1 2 3 4 / ROOMS 1 2 3 4	**C** STAFF 24 25 26 27 28 / ROOMS 14 15 16 17 18 **D** STAFF 37 38 39 40 / ROOMS 5 10 12 13
2ND YEAR	**C** STAFF 24 25 26 27 28 29 / ROOMS 14 15 16 17 18 22 **D** STAFF 37 38 39 40 / ROOMS 5 10 12 13	**D** STAFF 37 38 39 40 / ROOMS 5 10 12 13 **C** STAFF 24 25 26 27 28 29 / ROOMS 14 15 16 17 18 22	LANG. STAFF 54 55 56 57 58 / ROOMS 7 8 9 10 11 STAFF 48 49 50 51 52 REC. GYM HALL 1 HALL 2
3RD YEAR	LANG. STAFF 54 55 56 57 58 / 31 32 33 34 60 STAFF 48 49 50 51 52 53 REC.	**A** STAFF 5 6 7 8 / ROOMS 40 41 42 66 **B** STAFF 16 17 18 19 / ROOMS 50A 50B 51 52	**B** STAFF 12 13 14 15 / ROOMS 56 53 64 68 **A** STAFF 1 2 3 4 / ROOMS 31 32 33 34
4TH YEAR	**B** STAFF 16 17 18 19 20 / ROOMS 50A 50B 51 52 55 **A** STAFF 5 6 7 8 9 / ROOMS 40 41 42 66 67	**C** STAFF 30 31 32 33 34 35 / ROOMS 43 44 45 46 47 48 **D** STAFF 41 42 43 44 45 / ROOMS 35 36 37 38 39	**D** STAFF 41 42 43 44 45 / ROOMS 35 36 37 38 39 **C** STAFF 30 31 32 33 34 / ROOMS 43 44 45 46 47
5TH YEAR	**D** STAFF 41 42 43 44 45 / ROOMS 35 36 37 38 39 **C** STAFF 30 31 32 33 34 35 / ROOMS 43 44 45 46 47 48	LANG. STAFF 54 55 56 57 58 / 31 32 33 34 60 STAFF 48 49 50 51 52 53 REC.	**A** STAFF 5 6 7 8 9 / ROOMS 40 41 42 66 67 **B** STAFF 16 17 18 19 20 / ROOMS 50A 50B 51 52 55
6TH YEAR	STAFF 10 11 21 22 23 36 46 47 59 60	STAFF 9 10 11 20 21 22 23 36 46 47 59 60	STAFF 10 11 21 22 23 36 60

MATRIX 4	MATRIX 5

MATRIX 4 (left column)

F
37 38 39 40

S
5 10 12 13

F
24 25 26 27 28 29

S
14 15 16 17 18 22

F
1 2 3 4

S
1 2 3 4

F
12 13 14 15

S
19 20 5 6

F
30 31 32 33 34 35

S
43 44 45 46 47 48

F
41 42 43 44

S
35 36 37 38

F
54 55 56 57 58

S
31 32 33 34 60

F
48 49 50 51 52 53

S
16 17 18 19 20

F
50 50 51 52 55
A B

F
5 6 7 8 9

S
40 41 42 66 67

10 11 20 21 23 36 45 46 47 59 60

MATRIX 5 (right column)

LANG. STAFF
54 55 56 57 58

ROOMS
7 8 9 10 11

STAFF
48 49 50 51 52 53

REC. GYM HALL 1 HALL 2 FIELDS

B STAFF
12 13 14 15

ROOMS
19 20 5 6

A STAFF
1 2 3 4

ROOMS
1 2 3 4

D STAFF
37 38 39 40

ROOMS
31 32 33 34

C STAFF
24 25 26 27 28 29

ROOMS
56 57 58 59 60 61

A STAFF
5 6 7 8 9

ROOMS
40 41 42 66 67

B STAFF
16 17 18 19 20

ROOMS
50 50 51 52 55
A B

C STAFF
30 31 32 33 34 35

ROOMS
43 44 45 46 47 48

D STAFF
41 42 43 44 45

ROOMS
35 36 37 38 39

STAFF 10 11 21 22 23 36 46 47 59 60

NUMBER OF PUPILS
IN A YEAR GROUP (YEARS 1-5)
210

NUMBER OF PUPILS
IN SIXTH FORM
150

NUMBER OF STAFF
66

FACULTY DISTRIBUTION OF STAFF

MATHEMATICS (A)
1 2 3 4 5 6 7 8 9 10 11

SCIENCE (B)
12 13 14 15 16 17 18 19 20 21 22

CREATIVE ACTIVITIES (C)
23 24 25 26 27 28 29 30 31 32 33 34 35 36

HUMANITIES (D)
37 38 39 40 41 42 43 44 45 46 47

LANGUAGES (E)
54 55 56 57 58 59 60

RECREATION (E)
48 49 50 51 52 53

IN ADDITION THERE WILL BE TEACHING
TIME AVAILABLE FROM MEMBERS
OF THE ADMINISTRATIVE STAFF

2 Institutional Techniques

Some notes on the Matrix Timetable (Figure 5) by A. Chinn
It is envisaged that the teaching approach for much of the first three years would be an integrated one, while in the subsequent years the approach would be subject based.

The timetabler would produce an "Aunt Sally" which could be altered very easily in the light of staff requirements.

The matrix timetable lends itself readily to the production of option subject groups, e.g. in column 1, Year 4, the choice could possibly be:

$\frac{1}{2}$ Year Group   —   5 Sets of Maths

$\frac{1}{2}$ Year Group   — $\left\{ \begin{array}{l} \text{2 Sets of Physics} \\ \text{2 Sets of Chemistry} \\ \text{1 Set of Rural Science} \end{array} \right.$

There would be ample opportunity for preparation and marking time from a number of methods, e.g.:

(i)   Mutual arrangement within a "team".
(ii) The introduction of administrative staff for their teaching time.
(iii) The movement of "spare" staff from the fourth year and above.

3 Towards a Systematic Approach

INTRODUCTION

Education is undoubtedly one of the most difficult of human activities to manage. Reasons for this can readily be found, particularly:

1 the need to consider many economic, technical, organizational, behavioural and social factors;
2 conflict regarding the priorities amongst many aims and objectives;
3 considerable uncertainty in the relationships between resource allocations and outcomes;
4 an often long list of alternative decisions;
5 difficulties in the definition of quantitative measures of inputs to, and outputs from, an educational process.

Faced with these complexities and unknowns the decision-takers in education at various levels are forced to simplify reality and to abstract those factors and relationships which are believed (usually on a subjective basis) to have the greatest influences on the outcome. In other words a *model* of the situation is required. At one extreme the model may be a purely subjective idealization of the situation perceived by the decision-taker(s). At the other extreme a very detailed and formal mathematical model, requiring quantitative data for a whole set of factors, may be constructed. Somewhere between these extremes the decision-taker has to select a model to aid him in his decisions. While the use of a model in some form seems an obvious requirement, the necessity to select one from a whole range of possibilities poses a decision problem of fundamental importance.

The last seven articles contained in this Reader have been selected in order to introduce material about systems and systems concepts in education. Ideas of this type are having an increasing influence on the approach of social, management, political and economic scientists. The impetus towards systems thinking in education is arising from the considerable successes already achieved in other fields, particularly in industrial settings.

The article by Maurice G. Kendall emphasizes the model-builder's viewpoint and the difficulties he faces. It emerges clearly that to construct the test models of parts of the educational system is likely to need the skills of a group of people with varied background experience and expertise.

Next Roger L. Sisson introduces the systems approach and its application to planning in higher education. He compares the method by

265

which decisions are typically made at present with a possible systems approach. This is a valuable exercise and makes clear that systematic planning requires explicit and declared goals and measures of achievement towards them, as well as a formal analysis of alternative courses of action. Sisson feels that the basic problem of systematic planning is that it is very unfamiliar to educational decision-takers, requiring major changes of thinking and activity. This is a psychological problem and one which this book will, hopefully, go some way to overcoming. A particularly useful contribution in the paper is Sisson's analysis of the problems and benefits associated with systematic approaches.

The paper by Alexander M. Mood explores more deeply the possibility of applying systems analysis to educational decision problems. He sensibly proposes that the model-builder should make a study at the outset of whether the decision problem is amenable to a formal analysis. Mood implies that if the quantitative analysis is "forced", that is if it involves many subjective estimates and judgements, one might as well treat the problem as qualitative in nature rather than attempt some form of quantitative exercise. One of the most difficult problems in educational planning is to decide on objectives or, more specifically, to decide on what quantities are to be *optimized* in some sense. In systems analysis the expression of an overall goal is specified as a mathematical function, and this has so far proved to be the most difficult part of model-building exercises in education. Mood discusses this, using an illustration involving the allocation of classroom time to films. Not only is the definition of the objective different but, as Mood points out, multiple objectives are generally involved.

The paper by Tony Gear introduces a well-known management-science techinique, decision tree analysis. It appears feasible and desirable to apply this technique to a wide range of situations in education, both in short-term and long-term planning, and for strategic as well as tactical problems. Little information is available in education to relate quantitatively the achievement of objectives to the allocation of resources. For this reason the greatest benefit may come from constructing decison trees in order to set out clearly, in chronological order, the alternatives and uncertainties present. But eventually quantitative data and analysis would appear highly desirable. There is a challenge here to the ingenuity and flexibility of management scientists and systems planners who have, to date, done little work in the education area.

The paper by John L. Davies, commissioned for this Reader, presents a description and critical discussion of the usefulness of applying the techniques of Management by Objectives (MBO) and Planning Programme Budgeting Systems (PPBS) to education. At the present time there appears to be considerable uncertainty as to the usefulness of these examples of systems approaches, and it seems far too early to reach definitive conclusions.

We felt that the technique of linear programming, which is a well-established tree in industrial management, is likely to play an increasingly important role in educational management. We were therefore lucky to have the paper by William H. Stubbs available for inclusion, as it describes an actual application of the technique to the optimal allocation of money, under several budgetary headings, to five colleges of further education in Cumbria. The model is a very simple one, ignoring many complexities in the situation. But it is usually best to build a small model, extending it as limitations are revealed by its use.

"Making Claims for Computers" by Richard Hooper analyses some claims made for the use of computers in education. As far as management in education is concerned, computers become a necessity as models become too big to analyse by hand. Even the small linear programming model in the previous paper makes use of a standard computer programme. However, Richard Hooper is quite cautious regarding the usefulness of using computers to simulate the consequences of alternative resource allocations in education, stating that only limited successes have so far been achieved. He argues that the vast amount of data is uneconomic to collect. However, if the data really is relevant to a decision problem, it should be collected whether or not a computer is involved. And if a vast amount of data is needed, then the computer merely speeds up an otherwise tedious analysis.

Tony Gear

3.1   Models for Thinking With

Maurice G. Kendall

In recent years, the word "model" has been used, or misused, to describe almost any attempt at specifying a system under study in a scientific way. There are differences of opinion about what should truly be regarded as a "model" in the scientific sense. This bickering over fundamentals shows how difficult it is to lay down rigid classifications, but cannot disguise the fact that modelling is becoming a widely-used tool in business and industry.

The sort of model we are concerned with is not necessarily, or even usually, a physical representation like the scale models that an aircraft designer makes to test in a wind tunnel. The concentration in industrial and economic studies today is on models in the form of written specifications of the system under study, expressed in logical or mathematical terms. The idea of these models is that they express the inter-relationships between the parts of a system sufficiently clearly to enable its behaviour to be studied scientifically. In particular their object is often to show how the system should be controlled, and to predict its future movements.

USE AND PURPOSE

The applications of such "mathematical" models are many and varied. To take a more-or-less random selection of fields in which recent studies have relied on model-building and analysis, such methods have been applied to forest fire control, labour allocation, the rise of employees through a hierarchy, the behaviour of the stock-market, cloud formation, marketing strategy, the formation of social groups, the operations of an oil company, and traffic control (both air and road). The list could be extended almost indefinitely. There is hardly a branch of science or industry which is not coming under the model-builder's eye (despite the nature of these models, we still speak of "building" them).

It is not obvious at the moment whether or not all these different applications rest on a common body of theory, or a common collection of skills. On the face of it there does exist a set of basic problems and

---

Source: *New Scientist* (6 July 1967), pp. 13–15.

the necessity for a basic expertise shared by all model-building exercises. Whether or not it is possible to write a text book on *the theory of model building,* however, is another matter. The diversity of applications of model-building may have left those outside the fields a little mystified as to what it is all about. Not only do some of the methods used need explaining; some of the myths need exploding.

One important question to be clarified is the purpose of economic and industrial models. The fundamental idea of building models is to mimic the behaviour of a "real-life" system. In doing so, we can get increased understanding of the "real" situation and hence some guidance as to how to control it. What is not attempted is the construction of a microcosm of the system under study which mimics its behaviour in all respects. The systems which are studied are far too complicated to allow anything of this kind.

Models have to be built for specific purposes, not for all possible purposes. This means that there have to be quite different models of the same system, for different purposes. A model of a company for the purposes of planning capital investment, for instance, may be very different from a model of the same company for planning its information flow, and both would differ from a model of its manpower requirements.

Model-builders find it necessary continually to curb their natural ambition to build models of too great a generality. In practice it would seem that the best results are obtained by starting with simple—and by some standards, modest—objectives, and working towards more complicated systems, rather than by starting with attempts at comprehensive structures.

What sort of thing, then, can we fairly call a model? In a sense the organization chart of a company, notwithstanding the fact that it is always out of date, could be regarded as a "model" of the company structure. But, being only a static picture, it is of little use for control or prediction. Such "iconic" models (which include maps and flow diagrams) are, therefore, not of importance to the model-builder except perhaps as a preliminary to his work. He is interested in some sense or other in the movement of the system and in dynamic (as opposed to static) situations.

DISTINCTIONS OF APPROACH

It would be useful to be able to classify the different types of model. At this stage of the subject's development, however, it would be premature to do so. What is possible, and perhaps more relevant, is to compare the different approaches.

For instance, it may be in the nature of the system being modelled that all the relationships can be worked out absolutely precisely. More usually (particularly in economics), some random element is involved, which demands a statistical approach.

Again, some systems lend themselves to being described mathematically by means of general formulae, whereas others are so complicated as to defeat the mathematician's ideal. In the latter case we can very often simulate the behaviour of the system under a set of different assumptions and, as it were, form a picture of its behaviour by sampling from all the ways it might behave. If solvability is wanting, simulation provides the second line of attack.

There is also a choice between examining the reasons for phenomena and merely describing them. The difference here is more one of degree than of basic approach; it is frequently possible to start with a simple description of a situation, and to analyse it in more detail to find progressively deeper causal connections later on.

A number of such distinctions can be drawn between different classes of model: short-term and long-term; computable and non-computable; macro and micro. But the net result of all these different approaches is always the same—to give some indication of the nature of the system being modelled, as an aid to making decisions about its future.

A NON-IDEAL SCIENCE

Model-building is clearly a way of applying scientific method. It may not be obvious at first sight why it should be regarded as a separate subject. There are a number of reasons:

In the first place, unlike the scientist the model-builder has frequently to deal with concepts to which no concrete units of length, time, mass and so on can be given. In economics, sociology and psychology it is necessary to deal with variables such as value, utility and demand. In some cases these concepts are quantifiable, for example in monetary units, but the units themselves are frequently subject to changes in value so that correction factors have to be introduced. Even in models of manpower, where the primary units are countable human beings, some regard has to be made to quality in order to be realistic.

Secondly, many of the factors appearing in the equations of a model deal with inequalities rather than equalities. In fact, some models of an industrial plant, such as an oil refinery, consist almost entirely of inequality constraints expressing, for example, the maximum capacity of intake, or minimum requirements in output. These situations cannot be dealt with using the "classical" mathematic approach, and a special technique known as mathematical programming has been developed to cater for them.

Thirdly, classical economic theory has been found lacking as a basis for the construction of economic models because it is essentially qualitative. Even when economists did get as far as expressing relationships in mathematical terms, they did so in the manner of equations expressing static conditions. To deduce the dynamic behaviour of a system from such equations is like trying to deduce the laws of planetary motion from the principle of the triangle of forces (which accounts for the fact that mathematical formulation added little or nothing to economic theory).

3 Towards a Systematic Approach

Nowadays, economists realize that the behaviour of economic systems depends critically on the time-lags between stimulus and response. In fact, it has now been shown that the very stability of an economic system may depend on the time-lag between some measure being introduced and its full effect being felt, rather than simply on any causal law relating to the effect of the stimulus.

The length of a time-lag and the pattern of transient phases that follow a change are among the most difficult of economic effects to measure. It is surprising how little is known of them even in the best documented economics. How long, for example, does an alteration in bank rate take to exert its full effect? How far does production lag behind unemployment, or unemployment behind production?

Added to these problems, or perhaps causing them, are the difficulties of gathering economic data. In some circumstances it is possible to make up for deficiencies in given data by conducting *ad hoc* enquiries in greater detail. With a few exceptions, economic models built up to the present have had to rely on statistics that are produced by government departments, or central authorities of some kind, for quite different purposes. If governments are going to become seriously interested in model-building there will arise the necessity for collecting data for that purpose alone. This may have a far-reaching effect on the nature of the state's statistical service.

The model-builder is all too aware of the difficulties he faces. However, it would be wrong to paint too black a picture of his situation. It is not necessarily true, for instance, that the behaviour of a complicated system is itself very complicated. Statistics is full of examples of this fact. For instance, the circumstances and motivation which go to determine an individual's income are legion. Any model which tried to set out the situation in detail would soon get bogged down in sheer complexity. Nevertheless, the so-called Pareto law of income distributions, which is fairly closely followed in all Western societies, depends on only one parameter, yet it has proved remarkably stable over decades of fundamental change in economic control.

A second source of encouragement to the model-builder is provided by the electronic computer. In fact, it would be an an overstatement to say that econometrics and models have become practical possibilities only since the computer was developed. Early writers had many of the ideas, but the practical engineering of the subject had to wait for the technological breakthrough represented by the electronic machine.

THE MODELLER'S VIEWPOINT
As with many of the so-called management science methods, the mere discipline of expressing a situation in terms of a model can frequently advance our thinking about a system. For instance, most businesses have a chain of command expressible by the branching-pedigree type of diagram. The operations represented by this diagram work in both

directions; instructions flow downwards, information flows upwards. Decisions at defined levels are made at various points of the network. The attempt to express these operations in a precise way throws up some quite fundamental queries. Is it inevitable, for instance, that the (down-flowing) executive chain should be the same as the (up-flowing) information chain, or the decisional system the same as the executive system? Nature, in designing the human being, has provided at least four different systems for controlling the body (arterial, venous, vascular and nervous) and has linked them in a very intricate and roundabout way. In considering a social or commercial organism, ought we to take a leaf out of her book? I do not know the answers to these questions, nor indeed whether there are any answers. The point is that until we think about a situation from a model-building viewpoint such fundamental queries might not arise.

It would be pleasant to be able to offer a simple answer to the often-posed question: "How does one set about building a model?" This is one of those general questions like "How does one design a building?" or "How does one cure a disease?" The answer must be equally general—it all depends on what sort of model, and for what purpose. Granting that, it is still not possible to anatomize the model-building process. Perhaps, when a great many more models of all sorts have been built, it will be possible to lay down rules. At the moment it is only possible to examine the trends.

Certain facts have already emerged. For one thing: although, in limited fields, with limited objectives, it may be possible for one gifted individual to have at his command all the skills required to construct and test a model, the larger models must be a matter of team effort. A model of complete economy, for instance, requires the analytical training of the economist, the knowledge of available data of the descriptive statistician, the expertise of the theoretical statistician and perhaps of a specialized mathematician, the skill of the computer programmer, and the common sense of them all. The moral of this seems to be that we are in some danger of spreading our efforts too thinly on the ground. If, as I suspect, there is to be growing interest in the subject of model-building over the next 10 or 20 years, and if the amount of effort which can be put into the subject is limited in time, money and intellectual capacity, it would pay us as a nation (or perhaps some larger community) to strengthen our strong points and concentrate on setting up units for study bigger than the critical mass at which useful results are produced.

Of the many distinctions of type and use that can be made, there is one which may become a source of actual conflict: the difference between models produced primarily as a forecasting tool and those built for control purposes. A model of an economy may be useful to an individual firm to predict its environment, and useful to the government in the actual control of the economy. There is no conflict of aim in devising these cybernetic systems; but there may be a conflict among users in the sense that industry may want to rely on forecasts from a model, whereas government may want to falsify them. It will be interesting to see how this difference in emphasis will influence the development of model-building over the next decade.

3.2 How Did We Ever Make Decisions before the Systems Approach?

Roger L. Sisson

INTRODUCTION

The systems approach and its application to planning in higher education have long been the target of exhaustive discussion in administrative circles, as have such topics as the use of operations research, computer methods and the need for management information systems. After reading the current literature on the administration of higher education, one might conclude that decisions are never made except perhaps on the most capricious grounds. To date, no study has been made of the alleged shortcomings of our present planning processes. Does a new approach really need to be considered?

In this article I will attempt to answer that question by making at least an informal analysis of the method by which decisions are now made and of how that method compares with the systematic planning procedures so often proposed. I will then suggest a way in which the systems approach can be applied in higher education and will indicate what processes would be involved in effecting such a change. Finally, I will point out a few of the problems and some of the advantages of systematic planning.

PLANNING: A DUAL DEFINITION

We must look at planning from two points of view, that of the decision-maker or top administrator and that of the analyst or planner. The word has slightly different meanings in these two contexts.

For the decision-maker, planning is making decisions which commit the institution far into the future. Decisions about facilities (particularly special-purpose facilities), the hiring of tenured faculty and the implementation of a major new educational program, for example, are planning decisions.

Some decision-makers hire assistants, called "planning analysts", who gather and analyze data to facilitate the decision-making process. Thus, from the point of view of the planning analyst, planning is the collection, organization and analysis of information in support of planning decisions.

Source: *Socio-economic Planning Sciences* (Dec. 1972), Vol. 6, No. 6, Pergamon Press, pp. 523-9.

3 Towards a Systematic Approach

Decisions are indeed made and plans created and implemented in present-day higher education, but these tasks are now accomplished by a process most aptly described as a series of negotiations (see Cyert and March, 1959). In other words, the various people involved in the decision process bargain with each other to arrive at a common position, thereby making the decision.

Although real stories of such negotiation are readily available, an especially vivid picture of this method is delineated in the novel *Poetic Justice*, by Cross (1970). The setting is an American university, which includes an extension college. The main characters are the Dean of Arts, who is also the Chairman of the English department and the Dean of the extension college. The story takes place soon after the campus has been shaken by a series of riots and uprisings, as a result of which the senior members of the faculty and administration decide to "restructure" the curriculum and some of the regulations. No attempt is made, however, to define what this restructuring is or what it is meant to accomplish. *The absence of explicit goals is typical of the negotiating mode of planning.*

The Dean of Arts takes the opportunity to suggest that the extension college must be eliminated, his explicit reason being that the university should limit itself to degrees based on full-time participation on the campus. He attempts to carry out this aim through a series of bargains and negotiations with other members of the faculty. In the words of one character, "Dean Cudlipp (the Dean of Arts) had a lot of favors to trade" (p. 106). *Trading of favors is a prime basis for negotiating.* Typical are such trades as, "you vote for me as department chairman and I'll support your request for an increased budget".

The Dean of Extension, of course, insists that the extension service is a vital contribution to the community and a proper one for the university, sharply pointing, by way of justification, to the fact that the students of the extension college did not participate in the riots. As the novel progresses, he proceeds to strengthen his position by involving a female professor from the English department, thereby obtaining support within his opponent's own home ground. It seems that the lady has dared to allow extension students in her regular classes. He invites her to luncheons and makes it a point to enlighten her about the current school politics.

Here the novel contains a superb description of an English department faculty meeting, which is cleverly terminated by parliamentary procedures when the Dean of Arts feels he is losing his argument over the question of the extension college.

And so the negotiations ensue. At one point, the lady English professor, now won over to the side of the Dean of Extension, asks a colleague why the other colleges, such as engineering and the sciences, bother to support the extension programs. She is told:

"The secretaries in these various colleges take jobs in order to attend the extension college free: no extension, no secretaries.

It is really extraordinary the way one works one's ass off for important ideas and principles, only to find that decisions are made in the end for reasons and by people who have no more at stake in the quality or general movement of education, than I have in the changing rate of arbitrage" (p. 94).

As the plot thickens, the Dean of Arts dies under mysterious circumstances that look like murder, and, of course, some members of the college of extension are suspected. (I suppose murder is the ultimate form of negotiation!) However, it turns out that the death occurred for unrelated reasons, and at the conclusion of the novel it is still not clear whether the extension college is to continue its existence, though the implication is that it will survive.

THE SYSTEMS APPROACH

Let us suppose that the university in the above example had handled the question of creating and continuing an extension college, using a more systematic approach to planning, an approach that takes advantage of modern management and technical processes.

First, systematic planning assumes that planning decisions are made on a cyclical basis, every year or two. Thus, decisions are not triggered by crises, such as riots or an arbitrary dictum to "restructure". Rather they are examined on a regular basis so as to build a desired future and prevent crises. As part of the cyclical process, there are a series of specific planning analyses. I will review these analytic steps briefly.

The first step is to predict the environment. This means that a conscious effort is made to try to predict what demands might be made on the university. In our example, predictions could have been made of the number of students likely to attend the various colleges and programs. There would be a basis, thereby, for deciding, independent of faculty desires, whether or not the various colleges were providing a service desired by the community. An important feature of the systems approach is that predictions and forecasts are made by explicit, formal processes. There are often mathematical operations, computerized procedures which are called models. This formality ensures communicability. Anyone familiar with the procedure and having the basic data can repeat the prediction. All assumptions in the forecasts are explicit, if one takes the time to study the procedures.

The second step in a systematic planning approach is to predict the future status of the institution. This step describes how the university will operate and will meet various demands if no new planning decisions are made. Formal methods are used here also to predict such factors as faculty levels, number of students served, total costs of operations and comparisons of costs with revenues. Ideally, an estimate of the quality of the educational output should be made, but in connection with the present example, it would be impractical to make such a formal calculation. Planners could, however, estimate for the next five years the student enrolment in the extension college, the cost of operating the college and the number of graduates. These estimates would provide a "base case", or a guideline from which to judge the possible need for new decisions.

The third step of the planning process is to compare the predicted status with goals of the university. The assumption, of course, is that these goals have been established and have been made explicit, a point to which I will return below. If one of the goals is service to the community, then, obviously, the extension division may be a valuable program. On the other hand, if a particular goal is to promote basic research, then the extension division may be less essential. An examination of the base case prediction reveals the gaps between what is likely to happen and what we wish to occur.

The planning process proceeds with step four, the conscious development of alternatives to move the institution closer to the desired future. We might suppose, for example, that a goal of service to the community has been established, but there may be some alternatives to a classroom-oriented extension college. At this point, we enter a phase that is sometimes called program planning, the design of these alternatives. One alternative might be to eliminate the extension college. Another might be to give certain students a special status in the regular college programs. A third choice might be to develop some sort of independent study and test program, that is, a school without classrooms, for part-time students.

In this step, the alternatives are carefully designed and thought out. The description of each includes specifications of resource requirements and expected outcomes or results plus a scheme for implementation and operation over the planning period.

Step five in the planning process is to make an unbiased comparison of these alternative plans with the established goals. Predictions are made for the operation of the university, as for the base case, but it is now assumed that one or more of the alternatives has been adopted. These are the same kind of computations and estimates as those indicated in step two, but now we take new decisions into account. This procedure allows the comparison of alternatives in terms of resource requirements and in terms of the accomplishment of goals. Where possible, the predictions are made by formal techniques, which are used also for searching out the best combinations of alternatives. This last step involves the difficult problem of relating program (or alternative) goals to overall institutional goals.

Finally, the specific alternatives to be implemented are selected—a decision is made. Then the descriptions of the alternatives are used as a basis for preparation of budgets and authorization of program changes.

SUMMARY OF THE DIFFERENCES BETWEEN NEGOTIATED AND SYSTEMATIC PLANNING

Before we consider the possibility of a transition from present methods of planning to those based on systems analysis, it would be well to regard some basic differences between the two techniques.

In negotiated planning the goals are often not stated. Each negotiator prefers to leave his "fall back" position or ultimate goal a mystery so that he has room to maneuver and bargain. In systematic planning, both the goals and the measures of performance for judging progress toward the goals are to be made explicit and public. Most desirable, the goals are agreed upon by all parties before the planning starts.

The two methods also differ as to the use of data. A negotiator releases only those data which support his cause. The hope is that the combined effect of the data presented by various factions will ultimately bring forth a more or less total picture. In actual practice, however, many positions are not fully represented. Many parties to the negotiations do not have the resources to collect and organize even the data that would support their own case. In systematic planning, there is a common analysis group who collects, organizes and presents data for all to use. The data are to be made public and available to all interested parties. While this procedure is expensive, it does eliminate arguments about data, although not about its interpretation.

In negotiating, comparisons between alternatives, to the extent that explicit alternatives are presented at all, are made during oral arguments. In systematic planning, these comparisons are made by predicting the consequences of each alternative with formal analytics. All analyses are presented in writing and are available for study and for recalculation with differing assumptions.

Regarding the processes involved in making the decision, both methods are alike. By either one, value judgments are required to set goals (and in a few cases, to make predictions). The systematic method uses hard data and computational forecasting where possible, leaving the negotiations to the goal setting areas.

In a sense, the use of systematic planning "raises the level of debate" from arguing about specific alternatives to arguing about goals.

WHAT DOES IT TAKE TO USE A SYSTEMATIC APPROACH TO PLANNING IN HIGHER EDUCATION?

Suppose, for the moment, that one wishes to use a systems approach (without assuming that this is the best thing to do in all cases), several steps are required in order to define goals and to set up the data base and the predictive procedures required by the systematic method.

First, the decision-makers involved must agree on explicit goals. Expressions of basic goals are usually vague, such as, "our college should provide educational and research services to the community in which we exist". These goals, then, must be made more specific by agreement on the measures of performance, or *indicators*, which can be used to judge whether or not the system is moving toward the goal.

Indicators for the above-mentioned goal might be: the number of community residents who participate in a college program (perhaps measured by credit hours or contact hours) and the number of man-hours of faculty time devoted to projects designed to improve the community. Furthermore, these goals must be made explicit by establishing *desired levels* for the indicators. For example, the college might decide that at least 20 per cent of its student contact hours should be devoted to residents of the community and that at least 30 per cent of its faculty research time should be expended on community-related projects. (An extension service would, of course, contribute to at least one and perhaps both of these indicators and therefore to the goal.) Finally, since there will be several goals and many indicators, the decision-makers must set priorities among the indicators, to determine which deserve the most attention in a given planning phase.

Most "systems analysis" projects which fail do so because policy makers neglect to identify indicators and associated desired levels. Without these factors, there is no basis for either creating or evaluating alternatives.

The problem of setting goals in higher education is more difficult than it is in almost any other organization. There are obvious goals related to vocational training, such as the ability of the students to get jobs when they graduate. And there are goals related to the community, in two ways. First, the college, by its very existence, brings activity into the area and contributes to its regional economic product and to its economic health. Second, it can contribute to the community, beyond education. It can design and help implement improvements in community services.

Also, however, a college can be considered as an activity in which the students and/or the faculty participate for its own sake. In a sense, the college is an "art form", which one enjoys as a thing unto itself. It is very difficult to measure this last goal and to relate it to the others. Abstract considerations of this sort contribute to the difficulty of expressing priorities among various goals.

Goal-setting for higher education is further confused by the fact that a college can be considered as two almost separate entities: (1) the faculty, which is responsible for faculty–student interaction (the teaching and learning which go on) and for the research process; (2) the "administration", which is responsible for providing the services that the faculty and students need. Alternatively, the institution can be considered as an integrated whole with a single decision-making mechanism. The choice between these two views is significant. It affects everything from basic organization to the most trivial decision processes.

Yet, in my opinion, goal setting, while critical, is not as difficult as many imply. If faculty, students and administrators can be induced to think about what they really want the university or college to do—what they want the institution's future to be like—indicators which measure goals can be developed. A critical question to ask in this process is, what factors or indicators one would look at so that one could say that the institution is doing a better job than it did in "the past"? If the answers are the result of serious thinking, this question should evoke very explicit indicators, on which there will be general agreement. Differences may arise as to the desired levels and priorities, but the differences will be out in the open and subject to debate.

The second major effort which must be undertaken before systematic planning can be implemented is the development of a good data system. Most of the program planning and budgeting activities frequently proposed are efforts to establish good cost accounting and other data bases. Setting up such information systems is not conceptually difficult, but does take a great deal of time and effort. Perhaps it is largely this fact which inhibits the progress of an institution toward the implementation of systematic planning.

The third major effort required to implement systematic planning is the development of the analytic processes, or *models*, which will allow the prediction of resource requirements (manpower, space, costs), of effects and of other consequences of proposed alternatives. The development of some models is well within the state of the art, but again time-consuming and expensive. There are, however, many efforts underway to provide these models, along with generalized software to facilitate their use (see Casasco, 1970). Prediction of the consequences of behavioral processes or of the long-term economic consequences of alternatives is difficult and requires the judgment of experts.

Finally, of course, implementation of systematic planning requires decision-makers who understand what systematic planning is and how to use the models and data tools available.

In summary, setting up for systematic planning takes a high level of technical effort, concentrated negotiations for setting goals and priorities, money and time.

PROBLEMS WITH THE SYSTEMATIC APPROACH

We have discussed the process of planning and the steps required in preparing to plan by systematic means. To complete the picture, let us take a look at some of the problems which may result from the use of the systematic approach and then at some of the benefits.

The basic problem with systematic planning is that it is completely unfamiliar to decision-makers who have been trained and selected for years as good negotiators. The change from negotiating to explicating goals and analyzing on the basis of formal information is a major one. To some extent, the systematic approach takes away the negotiating base.

The psychological trauma associated with the transfer of orientation from negotiating to systematic planning is quite real and even impedes bringing groups together to establish goals.

K

As we have noted, systematic planning does involve money and man-power, not only to set it up, but also to operate the complex, extensive data systems. Technicians who can develop and use analytic models must be employed. Time on the part of decision-makers to analyze and absorb the data must be expended.

A more serious difficulty is that the systematic approach, by requiring explicit indicators may focus attention on goals or objectives which are too narrow. The phenomenon of inexpressible goals may be real and there may be alternatives which, though desirable, do not measure up well on a chosen set of quantitative indicators. Good systematic planning does *not* preclude the acceptance of such alternatives, but does tend to make them appear less attractive.

A final drawback to the systematic approach is that our understanding of human behavior is limited, and therefore we have no models or analytic methods for predicting the behavioral consequences of alternatives. In some work my organization [Government Studies and Systems, Inc., Philadelphia, USA] has done with the California Coordinating Council for Higher Education, there arose the problem of predicting the number of students who would come to very late or very early classes. No way was found to model the students' behavior. There was no prior data to serve even simple linear models. Another common educational planning problem is to predict the effect of increased faculty workload on faculty performance (both in educational and in research activities). There are, at this time, no formal ways of making such predictions. Still, systematic planning is valuable in that it eliminates the time required to make other predictions and gives the planner more time for concentration on these critical judgments. Also, an attempt to implement systematic planning pinpoints very clearly the need for fresh inputs in the behavioral area, thereby providing a pragmatic base for exploration by educational researchers.

BENEFITS OF SYSTEMATIC PLANNING

Despite the above problems, the systematic approach does offer a number of benefits. First, it provides a basis for communicating the institution's decisions to outside agencies. The negotiating mode may arrive at excellent decisions (in terms of application of resources to attain goals). But it does suffer from the fact that the negotiatior has trouble describing to outsiders why the decisions were made, what alternatives were considered and how those alternatives compared with one another. The systematic approach is explicit. Written justification for any decision is usually inherent in the documents produced as a normal part of the planning procedure.

Because the systematic approach depends on formal processes of prediction and comparison (models), it tends to offer more stability as managers and administrators change. There is less opportunity for the development of a personality cult and more for the continuity of efforts to improve performance and attain goals. (If an institution is already headed in the right direction, this independence of personality is an advantage. If, however, the organization is in serious trouble and needs a major "shakeup", the introduction of a charismatic leader to set new directions may be desirable and should not be precluded by a planning process.)

Because it is never possible to represent all aspects of a problem through negotiations and because there is never time to discuss all major alternatives, the negotiating approach often fails to lead to good decisions, especially in complex, dynamic situations. By reason of its formal, highly organized nature, the systematic approach is designed to produce sound decisions, by making wise use of resources in the attainment of clearly stated goals.

REFERENCES

CASASCO, J. A. (1970) *Planning Techniques for University Management*, American Council on Education.

CROSS, A. (1970) *Poetic Justice*, Knopf.

CYERT, R. M. and MARCH, J. G. (1959) "A Behavioral Theory of Organizational Objectives", in Haire, M. (ed.) *Modern Organization Theory*, Wiley.

3.3 On Some Basic Steps in the Application of Systems Analysis to Instruction

Alexander M. Mood

ABSTRACT

The Systems approach to the evaluation of instruction is treated. A mathematical methodology is presented and a discussion is provided of the major aspects of the procedure i.e. definition and scope of the problem, listing of the relevant variables and their measure and construction of the model of the formulation of criteria functions.

A discussion is provided of the advantages of the systems approach and the use of sensitivity analysis is treated.

1 INTRODUCTION

Systems analysis is often used interchangeably with the term *operations analysis*. It refers to a specific analytical technique which consists of constructing a mathematical model of an operation. The model is a set of mathematical equations which enables one to calculate changes in the outputs of the operation resulting from specified changes in the inputs. Thus a model of the operation of building a highway might show that increases of 10 per cent in the manpower and 5 per cent in the equipment inputs would result in an 8 per cent increase in the primary output—miles of highway completed per month. The model would allow one to calculate the outputs for any arbitrary selection of inputs.

There is also usually implied in the term, *systems analysis*, the notion of optimizing some aspects of the outputs. The thing optimized is called the *criterion*. In the case of highway construction the criterion might be cost per mile and the optimization would consist of minimizing the cost per mile. It would be done by trying all combinations of inputs and selecting that one which resulted in the lowest cost. There are a number of mathematical devices for simplifying a search of this kind.

A similar phrase, *systems approach*, refers to a much less definitive procedure. It is simply the idea of viewing a problem or situation in its entirety with all its ramifications, with all its interior interactions, with all its exterior connections and with full cognizance of its place in its context.

Source: *Socio-economic Planning Sciences* (1967) Vol. 1, Pergamon Press, pp. 19–26.

The two ideas are related because a systems analysis attempts to deal with a problem comprehensively; in setting up the mathematical model one uses the systems approach. However, one uses it primarily as a guide and as insurance against overlooking an important factor. The systems analysis does not attempt to be complete in its mathematical model. It attempts to be judiciously selective by including significant factors and omitting or aggregating minor factors in order to keep the model to manageable proportions for purposes of the optimization.

To have a convenient illustration during the course of the paper, we shall refer to a specific hypothetical investigation, namely: to what extent, if any, should films be used in high school biology courses?

2 POSSIBILITY OF A SYSTEMS ANALYSIS

The first problem to be faced is whether or not the question to be studied is suitable for a systems analysis. The only way to start exploring this problem is to make a quick try at setting up a model. Before that can be done one must decide upon the variables that may enter into the model. With regard to the question of using films in biology courses some of the variables suggested might be: (1) quality of available films; (2) quality of teacher; (3) capability of students; (4) proportion of class time devoted to films; (5) budget for biology course; (6) cost of films and related costs; (7) selection of material to be presented by films; (8) composition of instructional program (conventional classroom teaching, laboratory work, demonstrations, TV and radio); (9) time of day class meets; (10) size of class; (11) standing of school in its football league; (12) teacher's measurements (if female).

Without considering the relevance of these variables let us merely inquire into whether they are measurable. Certainly, the last few can be put directly in numerical terms. The first variable is not easy but critics do measure quality of films very roughly as one-star, two-star, three-star, etc. Unfortunately, critics are not altogether consistent in these ratings so that the best we can hope for is only a crude measurement. Similarly with the second variable, about the only quantitative measure we can hope for is some kind of consensus of persons in a position to make good judgments about the teacher's performance. The third variable is less troublesome; the average score of the class on some aptitutde test might be used. Better still, one might devote two variables to this factor and use both the average and the standard deviation of the scores to measure capability of class. Moving on to the seventh listed factor, one would need really an infinite number of variables to give a logically complete description of all the ways material could be selected from the course to be presented on film. However, reasonable people could probably agree on a classification of the subject matter which would allow this factor to be represented by half a dozen or so well-defined variables. The eighth listed factor suffers from the same kind of difficulty and also needs four variables merely to measure the time allocation to the different teaching means.

Thus the investigator faces at the outset the problem of whether his question is amenable, as a practical matter, to quantitative analysis or whether such an analysis would be forced. Forced, that is, in the sense that so many quantities rest on human estimates and judgments that perhaps one might just as well admit that the whole question is largely a matter of judgment and treat it by qualitative rather than quantitative analysis.

As a general rule it may be safe to state that the amenability of a question to quantitative analysis usually varies inversely with the generality of the question.

When an investigator decides that his question is not completely suitable for the systems analysis technique, he must then face the problem of whether some portion of his analysis might be a systems analysis. It is a problem which is largely a judgmental decision resting on the extent to which the analyst believes the outcome of such a systems analysis will substantiate important aspects of the qualitative analysis of which it will become a part.

3   CONFIGURATION OF THE ANALYSIS

The scope of an analysis is ordinarily limited by resources of one kind or another (e.g. time, money), thus presenting the analyst with the problem of what shall be included in and what shall be omitted from the investigation. The avenues available for limiting an investigation are: (1) omitting variables; (2) aggregating variables; (3) restricting the range of variables.

Omission of variables is primarily accomplished on the basis of the judgment of the analyst after careful consideration of his real goal and evaluation of the apparent relevance of each tentative variable to that goal. Rare happy occasions do occur now and then when a brief preliminary analysis will immediately establish the importance of certain variables to the central problem.

Rather than omit variables altogether, analysts often prefer to combine apparently correlated variables into a function or index of some kind which then enters the analysis as a single variable. Thus, in the list of twelve variables given in the preceding section, perhaps the last four could be aggregated into an index of environmental state with some variables making positive and some making negative contributions to the index. Again, considering the eighth factor (composition of instructional program), the matter of selection might be combined so that the eighth factor would be simply the proportion of time not devoted to conventional teaching. The fourth factor (time devoted to films) might then be merely a proportion to be applied to the eighth factor.

An analysis can be very effectively limited without great cost in information content by limiting the range of variables either in extent or by restricting a continuous variable to discrete values. Thus the fourth factor might be limited to the range 0–0.50 and might be further limited to the four values 0.05, 0.10, 0.20 and 0.40 if the analysis seemed to be getting unduly complicated.

4 THE ECONOMIC FACTOR

School boards know how expensive education is, how tight educational budgets are, how difficult it is to squeeze more money out of the taxpayers. There is not much value in informing school boards that their educational systems can be improved by spending more money. They already know that. An investigation which shows that biology students learn more biology when the teacher uses films has missed the point. A meaningful practical question is this: if the teacher's salary is reduced so that she must be replaced by a poorer teacher and if the money thus saved is used to buy film equipment and rent biology films to be used by the poorer teacher, what then is the effect on the amount of biology learned by the students? In other words, school boards must allocate resources; additional resources allocated to one sector must be subtracted from another sector. Boards need guidance for making such exchanges profitably from the point of view of overall educational goals.

There is another reason that costs must almost inevitably be a factor of every investigation. It is that conclusions often depend strongly on the operating level of the systems. Recommendations for a wealthy school system will usually differ quite significantly from recommendations suitable for a needy school system. For geometrically-minded persons the accompanying figure demonstrates the idea. The vertical axis measures some reasonable criterion such as amount of biology learned by students and the horizontal axis represents the total budget level of the school system. The curves represent different components of the criterion; one would expect them all to be monotonically increasing with increasing budget. However, they will surely not be increasing at the same rate except in pathologically improbable circumstances. Thus the curve marked x_4 may indicate that a priority portion of money should be

Figure 1

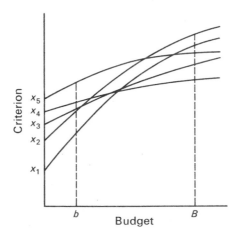

287

devoted to biology films at budget level b but that biology films may be at the bottom of the list at budget level B (which might include an excellent biological laboratory).

The primary effect of the cost factor is to place constraints on other variables in the mathematical model. Thus, supposing the twelve factors listed in Section 2 are each represented by a single variable or index and denoting those variables by $x_1, x_2, \ldots\ldots\ldots, x_{12}$ respectively, an economic constraint might appear as follows:

$$x_5 = C_1 + C_2 f(x_1) F(x_4) + C_3 g(x_2) G(x_4)$$

in which C_1 may represent some basic initial cost of using films (buying projector, etc.); C_2 and C_3 are unit costs by some definition; f, F, and g are increasing functions of the indicated variables; G is a decreasing function of x_4. This would be one of the equations comprising the mathematical model of a systems analysis.

5   RELATIONS BETWEEN VARIABLES

There are several problems involved in relating the variables of an analysis. There is first the problem of deciding what are the legitimate equational relations. An example is given in the preceding paragraph. That example was easy to write down from straightforward logical considerations. Others are not so easy to write down. What relation does "capability of students" fit into? How about "standing in football league", for another? Sometimes one has difficulty finding enough relations; sometimes one can put together too many. In the latter case, a mathematician must be called in to determine a complete set of independent relations.

Having one way or another determined a suitable set of relations, it is necessary to come to specific definitions about the functional forms that enter into the relations. Thus the equation above contains a function $f(x_1)$ which is said to be an increasing function of x_1. This says only that the cost of films increases as the quality of films increases. How does it increase? Linearly? In that case the function would be of the form $ax_1 + b$. This cannot be right. After the most lavish appropriation for a film which meets the director's every demand, will additional funds continue to increase quality at the same rate? Of course not. We need a function which increases steadily at lower values of x_1 but then levels off rapidly as one approaches high quality levels. The final choice might be made by having a mathematician supply a set of functions which have roughly the shape desired and then to have an expert in film production choose one from among that set.

After the equations have been determined and the functional forms selected for all the terms of the equations, one next faces the problem of fixing all the parameter values in the functions. The parameters are the constant (non-variable) elements in the functions and equations. In the illustrative equation above, C_1, C_2, and C_3 are parameters. It is possible that the function $f(x_1)$ might be taken to be linear over a limited range and then horizontal thereafter so that it would have the appearance shown in the accompanying figure with the slant portion given by $ax_1 + b$. Here a and b are parameters; b represents the cost of the very poorest quality film one could make. The parameter, a, measures the rate at which cost increases with quality; there might be some problem in determining what its numerical value is. All the functions will have parameter values to be pinned down.

Figure 2

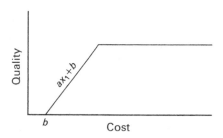

Some will require some digging through the literature; some, it will appear hopeless to determine except by the device of asking some expert to supply an educated guess. This last, incidentally, is a common and approved method of determining parameter values; it is upgraded, if possible, by obtaining several guesses from several experts in order to get an indication of their consistency and hence the reliability of the value used.

We have not been discussing solely the systems analysis in this section but also the qualitative analysis. A qualitative analysis must concern itself about all these things, the nature of relations, the elimination of dependent relations, the shapes of functions, the ranges of possible parameter values, the probable effects of all these on the criterion. An investigation which does not do these things is not an analysis but merely a pontification.

6 THE CRITERION

We recall that the criterion is the thing that the analyst is trying to optimize. It must be specified carefully and in the case of a systems analysis, specified with mathematical precision. Making the task difficult is the fact that the criterion nearly always seems to be the most elusive part of the whole analysis. It is an expression of an overall goal and once such a goal has been stipulated it rarely looks just right.

One aspect of the difficulty may be called the problem of philosophical pursuit. As an illustration we may suggest with respect to biology films that the goal is to optimize the proportion of classroom time to be devoted to films. To what purpose? Well, we want to maximize the amount of biology the students learn. Oh. So the real goal is to maximize the amount of biology learned. Yes, that's it. One thing you might do is drop history and maths so that three hours per day could be devoted to biology. No, no, no. The real goal is to maximize the amount of biology that can be taught in one hour per day. Oh? Even to the point of draining resources from the coaching of cheer leaders? God forbid! No! The real goal is to teach an amount of biology appropriate to a balanced education. What is a balanced . . .?

And so on and on the issue can be pushed until one is debating the fundamental aim of education. Is it to impart knowledge and information? Or, is it to generate understanding? Develop analytical skills? Develop capacities for imaginative creativity and ingenuity? Develop the capability of making sound judgments and decisions? Or is it all of these? If so, in what proportions or priorities? There is, of course, no point in getting off into this thicket. The investigation is certainly not going to settle these large matters. It is merely intended to shed a little light on the advisability of using films in teaching biology. The final statement of the goal should reflect that fact as accurately as possible and as consistently as possible with the general beliefs of the day about the larger matters. It is a good rule of thumb to phrase the goal about one level above that of the investigation in order to be sure that it does fit its immediate context. In a similar vein, the commander of an infantry company makes his decisions in the light of the goals of his battalion commander but does not wander off into the theater commander's plans or the national war aims.

The criterion must be a function of the variables in the analysis. That is why some of the variables are there in the first place—the criterion depends upon them. The other variables are there because those required by the criterion are entangled with them. One view is, then, that the criterion determines the model; certainly that is true to the extent that there is rarely anything to be gained by carrying along variables which do not affect the criterion either directly or indirectly.

Let us assume, for illustrative purposes only, that a suitable criterion for the film problem is maximization of the amount of biology learned as a function of the budget allocated to the one-year high school biology course. Restricting ourselves for simplicity to the first six variables only, we would seek (in symbols):

$$Y(x_3, x_5) = \max_{1,2,4,6} Y(x_1, x_2, x_3, x_4, x_5, x_6)$$

Where Y is the amount learned and is to be maximized over the first, second, fourth, and sixth variables. The actual maximization could not of course be carried out until the precise functional form of Y is specified.

Figure 3

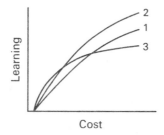

How does the amount learned by students vary with the quality of the films (x_1)? With the quality of the teacher (x_2)? And so on. To perform a qualitative analysis we must have at least some reasonably reliable impressions about how learning varies with these factors.

A very common problem in developing a criterion is that there is no suitable single criterion but two or more factors that one would like to optimize simultaneously. For example, one might desire not only to maximize the students' learning of biology but also to minimize the total cost C of giving the biology course. These two quantities work in opposite directions so that it is impossible to achieve both ends. Considering learning, Y, (e.g. measured by an achievement test,) and cost, C, for a fixed teaching system, the amount of learning might vary with cost along a curve such as one of those plotted in the figure. The curve labeled 2 is everywhere better than that labeled 1 because for any amount of learning it has lower cost and for any cost it gives more learning. But curves like 3 ruin any chance of selecting a system on the basis of the simple kind of comparison possible between 1 and 2. One must face the issue of how the criterion shall exchange dollars for achievement points and use a criterion perhaps of the form:

$$kY - C$$

if a constant exchange ratio k is to be used over the whole range of the variables. Thus, and this is generally true, multiple criteria must be combined into a single index or function before the optimization stage of a systems analysis can be carried out.

7 CONCLUSIONS OF AN ANALYSIS

The advantages of a systems analysis over a qualitative analysis are never so apparent as in the evaluation of the results of the analysis. The systems analysis with its precise mathematical statements is not an easy place to hide unconscious assumptions. Furthermore, a systems analysis can be subjected to a *sensitivity analysis* which is a replay of the whole analysis with modifications in some of the judgments and estimates that went into the construction of the model. Frequently very many replays of the analysis are done with whole sequences of variations in functional forms and variations in parameter values so that the analyst can see how seriously the results of the analysis depend on some of the less certain components of the analysis.

With all this, the role of judgment is nevertheless quite large in a systems analysis and it may be worthwhile to recapitulate some of the places where judgment has intruded: (1) definition of scope of problem; (2) specification of amount of resources to be devoted to investigation; (3) listing of relevant variables; (4) selection of factors to be included; (5) selection of factors to be excluded; (6) selection of factors to be aggregated; (7) selection of aggregating functions; (8) decisions restricting ranges of variables; (9) construction of model; (10) selection of functional forms; (11) estimation of parameters; (12) selection of criterion; (13) specification of criterion function; (14) selection of statistical design if data are to be gathered; (15) allocation of study resources to data gathering; (16) design of sensitivity analysis; (17) evaluation of sensitivity analysis. The eighth item may involve a number of decisions regarding selection of a standard model versus construction of a special model, regarding the handling of random variables by stochastic methods or simply by expectations, regarding a single analysis or a sequential analysis or the advisability of preliminary analyses, regarding the feasibility of more elaborate models considering the resources available.

If a systems analysis rests so heavily on judgment, what of a qualitative analysis? It rests practically 100 per cent on judgment. It may marshal hundreds of indisputable scientific facts and deploy them most ingeniously at strategic points of a coldly logical argument, but those facts were selected by judgment and the paths of that logical structure were selected by judgment from an infinite network of conceivable paths. Another analyst would never duplicate it.

The beauty of a systems analysis is that another analyst will frequently come fairly close to duplicating it. And the structure of the analytical procedure allows the two analysts to determine just where and why their analyses diverge. Often they will be able to come to some agreement or reasonable compromise that satisfies them both. In any case, there will eventually result, after publication and a period of review and criticism, some generally accepted position among professionals in the field as to what, approximately, the situation is. In this way there can be built up a body of verifiable quantitative knowledge about some of the complex processes and operations with which education must deal.

3.4 Applications of Decision Trees to Educational Planning

Tony Gear

ABSTRACT
A considerable proportion of national expenditures in western countries is devoted to education. Yet there are few descriptions of case studies of management science techniques in this area. The paper takes a particular technique, decision tree analysis, and demonstrates applications to important areas of educational planning. An example, spanning a 10-year planning period is described, arising from discussions with a local authority. The problem is concerned with the allocation of secondary school pupils in adjacent catchment areas. The decision tree demonstrates that the technique is able to present complex inter-relationships between local government, the schools involved, and central government departments.

INTRODUCTION
In complex environments, of which education is one, it is often necessary to take decisions regarding alternative courses of action when the outcomes of those actions are in some or all cases uncertain. Further, for a given course of action and uncertain outcome, subsequent decisions may be foreseen. As both the uncertain outcomes and the future decisions may have an effect on the "optimal" first stage decision, it may be relevant to include this information in any analysis.

The decision tree approach is a way of displaying the anatomy of sequential decision problems. It may also provide a ready means of analysing such problems.

The literature on decision trees is mainly concerned with applications in capital investment, marketing evaluation and military strategy, (e.g. see Beattie (1968), Gear, Gillespie and Allen (1972), Green and Frank (1966) and Hespos and Shassman (1965)). Two references which provide clear expositions of the technique itself are Magee (1964) and Raiffa

Source: Paper presented at the Joint National Meeting of the Operations Research Society of America and the Institute of Management Science (22–4 April, 1974) Boston, Mass. (Based in part on The Open University (1974) E221 *Decision-making in British Education Systems*, Unit 15 *Introduction to Planning and Decision Models*.)

(1968). This paper sets out to show that there are many potential applications of decision trees in educational planning and management. Six educational decision problems are described and associated decision tree diagrams are constructed. These are:

1   recruitment options;
2   school building decision;
3   school siting problem;
4   bussing option;
5   replacement problem;
6   school closure problem.

Each of the problems is fictitious but based upon actual situations described by school heads and local authority administrators. Lastly we look at a large and complex decision problem, developed in discussion with a local educational authority, to convert a region to a comprehensive secondary education system. The paper is concluded with a brief discussion of the problems of analysing the decision trees, which implies that educational objectives are clearly defined.

DECISION TREE EXAMPLES

1   *Recruitment problem*
The situation involves the science department of a comprehensive school, and the head of the department has to decide whether to press for the recruitment of one or two additional staff who can teach general science to ordinary level General Certificate of Education standards. His present staff size in this area is three (two married men and a newly married woman). Based upon his experience, he is aware of the chances of losing up to two members of his staff during the teaching year. He also has partly subjective and partly historical notions of the relative chances of losing none, one or two staff following the recruitment of one or two additions. The critical factor in his mind is the average pupil/teacher ratio for all the courses in general science for the coming year. The situation may be displayed as a small decision tree as shown in Figure 1.

This figure allows us to define the "building blocks" of decision-trees. Firstly, the square box or node labelled A indicates a decision point. The decision options are routes AB and AC, relating to the decision to recruit one or two additional staff respectively.

Nodes B and C depict uncertain outcomes. If the decision to recruit one addition is taken the wastage of staff (including the newcomer) is 0, 1 or 2 as shown by routes BD, BE and BF respectively. The subjectively based probabilities (denoted by "p" in the figure) of each of these possible future states are shown as p=0.3, p=0.3, p=0.4 for wastages of 0, 1 and 2 teachers respectively. Thus the chance (or if you prefer, the relative weighting) of route BD, for example, is 0.3 or 3.0 per cent.

Figure 1

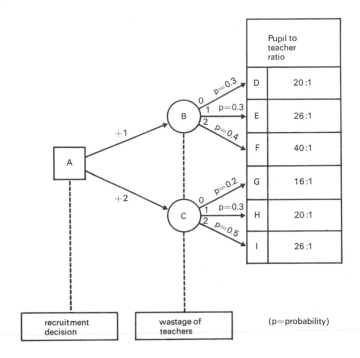

	Pupil to teacher ratio
D	20:1
E	26:1
F	40:1
G	16:1
H	20:1
I	26:1

Alternatively, if the decision to recruit two additional staff is taken (AC), the wastages of 0, 1 and 2 (CG, CH and CI) staff have subjective probabilities of p=0.2, p=0.3, p=0.5 respectively. Thus, in this particular situation, the chance of wastage is thought to increase if two rather than one extra staff member are recruited. In this example, six future positions, D to I inclusive, may be reached (or are foreseen). The parameter of special interest, the pupil/teacher ratio, is calculated and shown in the final column. It is assumed that there is no uncertainty regarding forecasts of pupil numbers.

2 *School building decision*
The decision problem facing a local educational authority is whether to build a small or large primary school for a given catchment area. If the small school is built to meet the present needs of a planned new housing scheme it would have to be substantially enlarged in about five years' time. The small school would cost £120,000, the large school £250,000. The cost of enlargements, necessary as the housing development scheme proceeds, cannot be exactly predicted due to uncertainties regarding

295

Figure 2

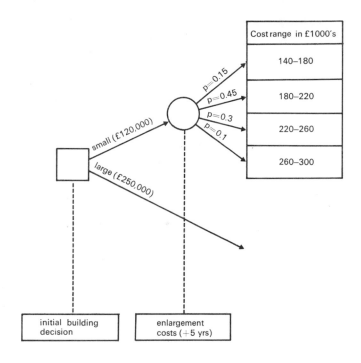

inflation in the building industry. Any of a range of values from
£140,000 to £300,000 are thought possible in five years' time. This
problem is depicted as a decision tree in Figure 2.

3   A school siting problem
In this example, a local education authority has two possible sites for the
building of an essential new comprehensive school. Site X is available for
purchase immediately at a price of £270,000. Alternatively, the Council
could consider applying to the Department of the Environment for
permission to build the school on some common land which is a local
beauty spot (site Y). The latter site would involve government departments and a public inquiry, the results of which would be uncertain.
Subjectively, the Chief Education Officer feels that there would be about
a 0.6 chance of obtaining approval for site Y, implying a 0.4 chance of
permission being rejected. Rejection would mean finally buying site X
about two years later, by which time the price would be inflated to an
uncertain degree, and there would be problems of overcrowding in existing schools. The situation is depicted in Figure 3.

Figure 3

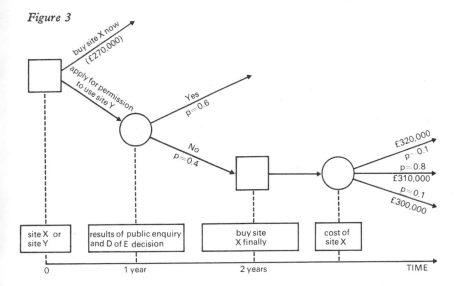

4 A bussing problem

In this example, the problem is whether a local education authority should accept responsibility for bussing a group of primary children from one area of a city to another where the school is sited. Legally, the council is not responsible, although there is a certain moral responsibility in terms of accident prevention at several trunk road crossings. Also it is known that not all the children will dutifully cross roads at manned points. The annual cost of bussing would be £2,000, inflating at 5% per annum. If the council decide not to provide buses, parental pressure-groups may form, especially if accidents subsequently occur. The situation is shown in Figure 4 (p. 298). Note that there are four decision nodes numbered in the figure, but those numbered 2, 3 and 4 are only there notionally, as only one course of action, i.e. one line, is drawn from these nodes.

Figure 4 does not include data for the probabilities of two or more, or less than two, accidents in the first year. Information of this kind could be obtained from the Transport and Road Research Laboratory, based on historical data from similar situations. Of course, the chance of two or more serious accidents is repeated in subsequent years, even if less than two accidents occur in the first year. This is an example of a trade-off of costs against accident risks by the Council. It could be that more lives may be saved by using the £2,000 per annum for another purpose, such as care of the elderly. So there could be an opportunity cost attached to using the money for bussing.

5 A replace or repair problem

Exchester College of Technology has a vigorous European Languages

297

Figure 4

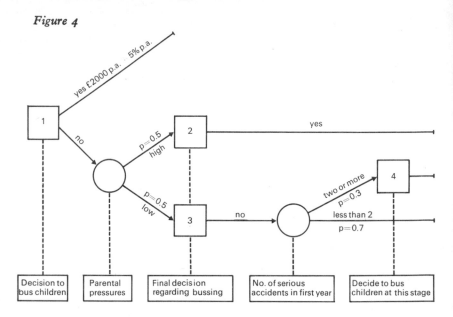

Department. The head of the department is faced with the problem of replacing an existing language laboratory with an improved facility at a cost of £5,000 or repairing the old laboratory at a cost of £2,000 initially, and £1,000 per annum thereafter, by signing a maintenance contract with the manufacturer.

The problem is made complicated as there is a new university college just down the road. This establishment, recently completed on a green field site, is highly likely to install its own language laboratory. This would be of much higher capacity, and could cope with its internal demands as well as any foreseeable demand from the College of Technology. In discussion, agreement is reached that the College of Technology would have free use of the laboratory once installed, but the timing of installation is uncertain. The University College estimate that installation could be in two, three or four years' time with probabilities of 0.25, 0.5, 0.75, respectively.

The problem is depicted in Figure 5: note that if the University College do not install until four or more years have passed the total cost on repairs and maintenance equal or exceed the replacement cost. However, the "repair" decision allows Exchester to spread out the cost of the laboratory over time. The head of the department must take this, and the associated probabilities, into account in order to reach a decision.

6   A school closure problem
The County Advisor for Primary Education, Cyril Butterfield, has advised the closure of Lower Nunswold County Infant and Primary

Figure 5

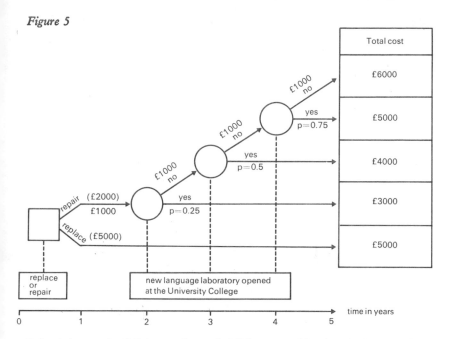

	Total cost
	£6000
	£5000
	£4000
	£3000
	£5000

repair (£2000) £1000

replace (£5000)

£1000 no   yes p=0.25

£1000 no   yes p=0.5

£1000 no   yes p=0.75

£1000 no

| replace or repair | new language laboratory opened at the University College |

time in years

0   1   2   3   4   5

School due to the fall in numbers of children, combined with the need for expensive repairs. Although closure is advised, from past experience the Chief Education Officer knows that this is not easy to carry out. In particular, he is aware that several members of the Education Committee are always reluctant to close a rural school, as a vital part of the social fabric disappears. Also, the School Managers have intimated to him that they will strongly oppose closure. Bearing these points in mind, he decides to construct a decision tree diagram, having recently acquired a working knowledge of the technique on a Civil Service Staff Management Course. This is shown in Figure 6 (p. 300) in which an attempt has been made to build in unexpected chance occurrences at three stages.

A COMPLEX EXAMPLE

A larger and more complex educational example is now presented based on discussions with the Planning Officers of a Local Education Authority.

The problem is concerned with the allocation of secondary school pupils in two adjacent catchment areas (S and T) of a city which are naturally divided by geographical features, as shown on Figure 7 (p. 300).

Accepting a policy decision to go fully comprehensive, the Planning Director for Education is faced with three major options:

1   to close school B, which is old and in need of modernization, transferring existing children at B to the comprehensive C in area T. This

3 Towards a Systematic Approach

Figure 6

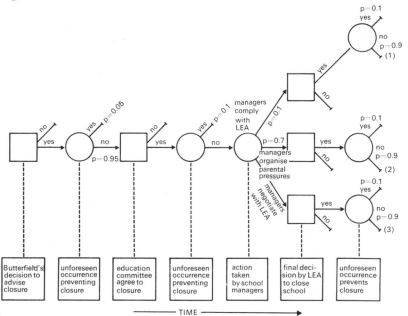

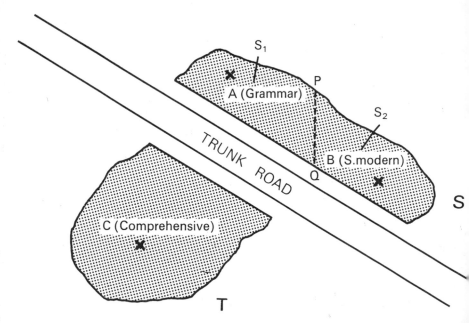

Figure 7

option would involve the enlargement and conversion of school A to a comprehensive for the whole area S, made up of areas S_1 and S_2;

2   to convert and modernize A and B into comprehensives serving areas S_1 and S_2 (divided by the broken line PQ) respectively;

3   to combine schools A and B into one comprehensive system serving the area S as a whole, without interfering with schools.

Option 1 is appealing to the Council, as a cash sum of £250,000 is obtained by selling site B. It would, however, be very expensive to enlarge A to serve area S; it would also mean bussing those children already at B to C, which would overcrowd C for about three years.

The policy decision and the three options are shown at the left-hand side of Figure 8. Option 1 has to gain the approval of the Department of the Environment and the Department of Education and Science. Assuming node 15 is reached, new posts would be offered for the staff at B to transfer to C. Resignations (node 26) would be expected, necessitating a recruitment decision (nodes 29, 30, 31). If node 16 is reached, following refusal of permission by the Department of Education and Science to close school B, then the decision would be taken to follow option 3, as this would be sure to gain Department of Education and Science approval. The decision to combine A and B would involve the reconstitution of two organizations into one. The resignation and recruitment problems of the key headmaster would be involved, as shown, from node 23 onwards.

DISCUSSION

The foregoing applications ignore to a great extent both the problems of applying decision trees in general and to education in particular. Some general problems likely to be encountered are:

1   The further into the future the diagram is developed, the more branches the tree has, bringing problems of data collection and analysis. An important consideration in this connection is that costs and benefits in the distant future may have small values when discounted to present time. One practical procedure is to assign "values" to the "tips" of a tree terminated at some horizon date in order to represent the subjective opinion(s) about the future beyond the cut-off point. The essential task is to experiment with more than one horizon date to see if these are sensitive to the *first* decision at "time now" on the tree.

2   It is simpler to construct the tree if essentially continuous probability distributions are approximated by treating them as discrete distributions. Again, a sensitivity analysis may be carried out in which the number of discrete values approximating the distribution is changed. Alternatively, a simulation approach may be adopted in which, by repeated sampling from each distribution on the tree, the relative frequency with which each alternative starting decision

Figure 8

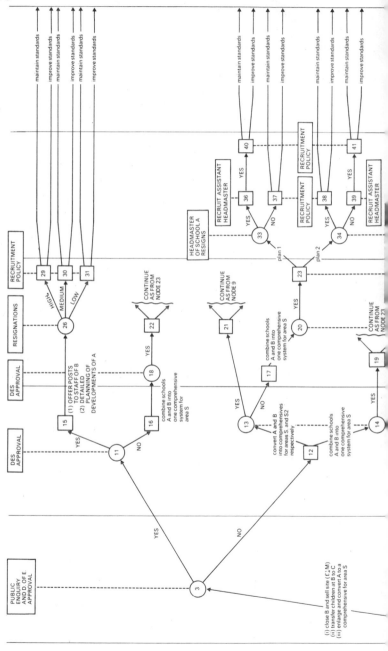

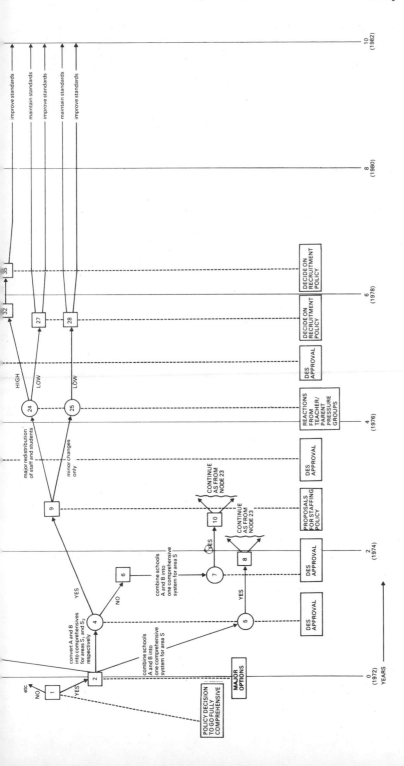

becomes the "best" can be found. One starting decision may completely dominate the rest; or the problem may be more complex, with the starting decision frequently changing. In the latter case one can present the results to the relevant decision-taker so that a starting decision in the face of uncertainty can be selected.

3   The whole decision tree concept implies that *all* alternative actions are analysed, and that *all* chance outcomes are included at chance nodes. The subjective probabilities on foreseen outcomes are scored so that they add up to one. But suppose an outcome is not foreseen, and hence excluded; the absence of the unforeseen path will introduce a bias into the analysis. This is a fundamental problem to which there is no easy answer. It may sometimes be possible to incorporate a branch labelled "unforeseen consequences", with a probability attached.

4   Care has to be taken to assess whether a particular cost or benefit should be attributed to a particular project. Questions to ask are: would the money have been spent, or the resources consumed, or the benefits accrued, independent of a given decision in the tree structure? For example, a cost may have been already committed by decisions made prior to those in the analysis, in which case the cost becomes one which is already committed (or "sunk") in the future.

5   Different parts of an organization may be responsible for different portions of the decision tree. Personnel in these areas may then each provide estimates to these sub-sections. This will lead to systematic errors between individuals due to different attitudes and skills regarding estimation. On the other hand, the technique can have an integrating effect on the personnel concerned, improving co-operation through a common vehicle of communication—the tree diagram. In some situations it may be desirable to apply forecasting techniques (such as the delphie technique) to provide data.

There are a number of factors which make *educational* planning to some extent distinct from many other planning areas. Specifically, these are:

1   The lack of methodology to develop working, that is operational, objectives. This immediately makes it impossible to perform some kind of quantitative analysis of the decision trees in this paper, except for trivial cases of, say, cost minimization to reach the same outcome under conditions of certainty.

2   The lack of known relationships, even of a stochastic nature, between the outputs ("educated" people) and the resource inputs to educate them (teachers, buildings, facilities, money).

3   The lack of known relationships between educational outputs and different methods and ways of utilizing the resource inputs.

4   The lack of means, other than some type of formal examination, to

measure the achievement in terms of student performance against pre-defined behavioural objectives.

CONCLUSION

It appears feasible and desirable to construct decision tree diagrams for a wide range of educational planning problems. It is also often possible to add data such as subjective probabilities, to chance branches. However, problems arise when the trees include alternative strategic (rather than tactical) decisions which it would be desirable to evaluate quantitatively, employing such techniques as "roll-back" analysis, bayesian analysis, simulation and portfolio planning. This is because difficulties arise when attempts are made to define objectives in an operational form; there is little information available which shows the relationship between the achievement of objectives and the allocation of resources to the learning process itself.

REFERENCES

BEATTIE, C. J. (1968) "Allocating Resources to Research in Practice", in Proceedings of NATO Conference entitled "Applications of Mathematical Programming Techniques", English Universities Press.

GEAR, A. E., GILLESPIE, J. S. and ALLEN, J. M. (1972) "Applications of Decision Trees to the Evaluation of Applied Research Projects", *Journal of Management Studies*, Vol. 9, No. 2, May 1972.

GREEN, P. E. and FRANK, R. E. (1966) "Bayesian Statistics and Marketing Research", *Applied Statistics*, Vol. 15, pp. 173–89.

HESPOS, R. F. and SHASSMAN, P. A. (1965) "Stochastic Decision Trees for the Analysis of Investment Decisions", *Management Science*, Vol. 11, No. 10, pp. 157–74.

MAGEE, JOHN F. (1964) "How to use Decision Trees in Capital Investment", *Harvard Business Review*, Sept.–Oct. 1964, pp. 157–74.

RAIFFA, H. (1968) *Decision Analysis: Introductory Lectures on Choices under Uncertainty*, Addison-Wesley.

3.5 A Discussion of the use of PPBS and MBO in Educational Planning and Administration

John L. Davies

INTRODUCTION

Planning Programming Budgeting Systems (PPBS) and Management by Objectives (MBO) are two examples of new techniques which have hit educational administrators in the United States and Great Britain during the last decade. As with several such techniques purporting to increase the effectiveness of educational organizations their origins are in other enterprises (Merevitz and Sosnick, 1971, Chapter 1). The fact that the origins of both sets of ideas are outside the educational system has produced major conceptual and practical difficulties of transplantation, which this article will be examining. Suffice it to say for the present that education differs from business in that it is not profit-oriented in terms of its objectives; it is concerned with providing a personal service; its success can only really be assessed over a long or medium time-scale; and decision-making is considerably influenced by the presence of politicians, whose relationships with professionals are a key variable in the whole debate.

It is a very difficult assignment to try to assess the success or failure of PPBS and MBO in education, a fact which will become clear in the course of this article (Frank, 1973). However, it may be that they should be considered in the light of their theoretical basis: both in fact originate from the open systems theory, which contains the following assumptions:

1 That any organization, to service, or to attain credibility, must be openly adaptable to the needs of its community.

2 That any organizational manifestations—structure, decision-making

---

Source: Commissioned for this volume by The Open University. Based in part on Davies, J. L. (1972, 1973) "Management by Objectives in Local Education Authorities and Educational Institutions" (Parts 1 and 2), *British Education Administration Society Bulletin*, Vol. 1, No. 1, Summer 1972 and Vol. 2, No. 1, Autumn 1973.

processes, information, sub-groups, personnel, etc.—are all inextricably linked; to modify any one will undoubtedly have some effect on the other elements, and managers ought to assess these likely consequences before making decisions.

3   That there are a number of key management activities which must be performed to ensure the effectiveness of the organization.

Figure 1 (pages 308–9) illustrates an approach to analysing public authorities using the systems concept. It is fairly self-explanatory, but some observations may assist:

(a) The organization is located within its environment or community, which comprises both the substantive environment (groups with a special and continuing interest in its activities: LEA, PTA, etc.) and the general environment (public opinion at large, which may only be mobilized on big, specific issues). The community will have various values of a political, social, religious and economic nature, which will influence how it is prepared to release the resources for educational purposes; it will also have something to say about the impact which the organization should have and to which goals it should be addressing itself. The community therefore provides, expects and criticizes or assesses. The three activities are quite clearly interrelated in a cyclical process.

(b) The organization itself therefore takes in raw *resources* (1), under the headings indicated, and by its various management and educational *processes* (2) converts them into a series of learning or teaching situations which can conveniently be regarded as its *provision* (3).

(c) Consumers of the service then make a behavioural *response* (4) to this offering, by taking up or rejecting the facilities and, in so doing, improving or not improving their own capabilities.

(d) Consumers who have used the service will then leave the orbit of the institution and, returning to society, will have an *impact* (5) on it, positively, neutrally or negatively. This impact may be in terms of their intellectual/physical contribution; their contribution to the community's economic prosperity; their cultural development, etc. The impact of their participation may well be felt by themselves in terms of increased earnings over a lifetime, or the joys of being a better citizen, or the ability to benefit more constructively from leisure. One may very well wish to define the impact in terms of the effect of the educational process on particular community problems (if this is possible) since it is according to one's perception of these problems that resources are put into the system in the first place.

(e) On the basis of the consumer going through the system and finding his way to the community, it is now possible to assess (in theory) just

3 Towards a Systematic Approach

Figure 1 A systems model of an educational institution in the context of organizational effectiveness

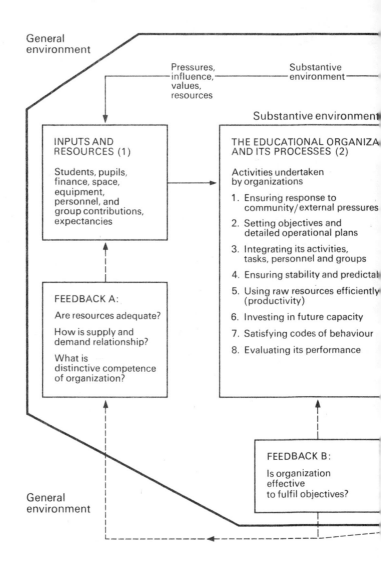

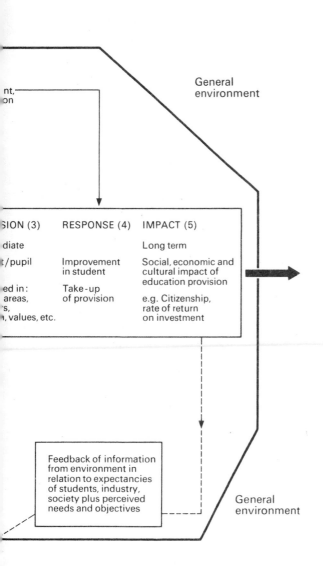

General
environment

nt,
on

SION (3)   RESPONSE (4)   IMPACT (5)

diate   Long term

t /pupil   Improvement   Social, economic and
              in student   cultural impact of
                            education provision
ed in :   Take-up
areas,   of provision e.g. Citizenship,
's,   rate of return
n, values, etc.   on investment

Feedback of information
from environment in
relation to expectancies
of students, industry,
society plus perceived
needs and objectives

General
environment

how successful the system has been; this necessitates the feedback loop. Here the purpose is to gain intelligence on causes of failure and scope for improvement by establishing relationships; without the systems model, and indicators, this cannot be done.

The common features of PPBS and MBO are:

1   a stress on the necessity of explicit objectives, and a recognition that they may be multiple and related to client satisfaction;
2   an emphasis on planning;
3   a conception of change in education as entirely normal, and something to be managed, controlled and phased, rather than something to be suffered;
4   a perception of the organization and its individuals as a means of transforming resources and expectations into achieved objectives;
5   a continuous review of whether the means employed in educational provision justify the ends;
6   The use of models, tools for making rational decisions and quantitative and qualitative means of measurement as a normal means of proceeding with administration;
7   the identification and use of alternative means of fulfilling goals;
8   the use of teams of specialists from many different disciplines to solve problems;
9   feedback and evaluation based on the extent of attainment of original goals, and accountability conceived also in these terms.

It very often follows that where PPBS and MBO systems have failed, the theoretical bases of the techniques have not been well understood. Short-circuiting adequate thinking on any of the above can lead to a great deal of trouble in the long term. For example, educational organizations have often set themselves objectives where the client figures only marginally; or have failed to examine all the courses open to fulfil a given purpose. In these cases the result has been a perpetuation of the *status quo*, and possibly spending more money on something which is increasingly irrelevant. To this issue, we shall return.

If the techniques have a common theoretical foundation, what then are the differences? PPBS is basically a system of budgeting around organizational objectives; a classification of anticipated expenditures around a set of programmes related to an end-product. PPBS incorporates a great deal of cost-effectiveness analysis, and the decisions which present themselves are concerned with how resources are to be allocated and used by the organization as a whole. MBO does not need many of the financial/ quantitative techniques necessary to PPBS. MBO is a personnel-oriented approach, which attempts to translate organizational objectives to individual and sub-group level, since it is here that the success of the school or college rests. Thus MBO incorporates features familiar to personnel administration—appraisal of staff effectiveness, motivation, control, staff development. Perhaps MBO is therefore a sub-system within PPBS, which reflects the needs of the wider organization. It is best, however, to regard the two systems as complementary and compatible.

Though we are considering PPBS and MBO in educational adminis- tration, we must not conceal the fact that education is part of a larger social service provision (Stewart, 1972 and Eddison, 1973). As such, if one is considering the objectives of provision organized by the local education authority or an institution, it is apparent that not only edu- cational objectives will be involved. A local education authority, for instance, provides facilities for school swimming and athletics, which could be used for wider community purposes at weekends and in the holidays. It provides technical education which, in some parts of the country, is a clear incentive to industries considering whether to invest in the area. Schools and colleges provide pastoral facilities which are often administered in close collaboration with the local services department. In short, educational organizations are fulfilling objectives which are not strictly educational—they may be based on wider economic, community care and recreational aims. In the past, education has not always formally and explicitly acknowledged these relationships in the planning and administration of its services. PPBS has been perceived to be a potent tool in demonstrating and activating these relationships, sometimes informally, in the rather tarnished name of "corporate management" (Bains, 1972). This aspect must nevertheless be considered in the discussion.

It is quite possible to consider PPBS and MBO in terms of the relationship of four groups with an interest in educational decision- making: politicians/elected members; clients/consumers; professionals in institutions at the front line; and educational administrators. Each of these groups has different things to obtain to further its own philosophy or interests. The purposes for which a specific PPBS or MBO system is used, and its design, will often reflect the strength or persistence of the various alliances of these groups. We shall attempt to demonstrate this aspect later.

It should be emphasized that both PPBS and MBO are only means to an end. If they become the end-product of the operation, education will only have created a self-perpetuating mechanism, something clearly to be guarded against.

PLANNING PROGRAMMING BUDGETING SYSTEMS

When any innovative management system takes root, it may be because of its own intrinsic worth, or because it was designed to overcome perceived deficiencies in the existing system. The latter is especially true of PPBS, and it will be useful at this stage to examine exactly what was thought to be wrong with the *status quo*. It follows that we have, implicitly, a series of expected advantages of using PPBS which can be tested against actual subsequent events.

It should be emphasized at the outset that not all authorities will necessarily subscribe to these reasons, but it is suggested that together they constitute a reasonably complete spectrum from which organizations may choose to use PPBS.

(a) There is a need to overcome the problem, evident in so many professional organizations, of separate, quasi-autonomous departments and lay committees, each one having its own particular policy which may not relate coherently to other empires' schemes; its own plans on a different magnitude or time-scale to others'; or its own resources which may never be available for fulfilling the needs of other services.

There may also be a prevalence of management by hunch or charisma, where all the facts pertinent to a decision may not be exposed. Furthermore, there may be little common understanding or wish to achieve common understanding of problems among the various groups. Here we would include mutual misconceptions by the public, elected members and professional officers at various levels. Misunderstanding leads to demotivation, and a complete failure of the authority to integrate its tasks, individual and group contributions.

What does PPBS offer us here? It offers the necessity of defining common objectives right across the whole local authority or institution to which a range of departments are likely to contribute. In the programme budgeting parlance, these are normally referred to as interdisciplinary programme areas, and departments such as Education, for instance, would contribute activities which would lead to the fulfilment of policy objectives for the Education, Leisure and Recreation, Community Care and Industrial Development programme. Libraries would also probably contribute to the same programmes, and both groups of professionals would have to organize their service to fulfil the requirements of several programme areas—quite a different situation from the present one.

(b) Corporate management purports to be a client-oriented system, and this is undoubtedly an attractive possibility in days of "community development" and "community politics". Ascertainment of need must not be confused with a well-articulated demand from a vociferous pressure group; neither should the information and demands of lay members be regarded as synonymous with a complete expression of public need, vital though this is. Supplementary information is required, collected objectively, with no doubts as to its validity, in areas like leisure and recreation provision, pre-school education facilities, housing, etc. This would seem to require (1) a group of officers with research and development and consumer survey functions; (2) a means of collating and analysing the vast amount of primary information possessed by rent officers, social workers, librarians and teachers, which is capable of wider usage (and, of course, the enormous amount of unsorted information possessed by elected members). Apart from this, if a PPB System is used, the way in which the choices are exposed at different levels should facilitate this client orientation. It is possible to design a programme budget for education, leisure or community care so that the sub-programme headings refer to particular population groups. In the case of the latter, groups such as problem families, old-age pensioners, physically and mentally handicapped, immigrants, etc., are quite feasible, though other structures may be preferable. The point is that PPBS lends itself to client orientation if this is required, since it is a system of output budgeting rather than input budgeting.

(c)   A client-oriented authority has to consider the satisfaction of needs over a long-period. Certainly any attempt to project the effect of investment in education and related services falls into this category. Perhaps, therefore, it is reasonable to project financial allocation and commitment over a similar period. This is extremely difficult, a fact reflected in the fact that capital budgets are normally forecast for five years ahead and that recently this has also applied to revenue estimates. However, the use of rolling finance programmes, whilst not caused by PPBS, is an essential part of any corporate management exercise.

(d)   The deficiencies of traditional methods of budget formulation have been a strong contributory factor in the movement we are describing. Apart from the projection problems already mentioned, we also have:

1   The expression of estimates in terms of inputs of expenditure rather than outputs or areas of projected achievement. Consequently, the implications of interrelated expenditure may not be recognized, and cuts may be made which make financial sense but managerial non-sense. For instance, it is quite possible for a committee to approve teaching staff provision for a given project under one heading but omit to grant the project non-teaching staff facilities under another heading, particularly since the latter may be subject to Establishment Committee control. It could be argued therefore that the traditional estimate statement clouds the real choices.

2   The separation of capital and revenue estimates, both in time and documentation. This is justified in finance terms, since one pays for one out of borrowing (longer-term mainly) and the other out of taxation (short-term). However, many decisions are made without the decision-taker (lay or professional) being fully cognizant of the fact that there may be an interrelationship. PPBS advocates a clear statement of activity/project together with the resource implications, from whatever origin.

3   There has been a traditional practice of "creeping incrementalism", i.e. adding $X\%$ to last year's budget. This has led to the assumption that what is, is good, and has often thwarted a proper scrutiny and justification of ongoing projects. In education this may not be justi-fied—courses become obsolete, as does anything else.

L

4 Associated with this is the "bottom-up" budget. The spending units
at the foot of the hierarchy (departments or schools) assemble their
demands for resources, which are aggregated at various levels in the
ladder until the political masters decide on the acceptable rate to be
levied; this usually means considerable cuts all the way down, often
without consultation with the officers concerned. Much executive
time may be wasted, and various authorities are now introducing a
global budgeting/rate rationing system, by which early in the
financial year (June/July) growth rates are indicated for each service
and each activity within it.

However, this can militate against effective client-oriented management since, irrespective of what needs may be identified by those at
the grassroots, provision has already been fixed in broad terms. This
is the contemporary dilemma of corporate management: reconciling
corporate resource supply with corporate service demand. Rate
rationing did not develop as part of PPBS, but PPBS is virtually
impossible to work without it.

5 If the purposes of estimate preparation are to offer choices for
expenditure, from what has already been said, the traditional system
may not offer us the right choices. Further, many authorities are
amending their system to a project orientation, which permits a selection of priorities.

(e) The search for productivity and cost-effectiveness is at least as
powerful a motive in authorities as any client orientation, though it can
convincingly be argued that to keep rates and loan charges down reveals a
considerable client orientation! It is perhaps not a coincidence that
PPBS, particularly in its financial aspects, gained great favour from the
period of the 1967 credit squeezes. It is certainly evident that many
politicians have espoused PPBS for the purpose of overcoming taxpayer
resistance to educational funding.

It is probably fair to say that whilst financial audit or work study tries
to save money at the margins by scrutiny, the audit associated with PPBS
is far more fundamental: "is the service needed anyway?", "have all the
alternative ways of fulfilling the objectives been identified and stringently
compared?"; "what was the result of the expenditure on the social condition it was intended to improve?". Savings are likely to be more convincing and accurately objective through this form of analysis. There is
still clearly a place for the traditional audit, but supplemented by these
newer skills of the corporate strategist and the social economist.

This development clearly involves the necessity of measuring the
effectiveness of expenditure—the indicators of performance, no less. We
need these indicators to cover the range from raw resources (inputs),
through process effectiveness, provision and response, to impact. It
further involves the use of techniques of selecting from alternatives
which have indicators attached, to which we shall refer shortly.

Figure 2 The usual conceptual framework of PPBS

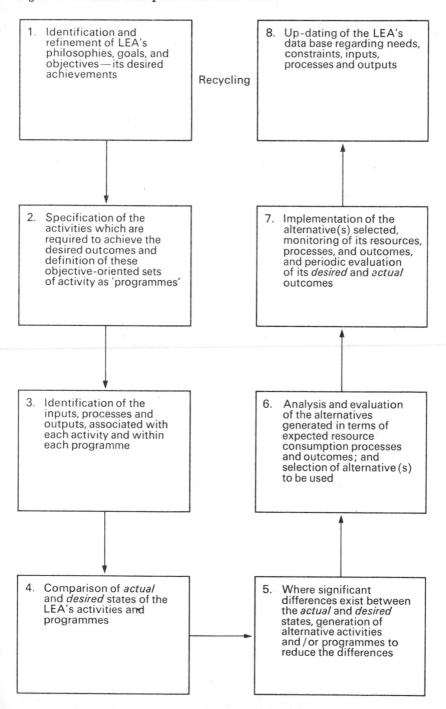

(f) The notion of an organization investing in its future capacity for coping with problems is not new: the immense increase in capital funding is testimony to this, and so is the growing attention to staff development. Acquisition of land is often not as prudent, and there may be no corporate policy for planning the incidence of detailed resource requirements in these three areas in relation to the principal objectives of the authority. The devices which we have considered, it is contended, facilitate this planned investment in the future problem-solving capacity of the authority.

(g) In the light of the above, PPBS is designed to increase the level of common understanding of the problems of institutional management, by not only improving the way in which information is presented, but by making clear the relationship between the various planning processes for the approval of courses, staffing, financial allocations, etc., which are present in education. Further, at its best it can be used to delegate responsibility, within defined targets and constraints, to a low level in the institution—the course tutor, head of department, etc., and this potentially is a good way of increasing staff morale.

(h) Finally, education is clearly in a period of extensive experimentation with new teaching methods and forms of organization and curriculum. If continuation of these has any legitimacy, it is important that educators evaluate in educational and economic terms the costs and benefits of the exercise.

There are two major points which emerge from the above analysis:

1 If one is to believe these statements of expected benefits to be derived by local education authorities from the use of PPBS, a great many things are being required of a finite management system/technique. The ability of PPBS to deliver these goods must be suspect, but perhaps the fault is that of the indiscriminate purchaser rather than the product itself! Indeed, Schick (1971) contends that the decision-maker may be falling between several stools, and strongly recommends dropping the B for Budgeting from PPBS, and using the technique mainly for purposes of policy clarification.

2 It is demonstrable in certain cases that some of the forms or manifestations of PPBS designed by local education authorities may not be suitable for their proclaimed purpose. A different form of PPBS or an allied technique could be much more profitably employed, and possibly with less dislocation to the organization. For example, if the main purpose of the exercise is to save money, some of the more traditional financial techniques such as value analysis, cost benefit analysis or organization and method studies might be deployed (Argenti, 1969).

It will be apparent that the business of introducing PPBS is very complex. The major features which we have identified to date demonstrate this:

1 budget-organized in a way which shows all the costs related to the true object of the expenditure;
2 long-, mid- and short-term forecasts of costs and outputs;
3 budgets based not on a departmental basis, but on the objectives of the whole organization;
4 budgets organized in a hierarchic manner to demonstrate all the courses to the fulfilment of a given policy;
5 a cycle of planning activity as indicated in Figure 2 (p. 315).

As we shall show later, there are few existing PPB Systems in education which are fully developed and exhibit all these features (Eidell and Nagle, 1970). This is partly because educational organizations have only wished to use part of the full PPB System at any one point in time, partly because of the immense technical problems of developing a full system, and partly because of the behavioural, organizational and logistic problems of implementation. The last-named particularly influence the acceptance or rejection of PPBS. We shall therefore examine these issues in more detail and, in so doing, attempt to show more of the mysteries of PPBS. It can be contended that education organizations leap into PPBS without adequate preparation in the areas discussed below.

The problem of devising goals and objectives in PPBS
The existence of a clear statement of organizational objectives within a PPBS framework is necessary to provide a backcloth against which any systematic making of decisions should take place. Without this statement, judgements about the adequacy and effectiveness of existing provision or proposed projects cannot be made.

A number of approaches to goals and objectives can be observed. New York State, in its early stages, focused on the long-term projection of needs and problems, and for each of its programmes provided a twenty-year estimate of trends and factors, a process well described by Schick (1971). Similarly, Burns and MacNamara (1974) describe the SWEP Project (Skyline Wide Educational Plan), which is a long-range planning project for the provision of comprehensive secondary education in the Dallas Fort Worth complex of Texas (see also Conrad et al., 1973).

The Department of Education and Science (1970) identifies a range of factors, variation in which will create a change in the level of resources required. Figure 3 indicates the factors determining the demand for resources in the Higher Education Sector at national level: a different range of factors may well be needed at local education authority or institution level (see p. 318).

An alternative method is that practised by Pennsylvania and Florida and, in this country, Coventry, Gloucestershire and Liverpool, where general goal statements were tied to the actual programme structures themselves. In each case, a hierarchy of a programme structure was created and objectives were attached to each level. The result is a broad statement of objective at the programme level, which is successively articulated and described in more detail at sub-programme, activity, element, and sub-element level. The degree of precision at the foot of the hierarchy is therefore quite evident, thus permitting practical and effective measurement and selection between alternatives.

There are a number of interesting issues emerging:

1   The goals must reflect the major values possessed by the dominant political force, or the professionals. For example, "to assist young persons and adults to identify their personal aims in life and to earn their own livelihood accordingly" is a more positive goal than "to provide a range of appropriate educational services for young adults in order to produce a supply of well-qualified manpower". The former has a philosophy of individual values, and the aim of enabling, whilst the latter's orientation is system based, impersonal and concerned with "doing things to people". One would therefore expect the programmes to be quite different to give effect to these contrasting aims.

2   The goals are likely to change as circumstances change. An objective of "caring for new minority groups within the population" (designed primarily to take care of immigrants) can become redundant if that particular objective is achieved. It could then change, of course, into an objective of "integration of minority groups"—a much more complex objective.

3   In the case of an education department of a British local authority it may operate activities and run organizations which contribute towards a

Figure 3 Variable factors on which to base projections for the future development of higher education

---

Maintenance of existing pattern and scale of provision for existing population change

Reduction of cost of provision to existing standards by intensive use of planned rationalization of subjects

Changes in proportion of age group attending

Changes in mix of institutions and subjects

Changes in standards and quality of accommodation

Changes in staffing ratios and standards

Changes in proportion taking different lengths of course

Other changes in scale of outputs

Changes in distribution of costs

Other (unallocable)

---

series of other programmes. Local authorities tend to evolve programmes in the following areas across the whole authority: education, community care, recreation and leisure, housing, transportation, environment, and industrial development.

Education departments have services which contribute to the programmes of education (schools, colleges); community care (aspects of special education, pastoral activity in schools, possibly pre-school provision); recreation and leisure (non-vocational, further education, school playing fields and swimming baths); housing (demands for student accommodation to be met from both specific provision and the general housing stock); industrial development (technical education, youth employment); transportation (school buses).

Under this type of PPBS therefore, within a corporate management system, education authorities and institutions are clearly likely to be subjected to multiple objectives.[1] These may create practical pressures for the individual school administrator: how far should school playing fields be subjected to intensive use? How far should the school caretaker be put out, or overworked, to allow the premises to be used twelve hours per day? They may intensify course planning problems: how far should a further education college shift its emphasis to programmes oriented towards industrial occupations in order to satisfy the pressures of the Industrial Development programme?

It could be argued that PPBS is merely bringing out into the open, for resolution and discussion, pressures which at the moment are concealed. Further, there is some evidence that where an activity administered by the education service is regarded by other local authority administrators as crucial to the fulfilment of their programme, those departments will be powerful advocates of increasing the spending on educational provision. Pre-school education is regarded thus by social service directors as well as industrial development officers, since it facilitates both child-care and child-minding. Educationalists may not be over keen on such attitudes, but they are nevertheless stimulated by PPBS.

4   The resolution of these possibly conflicting pressures and objectives can be approached through quantitative analysis (of which more later), the technicalities of programme design (see next section), and the setting up of inter-departmental working groups comprising other departmental heads and specialists (social researchers, finance staff, etc.) able to contribute informed judgement and information on the particular problem.

It should be noted that there is a strong body of feeling against the setting of precise goals. Alkin (1973) suggests that goals should be ambiguous, since they are thus able to accommodate more viewpoints, and are more likely to survive. In this way, they may acquire a greater degree of consent and legitimacy, though whether this is in any way helpful as far as the fulfilment of these objectives is concerned is highly debatable! James (1973) criticizes the whole national basis of policy planning. He contends that:

1   The definition of "need" is highly subjective, and will in any case change.
2   To replace "need" by "demand" (i.e. wants backed by the ability to pay) is not helpful in an LEA, since those who want may very well not have the resources to back their demands; this is why they would expect the LEA to provide.
3   The setting of objectives is often artificial, since most LEA administrators continually think actively and deeply about problems. To place creative administrators in a straitjacket may be seriously counterproductive.
4   The research and evaluation on which much policy planning is based is highly superficial in practice.

This debate is likely to continue for some time, but meanwhile, detailed experimentation in American schools supports the desirability of detailed objectives, for purposes of both effective implementation and subsequent evaluation.

THE DESIGN OF PROGRAMME STRUCTURES
The design of the programme structures themselves is a crucial matter, since it determines the choices presented to the decision-maker. By arranging the activities and services in various ways to correspond to different objectives, different options are presented. For example, one structure may be the objectives of education as laid out in the Education Act (1944). Whilst this is a true reflection of the purposes of education, it is exceedingly difficult to relate costs and apportion activities to many of these objectives; from the practical point of view, this has obvious limitations. A structure based on institutions can be criticized on the grounds that it is not the ultimate objective of an LEA to provide institutions. Institutions exist for higher purposes, and these are not defined in this structure. It is true, though, that in the 16+ category this budget does throw up a significant choice: does one provide education for the 16–19-year-olds within the school framework, the college framework, or both?
   It would also be possible to organize a further education budget to indicate what is being contributed in the way of particular subjects across the whole education authority. This could be a profitable enterprise, since institution-based budgets often conceal such things, and the exact subject position (and therefore the adequacy of provision in terms of market demand) is often not easy to assess across the whole authority. A further alternative would be to display the sub-programmes according to geographical communities or areas. This could be a useful categorization (suburbs, decaying inner-city areas, etc.) if the divisions are based on

Figure 4 Structures for an education programme in an LEA, using alternative target-group criteria

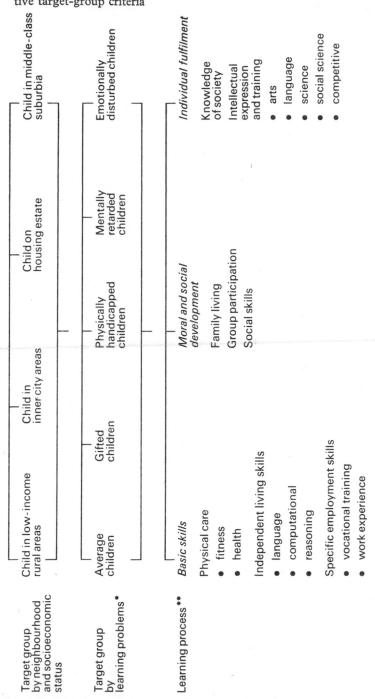

Target group by neighbourhood and socioeconomic status	Child in low-income rural areas	Child in inner city areas	Child on housing estate	Child in middle-class suburbia
Target group by learning problems *	Average children	Gifted children	Physically handicapped children / Mentally retarded children	Emotionally disturbed children

**Learning process **

Basic skills

Physical care
- fitness
- health

Independent living skills
- language
- computational
- reasoning

Specific employment skills
- vocational training
- work experience

Moral and social development

Family living

Group participation

Social skills

Individual fulfilment

Knowledge of society

Intellectual expression and training
- arts
- language
- science
- social science
- competitive

* Each of these categories refers to each of the types of community

** Each of the groups of learning processes refers to each of the target groups

distinctive socio-economic areas and the education authority's purpose is community planning; it can establish clearly the adequacy of local provision in relation to local problems and relate closely, if desired, to similar geographical divisions in the social services.

All these are possible but the structure most commonly adopted appears to be that of population target groups, which may reflect age bands, or perhaps groups categorized by types of learning problems (see Figure 4 p. 321). It is possible to define the needs of such groups fairly closely, and to relate the adequacy of educational provision to these categories. Each of these possible structures has its own advantages and disadvantages. The usefulness of a hierarchy structure for a local education authority is that any of these choices can be displayed at any of the levels, depending on the decision patterns which need to be exposed. For example, the sub-programmes tier could be based on age-bands, the activities tier on geographical area, the elements tier on institutions and the sub-elements tier on a traditional input budget. There must always be a correspondence of the sub-element with the input budget, since input headings are required for purposes of budgetary control.

We have discussed so far the technicalities of a programme hierarchy which is essentially two-dimensional. However, many sophisticated programme structures developed in the United States are emphasizing a multi-dimensional approach, which requires much more complex matrix structures and computerized information which will throw up all the necessary relationships between institution, client group, geographical area and educational objective (Frank, 1973 and Cleland and King, 1968). This sophistication is, as yet, not a common characteristic of local education authorities in the United Kingdom. It should also be made clear that different types of programme will be needed at institution level from those needed at local authority level.

Programme analysis

In the use of limited resources, officers, members and heads of institutions are faced with choices among various courses of action. The questions "why the expenditure?", "for whom the expenditure?", "what expenditure?", "when should the expenditure be made?", "where should it be made?" are therefore clearly pertinent, and in this programme structures can help by throwing light on questions such as "where should a new school be located?" "what provision should be made for the 16–19 age group?", "what is the potential of programmed learning in particular situation X?". Evaluation and analysis are hardly new to education, but perhaps their use in the administration of education may have lacked system in the past. Authorities have found the use of "position statements" or programme memoranda helpful here. Figure 5 (p. 324) indicates the lay-out of such a document, and from this emerge the questions which have considerable usefulness in clarifying the current situation (which should surely be uppermost at budget-time):

1 Is there any over-provision in terms of a particular objective?
2 Is there any clear under-provision in relation to the needs of a particular group, community or institution?
3 Is any of the provision *not* contributing to any particular objective? Has it lost the reason for its existence?
4 Have we any better ideas of the distribution costs, for example, in "central services" like administration, research and development? (It is perhaps worth mentioning here that one of the original purposes of an antecedent of PPBS in the United States was to keep manpower costs as low as possible.) Have these been allocated as far as possible?
5 In which alternatives of expenditure should we concentrate our investment, for the greatest return to the people receiving education?

An example of the way in which the value of capital projects may be assessed under this system is shown in Figure 6 (p. 326), drawn from one British local education authority.

If we return to the question of whether there are, in fact, more suitable alternative ways of meeting the objectives which have been defined, the programme structure should reveal a host of such alternatives. On the other hand, there may be other options not contained within the structure which will emerge through further systematic questioning. The next problem is, "how do we select the alternative, or mixes of alternatives, which may be the best solution to the problem at hand?" Many educational organizations have found the method of Issue Analysis to be of assistance. (This method sometimes goes under other names: Merewitz and Sosnick, for example, refer to Special Studies, which have procedures similar to those mentioned below, and emphasize that they must contain specific recommendations for action.) Figure 7 (p. 327) indicates the nature of Issue Analysis.

The central point is a statement of the question, in this case an analysis of what provision is needed for the education of handicapped children. To obtain various perspectives on the problem, the administrator would go to the programme objectives and there clarify his thoughts regarding the nature of the education proposed in the policy for handicapped children of different categories. Attached to the position statement, he would find details of the number of children in each category, and a summary of their characteristics; details of the existing volume and standards of provision; and an indication of likely available resources to meet the problem. Equipped with this information, he would evolve a range of likely alternatives, probably including 1–5 in Figure 7, and possibly some more. His main task would then be to select a series of criteria to apply to the alternatives in the light of the children's needs. These would be expected to include:

1 educational criteria needing to be satisfied: a minimum range of sub-

Figure 5 Example of position statement for youth employment service
Statement of standards, needs and deficiencies: youth employment service

Activities	Objective	Clientele	Standards	Needs	Provision	+ or −
1 Careers, information and advice	(a) To give information and advice to secondary school pupils that will help them to choose a career	(a) (i) Pupils aged 13 and over 1970 1973 1975 34000 39000 39000	Minimum of one group talk for every pupil before fourth year and subsequent contact	Group talks, etc., with pupils 1970 1973 1975 34000 39000 39000	Group talks, etc., with pupils 1970 18000	Group talks, etc., with pupils 1970 1973 1975 −16000 −21000 −25000
		(ii) 100 schools	Careers literature packages in every school	20000 books and pamphlets circulated	15000 books and pamphlets circulated	−5000 pamphlets circulated
		(iii) 100 schools	Careers conventions for every group of schools	20 careers conventions	16 careers conventions	−4 careers conventions
		(b) 14-year-old age group 1970 1973 1975 10500 10500 10500	Minimum of one personal interview with all 14-year-olds with parents present	10500 interviews with parents present	7500 interviews with 2500 parents present	−3000 interviews −8000 parents
2 Assistance with obtaining employment	(a) To help young people under 18 get suitable jobs	School-leavers for employment 1970 1973 1975 8000 3000 8000 (raised school leaving age)	(i) All leavers to be in suitable jobs within four months of leaving school	Suitable jobs for 1970 1973 1975 8000 3000 8000	1970 7800 jobs, 6200 of which were suitable	1970 −200 jobs (−1800 suitable)
			(ii) All leavers to register for employment	Registration by 1970 1973 1975 8000 3000 8000	Registration 1970 2900	−5100 registrations
			(iii) all vacancies to be notified by	In 1970 at least 7800 vacancies	6300 notified	−1500 notifications

				1970 2900 registered	*1970* 2000 found jobs	*1970* −900 new jobs
(b) To help unemployed young people find other work	Young workers under 18 *1970 1973 1975* 20000 15000 15000 of whom up to 25% may register for re-employment	Re-employment of all who register		2900 registered	2000 found jobs	−900 new jobs
3 Service to employers	To assist employers to recruit suitable staff, provide information about educational methods, and to stimulate interest in providing training	6300 employers in area	All employers to use services provided	6300 to use services	5400 use services	−900 do not use services
4 Staffing	To maintain high standards of service consistent with economy		One careers officer per 400 14-year-old pupils One careers officer per 200 handicapped pupils Equivalent number of supporting clerical staff	30 careers officers 30 clerical officers	27 careers officers 34 clerical officers	−3 careers officers +4 clerical officers

(Reproduced from Birley, 1972, by kind permission of Routledge and Kegan Paul.)

Figure 6   Format for the submission of capital projects under a PPB System

---

Formulation of proposals
11   All proposals for new capital schemes and changes in the specification of schemes should be accompanied by a written justification which should include the Team's best assessment of their proposals under the following headings:

(a) Programme Area Team; Committee and Scheme name.
(b) Objective to which the scheme contributes.
(c) Need for the scheme.
(d) Alternative means of meeting the need.
(e) Appraisal of alternatives leading to recommendation.
(f) Extent to which the scheme will:
    (i)   meet the objectives of the Programme Area;
    (ii) fill a gap in the provision of the service;
    (iii) improve the standard of service.
(g) Schedule of accommodation or other details indicating extent of scheme
(h) Capital cost—broken down over elements.
(i) Revenue cost—including details of staff requirements.
(j) Details of any revenue costs which will no longer be incurred where capital scheme supersedes an existing activity.

---

jects to be available; a commensurate number of specialist staff; the expected in terms of equipment; learning situations precisely designed for the pupils' needs, etc.
2   social criteria: handicapped children, it could be argued, should be encouraged to mix as much as possible with other children, etc.
3   geographical criteria: they should not have to suffer unwarranted travelling difficulties, etc.
4   economic criteria (similar costs criteria should be applied to each alternative): cost of support staff and teaching staff; initial costs and recurrent costs; extent of parental contribution; indirect and direct costs; fixed and variable costs, etc.

Clearly, this simple framework belies a very complex situation: there will be pressure groups for and against each alternative; some costs and some benefits are not at all easily quantified; it will not be possible to obtain all the necessary information in sufficient detail; it will certainly not be easy to handle all the variables in the equation. It is because of such factors that the method is imperfect.

Measurement problems in PPBS
Measurement of the gains and benefits to existing activities, or an analysis of what gains and benefits would be likely, given a certain course of action, are major requirements of any PPB System, as is evident from what we have already discussed. Measurement is necessary both for

John Davies

Figure 7 Issue analysis study on provision of education for handicapped children

Capable of being specified more precisely in terms of the various client groups affected

CRITERIA TO BE APPLIED TO ALTERNATIVES

EDUCATIONAL, e.g. range of staff available; variety of instruction; equipment

SOCIAL, e.g. medical care; school care required; mixing

GEOGRAPHICAL, e.g. location; transport; distribution of need

ECONOMIC, e.g. maintenance costs per place; occupancy ratio; staff/pupil ratio; support staff/pupil ratio; capital costs, etc.

ALTERNATIVE 1 Expand existing 'normal' schools, mix of children

ALTERNATIVE 2 Add extra handicapped units to existing schools

ALTERNATIVE 3 Build new special school for handicapped (day)

ALTERNATIVE 4 Use neighbouring LEA day and boarding schools

ALTERNATIVE 5 Extend home and hospital tuition

STATEMENT OF ISSUE What system of educating handicapped children should LEA adopt for expansion in the provision required for specified groups in specified areas?

PERSPECTIVE ON THE ISSUE

PROGRAMME OBJECTIVES To ensure provision of further education for handicapped children appropriate to age, need, ability and aptitude, and to secure their participation

PRESENT STANDARDS OF PROVISION X special schools; Y special schools; inadequate space, decaying fabric, rising costs; increased number of places required in various categories

AVAILABLE RESOURCES Revenue allocation, etc.

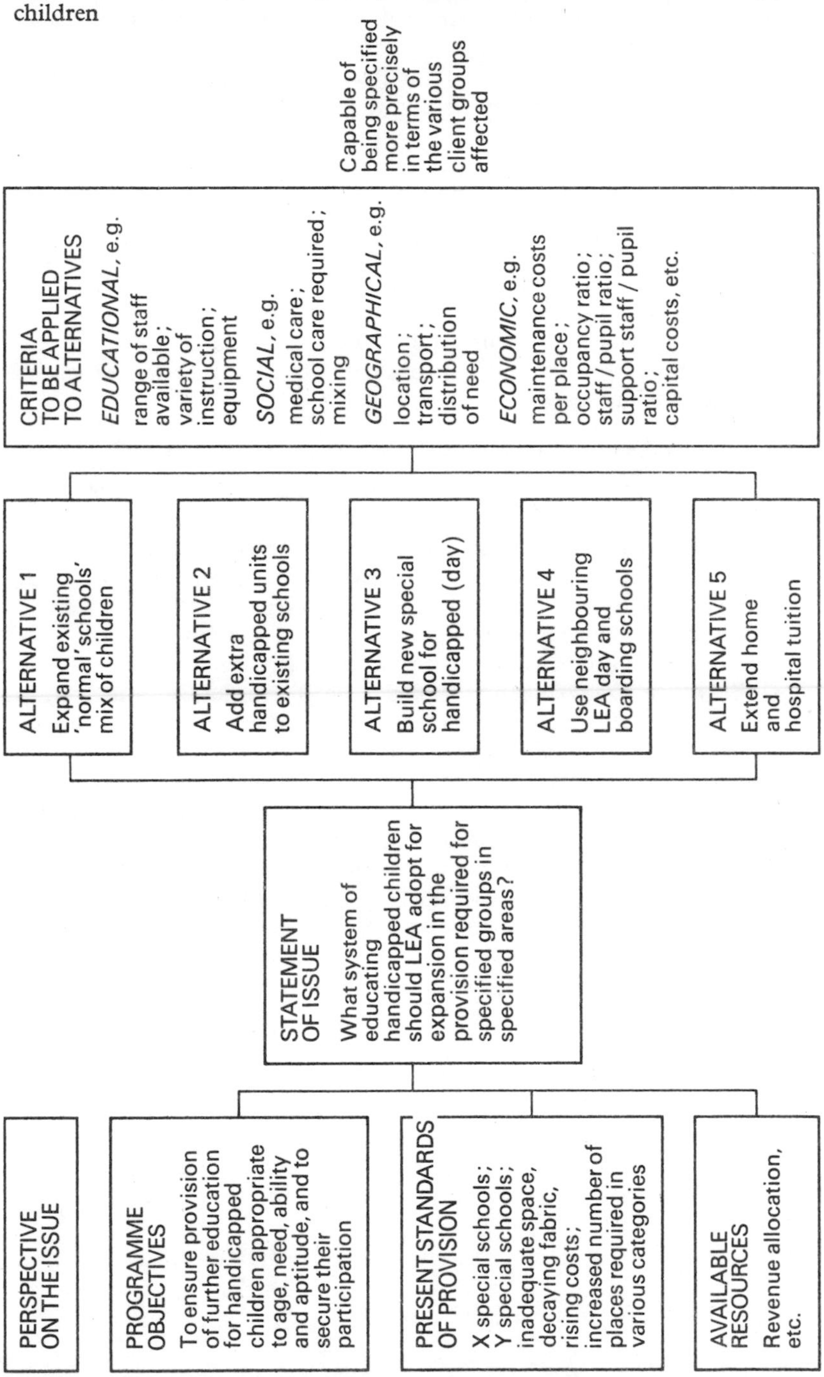

planning and assessment. In profit-oriented enterprises measurement of output is relatively straightforward, since one can talk of numbers and types of cars produced, and assess income from sales as against outgoings (purchase of raw materials, labour and administrative capacity). Traditionally, attempts to apply similar analyses to education and the rest of the public sector have not proved easy, and professionals have been swift to indicate that measurement in education can be impossible, dangerous or threatening (Aitken, 1974)—despite the fact that examinations have been part of the system for generations. The current economic climate, though, and the requests extended to education for a justification of the need for increased expenditure, have recently led to renewed efforts to come to grips with the problem. There is little doubt, however, that this still constitutes one of the major problem areas of PPBS.

In the PPB Systems currently in use, there appear to be five principal problem areas with regard to measurement.

(a)   Is the organization clear on the precise purposes for which measurement is being developed? I have outlined elsewhere a range of these purposes from a survey of British authorities (Davies, 1974). The conclusion has been drawn that there are considerable variations in the reasons why measurement is being undertaken. In some educational institutions measures are used primarily to assure external controllers, such as local education authorities, that the motivation is efficient and deserves more investment than do alternative institutions (the staff/student ratio is a good example of this). This comparison, of course, occurs also at departmental level. Others have tried to devise measures to shed light on the relationship between a particular type of learning situation (e.g. programmed learning) and the net effect on a student's achievement, or on his ability to work unsupervised compared with a traditional lecture situation. Each of these uses is quite valid, but many difficulties have emerged because measures have been used for the wrong purposes. One cannot use a student/staff ratio measure, for example, to comment on the overall effectiveness of student learning. All a SSR measure can tell us is how much staffing resource a given department or institution is consuming.

(b)   Is the organization clear on what it is trying to measure? This is a problem of specification requiring the design of standards, measures or indicators. Burkhead (1966) has derived a set of areas in which measures are needed by likening the educational organization to a production process. This yields measures in the categories of:

inputs   (student time and qualities; staff time and qualities; physical resources);
process (class size; teacher/pupil ratio; size of school);

Figure 8 Example of measures which could be used to compare effectiveness of existing alternative forms of providing special education for handicapped children, and to assess the best candidate(s) for additional expenditure

Type of measure	*Area in which measure is needed*	*Specimen measure*
IMPACT	To equip pupil so that he will be able to enter as full and active employment as possible	
	To maximize his earning powers	Salary profile of leavers over 10 years compared to normal children
	To enable him to play a full and active part in further education and adult education	Percentage of children enrolling in FE/HE and AE compared to normal children
	To enable him to play as full, independent and active a part as possible in the life of the community	
RESPONSE	To ensure that the facilities available are fully occupied	Occupancy ratio
	To ensure the satisfaction of both parents and children within the provision	Grievances/complaints Truancy/deviance percentage
	To improve the performance of handicapped children to a level at least as good as that of normal children	Reading attainment Oral ability measure Creativity measure Manipulative skills test Formal examinations
	To maximize their integration at social and educational level with normal children	Social adjustment measure Involvement in extra-curricular activities
PROVISION	To provide a number of places and learning situations for handicapped children which ensures: distribution in relation to geographical need, and therefore minimal travelling;	Analysis of places in relation to homes
	as much integration with other children as possible;	Extent of separate classes/provision
	co-education as far as possible;	?

Figure 8 (Continued)

Type of measure	Area in which measure is needed	Specimen measure
	a range of subject choices and curricula compatible with that of normal children; each child shall have the facilities appropriate to his particular disability	?
		Learning space per student —square metres per pupil, etc.
PROCESS	To create an efficient learning situation for handicapped children: optimum size of classes; learning situation which stimulates individual's effort; adequate staff supervision, teaching/support/medical; staff fulfilment;	Average class size Curriculum volume factor Staff background factor Staff/pupil ratio Labour turnover, vacancy ratio
	to maintain the provision at appropriate standards	Renewal period of furniture (15 years) Renewal period of redecoration (7 years) Renewal period of electrical wiring (20 years), etc. Staff training and development entitlements (weeks/2 years) Replacement period for teaching materials (?)
INPUT	Pupils at point of entry	Categories of handicap Numbers within category, broken down into sex, location, age Characteristics—attainment levels in reading, oral, manipulative skills, etc.— social adjustment
	Parents' expectations	Qualities and qualifications (+ and −)
	Staff	Expectations and values Numbers, types, grades, location

output (increased intellectual curiosity, creativity, skills and social adaptation of student; growth of informed electorate; increased national economic growth).

I have developed the basic systems model further (Davies, 1974), subdividing output into provision, response and impact, on the lines indicated in Figure 1 of the Introduction to this article. This permits a more meaningful and detailed analysis. The distinction between provision and response is particularly important: measures of provision will include numbers, types and location of student places available for potential students, whilst measures of response would include:

1 proportion of places actually taken up or not taken up (thereby identifying the need for further analysis as to why this was—poor credibility of institution, poor marketing of its services, lack of demand because the studies were perceived to lead to no advantage for the student?);
2 drop-out wastage or truancy (thereby enabling us to ask why—poor pastoral systems in the institution, perhaps?);
3 the improvement added to the student in terms of skills and knowledge acquired, attitudes changed, etc. (thereby enabling us to ask whether the improvement was in the desired direction and, if not, what light is shed on curriculum design, support services, or teaching standards?). One very important point thus emerges about the use of measures: potentially they enable us to ask fairly penetrating questions about the effectiveness of management processes within institutions. A series of sample measures is given in Figure 8 under the five headings discussed above. The reader is invited to fill in the blanks.

It will be clear that we have considerable problems here. Any single objective/project will probably need multiple indicators, to avoid drawing the wrong conclusion. We could take measures of attainment of children in relation to acquired knowledge or skills, but this would not tell us anything of their moral or attitude development. Many measures which we might need in order to proceed in the latter area are not in common use at all. Many projects/activities in education are going to require multiple measures because they have multiple purposes, which is likely to be a source of further complication. When we are trying to measure in the long term, it is much more difficult to determine direct causal relationship between an educational activity and an outcome, a problem well known in cost-benefit analysis studies. The fact that John Citizen, BSc (Engineering), may be a director of production in a company at the age of 35, earning £6,000, may be due to his degree. It may also be due to studies undertaken since graduation; a particularly good company training system; or the fact that he married the chairman's daughter! To attribute percentages of the £6,000 to these four factors would be difficult; when considered on a national basis the problems are compounded.

(c) Has the organization the necessary technical devices to produce the specified measures? This is a problem of "instrumentation" and involves a choice of methods for data acquisition and coding, the design of measurement scales and procedures for tabulating, accumulating and reporting information. Unless this is systematically done, considerable problems in researching, handling and using data will arise. One might therefore test any possible measure by ascertaining:

1 is it relevant to the objective or activity one is trying to measure?
2 how complete a measure is it? Does it quantify or qualify all significant aspects?
3 is it relatively simple to use by non-technical decision-makers in education?
4 is it possible to *obtain* the information required?

It is not the purpose of this paper to explore all the technicalities, since PPBS does tend to absorb a great many other systems and techniques at appropriate stages. Cost-benefit analysis is one of these and many PPB Systems founder because they either ignore its contribution or start using it without realizing the ramifications. We can, however, briefly examine some of the cost problems involved.

First, we have problems of attributing costs of inputs to objectives, activities or target groups. If costs were formerly displayed according to institutions or divisions, they may now have to be recast to correspond with the new categories. Consider a special education project (as in Figure 4). It may be said to contribute to programmes for education and possibly community care as well. If we wished to ensure that we knew the full cost of child care, then if special education were agreed to contribute to this secondary end, we could not omit their cost from the community care budget. It is common in such cases to employ one of several alternatives:

1 allocate the full cost to the dominant purpose of the activity, and regard the others as a bonus,
2 insert the costs under both programmes for decision-purposes, but only count it once for financial purposes,
3 split up the cost according to some usage formula, (based on percentage of children using the facility for purposes of care, percentage of mothers using the facility to enable them to go out to work, etc.) or merely an arbitrary basis.

It will be apparent to everyone that each of these methods of cost apportionment could be shot down in flames, and they undoubtedly create interesting problems of budgetary control.

Second, we have the task of ensuring that all relevant costs of the special education provision are included in the calculation, and where we are comparing these alternatives, clearly the same costs must be looked at. In the experience of authorities using PPBS, such costs would include revenue *and* capital costs; fixed and variable costs; direct and indirect costs; and single year and multi-year costs.

Third, if our projects are being considered over a fairly *long time scale,* we have to evaluate the likely costs and benefits over this period. Time involves uncertainty and an increasing limitation on our ability to predict. Over a period of time social and economic conditions change, rates of inflation vary, and the incidence of costs and benefits are not constant throughout a period. There is also the problem that many costs and likely benefits cannot be foreseen easily at the commencement of a project. Space does not allow us to enter the exceedingly complicated field of investment theories and cash flows. This is explored in some detail by Merevitz and Sosnick (1971, Chapters 7, 8 and 9), but it is worth observing that:

1 one cannot easily make judgements on future costs by simply referring to present monetary values. A considerable technical argument is therefore implied to try to establish appropriate interest or discount rates to gain the comparability in costs over a period of time;
2 some means of solving a particular problem look far less attractive than others when costs are analysed over the expected life-span of the problem or project (particularly in relation to borrowed money);
3 several writers prefer the construction of scenarios (see Kahn and Weiner, 1967) to forecast the expected elements of the socio-economic, physical, technological, political and educational environments of the future, as a means of clarifying perspectives;
4 the capacity of most British local education authorities to undertake analysis of the complexity described in the American journals is highly dubious.

Fourth, in considering alternatives such as in the handicapped children example, (Figure 5), one perhaps ought to identify what the economist calls *"opportunity* cost"—the value of lost chances to do other things. Thus, if the local education authority in this example decided to build a new special school, this precludes alternative use being made of that site for council houses, a library, etc. The authority has thus to establish its priorities not only in special education, but in special education in relation to other urgent, competing projects. If it is imperative that new council housing be built, then another alternative to Alternative 3 is necessary.

Fifth, there may be *associated costs* of different types. Building a special education unit in a certain place may well necessitate considerable transportation costs, to be met either by parents or the local education authority. If the local education authority has to bear these costs, it is a direct charge on the authority. If not, there are still additional costs to the community which must enter the equation.

One cannot, of course, only consider cost measures, since a great deal of what goes on in education is difficult to put into cost terms but may still be measurable. Other articles in this publication have considered the more technical problems involved in manipulating statistics in this context.

(d) There are a series of *organizational problems* in collecting the necessary information. Very often, programme structures and therefore sets of measures do not correspond directly with organization structures. Thus, information contained within educational institutions may need to be redirected to those administrators/politicians formulating and testing policies and projects in community care or recreation and leisure. There will thus be changes in the paths through which information flows and, at local authority level, combinations of selective data from various departments. Where the administrator of an institution is responsible for its effective operation it follows that, if that institution contributes to a number of policy programmes, his information system becomes rather complicated. The CASEA project (Eidell and Nagle, 1970) is a good example of the way in which new information needs have been generated. For an educational organization not to use a computer where possible is, of course, fairly inefficient. The whole question of the availability of necessary human and machine skills, and the capacity of the organization to be equal to the tasks of planning, direction, organization, control and motivation over the entire period of the project is thus highly significant.

(e) Finally, there is the question of *"who does the assessment?"* It is possible to argue that every line administrator, teacher and student is always assessing his own performance. This is true to a certain extent, but it is highly debatable whether he can be objective about his own work and achievements; whether he has all the necessary information which other people generate; or whether he does it systematically. As H. J. Hartley once observed, "when an administrator assesses his own performance, it is probably fair to say that it is doomed to success". There may therefore be behavioural and technical reasons why self-assessment has only limited potential in PPBS. If external agencies are to provide resources for an institution then, by definition, they have to satisfy themselves that the institution is worthy to receive them. They may wish to probe areas which the internal administrator would not normally consider, and may well be able to bring a more dispassionate view. Merevitz and Sosnick (1971, Chapter 6) analyse this point.

It would appear then that different groups will wish to do their own assessment for their own purposes:

1 Local education authorities advisers and HMIs are constantly evaluating the progress being made in curriculum developments in schools and colleges;
2 increasingly HMIs are concerning themselves with the total effectiveness of the institutions for which they have a responsibility. To assist them, various analytical devices such as Curriculum Notation, pioneered by T. I. Davies (1969), are being developed;
3 Pooling Committee and the Department of Education and Science have been concerned to establish the relative efficiency of various higher education institutions, particularly polytechnics, conducting advanced work. To accomplish this a series of cost norms has been developed, including staff/student ratios, curriculum volume factor (hours of classwork for students), staff deployment factor (hours of class contact for staff) and average class size (size of groups which are used for learning purposes) (Pooling Committee, 1972). The total effect of this is a series of guidelines to authorities controlling polytechnics centered on a staff/student ratio of 1:7.5–8.5 for laboratory-based departments and 1:9.2–10.2 for classroom-based subjects (Birch et al., 1974).

Local education authorities are constantly assessing institutions for resource purposes, and a growing movement has been that of indices of need to establish the relative claims of competing institutions, particularly in deprived areas, on a more objective footing. The Inner London Education Authority has an Index of Deprivation for this purpose, containing indicators of both an educational and a social nature;

Most higher education institutions have developed internal forms of assessment, for example of new course proposals, which may include some external measures of resource consumption.

Several school boards in the United States are beginning to clarify and make more explicit the purposes and substance of these types of assessment. It is clearly quite unfair to criticize schools profoundly for failing to satisfy criteria which they know nothing about! Perhaps, then, the trend in British education should be towards a similar public exposition, because confusion is fairly rampant in this area at present.

Behavioural problems in the development and use of PPBS
One of the areas of neglect in the development of PPBS in education has

undoubtedly been the lack of recognition in the peculiar problems of developing a complex system of resource-allocation and decision-making in organizations which are highly consumer-oriented, professionally dominated and politically controlled. Any one of this triad of interests produces a set of forces which can clearly destroy a system such as PPBS, by withdrawing its support. We must therefore look at the climate within the educational organization itself. The introduction of PPBS will provoke a quite different response among participants in the local education authority or institution if the major reason for its introduction is to stir up the organization, from the response it will provoke if the purpose is to help the organization cope with changing external circumstances. The whole issue puts into bold relief the necessity for the administrator to use strategies of implementation which maximize reception responses and minimize hostile responses from executive authority, legislative committees and external pressure groups.

Let us first consider the *political* aspects of the use of PPBS in education. Politics, according to McGivney and Bowles (1972) is the process by which society:

1   delegates the power to govern and administer;
2   allocates its scarce resources;
3   decides on its preferences from among competing values.

PPBS stresses the second element and, whilst it can clarify resource allocation, this is usually within a predetermined political and value-laden situation. PPBS therefore can be faulted for leading us to ignore political reality, because of its emphasis on the objective. This political reality may be apparent in the fact that the local education authority may have certain rules or conventions which members do not wish to see thwarted by PPBS:

1   Officers making decisions in areas which traditionally have been the preserve of members: a shift possibly in the focus of power (i.e. PPBS as an officer take-over).
2   The fact that political systems have rewards and sanctions: additional resources for certain "favoured" schools or wards, or the traditional power exercised by a chairman of committee in making appointments. Members perceiving PPBS as a threat to their privileges would naturally be suspicious. Disagreement is a fundamental aspect of politics which will not be compromised whilst PPBS assumes a certain consensus of goals and objectives.

We may also have situations of intense party political rivalry in local education authorities and one must ask whether it is possible for PPBS to play any useful part at all.

Depending on the situation, there are possibilities:

1 If there is a reasonable base-level agreement between opposing political forces, PPBS may force precision in the statement of objectives, generating alternatives and selecting an optimum solution.
2 In a situation where one party is trying to persuade another, PPBS may succeed in exposing a third alternative which may be mutually acceptable.
3 In a situation of political bargaining, PPBS can only be used to assist protagonists to evaluate the potential impact of policy aspirations, which they might then give up or retain. It cannot effect conflict resolution, therefore.
4 In a "win or lose" political situation, where dogma may be uppermost, PPBS is of little use. Moreover, it may itself be a ball in the power game.

Members therefore may not wish to be diverted from their political purpose by the rational framework of PPBS or, indeed, by its complicated information. Local education authorities or institutions which fail to present information as an aid to members, or who fail to recognize what makes members tick, cannot count on PPBS being at all helpful, despite its considerable potential for effective decision-making. Nonetheless, as Alioto and Jungherr (1969) mention, it is not at all unhelpful in certain cases, in assisting the public to judge the performance of political parties on the basis of achievement in relation to stated targets, and that cannot be too bad for democratic government.

Apart from elected members, of course, *educational administrators* also need motivation to accept PPBS in principle, and to make it work in practice. There are a number of reasons why PPBS has failed to stimulate the interest of administrators:

1 they may not have been party to the original deliberations on the introduction of the system, or to its design. It may even have been created as an imposition on them. (Educationalists often perceive PPBS to be the wicked product of the treasurer's mind!) Certainly initial hostility provoked by this lack of consultation and involvement over PPBS has proved a major cause of its subversion both at education-department and institution level. If it does not satisfy their own personal needs, such as ego satisfaction or professional fulfilment, then the system will have considerable difficulties;
2 they may be subjected to particular objectives and goals applied to their own spheres of work. One of the problems of the programme hierarchy is that people are often required to set objectives within goal parameters already established by the upper echelons, which may offer very little flexibility for creative thought and action. In complex institutions like schools, colleges and local education authorities it is quite impossible to legislate human behaviour completely, since professionals tend to resent non-professional, external controls

in the name of academic freedom, a phenomenon well developed at institution level. A system which attempts to give precise directions to school or teacher activity is thus perceived as a threat to traditional autonomy;

3   many administrators in local education authorities and institutions have evolved systems in which informal communication and influence networks have determined the manner by which resources are allocated—and there are quite clear advantages, in some situations, to this means of operating. When a system comes along which is characterized by open, rational allocations based on long-term considerations, those used to informality may well perceive their power slipping away. Others may see opportunities in the new method to develop a new power-base;

4   behavioural issues, of course, are not unconnected with technical aspects, and the technical problems of PPBS may be referred to as the reasons why PPBS should not develop. The limitations of administrators' know-how and technical prowess in developing position statements or performance measures, coupled with the almost frenetic desire of local governments to implement decisions as fast as possible, have produced considerable insecurity and feelings of helplessness. PPBS is therefore castigated as the "Planner's Folly". A rather more gradual installation to permit staff to develop confidence, knowledge and skills would be more appropriate;

5   PPBS does tend to spawn a great deal of paperwork, new rules and procedures, particularly related to time and date targets, performance measures, etc. PPBS may therefore be viewed as instituting a sophisticated form of accountability. Human beings have well-developed methods of neutralizing accountability systems based on targets; these usually consist of setting objectives which stand a very good chance of coming off—low-risk objectives;

6   people in educational organizations often tend to work as isolated individuals, and have little experience in group decision-making or problem-solving. Since one of the features of PPBS is the multi-departmental working party, this in itself produces a challenge for the educationalist. Such personal interaction is necessary both vertically and horizontally within the organization, and it is clear that barriers exist in both directions at present;

7   PPBS is, at worst, a structuring of the decision-making process. It is clear that if people do not want to make decisions in the categories proposed by PPBS programmes, they will not. Attitude change must come before any technical competence in PPBS;

8   shortage of time to develop fully PPBS plans is a universal complaint, particularly where external political pressures to get things moving are considerable, and where PPBS is imposed without discrimination on an existing system;

9   finally, there is the problem of incentives. PPBS, like MBO, is

designed to stimulate administrators to fulfil objectives. Having fulfilled them, so what? Is there any reward which can be offered? Certainly, extra resources may be employed in the section concerned as a result, and growth can well affect gradings of senior staff. But this need not at all be correlated with job satisfaction, or fulfilment in professional or student terms. Educational institutions in the past have been exciting places because of the sense of mission, intellectual curiosity and the warm feeling of having contributed to students' development. PPBS can extend this excitement, but only if it is seen as something contributing to educational progress rather than a bureaucratic device to screw down educationalists.

C. B. Derr (1971) is adamant that it is possible to develop PPBS in a manner which would preclude these behavioural difficulties. He advocates the deployment of the methods of Organization Development (OD) alongside PPBS. The purposes of OD are to change the culture of the educational organization so that it becomes "self renewing"—able to adapt itself to changing environmental problems and introduce processes for dealing with those problems. Further, it advocates that decisions would be made by persons who have the information, at no matter what point in the system; the assumption is that those at the top often lack the information. Self-renewing organizations have well-developed feedback mechanisms, commonly accepted goals, open, direct and clear communication and a capacity to bring conflict into the open instead of allowing it to be suppressed and thus to fester. The OD movement has quite clear implications for the manner and style by which PPBS should be introduced.

MANAGEMENT BY OBJECTIVES

Management by objectives (MBO) has many features in common with PPBS, since they each derive from a common conceptual parentage. Similarly, the problems of design, adoption and implementation fall into both behavioural and technical categories. There is in fact no standard MBO pattern, and the "first generation" classical MBO as developed by Humble (1968) is hardly to be found. We shall therefore explore some of the expressions of these MBO variations.

In essence, MBO seeks to integrate the organization's need for growth, fulfilment of its objectives and its client's expectations with the individual manager's needs to contribute to the organization, and to develop and satisfy himself in the process. To this end, MBO makes the organization define its objectives at various levels and assists the manager to define his own key results or key effectiveness areas within this total framework. The manager goes on to specify particular standards of performance indicating the conditions which exist when the result is achieved satisfactorily, and is encouraged to make suggestions for the improvement of the organization (e.g. procedures, structural, decision-making and communications machinery); for his own development; and for the structure and content of his job. At regular intervals, therefore, staff reviews are held, involving both superior and subordinate, to encourage a recycling of objective-setting and activity patterns. This pattern is generally common to organizations practising MBO.

The first significant area of variation observed has been the reasons (stated and unstated) why authorities and institutions have used MBO, and the quite different organizational malaises which have been attacked, using MBO as the principal medicine. It should be emphasized that not all bodies will subscribe to all these reasons; that not all managers in the organization would accept that the same needs exist; that some reasons will not be stated publicly; and that the rationale for the advantages of MBO often changes during the implementation process, which makes assessment of its effectiveness difficult. The following seem to be the major reasons for its use:

(i)   to develop a form of corporate strategy, in administrative, academic or social terms, which will reflect the total needs and objectives of the organization, particularly in response to its clients' demands; ensure compatibility and interlocking of personal and departmental contributions; release individual and group potential for creative thought through the challenge of participation; and to integrate managerial processes which traverse many departments, e.g. forecasting and controlling staffing and space;

(ii)   to increase the predictability of the organization by assessing critically its obsolescence in relation to fresh challenges and changing demands in objective-centred organization renewal;

(iii)   to improve the effectiveness of the communication system by questioning the degreee of ambiguity in job definitions, lines of accountability, relevance of information to decisions needing to be made;

(iv)   to focus attention on what should be the area of distinctive competence of the organization, based on its specific strengths and resources and the needs of its clients. At individual level, the aim has been to focus a manager's attention on his main priorities, in an attempt to preclude the possibility of his consuming large proportions of his time on activities of marginal significance;

(v)   to provide a relatively objective means of staff appraisal, where MBO is seen as a performance-based appraisal system which assesses achievement against defined standards, rather than a suspect personality-based system which lends itself to problems like the "halo" effect and favouritism;

(vi)   to enable a more realistic staff development scheme where training needs are identified by analysing the difference between what skills, knowledge and ability are expected of the individual to enable him to achieve certain targets, and the skills, knowledge and ability which he already has. This immediately focuses attention on on-and-off the job training, as well as traditional courses of a broader educational nature;

(vii)   to provide an effective system of delegation and participational mangement, based on broad guidelines (key results areas) and specific performance standards for the individual academic or administrator to enable him to organize himself, but with specific information flowing back to his superior as key areas of control data. Problems of control and freedom, it is felt, can be resolved in a system of management by exception. This has been a major problem in public bodies for some time, particularly following the advocacy of the Maud Committee (1967).

There are several motives which are rarely stated, for obvious reasons, but which nevertheless are present in some educational organizations:

(viii)   to provide a means of ensuring more effective control from the top by managers conscious of the tenuousness of their grip on departments and the inadequacy of their information, and convinced of the inferiority of their staff. MBO in this situation has been described as a "do-it-yourself hangman's kit"!

(ix)   to develop a sophisticated means of executive decision-making which might well force elected members and governors into an area of macro policy making, (based on objectives) and away from the area of trivia where they sometimes operate at present;

(x)   to keep up with the "municipal" or "educational" Joneses by either copying a rival body's system, or developing one's own for purposes of one-upmanship! This is what Bennis et al. (1969) would call an "emulative" motivation; and clearly, in the absence of anything more positive it is likely to be short-lived.

From our studies, therefore, educational organizations are looking to MBO to provide quite different brands of administrative salvation. These reasons imply that the organizations recognize weaknesses of a particular kind in their operation, but we would argue that MBO need not necessarily be the appropriate tool to overcome these deficiencies. There may be less painful and complicated means of sorting out appraisal, accountability, staff development and other problems. Its adoption may be a failure to diagnose accurately the true cause of trouble, and from this, other difficulties flow.

Problems of implementing MBO have arisen when education managers have treated MBO as a set of procedures quite independent of people, and they therefore have been unable to predict the outcome of setting in motion an MBO system, nor have their consultants been able to give them any real assurances. The vulnerability of MBO is therefore to be found not only in the technical aspects of the system but, more signifi-

Figure 9 The relationship between Schein's model of motivational assumptions, the type of "MBO" and the practical foci of the resultant "MBO" system (R. J. E. Tibbott)

Motivational assumptions	*Leadership practice*	*Nature of MBO system*	*Practical foci of MBO system*		
			Key results performance standard agreement	*Job review*	*Management development*
"Economic Man" assumptions: person motivated by economic considerations only	Tight administrative controls to maintain or increase wage-earner's effort; hire and fire according to task needs	Emphasis on accountability and control of managers; MBO provides tool for making effort more rational	Superordinate TELLS subordinate targets; subordinate bargains to gain more economic reward	Historic look at performance; a reward/punishment orientation	None
"Social Man" assumptions: person responds more to social pressure of work group than to control and incentives of superordinate	Use social pressure as an incentive	Emphasis as above but with a "human-relations gloss"	Superordinate SELLS subordinate targets by using subordinate's need for social interaction	Attempts to be objective and preserve group's relationships, but has underlying reward/punishment orientation	Specific training in techniques needed for efficiency of organization; no real consideration of the individual's needs for self-development, except in response to group pressure

"Self-actualizing Man": manager responds to opportunities for achievement and self-control	Staff tasks to maximize individuals' self-actualization needs	No need to ensure accountability or to control; emphasis on feedback and providing a creative atmosphere; MBO as a method of giving communication	Superordinate CONSULTS subordinate and a compromise agreement achieved	Concentrates on reasons, not blame or praise; future orientation	Management development programmes seek to integrate individual needs into the company plan; but naive expectation of programmed results from management development
"Complex Man": managers respond differently to others in similar situations	Adaptive leadership —according to knowledge of individual	Emphasis on feedback and providing a creative atmosphere; also on open and trusting relationships	Agreement based on a complete understanding of individual problems, and aspirations of subordinates	Recognition of individual problems and aspirations	As above, but realize effects of development will differ; need for highly individual management development programmes

cantly, in the highly complex environment of variable interpersonal relationships and leadership styles, about which there is still much to be learned. Several leadership theorists have suggested that the notion of an ideal leadership type for all managerial situations, as implied by McGregor (1957) and Wickens (1968) is erroneous. Thus, there must be other factors, such as the variations in technology, and the particular ethos and problems of the organizations. It would therefore appear that proponents of MBO as a system generally applicable to defence services, engineering, marketing, research and development, schools, colleges and local authorities are falling into the same trap as the "scientific" management writers, that of prescribing universal management principles to ensure success in planned organizational change.

The organizational situation then becomes the second major area of variation in MBO, and one may classify MBO systems in British education on the basis of their underlying motivational assumptions. R. J. E. Tibbott, formerly Research Associate at Sheffield Polytechnic, refining the work of Schein (1965) has produced the analysis indicated in Figure 9. It is not claimed that these ideal types exist in such bold relief, but that these are dimensions which exist in different proportions in the educational organizations we have studied. The MBO system introduced by a medium-size college of further education, for example, exhibits all the assumptions and features associated with the "Economic Man" classification. That of an education department in a county council displays many of the characteristics of the "Self-actualizing Man" classification and, moreover, has moved to this stage in order to make good some consternation originally caused by external consultants. The MBO of the education department in a county borough council reveals a combination of "Economic Man" and "Social Man" characteristics.

It is possible, therefore, that one may be able to predict the success and consequences of a particular MBO implementation by placing it with the classification suggested. It is not possible to indicate this with absolute certainty at present, because of the smallness of the sample involved and the limited time-scale of the operations. However, there are some points which are worthy of consideration, tentative though they may be:

(i)   The "Economic" and "Social" Man categories seem to be less likely to promote a creative atmosphere, so that to maintain the impetus of the exercise will require considerable inspiration and pressure from the top. In this way MBO has failed to generate a mood of organization renewal from within. It is interesting to note that where the head of the organization begins to insist on MBO, there develops basic contradiction in forcing people to accept what was supposed to be a participative system!

(ii) It seems to be the case that a comprehensive appraisal of the effectiveness of the organization as a continuing process will be more likely with the "Self Actualizing" and "Complex" Man classifications since these lend themselves far more to continuing growth and adaptation, and "second-phase" developments.

(iii) The acceptability of MBO to individual officers and teachers is closely related to their personal circumstances and security. Some senior managers have welcomed it as a means of demonstrating to peers their sophistication or managerial superiority. Some have felt threatened because it infringed their notions of job security, the conviviality of social surroundings and the satisfaction which comes from doing a professional job well. Others have been resentful of being pressed to indulge in innovative binges, at the expense of maintaining the effectiveness of the *status quo*.

LEA advisers, in particular, have felt uneasy about a system which, in their perception, has assailed the social and professional norms of their group, imparted a foreign jargon, produced a considerable amount of documentation, and has seemed to introduce a contractual relationship into their highly organic existence. If there appears to be a gulf between the perceptions of participants as to the purpose of the exercise and its implications, and if there are feelings of considerable insecurity, momentum and commitment usually begin to fade.

(iv) There is evidence of a failure of educational organizations implementing MBO to devise a means of solving problems which the system throws up. Instead, ways may be found to circumvent a problem which may sacrifice vital elements of the system. Thus, a conflict may be avoided, but with the results of slowing down the momentum of introducing change in the system without any corresponding gain in individual or group commitment. This raises the question of the capability of the organization to sustain and monitor the progress of the innovation.

This may well be due to insufficient thought being given to the question of a change agent charged specifically with carrying through MBO, diagnosing pressure points in social, educational, administrative and technical terms, and being constantly at hand to advise staff and management of possible solutions. Several types of change agent have been contemplated or used:

(i) an external consultant;
(ii) an establishment, management services or training officer of a local authority;
(iii) a senior line manager within the organization—director of education principal or headmaster, or their deputies, or a senior member of staff charged with administrative coordination;
(iv) a senior manager appointed as a management development adviser, with few line management responsibilities as such, but of sufficient status to carry weight throughout the department.

345

Given the scarcity of staffing resources in local authorities, (iv) is very rarely used and, given the reluctance of education departments to use the "O and M man", (ii) is used only very occasionally. Given the authority's decision to spend money for root-and-branch reform of departments, (i) is becoming popular, particularly since, as external catalysts, consultants tend not to be susceptible to internal politics, though one doubts their long-term effectiveness in some educational organizations because of paucity of ideas, reliance on a strong personality's opinion within the department, lack of specific knowledge of educational problems, and their short stay. (iii) is widely used, but unfortunately the person chosen often has myriad other duties which take up his time, and he is also a line manager associated with sanctions and control, which can produce problems. One is certainly not attempting to prescribe, but it does appear that, where used, (iv) is probably the most effective, in terms of momentum, commitment and quality of MBO. It should also be added that for a system like MBO, it is important to demonstrate results. For reasons mentioned above, these have not always been apparent: hence, a vicious circle develops.

It will therefore be evident that on questions of motives, organizational situations, leadership variables and commitment there is a wide variation in the manner in which educational organizations have approached MBO. It may shortly be possible to predict the success or otherwise of MBO in an institution by an analysis of these factors. Second- and third-generation MBO systems being developed, particularly on the Reddin (1971) model, already appear to be far more pragmatic and flexible than their predecessors (see also Merevitz and Sosnick, 1971). However, a further dimension to the MBO problem is the range of technical difficulties associated with its development, producing some fascinating socio-technical situations which we shall be able to consider only briefly in this article. It is to be hoped that the following analysis will prove to be a succinct summary of the current technical problems.

The basic principles of Management by Objectives are familiar, and are well described elsewhere (Reddin, 1971a, 1971b and Hives, 1971). It seems to be the case, however, that the model for the Management by Objectives process in education now emerging is similar to that indicated in Figure 10. In this, there are essentially four components—

1   the organizational planning process;
2   the individual objective-setting process within this broad framework;
3   improvement and development plans;
4   appraisal and review processes.

and it is proposed to examine the evidence available on implementation under these headings.

Figure 10 The MBO cycle and relationships with other elements in the management process

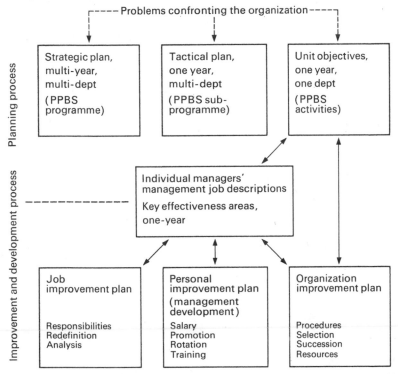

(i) *The organizational planning process*

One of the interesting variations in observed organizations has been the differing perceptions concerning Management by Objectives as an instrument of corporate management.

We have already observed in our discussions on PPBS that it, too, has been used as an instrument of corporate management. Many administrators in the United Kingdom have not been too bothered with the niceties of whether they are developing something called MBO or something called PPBS, and consequently the concepts and terms have been interchanged with confusing frequency. The main drift of this paper is that PPBS is mainly concerned with policy and financial matters, whilst MBO has a greater emphasis on the behavioural aspects of an organization. Thus when PPBS is translated to the level of an institution from the LEA to further the fulfilment of its macro objectives, its form is in educational and sub-objectives within financial resource targets. When MBO is used, it is to identify what a particular finite sub-group or individual must do to further those objectives. The fun starts when the two are quite unrelated!

Figure 11 Example of manager's guide

Job title	*Occupant*
Position in organization	(a) Directly responsible to
	(b) Subordinates directly supervised
Main personal activities	

Key results analysis

Key area no.	Key areas of job (1)	Standards of performance (2)	Sources of control data (3)	Suggestions for improving performance (4)
	Selected areas of work critical to the continued success of the person in the job	Processes and activities carried out by job holder to fulfil (1) and expressed in target terms of quality, quantity, time and cost	Sources of information indicating whether (2) is being achieved	What could be done to achieve a higher standard in: 1 job 2 organization 3 person

However, if MBO is an instrument of corporate management, those organizations with this motive have normally begun the exercise with an expression of corporate goals, and have worked out the individual objectives of numbers of staff from this starting point: in effect, a top-down process. In the light of observations, it would seem that this is more desirable than merely aggregating the individual contributions and describing these as the organization's objectives, since it tends to prevent the unfortunate effect of encouraging individuals to become more efficient at doing the wrong things! Nonetheless, there are problems in the top-down approach:

1 it assumes that it is possible to define organization level objectives satisfactorily to clients (pupils and parents, students and employers), laymen (elected members with political responsibility), professionals at various levels and (if one is considering the exercise at local education authority level) in various disciplines, including social services, recreation, finance, etc.;
2 it assumes that objectives can be made operational from a generalized aim.

Strategies may then be set up into precise targets in these areas, which can be translated into individuals' personal objectives, consistent, of course, with his management job description. Sheffield in their first phase of MBO adopted a similar approach which has subsequently become more sophisticated, and one suspects that, as corporate management systems develop within local government reorganization, this level of objective setting will be incorporated into a programme planning system. There are, as yet, few examples of education authorities using both MBO and PPBS, with the result that activities at branch and individual level may not be demonstrably connected to higher level objectives. It is interesting that where further education colleges are preparing detailed development plans, the transfer to individual plans is greatly facilitated.

3   there is often conceptual confusion where attempts are made to translate some higher level philosophical aim into operational terms. This often manifests itself in individuals selecting for themselves personal key areas, which in truth can only be achieved by the system at large, and not specifying what their particular contribution will be. Referring back to Figure 1, p. 308, the individual manager is principally carrying out his activities within the centre "box"—"the educational organization and its processes". The most one could hope to establish in causal relationships is that his activities will have an effect on provision (output) and response of the consumer. His personal key area analysis ought therefore to use performance standards from these categories, and exclude those of an "impact" nature.

4   if MBO is to be used at all in an organization then it should be used at all levels in the organization. This means that not only should senior administrators be full participants in the system, but also their committees of lay members, whether at full committee or governing body level. To take the latter as an example, if the principal of a college and his heads of department are attempting to fulfil their key results, there are surely obligations on the governing body to examine its own contribution to their achievement. The objectives of the principal and heads of department would presumably have been approved by the governors.

Clearly, to adopt this system with members is akin to the problem of belling the cat, but it does offer exciting possibilities of harnessing their undoubted energies and experience.

(ii) The individual objective-setting process
Ideally this process produces more positive effects if linked to higher organizational level objectives, but there is evidence that benefits have occurred even if the exercise is conceived as a reorientation of the individuals. However, the danger of the exercise being thus conceived is principally in motivational terms: the subject usually feels threatened.

The stages in the process are fairly well known, but again, certain problems have been evident:

3 Towards a Systematic Approach

(a) Where the key results analysis has been undertaken without a prior management job description, enormous problems of role uncertainty are created, particularly in relation to the confusion of responsibility channels upward and downward; areas of freedom to act, recommend, or act and report; limits on personal authority. It is unwise to have the dynamic of the key results analysis without the stability of the job description; both are necessary.

(b) The devising of key results in more traditional Humble terms can well produce difficulties of a conceptual nature in what is a non-profit organization. The Reddin notion of key effectiveness areas offers better possibilities, in that many administrators in education will recognize that their managerial contributions to the organization will be derived from a selection from the areas A–I in Figure 12. For example, an LEA general adviser may consider that the usefulness of his contribution to schools and the authority may well be based on effective performance in:

B (identifying the needs of his client heads and schools);
C (setting up recruitment and selection interviews, and advising heads on them);
H (developing new curricula in the authority).

Or a Head of Department in further education might find that:

A (using resources effectively);
B (developing good relationships with industry, etc.);
F (ensuring a well-motivated staff)

were his prime considerations. The possible presentations are endless, but it must be emphasized that they should be evolved on a team basis, to avoid unnecessary duplication and permit functional specialization by those who have skills and experience in a given direction. There is abundant evidence that as a reorientation exercise, many senior staff have found it useful. It permits them to analyse the methods by which they may be striving, often subconsciously, towards a given objective.

(c) The notion of performance standards has caused a great deal of difficulty in education, owing to the reluctance of educationalists to be fooled by the fatuous and facile "measures" which have been produced in some published MBO schemes. It has been found helpful to consider such standards in relation to various activities which may have to be carried out in fulfilment of the key area. Thus within key area F, for example, in Figure 12, it is quite possible to devise standards for the subdivisions indicated. Where these standards are ignored, any subsequent management activity based

Figure 12 Effectiveness areas: component parts

*A Processing resources production
    area*
Quality
Quantity
Timing
Wastage
Inventory levels and ratios
Labour costs
Material costs
Equipment and space utilization
Unit cost
Staff/operative/pupil ratios
Staff mixes
Staff workload analysis

B Client area
Consultative process
Identification of need and social
    research
Market strategy (further education)
Market plans and penetration/
    persuasion/public relations
Distribution costs

C Personnel area
Selection
Management succession
Personnel information and appraisal
Reward policy
Safety
Attitude and behaviour change
Training and development

D Finance area
Availability of finance
Financial information—quantity
                        quality
                        timing
Realiability of information storage
    and retrieval
Cost effectiveness
Audit variances
Accuracy of forecasting

E Supply area
Acquisition cost
Processing cost
Distribution cost
Numbers
Size
Damage
Complaints
Dates fulfilled
Stock control

F Integrative area
Communication system
Networks
Coordinating machinery
Commitment morale/job
    satisfaction
Labour turnover/stability
Frustration symptoms

G Predictability of organization
Rules
Conventions
Targets
Supervision
Commitment
Roles

H Development and innovation area
Human skills acquisition
Technical skills acquisition
Conceptual skills acquisition
Work habit modification

I Systems effectiveness area
Maintenance of budget
Procedural and control

Figure 13 Criteria for an effective analysis

An effective analysis is one that assists in improving the performance of the organization and its managers. There are varied "technical" considerations in undertaking analyses which contribute to their success; these are listed below. It should be remembered, however, that commitment to a rough-and-ready analysis will produce better results than lip-service paid to a technically perfect analysis.

Criteria

1　Has the analysis identified the ends, not the means, of the job in the key effectiveness areas column? (*result-centred*)
2　Is the total number of key effectiveness areas too many for the individual to achieve, or are the areas themselves not sufficiently stretching?
3　Do the performance standards measure a range of subordinate activities relevant to the main effectiveness area? (*measurable*)
4　Is there a logical continuance from key effectiveness areas through performance standards and control data to improvement plan? (*integrated*)
5　Is the analysis precise enough to permit of effective appraisal at the end of, and during, the period in question? (*specific*)
6　Does the analysis indicate the relationships with other people's targets and activities? (*related*)
7　Does the target give time for the achievement of the objective specified? (*time bounded*)
8　Is the analysis worked out with the person concerned or imposed upon him? (*participative*)
9　Is the analysis on-going, and generative of improvement ideas within the manager? (*dynamic*)
10　Does the analysis stimulate him to greater job satisfaction? (*enriching and motivating*)

The above questions should be applied to the drafts of analyses so that the coherence of their construction is continually refined.

---

on MBO becomes practically impossible—activity geared to the targets Appraisal of Staff, Staff Development, etc. In short, performance standards of necessity have to be result-centred if the exercise is to be more than just a philosophical inquiry, and the following categories are suggested:

1　quantitative standards may very well be used to denote measurable features such as time spent, costs, curriculum volume, staff deployment, unspent balances;
2　indirect and qualitative standards are necessary to avoid undue credence being placed on the first category, and here adverse conditions (morale low, ineffective group decision making, user/client dissatisfaction), are examples of possibilities.

(d) Having detailed key areas and a battery of standards was found by several administrators to be of limited value without the existence of control information to enable them to take remedial action when necessary, and in ample time. Essentially, there should be sufficient information to enable administrators to manage by exception, but this remains one of the major problem areas in MBO to date.

Figure 13 indicates in the light of the author's experience the type of technical criteria which need to be applied to an analysis.

(iii) Improvement and development plans
These are the MBO expression of organization renewal. Deficiencies will emerge as a result of the key area analysis: deficiencies in the capacity of the manager to achieve all he wishes, and all that is expected; deficiencies in the capacity of the organization itself to facilitate the expected developments. Unless these deficiencies are identified and steps taken to remedy them, the organization will not be a learning organization and its health will be in jeopardy. Unfortunately, several factors have tended to militate against the full development of improvement plans in education —the erection of professional barricades against alleged interference in traditional sanctums; the inertia which exists in large organizations; the tendency to initiate structural and procedural reforms separately from an objective analysis of deficiencies; and the notice of some senior administrators that deficiencies are necessarily those of more junior staff rather than of the systems they themselves have created.

(a) Frequently insufficient thought is given to the reconstruction of a person's job to ensure a more cohesive set of activities, a more enriching job, and a workload commensurate with personal capacity.

(b) Whilst there are some notable advances in organizational improvement, deficiencies are not picked up and resolved early enough, particularly in the case of institutional MBO. This is partly because, unlike the local educational authority MBO schemes observed, the resolution of a given deficiency was not clearly made the responsibility of a particular officer. It should be mentioned that changes in this area range from procedural improvements over a broad front, as typified by Somerset CC Education Department—to a thoroughgoing reform of departmental assumptions, processes and structure, well displayed by the Sheffield developments (Mann, 1973).

(c) There is still a tendency to regard personal improvement plans as being synonymous with courses. A variety of other means more relevant to the particular situation need to be used—job rotation, on-the-job training, etc. Too many training needs identified seem to be concerned with the person's ability to work the MBO system, rather than with his major missions as an educational manager.

(iv) Appraisal and review processes
The final problem area in MBO is most assuredly that of appraising results. The main causes of the rejection of MBO have been, on the one hand, the failure to assess systematically what has been achieved and, on the other, the fear and insecurity engendered by the very idea of assessment. Failure in this area has meant a failure to reset objectives in the light of experience, and the cyclical basis of MBO has thus foundered. The author has observed many reasons why problems are evident here, but the following, drawn from a range of situations, seem to deserve the greatest attention from those actually in an MBO system, and those contemplating it:

(a)   The purposes of the appraisal have not always been made clear in colleges or LEAs: are they to allocate blame; sharpen up the subject's sense of accountability and obligation; identify management obstacles to his effectiveness; identify training needs; or what?

(b)   Despite the fact that MBO was designed partly to permit a more objective staff appraisal, based on targets rather than personality traits, there is some evidence that well-known phenomena like "halo" ratings, preoccupation with personality rather than performance, and prejudice, are still present. The behavioural factor is still powerful.

(c)   Appraisals with MBO are still not closely enough linked to other personnel functions such as training and reward systems.

(d)   In institutions there is a tendency, not commonly found in LEAs for the headman to be exempt, particularly if his governing body is not involved in the scheme.

(e)   There are still conflicting views as to the appropriate length of the performance/assessment period, varying from three months to one year, and these do not necessarily correspond with any particular situational variables.

(f)   Assessors often seem to be in doubt whether they are assessing past performance, current activities or future potential.

(g)   Some assessors are clearly unhappy with their role in a counselling/ appraisal interview, perhaps because of lack of training, perhaps because this form is foreign to their leadership style.

In conclusion, one must concede that the sample of educational organizations studied has not been considerable: more organizations are talking about MBO than are actually doing it. One could go further, and say that

MBO in some organizations (Sheffield Education Department) has evolved into something else, and has therefore fulfilled its purpose as an instrument of change. Though we have concentrated on the problems, it should not be deduced that MBO has been a disaster. Many have seen the benefits, but these must be made more demonstrable if MBO is really to take root as a system, rather than to function as an interesting annual diversion from the job itself. In short, MBO is at a crossroads, conceptually and technically.

NOTE

1 See the ongoing correspondence on corporate management in *Education* from September 1972.

REFERENCES

AITKEN, R. (1974) "Output Budgeting for the Local Education Authority", *Output Measurement in the Education Service*, Institute of Public Finance and Accountancy.

ALKIN, M. (1973) "Evaluation and Decision Making", *Planning and Changing*, Vol. 3, No. 4, Winter 1973.

ALIOTO, R. F. and JUNGHERR, J. (1969) "Using PPBS to Overcome Taxpayers' Resistance", *Phi Delta Kappan*, Vol. 11, No. 3, Nov. 1969.

ARGENTI, J. (1969) *Management Techniques*, Allen and Unwin.

BAINS, M. A. (1972) "The New Local Authorities: Management and Structure", Department of the Environment.

BENNIS, W. G., et al. (1969) *The Planning of Change*, Holt, Rinehart and Winston.

BIRCH, D. W., CALVERT, J. and DAVIES, J. L. (1974) *Academic Staffing Formulae, with Particular Reference to Advanced Further Education*, Nelpress (North East London Polytechnic).

BIRLEY, D. (1972) *Planning and Education*, Routledge and Kegan Paul.

BURKHEAD, J. (1966) "A New Way to View the Educational Process", in *Education in the States*, National Committee for the Support of Public Schools, Washington.

BURNS, R. J. and MACNAMARA, J. F. (1974) "Technological Forecasting and Long-range Planning in an Urban School District", *Planning and Changing*, Vol. 4, No. 1, Spring 1973.

CLELAND, D. J. and KING, W. R. (1968) *Systems Analysis and Project Management*, McGraw-Hill.

CONRAD, M., BROOKS, K. and FISCHER, G. (1973) "A Model for Comprehensive Educational Planning", *Planning and Changing*, Vol. 4, No. 1, Spring 1973.

DAVIES, J. L. (1974) "The Refinement of the Conceptual Framework of Output Measurement in Education", in *Output Measurement in the Education Service*, Institute of Public Finance and Accountancy.

DAVIES, T. I. (1969) *School Organisation*, Pergamon.

DEPARTMENT OF EDUCATION AND SCIENCE (1970) "Output Budgeting for the DES", Planning Paper No. 1, HMSO.

DERR, C. B. (1971) "Organization Development PPB for Education", paper delivered to the American Educational Research Association Convention.

EDDISON, A. (1973) *Local Government: Management and Corporate Planning*, Leonard Hill Books.

EDUCATION ACT (1944) Ch. 31, HMSO.

EIDELL, T. L. and NAGLE, J. M. (1970) *PPBS and Data-based Educational Planning*, National Schools Development Council, Washington.

FRANK, J. E. (1973) "A Framework for the Analysis of PPBS Success and Causality", *Administration Science Quarterly*, Dec. 1973.

Hives, P. (1971) "The MBO Movement", *Management by Objectives Journal*, Vol. 1, No. 1.

HUMBLE, J. W. (1968) *Management by Objectives*, Industrial, Educational and Research Foundation.

JAMES, R. (1973) "Is There a Case for Local Authority Policy Planning?" *Public Administration*, Vol. 51, Summer 1973.

KAHN, H. and WEINER, A. J. (1967) *The Year 2,000*, Macmillan.

McGIVNEY, J. H. and BOWLES, B. D. (1972) "The Political Aspects of PPBS", *Planning and Changing*, Vol. 3, No. 1, April 1972.

McGREGOR, D. (1957) *The Human Side of Enterprise*, McGraw-Hill.

MANN, J. F. (1973) "3D Management", *Municipal and Public Services Journal*, 12, Jan. 1973.

MAUD COMMITTEE (1967) *The Management of Local Government*, report of the committee appointed under the Chairmanship of Sir John Maud, Ministry of Housing and Local Government, HMSO.

MEREVITZ, L. and SOSNICK, S. H. (1971) *The Budget's New Clothes*, Markham.

POOLING COMMITTEE (1972) "Assessment of Curricular Activity and Utilisation of Staff Resources in Polytechnics and Further Education Colleges", Councils and Education Press.

REDDIN, W. J. (1971a) *Effective MBO*, British Institute of Management.

REDDIN, W. J. (1971b) "Do MBO Systems Differ?" *Management by Objectives Journal*, Vol. 1, No. 1.

SCHEIN, E. H. (1965) *Organizational Psychology*, Prentice-Hall.

SCHICK, K. (1971) *Budget Innovation in the States*, Brookings Institute, Washington.

STEWART, J. D. (1972) *Management in Local Government: A Viewpoint*, Charles Knight.

WICKENS, J. D. (1968) "Management by Objectives: An Appraisal", *Journal of Management Studies*, Vol. 5, No. 3, pp. 365–79.

3.6 Allocating Budgets to Colleges of Further Education: A Case Study in Cumbria[1]

Tony Gear, John S. Gillespie and William H. Stubbs

INTRODUCTION

The allocation of the financial budget to all sectors of local government has become more difficult in recent years because of the increased demands which are being made on the limited financial resources available. Whilst some of the increased demands for finance are due to a greater provision in the services provided for the public by local authorities, most of the increased expenditure results from the severe financial inflation which has occurred recently. As a result local authorities are examining more carefully than ever all requests from departments for increased financial allocations.

The reorganization of local government in April 1974 further complicated this budgetary problem. New local authorities became responsible for providing services which previously had been the responsibility of the old authorities, not all of which had made similar provision for the various services.

An example of this situation is in Cumbria where the new local education authority (LEA) assumed responsibility for the colleges of further education in an area which had previously been administered by four different local education authorities.

This paper describes an investigation of the feasibility of using a formal method to assist in allocating a limited financial budget between five of the colleges of further education in Cumbria in order to help in achieving a closer equity of distribution of resources amongst the colleges. The method used attempts to recognize the elements of discussion and competition which are present when the annual budgets of colleges are fixed and to assist in the making of an objective allocation of funds.

Source: A preliminary report in an ongoing applied research project undertaken by The Open University (Tony Gear) in collaboration with Corporate Management Consultants Ltd (John S. Gillespie) and Cumbria County Council (William H. Stubbs).

FINANCE OF COLLEGES OF FURTHER EDUCATION

The financing of colleges of further education is made from two main sources: the annual revenue budget and the capital budget of the LEA. This model is concerned only with a part of the revenue budget. All of the expenditure headings in the revenue budget are shown in Table 1a and those included in the model are marked with an asterisk.

Table 1a Categories of expenditure in colleges of further education

Employees
Salaries and wages
    Teaching staff
    Other staff
National insurance
Superannuation

Running expenses
Premises:
    Repair and maintenance
    Alteration to buildings
    Fuel, light, cleaning materials and water
    *Furniture and fittings
    Rent and rates

Supplies and services
*Books, stationery, educational equipment,
    other equipment and materials
*Protective clothing and laundry
*Examination fees

Transport
Car user allowances

Establishment expenses
*Stationery, postage, telephones
*Travelling and subsistence
Insurances

Miscellaneous
Refectory

The largest proportion of the college revenue budgets is allocated for staff and premises and any aid to resource allocation would be more useful if it was capable of examining these major items of expenditure. In order, however, to examine the feasibility of this particular method, it was decided to concentrate on certain non-staffing costs, particularly those of educational equipment.

Unlike LEA maintained schools, which each receive annual money allocations for books and equipment (i.e. capitation allowances) based on the number of children on the school roll, allocations to colleges are based on an estimate of the requirements of each college in the next financial year.

The estimates of college expenditure are made in the light of the expenditure in the current financial year and the likely cost of any developments planned for the next year. Although such estimates are examined for each individual college and also as a gross amount for all colleges in the county, it has not been the practice to base the budget on unit allocations, which would allow a comparison to be made of the relative demands of each college.

THE BASIC MODEL

This study is a first attempt to find a basis for comparing colleges in terms of their relative cost in order that running expenses may be allocated in the most equitable fashion possible. The model used is based on the concept of relating the resources which a college receives to the amount of teaching carried out in that college.

As a first step towards measuring the amount of teaching it was decided to use the Burnham Unit total of each college. In recent years it has become necessary for each LEA to determine this unit total as part of a separate exercise concerning the number of graded posts in each college. The units are related to the number of students attending the various courses and are weighted according to the level of the course attended in the following manner: [2]

Standard of work	Units
Courses leading to a university degree (A1)	For each 300 student hours: 1 unit
Courses of equivalent standard to those above (A2)	For each 375 student hours: 1 unit
GCE Advanced level courses (B)	For each 600 student hours: 1 unit
Other courses	For each 1 000 student hours: 1 unit

For each college, the following quantities are incorporated in the model:

(i)   The total *present* annual allocation in £s to each college, represented by Ti where i is the identification number of each college. (i.e. i=1, 2, 3, 4 or 5)

(ii)   The *present* allocation, in £s per Burnham Unit, to each college under each budgetary heading, represented by Aij where i=1, 2, 3, 4 or 5 and j=1, 2, 3, 4, 5 or 6 for the following headings:

Budget heading
1	Furniture and fittings	1
2	Books, stationery, educational equipment and other equipment	2

3	Protective clothing and laundry	3
4	Examination fees	4
5	Administration —stationery, postage and telephones	5
6	Travelling and subsistence	6

(iii)   The *present average* annual allocation in £s per Burnham Unit to each of the six budget types, the average being taken over the five colleges and represented as A_j where $j = 1, 2, 3, 4, 5$ or 6.

(iv)   The proposed *new* allocation in £s per Burnham Unit to the budgetary heading, represented by R where $j = 1, 2, 3, 4, 5$ or 6.

(v)   The *penultimate*[3] Burnham unit total for each college i, represented as N_i.

(vi)   The *most recent* Burnham unit total for each college represented as M_i for college $i = 1, 2, 3, 4$ or 5.

(vii)   The anticipated *overall* budgetary limit for the budgetary headings 1 to 6 for all of the five colleges in Cumbria, represented by C (in £s).

(viii)   The *change* (in £s) of the proposed allocation for college i from the previous allocation, represented by Z_i $i = 1, 2, 3, 4$ or 5.

With these definitions of quantities, the present average annual allocations to the six expense headings (i.e. the quantities A_j) can be regarded as a calculated average goal. The model is designed to "reward":

Colleges with an individual A_{ij} less than the average A_j
and/or colleges which propose high values of planned Burnham units, M_i.

The "reward" comes in the form of high positive values for the change in budget allocation, i.e. in high positive values for the quantities Z. More generally, the model is designed to assist in placing the method of resource allocation on a more objective and consistent footing than hitherto, treating all colleges in a similar manner. The model, in mathematical form, is composed of constraints (that is, limits) on certain of the above quantities, together with a formula to be optimized. In its present form, the model includes the following constraints:

(i)   The changes, Z_i, must be positive for each college, that is, the budget allocation must increase (this point is raised in the next section).

(ii)   The variables, R_j, which represent the proposed new average annual allocations per Burnham unit, must equal or exceed a given percentage of the corresponding *present* average annual allocation, A_j. This

Tony Gear, John S. Gillespie and William H. Stubbs

can be used, for example, to ensure that allocations are at least increased in line with inflation.

(iii) The variables, R_j, must be less than or equal to a different, and higher, percentage of the corresponding A_j. This constraint sets an upper limit which will be tolerated between the present average allocation and the new average allocation determined by the model.

(iv) The total budget allocation in the coming year to all the colleges in the study, summed over the six expense categories, must be equal to, but not greater than, the overall limit, C.

The objective chosen is to maximize the total sum of the budget changes (i.e. new allocation minus old allocation) for the five colleges up to the allowable limit of total expenditure.

DATA USED FOR TESTING THE MODEL

In order to evaluate and investigate the usefulness of this model, existing data for the financial year 1974/75 and the 1973 and 1974 Burnham Reports were used. The data is given as follows:

Present total budget allocations to the 5 colleges in 1973/74

$T_1 = £35\ 215$
$T_2 = £81\ 508$
$T_3 = £32\ 030$
$T_4 = £87\ 600$
$T_5 = £23\ 820$

_____

£260 173

Minimum values for each R_j were defined as 1.02 A_j. Maximum values for each R_j were defined as 1.12 A_j.

Present average annual allocations to each of the 6 budget categories in 1973/74 (£/unit)

$A_1 = 1.79$
$A_2 = 43.90$
$A_3 = 0.72$
$A_4 = 8.12$
$A_5 = 4.00$
$A_6 = 1.11$

These A_j values (averages) were calculated as shown in Table 1b, which gives the A_{ij} values (£s per Burnham unit) for each college.

For this particular run, the total budget for running expenses for allocation to Cumbria colleges (i.e C) was limited to £331,875, i.e. a 19 per cent increase on the current financial year.

The 1973 and the 1974 total Burnham units for the five colleges were as shown in Table 2.

361

Table 1b A_{ij} values; numerator in £s, denominator in Burnham units

Budget category	College 1	College 2	College 3	College 4	College 5
1	$\dfrac{915}{995}$	$\dfrac{2083}{25}$	$\dfrac{380}{427}$	$\dfrac{3500}{1320}$	$\dfrac{920}{368}$
2	$\dfrac{26400}{995}$	$\dfrac{61750}{25}$	$\dfrac{23100}{427}$	$\dfrac{61200}{1320}$	$\dfrac{19100}{368}$
3	$\dfrac{250}{995}$	$\dfrac{1150}{25}$	$\dfrac{250}{427}$	$\dfrac{1000}{1320}$	$\dfrac{500}{368}$
4	$\dfrac{6500}{995}$	$\dfrac{13350}{25}$	$\dfrac{4050}{427}$	$\dfrac{10000}{1320}$	$\dfrac{1500}{368}$
5	$\dfrac{1050}{995}$	$\dfrac{1700}{25}$	$\dfrac{3400}{427}$	$\dfrac{10600}{1320}$	$\dfrac{700}{368}$
6	$\dfrac{100}{995}$	$\dfrac{1475}{25}$	$\dfrac{850}{427}$	$\dfrac{1300}{1320}$	$\dfrac{1100}{368}$

Table 2 Burnham units corresponding to each college in 1973 and 1974

	College 1	College 2	College 3	College 4	College 5	Total
1973	995	1425	427	1320	368	4535
1974	1003	1424	423	1284	371	4505

RESULTS

The above model and data were analysed using a standard technique known as linear programming. This allows the objective to be maximized in accordance with the set of given constraints listed on pp. 360–1.

However, initial calculations showed that no answer to the stated problem could be found which would ensure that *all* the constraints could be simultaneously met. This meant relaxing one or more of the constraints in some way. It was decided that the restriction making the change in allocation to each college (Z_i) positive would be removed from the problem, meaning that it would then be possible for one or more of the colleges to receive a lower allocation in 1975/76 than in 1974/75. There are, however, other ways in which the constraints could be modified, e.g. by allowing the values of the new average allocations, R_j, to lie between broader limits than 2% to 12% of A_j. The model can be run with a series of modifications to the constraints in order to examine the budgetary implications. By allowing the changes, Z_i, to be positive or negative, the following solution was given:

	Old (1973/4) allocation (T_i)	Change (Z_i)	New (1974/5) allocation ($T_i + Z_i$)	Percentage change
College 1	£35 215	£29 233	£64 448	+83%
College 2	£81 508	£9 990	£91 498	+12%
College 3	£32 030	−£4 850	£27 180	−15%
College 4	£87 600	−£5 099	£82 501	−6%
College 5	£23 820	£19	£23 839	0
Total	£260 173	£29 293	£289 466	11%

A more detailed version of the results is shown in Table 3:

Table 3 Allocations to each college proposed for 1975/6 and the allocations made in 1974/5

Budget category	Financial year	College 1	College 2	College 3	College 4	College 5	Total
1	1974/5	915	2083	380	3500	920	7798
	1975/6	1932	2743	815	2473	715	8678
2	1974/5	26400	61750	23100	61200	19100	191550
	1975/6	47451	67368	20012	60744	17552	213127
3	1974/5	250	1150	250	1000	500	3150
	1975/6	775	1100	327	992	287	3481
4	1974/5	6500	13350	4050	10000	150	35400
	1975/6	8774	12456	3700	11231	3245	39406
5	1974/5	1050	1700	3400	10600	700	17450
	1975/6	4325	6140	1824	5537	1600	19426
6	1974/5	100	1475	850	1300	1100	4825
	1975/6	1191	1691	502	1524	440	5348
7	Total 1974/5 (T_i)	35215	81508	32030	87600	23820	260173
	Total 1975/6 ($T_i + Z_i$)	64448	91498	27180	82507	23839	289466

It can be seen:

1   That despite the relaxation of the constraint allowing Z_i to be positive or negative, the solution shows a total allocation of £289,423 which is considerably below the allowable maximum of £331,875. Thus the total budget was not a limiting factor in that, increasing the range within which the R_j values have to lie, the budgetary limit would eventually become an active constraint on the solution.

2   That college 1 has a large increase in allocation, College 2 has a medium increase, College 3 has no change and Colleges 4 and 5 have reductions.

CONCLUSIONS
1   The present model appears to have some useful features, particularly in its ability to discriminate between colleges in terms of their student enrolments as measured by the unit totals.
2   The present model is simple, and only requires data which is already available.
3   The calculation of present annual allocations in £s per Burnham unit for each budget type (the A_js) is empirically based. Looking at the data from which the A_js were derived (Table 1), the range of individual ratios for each budget type for the five colleges varies very considerably, and hence the average ratio, A_j, has great dispersion. This may be due to fundamental differences between colleges in terms of the balance of course types offered; or, indeed, it may reflect differences in definition of the budget types within each college.
4   The ease with which the model can be formed and analysed indicates that this approach could provide valuable assistance to the Education Committee and to the principals of the colleges; its ability to examine alternative allocation policies seems especially important.
5   The results from the model are useful mainly as a guide to management decision making. It is necessary for consideration to be given to special features of each college, e.g. new developments in the oncoming financial year, unavoidable commitments arising from previous decisions which will have continuing financial implications.
6   The model provides a set of terms, such as the changes in allocations, which can be used by all concerned in resolving budgetary issues; however, the model can only provide guidelines for further discussion of the wider implications. It in no way replaces the decision-taking functions of the Education Committee and college principals.

DEVELOPMENTS OF THE MODEL
In view of the above conclusions the next stage is to investigate the possibility of breaking down each college's budget not by the above budget types, but instead to the departments which exist in each college. It seems

likely that this would give a sounder basis for comparing the requirements of similar departments in more than one college.

This was, in fact, the approach which was initially planned, but it had to be modified in view of the availability of case study data. However, this problem cannot be insuperable, and the results of the above model indicate that it might be desirable to develop accounting procedures in keeping with a departmentally based model.

In addition to dealing with the running overheads in the short term only, the model could be expanded to consider the *total* capital and revenue allocations to the colleges over a number of future years. The benefits of this development would be to analyse longer-term policies in further education such as new colleges and/or extensions, changes to the departmental emphasis and size, recruitment policy, and so on. The above study, therefore, is a first step towards the total planning of further education in Cumbria.

NOTES

1 The authors are grateful to J. Robin Barron, Cumbria Education Department, and to Chris Orton, The Open University, for assistance in developing the model described in this paper.

2 Following the Report of the Committee of Inquiry into the pay of non-university teachers (The Houghton Report) amendments have been made in the weighting of the Burnham units.

3 For the calculation shown the budget being prepared is for the 1975/76 financial year. N_i and M_i refer to the unit total under the 1973 and 1974 Burnham Reports, respectively.

3.7 Making Claims for Computers

Richard Hooper

The claims made for the computer as an educational technology have come thick and fast over the last decade and a half—and continue to come. "The computer has a potential for higher éducation," wrote the influential Carnegie Commission on Higher Education's 1972 study of computers in higher education, "comparable to the potential that the motor had for nineteenth-century industry. Eventually, it may transform higher education" (Levien, 1972, p. 8).

It is symptomatic of educational technology boosterism generally that the claims are seldom scrutinised in any detail. Much detail, however, is lavished on the requirements for operating systems and programming languages, the terminal interface, the characters per second—all the bits and bytes of computer technology.

I would like to examine three major claims made for the computer in assisting learning—or rather categories of claim. Under one of these three categories (sometimes more than one) are subsumed most of the claims that one encounters—either consciously stated or unconsciously assumed—in the literature and in conversation with practitioners. The three claims are:

1 Computers can provide more effective education at lower cost.
2 Computers can individualise instruction.
3 Computers can provide learning opportunities that can be provided by no other educational media.

I am *not* talking about the claims made for using the computer to teach computing and spread computer awareness—since it is a self-evident claim. Whether computing and computing education have a claim to a place in the curriculum is not self-evident, however.

Source: Paper given at the conference "Computers in Higher Education" at the University of Lancaster (26–29 March 1974) and published in the *International Journal of Mathematical Education in Science and Technology* (1974), Vol. 5, pp. 359–68.

1 COMPUTERS AND COST-EFFECTIVENESS

With the costs of labour-intensive industries such as education and the demand for education both rising, but with income flattening off, it is not suprising that the development of education technology is seen by some to be synonymous with the attainment of cost-effectiveness. In one of the early NCET studies which eventually led to the creation of the National Development Programme in Computer Assisted Learning, it was stated that "the introduction of computer based learning will be justified if (and only if) it is likely to do the job as effectively as and more cheaply than ... alternatives" (NCET, 1969). The CAI [Computer Assisted Instruction] literature in the States is replete with elaborate cost analyses, comparing conventional teaching costs per hour with computerised teaching costs. But comparisons such as these, and cost-effectiveness arguments generally, are a minefield of good (and bad) intentions.

If we are to make any significant cost reductions in, for example, higher education (forgetting about the "effectiveness" dimension for a moment), there are only two ways—putting to one side the most effective way of all, reducing the number of students permitted into higher education. Costs can be significantly reduced in higher education if the ratio of teacher and administrative staff to students goes down—that is to say, if a teacher teaches more students than he does at present. The other way is to reduce capital requirements, for example by getting more students to live, and study, at home. These two methods of achieving cost reductions—less teachers and less buildings—have been used most obviously by the Open University. If computers do not assist either or both of these to happen, then all talk of cost-effectiveness is empty.

Some 95% of recurrent educational costs go on staff salaries and building upkeep of one sort or another. Any reallocation of moneys within the remaining 5% spent on books, laboratory equipment and other instructional materials is of little or no consequence. To be truly cost-effective, the computer has got to eat into that 95%. Yet, far from the computer being permitted to eat into that 95%, the pressures are all the other way. The latest estimate I have come across of the cost per student hour of the famous PLATO CAI system in Illinois, when it is fully developed to 4,000 terminals, is 14.17 pence (Glasgow Education Committee, 1973). Now this cost of a computerised teaching hour is only worth comparing with the cost of a conventional teaching hour if the one is to replace the other. But will it be allowed to? The answer in today's secondary and post-secondary educational institutions in this country is almost certainly no—for the simple reason that the demand from teachers and teachers' unions, is always to increase the teacher-student ratio, not reduce it (by machine substitution or any other method). What is more, teachers' salaries are steadily increasing, as are land and building costs. Despite the bestseller status of Ivan Illich, there is no significant move to deschool higher education and thus reduce capital spending.

But there is a further, even more painful realisation for computer assisted learning proponents. Where an educational technology such as computers has been introduced, there has almost always been an *increase* in staff required, and an *increase* in space required. Now it can of course be argued that computers are still in their experimental stage and that these extra staff will disappear when the "steady-state" state is reached. The person who argues this has heard nothing about higher education's propensity for empire-building. The closed circuit television units installed in British universities from around 1967 onwards have in some cases today large staffs and extensive space utilisation. In no case that I know of has there been any sign of teacher reduction or teaching space reduction to offset this. It is an abiding irony of educational technology that, even where it has been sensitively and creatively applied, more staff seem to be needed, *and* better trained, more imaginative teachers. Yet that very educational technology was originally justified to decision-makers as a means of reducing staff and eking out the fare of poor and inadequately trained teachers.

Turning from the cost to effectiveness, the problems are, if anything, more complex. Here, the argument runs as follows: the introduction of computer assisted learning will increase the budget of a given educational institution or system; this *add-on* cost can only be justified by increased effectiveness—i.e. more, or better, educated products. But how do you measure a "better educated product"? At this point the consensus collapses.

Where evaluation has been done of American CAI projects, the results are not conclusive. The PLATO project is only now being independently evaluated—some thirteen years after the horse began bolting. Where there have been some conclusive results, with CAI achieving that magic "significant difference", the research designs have often been found wanting. The much publicised Russian language course at Stanford University, taught entirely by computer and language laboratory, showed significant gains for the experimental group against the control group, but the sample was small and the selection of control and experimental groups was not done on a random basis (Levien, 1972, p. 357). The Russian CAI course was closed down some while ago, anyway. It was said to be costing three times as much as conventional instruction—after many years' development and operation. (Hammond, 1972). This is real evaluation—educational decision-makers voting with their feet, or rather with their wallets.

In 1972, the Educational Products Information Exchange (EPIE), the *Which?* of US educational technology, commented: 'Nowhere has there occurred objective and systematic evaluation of the effectiveness of CAI." This independent judgement needs to be set against the claims of over ardent project directors, who have a career stake in proving significant difference for their own brand of technological solution.

There have been other claims, notably in the USA, that the computer will prove most cost-effective as a tool for educational planners. A computer-based model of the educational system or sub-system would, it is argued, allow decision-makers to simulate decisions about the future use of resources (cash, staff, equipment, buildings). As a result, such resources would be used optimally. In theory, this sounds fine. In practice, the experiences with such an approach have not been satisfactory. It has proved uneconomic to model educational systems in any realistic manner because of the vast amount of data that needs to be collected, classified, manipulated and, at regular intervals, updated. In addition, such exercises in resource optimisation tend to remain rather "academic" in the real political world of annual or quinquennial funding. In the USA some limited successes have been achieved with computer-based modelling in private institutions of higher education, in limited areas of educational planning such as student fees and enrolment patterns.

In summary, then, the claims for cost-effectiveness cannot be taken too seriously at present—even remembering the awe-inspiring cost reductions being quoted for computer hardware. It is difficult to establish cost (PLATO makes all sorts of major, and some would say dubious, assumptions to achieve its estimated figure of 14.17 pence per student terminal hour). It is difficult to establish educational effectiveness. It is difficult to relate the one to the other. But even if all this is done, computers are not likely to be permitted by existing educational structures to *be* cost-effective.

Yet the cost-effectiveness claim file cannot be closed, since the argument really rests on what you use the computer to do. Cost-effectiveness is, after all, only a means to an end.

2 COMPUTERS AND INDIVIDUALISED INSTRUCTION

Turning to the second major claim—computers can individualise instruction—this is the point at which CAI enthusiasts wax lyrical:

"One can predict," claimed one of the CAI elders, Patrick Suppes, in 1966, "that in a few more years millions of school children will have access to what Philip of Macedon's son Alexander enjoyed as a royal prerogative: the personal services of a tutor as well-informed and responsive as Aristotle" (quoted in Oettinger, 1969, p. 178).

Being at present fashionable, the term "individualised instruction" can mean almost everything. It is often confused with independent learning and self-instruction, for example. Sometimes it refers to a situation where students are permitted to move at their own pace through uniform sets of material. Individualisation can also mean students moving through dissimilar sets of materials according to their own individually prescribed objectives, needs and interests. It can imply students being routed off on to branch lines of instruction, or forward to more difficult modules, leaving out certain intermediate steps. Some would argue that individualised instruction involves the identification of the individual student's learning style and the design of materials which match it. The Leeds University

Computer Based Learning Project stresses the importance of *feedback* as the means of achieving what they term "adaptive teaching systems".

The problem raised by individualisation is that, frankly, we do not know very much about implementing it at any very sophisticated level. Whilst we may be fairly certain that feedback is an important component of an individualised system, we are far from certain about the sort of feedback it should be. Following Skinner, it should be feedback which basically confirms correct responses, with the learner seldom being allowed by the instructional designer to make errors. Taking the Crowder line, the emphasis is on diagnostic feedback as a result of the learner being "forced" into making errors. Skinner, after a period in the wilderness, is having a comeback in a different guise. Some people working in remedial reading are asserting that the act of error detection may actually reinforce error, by reinforcing the poor self-image of the learner.[1] Instead, the child's competence should be detected and built upon, thus improving the child's all-important self-confidence. But even if we know the type of feedback that is optimal, there are still other uncertainties relating to, for example, the frequency of feedback provision, and to the whole complex area of diagnostic assessment. To know that Johnny has made an error of computation does not constitute diagnosis. The crucial question is causal—why did he make this error?

But given that we could individualise instruction in a theoretical sense (and we can't), is it as universally desirable as the individualisers often take for granted? There are some subjects where individualisation of instruction might work actively against the message of the subject. In the RAF, for example, it is probably not desirable to individualise the training of pilots in close formation flying! A more familiar example might be the teaching of social studies. An individualised course on man as a social animal might prove something of a paradox.

But given that it is desirable, is individualised instruction using the computer as a tutorial teaching machine practicable? Not only is the educational technology—i.e. the learning theory—largely deficient in this area; so is the computing technology. The computer is still today very restricted in the responses it can understand from the learning and the responses it can itself make. To suggest that the computer today (or in the near future) even approximates a human tutor, in either the structural or the functional sense,[2] is to indulge in pure fantasy. As Don Bushnell (1971) said in his paper for President Johnson's Commission on Instructional Technology, "the early promise of CAI was that it would give the learner rapid access to a body of information organized to his particular style of learning. Somehow we lost the way. ..."

But the severest test of practicability is cost. Individualising instruction by stuffing the computer with teaching materials must be the most expensive possible way of doing it. Many of the important individualising dimensions can be achieved by print, for example, at a fraction of the cost and inconvenience. Print is very adaptive to student pace, and to students' differing requirements for content. Print can be accessed easily, at any time, and in whatever sequence is individually appropriate. Print can also provide quite skilful feedback, as has been shown by some programmed texts and by the Open University correspondence texts. In the present state of the art, there is no hard evidence that the computer can more skilfully individualise instruction than a range of other cheaper non-human media. Even where the computer has the edge, the cost differential between it and the other media cannot begin to be justified in relation to that marginally increased edge of effectiveness. Given a need to work within continuing cost constraints, it is of course idle to assume that we could fully individualise instruction—in a society committed to universal, mass education. The real education design problem is achieving a good balance between individualised and mass instruction. Individualised instruction by itself yields too few economies of scale. Mass instruction by itself is likely neither to be effective nor to be philosophically acceptable.[3]

But finally, and I feel most important of all, it may be tactically unwise to develop the computer solely as an individualising teaching machine. The live human teacher medium is already very equipped—in a technical sense—to be just that. The history of educational technology is full of technological graveyards, where lie the valves, circuits and transistors of new media that attempted to ape the classroom teacher. Whether the computer can or cannot individualise instruction is not the issue here. Even if it could, its backers will sooner or later find themselves on a collision course with the teaching establishment, which will say simply this: "instead of spending money on computers and systems analysts, let us spend it on more and better-paid teachers".

This brings me naturally to the third major claim made for computers in education: computers can provide learning opportunities that can be provided by no other educational media (*including* the live teacher medium).

3 COMPUTERS AND "UNIQUENESS"

The significant and recognisable feature of the many claims made for computers in this third category is that references to individualisation, to educational psychology and technology are seldom, if ever, made. Instead the language of justification is the language of the particular subject matter for which the computer is employed. The uses of the computer, here, derive not from learning theory or even educational considerations, but *specifically from the requirements and nature of the subject matter*. The use of the computer to individualise instruction is essentially content-free in inspiration, deriving from educational and psychological considerations, and is applicable—in theory at least—to any subject that is taught. The use of the computer to teach physics derives from the nature of physics and is essentially content-specific.

Here are samples of the claims made by staff from science and engineering departments in higher education in the UK. The computer, it is claimed, allows the student:

1 to obtain firsthand experience of more realistic problems and experiments, without becoming bogged down in mathematics and data analysis;
2 to explore and practise numerical approaches to problem-solving, thus complementing traditional analytical procedures: given these numerical techniques, the student can then tackle the more realistic problems;
3 to integrate different approaches and disciplines in an authentic, multivariate simulation model;
4 to develop skills of synthesising as well as analysing (circuit design may be best learnt by designing circuits rather than analysing circuits already designed);
5 to close the gap between theory and practice, lecture and lab session, by being able to manipulate in practice theoretical concepts, changing, for example, the input values and parameters of a given model to test a given hypothesis;
6 to develop problem-solving skills, particularly with regard to decision-making, for example in the planning of scientific experiments or in the carrying out of a medical diagnosis;
7 to perform simulated experiments which are *expensive, dangerous, time-consuming, impossible* to do in the normal science teaching laboratory.

Computer assisted learning, deriving from these claims, is substantially different from CAI. It provides the student and teacher with a flexible and open-ended learning resource. The computer is, using Tony Oettinger's classification in *Run, Computer, Run* (p. 200) both instrument and actor. In its instrument role, the computer is most obviously providing fast calculating facilities. In its actor role, it is providing predictive models which can act out "what would happen if . . .?" scenarios.

Most of the applications of the computer in this *laboratory* role, as I have previously called it (Hooper, 1973), have for obvious reasons gone on in higher education and in the numerically based disciplines. Seymour Papert at the Massachusetts Institute of Technology has, however, developed the programming language LOGO in order to introduce similar approaches with young children. Papert (1972) claims that LOGO provides "rich soil for the growth of intuitions and concepts for dealing with thinking, learning, playing. . . ." LOGO, like APL, is not so much a programming language, more a way of life.

Assessing these claims is very difficult, since they are so varied and so content-specific. Many of the claims imply a shift in the curriculum, and also a shift in the jobs to which graduates are going. Thus the arguments are about curriculum development and vocational requirements, about ends more than means. An obvious example is the relationship in engineering between "old-fashioned" analytical approaches and "new-style" numerical approaches.

The difficulties of evaluation are heightened by the fact that the computer in these claims is not being used to teach what was taught last year by conventional methods. Control group experiments and comparability studies (conventional teaching versus computerised teaching costs) are not so obviously appropriate where there has been a qualitative shift in the content of teaching as a result of a new method being introduced.

Yet some general comments on these claims should and can be made. If previous experience of educational claims to uniqueness for this or that new medium, this or that curriculum innovation, is heeded, then many of these claims need to be consumed with reasonable amounts of salt. In some cases, the assertions are so grandiose that they defy assessment. The LOGO claims, for example, accelerate out of teaching geometry, to teaching mathematics, to teaching thinking—almost before you can say "CPU". In other cases, the people using the computer as laboratory are not even aware of the claims that actually underlie their approach. To describe these people, we need a special slogan: "computers are the answer—but what was the question?"

Just because you can simulate on a computer a high energy physics experiment which can't be done in the undergraduate laboratory, it does not mean that this is *worth* doing, or that it materially contributes to the educational objectives of laboratory work.

The claim that a computer model provides the student with *firsthand* experience of *more realistic* phenomena must clearly be treated with care. The model is only as good as the person who thought it up, and putting it inside a computer does not perform any alchemy upon its validity—or upon its realism. In no sense can a computer-based simulation be "more realistic"—it can only be a "more accurate model of the physical situation". The danger must always remain that students believe that the physical world behaves as the model behaves. But then, of course, the same argument can be made against most lectures that handle theory. Physics itself is a theory. The computer can in black-box fashion hide the model or theory from the student—yet it is the model and its mode of construction which are at the heart of the higher education scientific curriculum.

A further problem with this computer-as-laboratory approach is highlighted if one examines the use of computer-based games and simulations in management studies. It is felt by some teachers that students play the game or simulation but do not actually *learn* anything from it. The educational objectives are not clear and the educational message is not received. If the games are not integrated into the whole teaching plan, and related specifically to the theory sections, then they remain games, probably good for motivation but little else.

Another problem with the computer acting solely as a calculating device is that it allows students to put nonsense figures in and get nonsense figures out. This is fine if, *and only if*, the student has learned to recognise the nonsense. If he hasn't then we are indulging in computer assisted GIGO—garbage in, garbage out.

Finally, there is a persistent danger with all these computer uses for problem-solving, modelling, simulation, that the student only learns one thing—how to program a computer.

Perhaps the most awkward deficiency in these claims for the computer as laboratory concerns cost-effectiveness. For one thing, the subject of cost-effectiveness is all but totally evaded by the laboratory supporters, in sharp contrast to the supporters of computerised individualised instruction. The reason is obvious. These uses of computers almost all constitute straight add-on cost to the educational institution adopting them. Computers are not being introduced to teach—more effectively—what was taught last year. Thus, we have another good reason for talking here of the "computer as laboratory". Laboratory equipment is typically an add-on cost, requiring more space and more technical, supervisory and teaching staff, *not* less. The word "enrichment"—a notorious word in the annals of audio-visual history—is used a lot by the computer-as-laboratory claimants, and it is not only the curriculum which is being enriched! At a time of expenditure squeeze such as the present, enriching costs of this sort are hardly popular. Educational decision-makers would much prefer to hear the soothing music of cost-effectiveness from educational technologists—even if it is spurious.

But, of course, *tactically* this third claim for the computer as laboratory is a winner—even though it represents add-on costs. The reasons for this are important to identify. First of all, the subject matter of certain disciplines is becoming indistinguishable from computing. It is already very noticeable in physics and electrical engineering, increasingly noticeable in biology and subjects like geology. The same trend is under way, more slowly, in the social sciences—for example, quantitative geography and economics—and of course it is very obvious in management studies. An interesting analogy emerges here between computing and the educational medium of *print*.

Ever since the various inventions concerning moveable type made by Gutenberg and his contemporaries, print has been intimately linked to the needs of the learned profession: "the printer-publishers carried on their work in close connection with the university: the books were written by university professors, were read and corrected for errors of printing and fact by men in universities or trained by them, and were sold most freely in university circles" (Taylor and Arlt, 1941). The invention and subsequent development of print not only were identified with the educational world (school and church being practically synonymous), but also came to help shape academic disciplines and the way they are taught. At certain universities you "read for a degree". What academic discipline today would be thinkable if it did not have recourse to print as a medium of record and communication? What funding agency in recent years has financed a cost-benefit study comparing one education system using print with another one not using it?

Now computing follows a remarkably similar path. Charles Babbage, for some years a (rather inactive) professor of mathematics at Cambridge University, invented his calculating engines for mathematical and scientific purposes in the middle of the nineteenth century. A century later, today's digital computers were being invented *in universities* (including notably Cambridge), to "ease the severe computational tasks arising in ballistics, nuclear-weapon design, meteorology, and navigation" (Levien, 1972, p. 11). Digital computers have, like print, begun to alter the shape of knowledge and the way that this knowledge can be taught. It is for this reason that computer assisted learning in the laboratory sense has a distinct air of inevitability about it. The computer, like print, is academically respectable. By contrast, educational television and film are less respectable, since the technology there grew up in the commercial and entertainment world and does not have, with obvious exceptions such as twentieth century studies, any close relationship to academic subject matter. Computers, being academically respectable, are of course academically *acceptable*, since they talk the language of, say, physics to physicists. Programmed texts and CAI have difficulty in being academically acceptable, since they talk the language of educational theory/psychology/technology—a language that is foreign to most teachers in higher education, whether one likes it or not.

A second major reason why the computer as laboratory is a tactical winner, is that it is in tune with certain educational trends already noticeable in the classroom. In the wake of Dewey, Piaget and Bruner, methods of learning-by-discovery are becoming well-established in the primary school and filtering upwards into secondary education. In addition, in post-secondary education, there is a noticeable trend to bring project work downwards from post-graduate into the undergraduate curriculum. The computer as laboratory, in sharp distinction to computerised programmed learning, implies a modern version of "learning by doing".[4]

Finally, the computer as laboratory is a tactical winner because it is not competing with the human teacher medium. Most human teachers are happy to agree that a computer is better at solving partial differential equations. Where the computer as laboratory has been sensitively developed, it can be said with reasonable confidence that the computer is providing learning opportunities that other educational media—human or nonhuman—cannot. Thus, it refutes the argument that the same results could be achieved if only there were more and better paid teachers. This is also in tune with current thinking in educational technology, which suggests that the various educational media—teachers, books, films, computers—should be orchestrated to do what each is best at, within specified budgetary limits of course. Whilst admitting that we have no hard evidence of what each is best at, we can make certain common-sense statements. For example, it is probably better to use film to show moving pictures, which a teacher can't, rather than a talking face, which a teacher is. Similarly, it is probably better to use the computer either as a calculator or a data processor, than as an imitation human tutor.

CONCLUSION

But the story of the three claims does not end there. A conflict exists between the individualisers and the laboratory problem-solvers, for example. LOGO proponents abhor the CAI approach, seeing it as machine-dominated, passivity-inducing, uncreative, non-Brunerian, pre-ordained and pre-chewed instruction. The individualisers counter with the argument that many of the laboratory uses do not even constitute computer assisted learning, any more than the use of a slide-rule does. A useful distinction has been made by Roger Miles (1973) with regard to computer-based simulators in the armed services. These simulators cannot really be classified as computer-assisted learning since the computer's role is solely to help reproduce with as much fidelity as possible the actual operational experience of flying a Nimrod or controlling air traffic on a radar screen. The computer is in no sense teaching, that is to say responding to the student's learning state. The teaching is done conventionally (and very expensively) with one-to-one human tuition in the simulator.

The battle lines have been historically joined in the United States between the followers of Patrick Suppes and programmed instruction, and the followers of the Dartmouth College approach. The sides were well delineated in two presentations to the 1971 Dartmouth College Conference on Computers in the Undergraduate Curricula. In the red corner, representing the computer as laboratory, we have Arthur Luehrmann, himself of Dartmouth College. In the blue corner, representing CAI and individualisation, is Victor Bunderson, formerly of Texas, now of Brigham Young University, Utah.

Luehrmann (1971). For the undergraduate curriculum in mathematics, physics, and engineering and most other sciences, the maximum return on a modest investment of developmental effort comes from work in [problem-solving; simulation; laboratory data analysis] in that order. Furthermore, I contend that work in these computational uses leads to a *qualitative* improvement in the teaching of the essential subject matter of these courses, in that it makes some central concepts possible to teach that were not possible or very difficult before. Third, I contend that these three categories of use develop in the student a sense of mastery of a powerful general tool. And finally, I contend that these uses, which are student-dominated rather than computer-dominated, are more in keeping with the liberal tradition of enquiry.

Bunderson (1971) Extensions of present labor-intensive patterns for instruction cannot meet the coming crises in higher education ... the adjunct use of the computer, being an expensive additional cost, cannot be considered to be a solution of these critical problems ... adjunct instruction depends heavily on individual instructors. It also emphasizes strategies which require rather bright and highly selected students. It therefore [is] not seen to constitute a direct solution to the problems of increased enrollment and reduced entrance requirements. Mainline instruction [using computers], on the other hand, [is] seen to offer an economically attractive and educationally effective alternative.

The conflict between "mainline" and "adjunct" factions is not trivial. Much of the technological argument relates specifically to one or other use. For example, it is not coincidental that author languages have been eagerly championed by the mainline supporters, on the (now increasingly dubious) assumption that general-purpose high-level programming languages cannot match answers, manipulate text, keep dynamic records of student performance, and be easy for teachers to use. The adjunct supporters tend not to bother with author languages and prefer BASIC, the language which was, of course, developed in New Hampshire at Dartmouth College.

The answers to the conflict between mainline and adjunct, between the computer as individualiser and the computer as laboratory, must surely be found somewhere between the two extremes. The development of models and problem-solving situations that do not have an educational justification in the curriculum development sense, and an individualising framework, is not likely to "assist learning", and is certain to be expensive in terms of add-on costs. On the other hand, developing computerised tutorials is likely to be cost-ineffective and, more important, hostility-arousing. The middle way between the second and third claims might very well be an adaptive laboratory which uses the particular characteristics of the computer as both calculator and data processor within a well-thought-out educational and curriculum context, permitting the learner to explore and manipulate information in a flexible manner but guided by feedback. This idea of an "adaptive laboratory", which has been developed by the Leeds Computer Based Learning Project in this country and people such as Professor Alfred Bork in the United States, is not likely to be suitable for all subject matters since the laboratory in question is not only adaptive to the learner. To be successful, it must also be adaptive to the special requirements of the subject matter. It is not co-incidental that the Leeds group has developed the idea of the adaptive laboratory furthest in the teaching of statistics, and that Bork's work has been mainly in the teaching of physics.

As for the first claim—cost-effectiveness—there is no easy answer. If there were, there would be no requirement for a National Development programme in Computer Assisted Learning. To find answers, it would seem best at the present time to travel in the direction of the computer's being used as a management device. The computer is beginning to establish itself quite securely as a manager of learning. It stores student records, marks and generates tests, routes students to appropriate learning materials and bibliographic references, and performs a range of administrative functions. Given a well-designed override facility that both teacher and student can use, the computer as manager may, far from creating hostility, liberate the teacher to be that interactive tutorial "machine". The computer as manager does not become an expensive store of teaching materials that can be quite effectively and much more cheaply stored in other media—including human beings. The computer may help the teacher and student to orchestrate the range of media now available in the classroom—teachers, print, tapes, and, of course, the new medium of the computer assisted adaptive laboratory.

Perhaps the greatest challenge for the computer as manager will be—the individualisation of instruction.

NOTES

1 See Peter Young's work at the Cambridge Institute of Education, and also Lawrence (1973).
2 For the distinction between "structural" and "functional" models see Oettinger (1969), p. 21.
3 For a detailed analysis of the mass/individualised dilemma see Oettinger and Zapol (1972).
4 I am grateful to Bob Lewis of Chelsea College for pointing out this tactical reason during the discussion following the paper. I have included it here in the published version.

REFERENCES

BUNDERSON, VICTOR (1971) "The Computer as a Means towards Controversial Educational Ends", Conference on Computers in the Undergraduate Curricula, Dartmouth College, p. 10.
BUSHNELL, D. D. (1971) "Introducing the Docile Technology in Memoriam of CAI", in Tickton, S. G. (ed.) To Improve Learning, Bowker, p. 168.
GLASGOW EDUCATION COMMITTEE (1973) Computers in Education in North America, a report to the Education Committee, Corporation of Glasgow, p. 38.

EPIE (EDUCATIONAL PRODUCTS INFORMATION EXCHANGE) (1972) *Report No. 45*, p. 35.

HAMMOND, A. L. (1972) "Computer-assisted Instruction: Many Efforts, Mixed Results", *Science*, Vol. 176, June 1972, p. 1006.

HOOPER, R. (1973) *The National Development Programme in Computer Assisted Learning*, Council for Educational Technology, p. 2.

LAWRENCE, D. (1973) *Improved Reading through Counselling*, Ward Lock Educational.

LEVIEN, R. E. (1972) *The Emerging Technology*, McGraw-Hill.

LUEHRMANN, ARTHUR (1971) "Dartmouth Project COEXIST", Conference on Computers in the Undergraduate Curricula, Dartmouth College, p. 2.

MILES, R. J. (1973) *Computer Applications in a Systems Approach to Training*, Army School of Instructional Technology.

NCET (NATIONAL COUNCIL FOR EDUCATIONAL TECHNOLOGY) (1969), *Computers for Education*, Working Paper No. 1, p. 25.

OETTINGER, A. G. (1969) *Run, Computer, Run*, Harvard University Press.

OETTINGER, A. G. and ZAPOL, N. (1972) "Will Information Technologies Help Learning?" *Teachers College Record*, Vol. 74, No. 1, Sept. 1972, pp. 13–19.

PAPERT, S. (1972) "Teaching Children Thinking", *APLET Journal*, Vol. 9, No. 5, September 1972, p. 247.

TAYLOR, A. and ARLT, G. O. (1941) *Printing and Progress*, University of California Press, p. 31; quoted in Oettinger and Zapol (1972), p. 34.

INDEX

Index

teacher/administrator animosity, 83, 84; absence of faculty and student participation, 85; and recurrent education, 86; formal and expensive institutional structure, 86; correlation with four-fold development sequence, 87; effects of specialization on staff numbers, 87; boards of governors and decision making, 87, 88; process of bureaucratization, 88; proposed abandonment of comprehensiveness, 89, 91; should exhibit parsimony towards claims, 90, 91; use of external evaluation audit, 90; total involvement of personnel in budgetting, 90–1

Canada, Western, characteristics of education, 82, 86, 91; nature of government organizations, 88–9

Carnegie Commission on higher education, 366

CASEA Project, generation of new information needs, 334

Colleges of Advanced Technology (CATS), Ontario 85; UK, 119, 120

CEGP, Quebec, authoritarian administration, 85

Collective bargaining, and security of tenure of unskilled workers, 67n4

Colleges of education, 51; training places needed by 1981, 54–5; Weaver Report, 120, 121; gain autonomous governing bodies, 120; reform, 120–1

Colleges of further education, gain autonomous governing bodies, 120, 125; Circular 7/70 on their government, 121, 123, 125, 127, 132; and student governors, 132; sixth forms,

241; MBO system ("economic man"), 344; transfer to individual plans, 349; (Cumbria), allocation of budgets after reorganization. 357, 359; main sources of finance, 358; annual revenue budget, 358; categories of expenditure, 358, 360; allocation to educational equipment, 358; comparison between colleges (relative costs), 359; measurement of amount of teaching, 359–60; "reward" system, 360; constraints included, 360–1, 362; data used for testing the model, 361; use of linear programming to obtain results, 362–4

Committee of Vice-Chancellors and Principals (CVCP), "Enquiry into the use of academic time", 203–4; data for expenditure allocation, 212, 213

Comprehensive reorganization, need for management techniques, 241; Circular 10/65, 241; use of decision-tree analysis, 294, 296; involvement of planning officers, 299, 301, (Fig. 8) 302–3; resignation and recruitment problems, 301

Computer Assisted Instruction (CAI), US literature on cost effectiveness, 367; inconclusive evaluation, 368; and individualization of instruction, 369–70; alien language, 375; criticized by LOGO, 376

Computers, computer technology, 26, 29; as a means of reducing salary costs, 83; basis of teacher resistance, 83, 367; in university accounting, 215–16; and timetabling, 256; analysis of claims made for in education, 267, 275, 366–8; and model